Historical Dictionaries of Ancient Civilizations and Historical Eras
Series editor: Jon Woronoff

Historical Dictionary of the Vikings

Katherine Holman

Historical Dictionaries of Ancient Civilizations and Historical Eras, No. 11

The Scarecrow Press, Inc.
Lanham, Maryland, and Oxford
2003

SCARECROW PRESS, INC.

Published in the United States of America
by Scarecrow Press, Inc.
A wholly owned subsidary of
The Rowman & Littlefield Publishing Group, Inc.
4501 Forbes Boulevard, Suite 200, Lanham, Maryland 20706
www.scarecrowpress.com

PO Box 317
Oxford
OX2 9RU, UK

British Library Cataloguing in Publication Information Available

Library of Congress Cataloging-in-Publication Data

Holman, Katherine.
  Historical dictionary of the Vikings / Katherine Holman.
      p. cm. — (Historical dictionaries of ancient civilizations and
historical eras)
  ISBN 0-8108-4859-7
  1. Vikings. 2. Scandinavia—History—Dictionaries. I. Title. II.
Series.
DL65 .H62 2003
948'.022'03—dc21
                                        2003010010

Contents

Editor's Foreword

Of the many volumes in this series on ancient civilizations and historical eras, few deal with a topic that exudes as much adventure as this. The Vikings set forth and discovered unknown lands or conquered more settled territories in a huge area stretching from the North Atlantic and North America, in and around the British Isles, through France and into Spain and the Mediterranean, to the vast reaches of Russia. All this was done in an amazingly short period of time by incredibly small, if intrepid, bands of people. Yet, while this is definitely the stuff of adventure for us, for them it was almost just a job, another more promising way of living than was offered at home, with tantalizing but not always realized potential, as well as substantial risk. It is therefore appreciated that *Historical Dictionary of the Vikings* can convey the awesome achievements (and periodic disasters), sense of adventure, and more prosaic details of Viking life.

The adventure does not have to be writ large—it emanates from the dictionary entries on numerous leaders, warriors, and kings, many of whom were warriors not long before, as well as the battles and sieges, discoveries and conquests. Other entries trace the Viking penetration of the many regions where they appeared as raiders, traders, and sometimes eventually rulers. The nitty-gritty appears in entries on their weapons, customs, art and burial practices, and sagas and mythology. Who the Vikings were, where they came from, and what they did is summed up in the introduction. How much they accomplished over a mere three centuries is traced in the chronology. This book is a good reference work, but anyone interested in the Vikings will certainly want to know more, so further resources are included in the bibliography.

This volume was written by Katherine Holman, formerly a lecturer in Scandinavian Studies at the University of Hull. In this capacity, she taught both the history of the countries from which the Vikings came

(Denmark, Norway, and Sweden) and the places they visited, as it were, in modules on the Vikings at home and abroad, and especially in the British Isles. Aside from this, she has undertaken several research projects dealing mainly with runic inscriptions. Dr. Holman has also published a number of articles, again largely on runes, but also on other aspects of the Vikings and Viking Age. Her specialization requires method and precision, something perhaps a bit remote from adventure, but fortunately providing a stronger foundation for any interpretation or conclusions.

Jon Woronoff
Series Editor

Reader's Note

A dictionary is, of course, organized alphabetically, but when it comes to the Vikings, this is not as easy a task as it may sound: there are a number of additional characters in the Scandinavian and Icelandic languages, *å, æ, ä, ö, ø, ð, þ*, which have to be included. As this dictionary is primarily designed for an English-language audience, which may include people unfamiliar with the conventions of the Scandinavian and Icelandic languages, I have chosen to anglicize these characters. Thus, *å* and *ä*, are treated simply as the letter *a*; *æ* as the letters *ae*; *ö* and *ø* as the letter *o*; sometimes I have replaced *ð* and *þ* with the letters *th*, which corresponds to the sound represented by *ð* and *þ*; however, where a spelling with the Icelandic characters is very well known, I have kept the original letters but treated them as *th* for the purposes of alphabetizing. The length markers over vowels (´) have been retained in spellings where there is no generally accepted anglicized form but ignored in the alphabetical ordering of entries. Hooked *o* has been normalized as *ö* and hooked or nasal *a* as *ã*.

The forms of personal and place-names are a further source of headaches for the person seeking to provide a work of reference such as the *Historical Dictionary of the Vikings*. In this book, I have used anglicized spellings of place names where these exist and are presently well known (e.g., Copenhagen not Danish København; Reykjavik not Icelandic Reykjavík), but otherwise I have used the form found in the relevant country of origin (e.g., Swedish Skåne not archaic anglicized form Scania; Danish Sjælland not archaic anglicized form Zealand). Personal names are tricky because all original forms are, to some extent, normalized, sometimes according to different conventions; and many also exist in different, more modern forms, as well as in a variety of anglicized forms. It is hard to be consistent, but I have generally used anglicized or modernized English and Scandinavian forms where these exist and are well known in English-language historiography; otherwise I have used the standardized Old Norse forms. The names of people from other areas—particularly Arabic and Byzantine figures—are given in the form most commonly found in modern works on the Vikings.

In order to help the reader, I have also cross-referenced entries with a number of different forms. For example, the entry for King Cnut the Great is found under CNUT, but people who look under CANUTE or KNUT will be redirected to CNUT. Where names are given in their anglicized form, I have tried to include their original form in brackets to assist the reader in further research. Readers should also note that, as is the convention, historical figures are listed under their first names not their surnames (if indeed any surname is known). Thus Snorri Sturluson appears under SNORRI rather than STURLUSON.

The titles of written works are generally listed in both their original language and in English, when a well-known translation of the title exists. Where two or more versions of a title are in common usage, the full entry is normally given under the English title, as befits a dictionary designed for an English-speaking audience (e.g., The entry for the Icelandic work *Íslendingabók* is given under *Book of the Icelanders*, but those who look up *Íslendingabók* will be referred to the correct place in the dictionary). All entries are provided with either a translation of the title into English or the original form of the title as is appropriate.

Some standard acronyms are used in the text of the dictionary: OE for Old English and ON for Old Norse. When referring to runic inscriptions, I have supplied the reference numbers of the individual inscriptions as found in the published editions. For example, DR refers to the number of the inscription as found in *Danmarks Runeindskrifter*; U refers to an inscription published in *Upplands Runinskrifter*; and N refers to *Norges Innskrifter med de Yngre Runer* (*see* Bibliography: Scandinavian Sources).

Finally, cross-references are given in bold type.

Chronology

***c*. 705** Foundation of Ribe, Denmark.

***c*. 710** Willibrord's mission to Denmark.

737 Earliest sections of *Danevirke* constructed in Denmark.

***c*. 750** Foundation of Birka, Sweden, and Staraja Ladoga, Russia.

786–802 Reign of King Beorhtric of Wessex; *Anglo-Saxon Chronicle* recorded attack on Portland, Dorset, England, by men from Hordaland, Norway.

793 Monastery of St. Cuthbert on Lindisfarne, Northumbria, England, attacked by Vikings on 8 June.

795 Viking attacks on *Rechru* (=Rathlin Island off northern Irish coast?) and Scottish Hebridean island of Skye recorded by *Annals of Ulster*.

799 Vikings attacked monastery of St-Philibert on Noirmoutier, off Brittany coast, Frankia.

800 Coastal defenses against Vikings organized by Charlemagne.

802 Monastery on Hebridean island of Iona attacked by Vikings.

806 Another Viking attack on Iona left 68 monks dead.

***c*. 808** Danish king, Godfred, destroyed Abodrite market at *Reric* and established trading town at Hedeby.
Danevirke extended to protect new trading center.

810 Danish attack on Frisia.
King Godfred of Denmark killed and succeeded by nephew, Hemming.
New king made peace with Charlemagne.

812 Death of Hemming of Denmark.
Hemming's kinsmen, Harald Klak and Reginfred, became joint kings of Denmark after battle for power.

813 Harald Klak and Reginfred forced into exile by rivals, sons of Godfred.

814 Death of Charlemagne. Succeeded by son, Louis the Pious.
Reginfred killed in unsuccessful bid to regain Danish throne.

819 Harald Klak and Horik became joint rulers of Denmark following truce negotiated by Louis the Pious.

823 Archbishop Ebo of Rheims led mission to Denmark.
Appeal from Harald Klak for Frankish support against sons of Godfred.

825 Vikings attack Hebridean island of Iona again, killing its prior, Blathmac.

826 Harald Klak, his family, and his followers baptized at Mainz, with Louis the Pious standing as sponsor.
Missionary priest, Ansgar, accompanied Harald to Denmark.

827 Harald Klak of Denmark forced into exile.

829–831 Ansgar visited Birka in Sweden.

832 Ansgar appointed as bishop of new see of Hamburg.

833 Louis the Pious driven out of power by sons.

834 Oseberg ship burial in Vestfold, Norway.
Louis the Pious restored.
Frisian market center, Dorestad, attacked by Vikings.

835   Dorestad attacked by Vikings.
Isle of Sheppey in Thames estuary, southeast England, attacked by Vikings.

836   Monks of St-Philibert abandoned island of Noirmoutier.
Dorestad attacked by Vikings.

837   Dorestad attacked by Vikings.

839   Byzantine diplomatic mission to court of Louis the Pious included men called "Rus."

840   Death of Louis the Pious followed by civil war in Frankia.
First overwintering of Vikings in Ireland, on Lough Neagh.

841   Vikings established settlement (*longphort*) in Dublin, Ireland.
Island of Walcharen given to Viking leader, Harald, by Lothar.

843   Treaty of Verdun divided Carolingian empire into three: Charles the Bald received western kingdom, Lothar received central kingdom, and Louis the German received eastern kingdom.

844   Viking attack on Seville, southern Spain.

845   Paris ransomed for 7,000 pounds of silver.
Hamburg sacked by Danish fleet.
Pagan backlash against Christian mission in Birka.

848–849   See of Hamburg amalgamated with Bremen, under Ansgar.

849   New Viking fleet arrived in Ireland.

c. **850**   Ansgar built churches in Hedeby and Ribe.

851   First overwintering of Vikings in England, on Isle of Thanet, Essex.
Clash between incoming "dark" (= Danes?) and established "fair" (= Norwegians?) Vikings in Dublin.

852 Ansgar returned to Birka to revive the mission there.

853 All Vikings in Ireland submitted to Olaf the White.

854 Horik I, king of Denmark, killed in battle; Horik II succeeded him.

859 Varangians first exacted tribute from people of northwest Russia. Björn Ironside and Hastein led Viking fleet into Mediterranean.

860 Rus attack on Constantinople.

862 Rurik and brothers invited to rule over people of northwest Russia.

865 Great Army arrived in East Anglia, England, commencing long campaign that resulted in first Scandinavian settlements of England.

866 English town of York captured by Great Army.

867 Kings Ælla and Osberht of Northumbria killed during attempt to recapture York from Vikings.

870 Traditional date for first Scandinavian settlement of Iceland. Edmund, king of English East Anglia, is killed by Vikings.

871 Alfred became king of English kingdom of Wessex. Death of Olaf the White of Dublin. Succeeded by kinsman, Ivar.

873 Death of King Ivar of Dublin. Great Army winters in Repton, England.

874 Ceolwulf established as puppet ruler of Mercia. Split in Great Army.

876 Part of Great Army, led by Halfdan, settled in English kingdom of Northumbria.

877   Eastern half of Mercia settled by Scandinavians.

878   Following surprise Viking attack on Chippenham, Alfred the Great of Wessex forced to take refuge in marshes of Athelney, Somerset.
Vikings defeated by English under Alfred of Wessex at Edington.
Treaty of Wedmore established border between Wessex and Scandinavian army in East Anglia; treaty included conversion of Viking leader, Guthrum.
First overwintering of Vikings in Wales.

879   English kingdom of East Anglia settled by Great Army under Guthrum.
Death of Rurik of Russia. Succeeded by Oleg.

885–886   Siege of Paris.

886   Terms of Treaty of Wedmore reconfirmed by King Alfred and Guthrum.

c. **890**   Harald Fine-Hair defeated alliance of chieftains at Hafrsfjörd in southwest Norway.
Death of Guthrum of East Anglia.

899   Death of King Alfred of Wessex. Succeeded by son, Edward the Elder.

c. **900**   Olaf dynasty established in Denmark.

902   Vikings expelled from Dublin by Irish.

911   Viking leader, Rollo, given French province of Neustria (later Normandy) by Charles the Simple.

912–920   English reconquest of Danelaw.

917   Norse settlement of Dublin is re-established by Sigtrygg Cáech.

919   Ragnald recognized as king of York.

c. 922   Ibn Fadlan recorded encounter with Rus on River Volga in Russia.

924   Death of Edward the Elder. Succeeded by Athelstan.
William Longsword succeeded Rollo of Normandy.

927   Athelstan reconquered York from Guthfrith, brother of Sigtrygg Cáech.

930   Traditional date for end of colonization of Iceland.
Icelandic assembly, the Althing, is established at Thingvellir.
Hardegon ousted the Olaf dynasty in Denmark.

c. 935   Hákon the Good conquered Norway and deposed his half-brother, Erik Blood-Ax.

937   Battle of *Brunanburh* fought by English king, Athelstan, against Hiberno-Norse alliance.
English victory recorded in poem in *Anglo-Saxon Chronicle*.

954   Erik Blood-Ax, last Viking king of York, killed at Stainmore in Yorkshire, England.

958–959   Death of Gorm the Old. Succeeded by his son, Harald Blue-Tooth.

960   Hákon the Good killed in Battle of Fitjar by sons of Erik Blood-Ax.

965   Harald Blue-Tooth, king of Denmark, converted to Christianity by missionary Poppo.

974   Otto II of Germany invaded and occupied southern Denmark.

978   Æthelred II crowned king of England.

980   Vikings of Dublin defeated in Battle of Tara in Ireland.

985–986   Erik the Red discovered and colonized Greenland.

c. **987**   Death of Harald Blue-Tooth of Denmark. Succeeded by son, Svein Forkbeard.

988   Vladimir of Russia converted to Christianity.

989   Sigtrygg Silk-Beard became king of Dublin.

991   Battle of Maldon in Essex, England.
First Danegeld paid after Olaf Tryggvason's Viking army defeated English under Ealdorman Byrthnoth.

995   Olaf Tryggvason returned to Norway and claimed throne.
Death of Erik the Victorious of Sweden. Succeeded by son, Olof Skötkonung.

1000   Olaf Tryggvason killed by a Dano-Swedish alliance in Battle of Svöld.
Iceland accepted Christianity as official religion at Althing.
Discovery of Vinland.

1002   King Æthelred II of England ordered massacre of all Danes in England on St. Brice's Day.

1009–1012   Viking army of Thorkell the Tall harried southern England.

1013   Svein Forkbeard of Denmark received submission of English.

1014   Death of Svein Forkbeard.
Æthelred II returned from exile in Normandy, and Cnut left for Denmark.
Battle of Clontarf fought near Dublin, Ireland, on Good Friday. Irish high king, Brian Boru, killed.

1015   Olaf Haraldsson returned to Norway and declared king.
Began campaign to convert Norway to Christianity.
Cnut returned with army to England.

1016   Death of Æthelred II. Succeeded by his son, Edmund Ironside.
Edmund defeated by Cnut at Ashingdon.
England partitioned between Cnut and Edmund at Olney.
Death of Edmund.
Olaf Haraldsson defeats Norwegian rivals in Battle of Nesjar.

1017   Cnut, son of Svein Forkbeard of Denmark, crowned king of England.
Cnut married Emma of Normandy, widow of Æthelred II.

1019   Cnut became king of Denmark after death of brother, Harald.

1026   Battle of Holy River.

1028   Olaf Haraldsson driven out of Norway by Danish-backed revolt.
Took refuge in Russia with Jaroslav the Wise.
Cnut installed son, Svein, and Svein's English mother, Ælfgifu, as representatives in Norway.

1030   Olaf Haraldsson returned to Norway and killed in Battle of Stiklestad, near Trondheim, on 29 July.

1035   Death of Cnut, king of England, Denmark, and Norway.
In England, Cnut succeeded by son, Harold Harefoot; in Denmark, by son, Harthacnut, and in Norway, by Olaf Haraldsson's son, Magnus the Good.

1040   Harthacnut became king of England following death of Harold Harefoot on 17 March.

1042   Death of Harthacnut marked end of Danish rule in England. English royal line restored with coronation of Edward the Confessor, son of Æthelred II.
King Magnus of Norway became king of Denmark.

1046   Harald Hard-Ruler became joint king of Norway with half-nephew, Magnus.

1047   Svein Estrithsson, Cnut's nephew, became king of Denmark. Death of Magnus the Good.
Harald Hard-Ruler became sole king of Norway.

1066   King Harald Hard-Ruler of Norway killed in Battle of Stamford Bridge.
William the Conqueror defeated English king, Harold Godwinsson, in Battle of Hastings.
Magnus Haraldsson became king of Norway.

1067   Olaf the Peaceful became joint king of Norway with brother Magnus.
Ari Thorgilsson, author of *Book of the Icelanders*, born in Iceland.

1069–1070   Svein Estrithsson invaded England.
Death of Magnus Haraldsson.
Olaf the Peaceful became sole king of Norway.

1074   Death of King Svein Estrithsson of Denmark. Succeeded by son, Harald Hén.
Adam of Bremen finished *History of the Archbishops of Hamburg-Bremen*.

1075   Last Danish invasion of England by Knut II.

1079   Godred Crovan became king of Man after victory at Battle of Skyhill.

1080   Death of Harald Hén of Denmark. Succeeded by Knut II.

1085   Knut II of Denmark planned invasion of England.

1086   Murder of Knut II of Denmark in Odense. Succeeded by half-brother, Olaf Hunger.

1095   Death of Olaf Hunger. Succeeded by half brother, Erik Eje-good.

1098 King Magnus Bare-Foot of Norway's expedition to Norse colonies in the west.
Deposed earls of Orkney; captured king of Isle of Man; defeated the Normans off Anglesey, and signed treaty with king of Scotland.

1103 Death of Magnus Bare-Foot in Ireland.

Introduction

The Vikings, those medieval Scandinavian warriors who launched ferocious and much-lamented attacks on western Europe, continue to evoke vivid images and lively public interest today, some 1,200 years after they first came to the attention of contemporary monastic chroniclers. One only has to search for the word *Viking* on the Internet to realize the extent of this enduring popularity and to see just how valuable a commodity it has become in 21st-century commerce and tourism. This is perhaps rather surprising given that popular images of the Vikings nearly always begin with swords, axes, helmets (*see* **weapons**), **ships**, pillage, looting, and of course slaughter and destruction. This bad press dates right back to the earliest sources for the Vikings, where the Christian victims of their attacks complained about the destruction inflicted on their churches and congregations, and perhaps this supports the idea that there is no such thing as bad publicity!

However, the enduring interest in the Vikings lies not only in their reputation as barbarians who harried the Christian civilization of western Europe. In the 19th century, Romantic artists, musicians, and writers were interested in the heroism of these warriors, who were free and unbound by the constraints of later feudal structures, who were loyal to their brothers-in-arms, who would continue to fight even if the odds were against them, and who sailed overseas in search of adventure. This heroic Viking figure was equipped with appropriately dramatic trappings, most notably the horned or even winged helmet (which in fact seems to have had a ritual rather than battle purpose in early Germanic cultures) and the double-headed battle-ax. Translations of Icelandic sagas allowed international audiences to read about the pioneering society established by these Vikings in the North Atlantic: a collection of free men, ruled by their own laws rather than a king, on the very fringes of the habitable world—a society that had undoubted appeal to Europe and **North America**, where new ideas of personal liberty and universal suffrage were beginning to take hold.

Under the impact of modern scholarship, particularly archaeological excavations, this image of the free and heroic *Viking* has been supplemented with other, perhaps more everyday, images. The raider might also have been a trader, who traveled about selling goods, and a colonist, who left his homeland behind him and began a new and peaceful life in a different country. Archaeological finds have revealed that Viking craftsmen produced elaborate and beautiful jewelry and sculpture, as well as weapons, and the technical skill of the Viking shipwright was second to none. There are also the large numbers of Scandinavians who chose to stay at home, those who supported the conversion of their compatriots to Christianity, and the social groups neglected by written sources: women, children, the poor, and the enslaved. None of these Vikings are so attention-grabbing as the more dramatic warrior figures, but our knowledge about these people and their lives certainly helps to paint a more complex and realistic image of the period and also to explain why people continue to find the Viking Age a compelling and fascinating period to study.

DEFINITIONS: VIKINGS, THE VIKING AGE, AND SCANDINAVIA

This is a historical dictionary of the Vikings, but who were the Vikings? The word *Viking* has come to be used in a general sense for those people from the area covered by the modern Nordic countries of Denmark, Iceland, Norway, and Sweden in the historical period *c.* 800–*c.* 1100. However, strictly speaking, *Viking* is not merely another way of referring to a medieval Scandinavian. Technically, the word has a more specific meaning, and it was used (only infrequently by contemporaries of the Vikings) to refer to those Scandinavians, usually men, who attacked their contemporaries. There were also large numbers of those people who sailed across the North Sea, the Baltic, and down the Russian rivers into the Black Sea and beyond, trading and settling as well as raiding (*see* **Viking**).

The activities of these people led historians to name the period in which they undertook raiding, trading, and colonizing as the Viking Age. As with all historical epochs, the Viking Age is an artificial scholarly construct; for example, in English scholarship, the first *recorded* raid on the monastery on **Lindisfarne** in 793 marks a convenient starting point, and the Norman Conquest, in 1066, has been selected as a suitable end to the Viking Age. The *Concise Oxford Dictionary* (9th ed. Oxford: Oxford University Press, 1995) therefore defines a Viking as "any of the Scandinavian seafaring pirates and traders who raided and settled in parts of NW Europe in the 8th to the 11th c[enturies]." However, in Scandinavia itself, there are no contemporary written sources that allow historians to select a particular date as either a beginning or an end to the Viking Age, so here the periodization is much more of an approximation, covering the years from *c*. 750 to *c*. 1100.

For the purposes of this dictionary, this longer time span (*c*. 750– *c*. 1100) will be used. Although, strictly speaking, Scandinavians who stayed at home during this period were not Vikings, to study the Vikings without making reference to their compatriots and their home life would, of course, be meaningless. Even Vikings were not always Vikings, for it often appears to have been a seasonal activity, undertaken in the summer when the seas were relatively calm, while winters were spent at home in Scandinavia. Therefore this dictionary will actually focus on the archaeological, art historical, epigraphical, historical, linguistic, and literary evidence for Scandinavia and Scandinavians in the Viking Age. It has also been necessary to include separate entries on some historical figures who were not Scandinavians, but who had considerable interaction with Scandinavians; for example, to omit a separate entry for King **Alfred the Great**, who spent much of his reign repelling Scandinavian raiders, would be pedantic, even though he is not of course a Viking in any sense of the word. By the same token, there is much in this dictionary that postdates the Viking Age: apart from runic inscriptions carved on to memorial stones, all the Scandinavian written evidence for the society, economy, politics, personalities, and culture of the Viking Age comes from the medieval period. Although the value of these sources to historians of the Viking Age is not straightforward, to omit references to Icelandic sagas or **Eddic poetry** because they were written down in the 13th and 14th centuries, for example, again would be taking an unnecessarily narrow view of the Vikings. Any student of the period has to use these sources, imperfect as they may be.

It is also necessary at this point to discuss the meaning of the word Scandinavia. Scandinavians use this word to refer to the three present-day countries of Denmark, Norway and Sweden; in other words, both Iceland and Finland are excluded from this definition of *Scandinavia*. The Scandinavian word to describe all five of these present-day countries is *Norden*, which can be loosely translated into English as "the Nordic countries." This usage of the term *Scandinavian* has been followed in this dictionary: certainly Finland was and indeed is ethnically and linguistically quite distinct from the other four countries, which during the Viking Age spoke a common language, known to contemporaries as *dönska tunga* or *norrænn*. In fact, very little is known about Finland during the Viking Age, and although Scandinavians heading east are likely to have traveled through the country, there is little evidence that they spent much time there. At the beginning of the Viking Age, Iceland was of course not part of the Scandinavian world, but it was colonized by a Scandinavian-speaking population in the ninth century and maintained close contacts with Norway, in particular. Although Iceland is therefore ethnically and linguistically part of the Scandinavian world, there are significant differences that placed it outside the Scandinavian mainstream: politically, it was not a monarchy—at least not until it acknowledged the Norwegian king, Hákon Hákonarson, as its king in 1262–1264; ethnically, there appears to have been a small but significant Celtic strand in the Icelandic population, following the settlement of some Scandinavian families who had previously spent time in parts of the British Isles; economically, it lacked its own towns during the Viking Age and was instead dependent on trade with Scandinavia; and geographically, it was, of course, a considerable distance from Denmark, Norway, and Sweden. Nevertheless, although Iceland is not treated as part of Scandinavia *per se* in this dictionary—it is a crucial piece in the puzzle of the Viking and the Viking Age—as it was of course here that a flourishing literary and historiographical culture developed in the Middle Ages.

GEOGRAPHY AND HABITAT

Although Scandinavia is a convenient umbrella term for the three present-day countries of Denmark, Norway and Sweden, lying on the northern edge of the European continent, it masks significant differences between these three countries. Most fundamentally, the geography and topography of Scandinavia varies considerably. This is hardly surprising given that Scandinavia stretches from the base of the Jutland Peninsula in the south (about 55° latitude) to Nordkapp or North Cape in the north (71° latitude). Geographically and topographically, Norway and Denmark are totally different. While Denmark is just approximately 375 kilometers from north to south, Norway measures about 1,770 kilometers. Similarly, in contrast to the predominantly flat, arable lands of Denmark, only one-fifth of Norway lies below 150 meters. Most of Norway is marked by high mountains that are cut by long, narrow valleys that follow the fjörds, and the only region that can be described as coastal lowland lies in the area surrounding Oslo. Sweden, like Norway, is a long country, stretching from the Baltic in the south to beyond the Arctic Circle, and conditions within this area vary considerably. There are larger tracts of flat, arable lands in Sweden than there are in Norway, but also much uncultivable marshland and forest. Communications with inland areas in Sweden were difficult as, unlike Norway, there were no fjörds to provide a relatively quick and easy means of transportation, and the climate of northern Sweden did not benefit from the Gulf Stream that warmed the north Norwegian coast. These geographical and topographical conditions played a crucial part in the development of Scandinavia during the Viking Age.

THE VIKINGS AT HOME

The most visible and obvious characteristics of the Viking Age are the expeditions that the Vikings undertook in their ships, across seas and along rivers. The Viking Age is when Scandinavia really made its entrance on to the stage of European, indeed world, history. However, at home in Scandinavia, the Viking Age also saw important changes and developments, many of which were partly the result of increased contact with Europe: Scandinavian kings sought to establish themselves as the rulers of more clearly demarcated and unified kingdoms, modeling themselves on European rulers such as **Charlemagne**, emperor of the Franks; Christianity and the institutions, liturgy, and learning of the Catholic Church were introduced to Scandinavia, replacing pagan beliefs and rituals; and the growth of trade with Europe and beyond led to a degree of urbanization in Scandinavia, as well as an increased awareness of European politics, society, and culture.

At the start of the Viking Age, Denmark, Norway, and Sweden did not exist as three separate kingdoms; instead there appear to have been a number of regional chieftains in each "country" who ruled over the inhabitants of smaller districts. Politically, the Viking Age is characterized by the gradual centralization of power into the hands of a much smaller number of kings and the emergence of political units known as Denmark, Norway, and, somewhat later, Sweden. This development was uneven across Scandinavia: already, at the beginning of the Viking Age, there is evidence that there were some people claiming to be kings of "Denmark," but in Sweden, no king had effective power throughout the whole country until well after the end of the Viking Age. A final and further point here is that the borders of the modern Scandinavian countries of Denmark, Norway, and Sweden differed from those in the Viking Age. Most importantly, the part of southwestern Sweden that is today the province of Skåne was, in fact, part of the kingdom of Denmark throughout the Viking Age.

Denmark ("Land [March] of the Danes")

At the beginning of the Viking Age, the peninsula of Jutland appears to have been the most important part of Denmark. There is archaeological evidence for a number of important and large-scale building works in eighth-century Jutland that suggest that there was already someone in the area powerful enough to organize this work. For example, the town of **Ribe** was founded *c.* 700; the **Kanhave Canal** was constructed on the island of Samsø *c.* 726; and, most significantly, around 727 building work on a long fortification, known as the **Danevirke**, running across the base of Jutland, was begun. It provided a defensive line where the naturally marshy terrain did not and consisted of large turf and timber ramparts. This suggests that someone with considerable political and economic power in Jutland was worried by expansion from Germanic tribes to the south into Danish territory, and that, already at this period, there were some political attempts to differentiate Denmark from the European mainland.

Much of our knowledge of the early history of Viking-Age Denmark comes from continental chronicles, reflecting in particular the close geographical relationship between Denmark and the kingdom of **Frankia**. Frankia is the name given to the kingdom that, roughly speaking, covered the area of present-day France and Germany, and at the beginning of the Viking Age it was ruled by the Emperor Charlemagne from his capital in Aachen (in present-day Holland). The province of Saxony, on the southern border of Jutland, was taken over by the Frankish emperor in the eighth century, bringing this expansionist power right onto Denmark's doorstep. The **Royal Frankish Annals** record a Danish king called **Godfred**, who was in power around 800–810, and who attacked Charlemagne's Slavic allies. Godfred is also said to have settled merchants in the early Viking-Age town of **Hedeby**. Two other ninth-century Danish kings, called Horik the Older and Horik the Younger, are known (*see* **Horik**). Horik the Older allowed the German missionary, **Ansgar**, to build churches in Hedeby and Ribe in the 850s. Like Godfred, they were also involved in continental politics and launched an attack on Hamburg. However, for much of the second half of the ninth century and the early 10th century virtually nothing is known of events taking place in Denmark or of the power struggles that were probably taking place between various chieftains. Then, in the middle of the 10th century, a new Danish royal dynasty appears, that of **Gorm the Old**, based in **Jelling** in central Jutland. This family appears to have won total political dominance in Denmark, and the current queen of Denmark, Margrete II, can in fact trace her ancestry right back to Gorm.

Gorm is thought to have died in the 950s. Not very much is known about him or the events of his reign in Denmark, but it is clear that he was buried in a large burial mound at Jelling. At Jelling, there is also a commemorative inscription, carved in runes, that was commissioned by Gorm's son and successor, Harald, who is usually known as **Harald Blue-Tooth**. In 987, Harald was deposed by his own son, Svein, who had the nickname Forkbeard. **Svein Forkbeard** was involved in many of the Viking campaigns in **England** and died in Gainsborough (Lincolnshire) in 1014, after having defeated the English king, Æthelred II the Unready, and having won control of the kingdom of England. Two years later, in 1016, Svein's son, **Cnut I the Great**, became king of England, and two years after that, in 1018, Cnut also succeeded his brother (Harald) to the Danish throne. Cnut became king of a great "empire," which at its maximum extent included Norway and possibly even parts of southwest Sweden, as well as Denmark and England. This empire started to crumble before his death in 1035, and after he died, Denmark went briefly to his son **Harthacnut**, before passing, for an equally brief period, to the Norwegian king, **Magnus the Good**. After Magnus's death in 1047, Cnut's family, in the form of his nephew, **Svein Estrithsson**, regained the Danish throne. While Svein harbored plans to win back England for the Danes, he had enough trouble at home for much of his reign. For example, in 1050 and 1066, the lucrative trading place at Hedeby was attacked, firstly by **Harald Hard-Ruler** of Norway and then by Slavs. Svein was succeeded in turn by his five sons, one of whom, also called Knut, was declared a saint after his murder in Odense at the shrine of St. Albans. His assassination takes us more or less to the end of the Viking Age, to 1086. With him also died the last hopes of the Danish kings for regaining England.

Norway ("North Way")

Norway was more remote from the continent than Denmark, although it had connections in the west with the British Isles, and it was also harder to unite politically because of its geography: huge distances, isolated valleys, and mountainous terrain. Thus, at the beginning of the Viking Age, there was, again in contrast to Denmark, no evidence of any central political power in Norway. The country appears to have been divided up into small territories, ruled by local chieftains, which were separated by large tracts of unoccupied mountainous land.

However, we learn about the emergence of a more powerful king in southern Norway in the 880s. He was called **Harald Fine-Hair**. Harald was king of Vestfold, a district that lies to the west of present-day Oslo. Around the year 900, he is said to have fought and won a battle at **Hafrsfjörd**, near modern Stavanger, on the southeastern coast of Norway. Here, Harald defeated an alliance of petty chieftains, and he promptly declared himself king of Norway. In reality, his kingdom probably only consisted of southern Norway, and there remained considerable opposition to his rule. In particular, the Earls of **Lade**, who controlled the district of Trøndelag (around modern **Trondheim**), resisted all attempts to be incorporated into the kingdom of Norway. Harald died around 930, and his immediate successors were unable to build on his achievements: his son, **Erik Blood-Ax**, was deposed and set off to find fame and fortune (and ultimately his death in 954) in England, while Erik's brother, **Hákon the Good**, returned to Norway from England and ruled as king until Erik's sons killed him in 960. The following decades saw political power in Norway more or less divided between the Earls of Lade and the Danish king, who was looking to extend his realm—the coastal lowlands around Oslo naturally attracted Danish attention. In particular, Harald Blue-Tooth of Denmark defeated various sons of Erik Blood-Ax and drove them out of Norway, setting up **Hákon Jarl** of Lade as his regent.

At the end of the 10th century, Norway took a decisive step toward political unity when the great-grandson of Harald Fine-Hair, **Olaf Tryggvason**, returned to Norway after campaigning in England, secured a base in Trøndelag, and challenged Danish rule of the country. Olaf had been baptized in a period of exile in England, and he tried to force Norwegians to accept Christianity—a policy that enjoyed only mixed success. But his was a short-lived reign, ended by Olaf's death in the Battle of **Svöld** in 1000, when the combined forces of the Danish king, Svein Forkbeard, and the Swedish king, **Olof Skötkonung**, together with Jarl Erik of Lade, defeated the Norwegians. The following 15 years again saw Norway divided into different political spheres of influence, under Svein of Denmark, with the Earls of Lade dominant in central and northern Norway and the Swedish king, Olof Skötkonung, holding power in the province of Ranrike (along the eastern coast of Oslofjörd). The next Norwegian king to emerge was another Olaf who had been campaigning as a Viking for many years. **Olaf Haraldsson** was also a Christian and tried to convert Norway to his religion during his 13-year reign between 1015 and 1028. However, this provoked opposition, particularly in Trøndelag, and in 1028, Olaf was temporarily driven out of the country by Cnut of England and Denmark. On his return in 1030, he was defeated and killed in the Battle of **Stiklestad** on 29 July 1030. However, the tide turned against the Danes shortly after this, in protest at the oppressive rule of Cnut's son and consort. The dead Olaf was promoted to sainthood, and his son Magnus the Good was called back from exile in Russia and made king of Norway. Magnus was strong enough and Denmark weak enough to reverse the traditional Danish domination of Norway, and Magnus appears to have ruled Denmark too between 1042 and 1047. His uncle, Harald Hard-Ruler, succeeded him. Harald is most famous for dying in the Battle of **Stamford Bridge** in East Yorkshire in 1066—defeated by King Harold Godwinsson of England a few days before Harold fought William the Conqueror at the Battle of Hastings. This date is often used to mark the end of the Viking Age in England, because it was the last real Scandinavian invasion of England. One of Harald's sons, **Olaf the Peaceful**, ruled Norway until 1093. As his nickname suggests his reign was a relatively uneventful, if prosperous, period. His son, **Magnus Bare-Foot**, was more active abroad and tried to extend Norwegian royal authority over the Scandinavian colonies in the British Isles. However, he was killed while campaigning in Ireland, and after this date the kings of Norway were increasingly preoccupied with conflict and civil war at home.

Sweden ("Kingdom of the Svear")

Sweden was the last of the Scandinavian kingdoms to be established, and it is also the country about which the least is known. This is partly because the country, remote from the continent and the British Isles, naturally looked to the east and the emergent kingdoms and rather less literate cultures of the Baltic and Russia. However, it is known that during the Viking Age, Sweden essentially consisted of two separate kingdoms: in central eastern Sweden, the kingdom of the Svear tribe, around modern Stockholm and Uppsala, and in the west, the kingdom of the Götar tribe, part of the modern provinces of Västergötland and Östergötland. These two areas were effectively divided by a large tract of heavily wooded and marshy land. **Götaland** was less remote than **Svealand**, and there seems to be evidence of contact between Götaland and the kingdom of Denmark, quite natural given the importance of sea communications in this period and the difficulty of land travel.

The first kings of Sweden whose names are known are mentioned by a Frankish writer called Rimbert. Rimbert was the author of the ninth-century *Life of St. Ansgar*. The **Ansgar** that he wrote about was his deceased mentor and a Christian missionary from Frankia, who was welcomed by a King **Björn** and later a King Olaf to the important Swedish trading town of **Birka** in the 820s and 850s respectively. How much power they had in Svealand is unclear, but the kings of the Svear do seem to have been sufficiently powerful to control the Baltic islands of **Gotland** and Öland by the end of the ninth century. The first king who is known to have exerted power in both Götaland and Svealand is another king called Olof. His nickname was Skötkonung ("Tribute-King"), which suggests a degree of political subservience (*see* **Olof**

Skötkonung). Olof's reign can be dated roughly to the period 995–1020, and he issued his own coinage from the new royal center at **Sigtuna**, proclaiming himself as a Christian king of the Svear. Nevertheless, many of his subjects appear to have still been pagan—and in the 1070s the German writer, **Adam of Bremen**, records that pagan rituals were still taking place at the cult center of **Gamla Uppsala**. Olof's power was not unchallenged, and he seems to have lost control of Svealand at some point. He was, however, succeeded by his son in Sigtuna, **Anund Jakob**, and when Anund died around 1050, his half-brother **Emund**, another son of Olof, became king. While these kings exercised some power throughout the country, it is really not until after the Viking Age, in the 1170s, that the whole of Sweden was properly united under one king—Knut Eriksson.

THE VIKINGS ABROAD

It is possible to divide Viking activity abroad into a number of distinct geographical spheres, reflecting the character of this activity. Most simply, historians talk about an eastern and western sphere of Viking influence. The west, including those lands surrounding the North Sea, the North Atlantic, and, to a lesser extent, the Mediterranean, was the main sphere of activity for Danish and Norwegian Vikings. Viking activity in the east affected Finland, Poland, the Baltic States, **Byzantium** (the empire including present-day Turkey and Greece), **Russia** and the area covered by the former Soviet Union, and was dominated by Swedish Vikings. However, although geography meant that Norway was orientated to the west, Denmark to the south, and Sweden to the east, Swedish Vikings were, for example, involved in raids in England, and it is known that there were Norwegian visitors to Russia. The traditional view of Viking activity in the East and West respectively was one that contrasted trading with raiding, with settlement taking place in both spheres of influence.

However, more recently, Viking scholarship has distinguished a number of subspheres: the North Atlantic, the British Isles, continental Europe, the Baltic, European Russia, and Byzantium. This reflects in part the increase in archaeological data, which has allowed scholars to present a more complex picture of Viking activity abroad, but it is also a result of the desire to move beyond the simplistic image of the Vikings as destructive raiders in the West and constructive traders in the East. There is much archaeological evidence that the Vikings were involved in trade in the West, and the real difference between East and West may be the absence of rich religious establishments and contemporary monastic chroniclers in the East. Obviously the motives for and the nature of Viking travel abroad varied considerably over the 300-year period that is the Viking Age, given that the people known as Vikings come from areas as different and as far apart as Denmark, Norway, and Sweden. When trying to present a summary or survey of Viking activity abroad it may therefore be more useful to talk about the different types of activity, rather than where it took place. In the final analysis, Viking activity was nothing if not opportunistic.

However, it is important to realize that not all Scandinavian travel in the Viking Age was necessarily "Viking" in character. For example, some Scandinavians went on pilgrimages to Rome and Jerusalem, and others paid diplomatic visits to the courts of kings and emperors. It used to be common to regard the Vikings as barbarian outsiders who inflicted themselves on the rest of civilized, Christian Europe. However, the Vikings were not more savage or primitive than their neighbors. What separated them from the rest of western Europe was religion: the Vikings believed in the pagan gods **Odin**, **Thor**, **Frey**, and a whole range of different deities at the beginning of the Viking Age. Yet in the course of the Viking Age they were converted to Christianity; they gradually abandoned their old writing system, **runes**, in favor of the Roman alphabet; and they were integrated into the mainstream of European culture and Christendom.

Viking Raiding

Raiding is what most people think of when they hear the word *Viking*. Attacks characterized by violence—looting, pillaging, burning, raping, slaughtering—and made possible by the longships that carried these warriors across the seas from Scandinavia to foreign shores. Moreover, in popular belief, these warriors were pagan barbarians who targeted Christian monasteries for the sole reason that they were Christian places of worship. Of course, Vikings did target monasteries and they did loot, burn, and kill. However, it seems that this type of raid was very much a feature of the early years of the Viking Age and, certainly in the British Isles and Frankia, Vikings later devoted much of their energies to the acquisition of land, wealth, and political power, confronting armies in battle, rather than attacking monastic targets. This probably partly reflects the realization by the inhabitants of monasteries that they were vulnerable and unable to adequately protect the wealth that they had accumulated, and the resultant action that they took to protect their establishments: for example, the monks on Lindisfarne and **Noirmoutier** in England and Frankia respectively relocated from their deserted islands to safer locations on the mainland. But the Vikings too must also have realized that greater wealth could be acquired through blackmailing secular authorities to pay them tribute or **Danegeld**.

In this way, the early raids by small numbers of men on isolated coastal monasteries were soon supplanted by larger expeditions: more ships, more men, and wealthier, bigger targets, such as the trading towns of **Dorestad** and **Quentovic** in **Frisia**. In part, the raiders in both Frankia and England took advantage of political problems there—and so Viking activity often peaked when the kings in Frankia or England were weak and lacked political power. For example, there were many raids following the death of **Louis the Pious** in 840, when his Frankish empire was divided among his three sons, **Lothar**, **Louis the German**, and **Charles the Bald**. These brothers were bitterly opposed to each other and hoped to expand their kingdoms to include their siblings' thirds and were happy to employ the Vikings in their wars against each other. Scandinavians also served as mercenaries in other kings' and princes' wars—for their own financial gain rather than political gain. For example, it is known that Scandinavians served in the bodyguard of the emperors of Byzantium. This predominantly Scandinavian bodyguard was known as the **Varangian Guard**, and the most famous Varangian was the Norwegian king, Harald Hard-Ruler. Scandinavians in Byzantium certainly seem to have played an important part in the internal politicking that led to the blinding and deposition of the unfortunate opponent of the emperor, Michael Calaphates, when he attacked the Empress Zoe in 1042. In England, the weakness of King Æthelred II's rule led to the victory of Svein Forkbeard, king of Denmark, whose son Cnut was crowned king of England in 1017. The so-called *Russian Primary Chronicle* also suggests that sometimes Scandinavian involvement in internal politics was actually encouraged by natives. This 10th-century source writes that in the years 860–862, the Scandinavian **Rus** were invited by quarreling Slavonic tribes in the area to come and rule them. Three Rus brothers, the most famous of which was called Rurik, are credited with establishing the state of Russia, centered on the towns of **Kiev** and **Novgorod**.

Viking Colonists

The Vikings who left Norway, Denmark, and Sweden also founded permanent settlements abroad in eastern England, **Ireland**, the Scottish Isles, in **Normandy**, in Russia, and, most famously, in **Iceland** and **Greenland**. In Iceland and Greenland, both of which were virtually uninhabited at the beginning of the Viking Age, the colonists were able to establish their own society in relative peace. However, Viking settlers elsewhere had to deal with pre-existing native populations. In **Orkney** and **Shetland** the incoming Norse appear to have overwhelmed the native Pictish population (*see* **Picts**), who completely disappeared from the islands. At the other extreme, in Russia and Normandy, the Scandinavian settlers only formed a small if politically significant minority and were rapidly assimilated into native society. The scale of the Viking settlements in the **Danelaw**, eastern England, is still very much a matter of scholarly contention. Certainly, the Norse settlers made a significant contribution to the English language, but scholars disagree as to whether large numbers of settlers are needed to explain the extent of this linguistic impact. Yet another colonial experience can be traced in Ireland, where the Scandinavians established themselves in newly founded towns that became the economic, and eventually, the political centers of the island. There is little evidence for any Scandinavian settlement or long-term influence outside these urban sites.

Viking Trade

Commercial journeys were another and an important form of Viking activity. The produce of Scandinavia and the Baltic lands were highly prized in western Europe: the thickest and best-quality furs came from the cold North, there was also the ivory from walrus tusks, and the semiprecious stone, amber, was particularly abundant around the shores of the Baltic. Compared to raiding and colonizing ventures, there is very little written evidence for the trading activities of Scandinavians during the Viking Age. However, archaeological excavations in urban areas and rural settlements across the Viking world are now filling in this gap, by revealing the trading connections of Scandinavia. The evidence of coins and hoards also demonstrate the extent and importance of these links.

CAUSES OF THE VIKING AGE

Historians and writers, from the Viking Age onward, have suggested many different reasons why, between the years 800–1100, there was this sudden surge of activity on the part of the Scandinavian people:

- Monastic writers thought it was God's punishment.
- European clerics, such as Adam of Bremen and **Dudo of St-Quentin**, attributed it to over-population and land shortage in Scandinavia. However, there is no real evidence for this, and in some places, such as Rogaland in southwest Norway and the Baltic island of Öland, archaeological evidence suggests that the population seems to have been larger in the sixth century.
- The development of the classic Viking ship has been seen as a key to the Viking Age, and certainly without it the Viking Age would not have been possible.
- Icelanders, such as **Ari Thorgilsson** and **Snorri Sturluson**, thought the Vikings left Scandinavia to avoid the growing power of kings. Certainly during the Viking Age, the kings of Denmark and Norway had much more power and control over their countries than had previously been the case.
- There also appears to have been a trading boom in Europe—improved ships made it possible to travel and exchange goods farther afield than before.

The account that the Norwegian trader, **Ohthere**, gave to King Alfred of England also provides an insight into some of the reasons why Scandinavians traveled in the Viking Age. He mentions trading as one of the reasons for his journey, but also curiosity—he wanted to explore the regions of north Norway because he did not know what type of country and, perhaps more importantly, what resources he might find there. He discovered the existence of a number of Sámi tribes and was able to impose tribute on them, and so to exercise a sort of economic power. Certainly the desire to acquire wealth—either moveable wealth in the form of loot or fixed wealth in the form of land or even wealth through employment—was an extremely important motive that helped to trigger the journeys of the Viking Age and that underlies many of the expeditions. The desire to gain political power was also important and was an extension of this economic motive: political power meant that you could impose taxes and tribute and control trade. However, there can be no one single explanation of the Viking Age: motives varied over the three hundred years for which it lasted and across the vast distances of Scandinavia. The only real agreement today is that many different factors played a part in triggering this wave of outward activity.

AFTER THE VIKING AGE

Traditionally in English-language scholarship, little attention has been paid to the relationship between Scandinavia and Europe after the Viking Age drew to a close. This is perhaps partly due to the civil wars that dogged Scandinavian politics from the end of the 11th century. Scandinavia seems to have turned in on itself in the centuries after the Viking Age, a development that ultimately resulted in the creation of a pan-Scandinavian union, the so-called Union of Kalmar, which was established in 1397. More important, however, is the fact that although Scandinavia still of course lay on the northern periphery of Europe, it was considered to be part of Europe culturally following its conversion to Christianity. The Danes and the Swedes undertook a series of crusades against their pagan neighbors who lived on the southern shores of the Baltic and in Finland, but this kind of activity was not considered to be "Viking" by contemporaries as it fitted into accepted European models of warfare. Through the Church, Scandinavians were influenced by European models of kingship, law, social organization, and literature. This kind of influence, although less dramatic than Viking activity, ultimately had a more insidious and long-term effect than the raiding that had preceded it.

The Dictionary

– A –

ABBASID CALIPHATE. The Abbasids were an Arab dynasty, descended from al-Abbas, the uncle of the Prophet Mohammed. They displaced the ruling Umayyad dynasty and came to power in the Islamic world around 750, establishing their capital city, Baghdad, on the River Tigris. The lands of the Abbasid caliphate (a caliph was a ruler) were a rich source of silver, and over 60,000 Arabic coins have been found in more than a thousand Scandinavian hoards. This silver, from mines in present-day Afghanistan, Uzbekistan, Kirghizia, and Tajikistan, was an important source of wealth in Scandinavia in the early ninth century but became less important as the mines were exhausted and the caliphate was engaged in civil and foreign wars toward the end of that century.

ABODRITES. Also known as Obodrites. A Slavic people that lived in the area between the lower stretches of the River Elbe and the shores of the Baltic Sea, to the north and northeast of Hamburg, in West Mecklenburg and East Holstein, in present-day Germany. The Danish king **Godfred** appears to have levied tribute from the Abodrite port of *Reric* and to have enjoyed some kind of overlordship over them at the end of the eighth century, but during **Charlemagne's** campaign in Saxony, the Abodrites realigned themselves with the Franks and were rewarded with Saxon lands beyond the Elbe following Charlemagne's conquest of the region in 804. However, Godfred defeated the Abodrites in 808, and he removed their merchants from the unidentified *Reric* to his own new market place at **Hedeby.** Later on, in the 10th and 11th centuries, several marriage alliances were made by Danes with the Abodrites, including **Harald**

17

Blue-Tooth, who married an Abodrite princess, Tove, the daughter of Harald's ally, Mistivoi; the daughter of **Svein Estrithsson** was married to the chieftain, Gottschalk, who was himself descended from Mistivoi (Gottschalk's great-grandfather) and **Svein Fork-beard** (Gottschalk's grandfather).

ADAM OF BREMEN (d. *c.* 1085). The German cleric Adam of Bremen is most famous for his *History of the Archbishops of Hamburg-Bremen*, written between around 1072 and 1075. In his prologue, Adam tells us that he came to Bremen as "a proselyte and a stranger" in 1066–1067 at the request of Archbishop Adalbart, but otherwise very little is known about Adam's background and life. Indeed, his full name is supplied from a later chronicler, Helmold, as Adam refers to himself as "A., the least of the canons of the holy Church at Bremen." As well as being made a canon of the cathedral chapter at Bremen, he may have been the *Adam magister scolarum* in charge of its school in 1069. Scribal annotations later made to the fourth book of Adam's history state that their author, probably Adam, was from upper Germany, and their date suggests that he lived into the 1080s. While Adam of Bremen seems to have made a brief trip to Denmark, where he met the Danish king, **Svein Estrithsson**, there is no evidence that he ever visited Sweden or Norway.

ADMINISTRATION OF THE EMPIRE (Latin *De Administrando Imperio*). A work of guidance compiled by the Byzantine emperor **Constantine VII Porphyrogenitos** for his son Rhomanós II between 948 and *c.* 952. The book consists of some 53 chapters on the geography of the Byzantine Empire's neighbors and on the empire's relations with those countries in the mid-10th century. The original has no title, just the dedication to Rhomanós II. The *Administration of the Empire* is a collection of files rather than a coherent composition, and although some attempt has been made to order the files into logical groupings, this was not fully realized. It has been suggested that Constantine may have been waiting to add material relating to Bulgaria, **Russia**, Khazaria, and Germany before attempting a second reorganization of the documents. While some of the chapters are clearly instructional (such as chapters 1–8 on how to deal with the Pechenegs), others appear to be merely descriptive (chapters 9, 13–53), lacking any evidence of an editorial hand.

Chapter nine is an account of the annual expedition down the River **Dnieper** to **Byzantium** by the Scandinavian **Rus** of **Russia**. It describes the hazardous journey, undertaken in *monoxyla* ("[boat] made from single tree trunk"), in some detail, including "Russian" and Slavonic names for seven of the nine treacherous rapids along the river. At least three of the "Russian" names appear to be Scandinavian: "Oulvorsi" from *Hulmfors* "islet-rapid"; "Gelandri" from *Gællandi* "howling, clanging"; "Leanti" from *Leiandi* "laughing"; possibly too "Varouforos" is from Scandinavian *Bárufors* "wave-rapid," and "Stroukoun" from *(at) strukum* "the narrows, swift currents." In addition to this, chapter nine details the relationship between the Rus and several of the tribes living in the regions around the Dnieper, down to **Kiev**: the Slavic Krivichians and Lenzanenes paid them tribute, but the Pechenegs were hostile; and there is also mention of some pagan rituals performed by the Rus on the island of St. Gregorios on their journey south. Most of this chapter reads like an eyewitness's account, and it has been suggested that Constantine's source was a Byzantine diplomat or perhaps a Scandinavian from Russia, familiar with both the Slavonic and Scandinavian languages.

ÆLFGIFU OF NORTHAMPTON. Known as Alfiva in Scandinavia. Ælfgifu belonged to an aristocratic Mercian (*see* **Mercia**) family and was the daughter of Ælfhelm, who was appointed ealdorman of **Northumbria** in 993. King **Æthelred II** had her father murdered and her brothers blinded in 1006. Ælfgifu married **Cnut I the Great** in 1013 and bore him two sons, **Svein Cnutsson** and **Harold Harefoot**. Although Cnut subsequently married **Emma of Normandy**, widow of Æthelred II of England, in 1017, he continued his relationship with Ælfgifu, which also offered important political advantages. Ælfgifu ruled Norway on behalf of her and Cnut's son, Svein, between 1028–1035, but her rule was unpopular and they were driven out of the country by **Magnus the Good** shortly before Cnut's death. Although her second son, Harold, became king of England in 1035, nothing more is known about Ælfgifu after her departure from Norway.

ÆLLA (d. 867). Anglo-Saxon king of **Northumbria**. Ælla was killed during the Northumbrian battle for **York** against the **Great Army** in March 867. According to the *Anglo-Saxon Chronicle*, the Northumbrians had chosen Ælla, "an unnatural king," over their existing king, Osberht, after the Viking occupation of York in 866. Osberht was also killed in the Northumbrian attempt to recapture York.

According to the legendary 13th-century *Saga of Ragnar Loðbrók* (*see* **Ragnar Loðbrók**), Ælla had its eponymous hero, Ragnar, killed in a snake pit after his attempted invasion of England. The same saga attributes the death of Ælla in 867 to a revenge killing by Ragnar's sons, **Ivar the Boneless**, **Björn Ironside**, and Sigurd, who it is claimed carved a **blood-eagle** on Ælla's back. However, while the three sons are historical figures, there is no evidence for the existence of a man called Ragnar Loðbrók, and the story of the snake pit is a complete literary fabrication.

ÆLNOTH. English monk and author of the *Gesta Swenomagni Regis et Filiorum Eius et Passio Gloriosissmi Canuti Regis et Martyris*, a history of the Danish king, **Svein Estrithsson**, and his sons, including an account of the martyrdom of **Knut II Sveinsson**. Ælnoth was a member of the Benedictine community of Evesham, which established a daughter cell in Odense, Denmark, just before 1100; he wrote his history *c*. 1122.

ÆSIR. One of the two families of Norse gods, including **Odin** and **Thor**, who lived in **Asgard**. According to **Snorri Sturluson's** prologue to the *Prose Edda*, the Æsir originally came to Scandinavia from Troy and their collective name, *Æsir*, meant "men of Asia" (it is in fact the plural form of the Old Norse noun *áss* "god"). *Gylfaginning* describes how these "men of Asia" tricked the people of northern Europe into believing that they were gods. Although Snorri mentions the other family of gods, the **Vanir**, he also includes the Vanir in his list of Æsir at the very beginning of *Skáldskaparmál*, reflecting the use of the word in a wider sense to mean all gods. Similarly his list of goddesses, *Ásynjar*, includes members of both families. For example, Odin's wife, **Frigg**, is named first, but she is followed by one of the Vanir goddesses, **Freya**.

ÆTHELRED II THE UNREADY (d. 1016). King of England 978–1016, Æthelred was the son of the English king, Edgar (d. 975), and his wife, Ælfthryth (*c.* 944–999/1001), and was perhaps nine years old when his father died. His elder half brother, Edward the Martyr (d. 978), became king, but was murdered by a faction linked to Æthelred's mother. Æthelred was formally consecrated king on 4 May 979. He was married twice, firstly to Ælfgifu, by whom he had six sons (Athelstan, Ecgberht, **Edmund Ironside**, Eadred, Eadwig, and Edgar), and secondly, in 1002, to **Emma of Normandy**, by whom he had two sons (Edward the Confessor and Alfred the atheling) and one daughter (Godgifu).

His nickname is derived from Old English *unræd*, which means "poor counsel," and is a pun on the literal translation of his first name ("noble counsel"). However, although the *Anglo-Saxon Chronicle* is critical of Æthelred's policy toward the **Vikings** attacking his kingdom, this nickname is not contemporary and is not evidenced in written sources until the 13th century. Indeed, the *Anglo-Saxon Chronicle*'s account of Æthelred's reign was written after his death and the accession of **Cnut I the Great** and therefore seems to reflect the benefit of hindsight in its assessment of Æthelred's rule. However, Æthelred certainly seems to have been led astray by his counselors in the period 984–993, seizing church lands and granting them to nobles, before repenting in a charter; and after 1006, the growing influence of Eadric Streona, a treacherous ealdorman from **Mercia**, also seems to have caused problems. Nevertheless, there were some internal accomplishments, such as the issuing of the Wantage Code, which extended royal control in the **Danelaw**.

Æthelred's accession to the English throne almost exactly coincided with the resumption of Viking raids in England in 980. The character of these expeditions was quite different from the earlier assaults, with well-organized armies, operating under Scandinavian kings and princes, demanding large payments of silver. In 991, the future king of Norway, **Olaf Tryggvason**, arrived with 93 ships at Folkestone in Kent and succeeded in extracting a **Danegeld** of £10,000 following the English defeat at **Maldon**. Olaf subsequently joined forces with King **Svein Forkbeard** of Denmark and together they ravaged southeast England and attacked London in 994, receiving yet another large tribute from the English (£16,000). In 1002, an even larger sum of money was paid out (£24,000), and in response to a supposed plot against his life, King Æthelred ordered that all the Danes in England should be massacred on **St. Brice's Day** in 1002. However, this presumably antagonized his Scandinavian subjects living in the Danelaw and failed to keep the Viking threat at bay: raids continued and Danegelds were paid again in 1007 (£36,000), 1012 (£48,000), and 1014 (£21,000).

In 1009 a large army under the leadership of **Thorkell the Tall** arrived in England and campaigned extensively in southern and southeastern England for the next three years. Before it dispersed in 1012, virtually the entire area was under Scandinavian control according to the *Anglo-Saxon Chronicle*. However, Thorkell then decided to enter the service of Æthelred, and help him to combat a new Scandinavian army threatening England. In 1013, Svein Forkbeard landed at Sandwich before moving north. He quickly received the submission of **Northumbria**, Lindsey (North Lincolnshire), and the **Five Boroughs** at Gainsborough and then headed back south, taking hostages at Oxford and Winchester, and finally receiving the submission of **London** at Bath. Æthelred, his wife, Emma, and their two sons, Edward and Alfred, fled to **Normandy** and the protection of Emma's family in 1013. However, Svein's death on 3 February 1014 heralded a period of considerable political confusion: while the Danish fleet chose his son, Cnut, as king, the Anglo-Saxon councilors advised that Æthelred should be recalled from exile in Normandy, and he arrived back in his kingdom in 1014. Æthelred's army proceeded to ravage Lindsey, and the king was involved in the murder of two leading figures in the Danelaw (Sigeferth and Morcar), actions that made him unpopular with his subjects in eastern England. Cnut returned to Sandwich in September 1015 and campaigned throughout the country, winning the support of Æthelred's former ally, Eadric Streona of Mercia, and receiving the submission of the West Saxons in 1015. Cnut's armies moved north into the Midlands and Northumbria in spring 1016, but following the death of Æthelred on 23 April, Cnut returned to London. Æthelred's son, Edmund Ironside, was immediately declared king by the councilors and people of London, and later came to terms with Cnut at Olney.

AGGERSBORG. *See* TRELLEBORG FORTRESSES.

ÁGRIP AF NÓREGS KONUNGA SÖGUM ("Summary of the Sagas of the Kings of Norway"). The oldest preserved history of the kings of Norway in the Old Norse vernacular. It is today found in only one 13th-century manuscript, which is an Icelandic copy of a Norwegian original. However, the original text is believed to have been composed in the final decade of the 12th century in **Trondheim**. This strongly patriotic history covers the period of Norwegian history from **Halfdan the Black** to 1177, when Magnus Erlingsson was ruling the country. The author apparently made use of Theodoricus's *Historia de Antiquitate Regum Norwagensium* and possibly *Historia Norwegiae*, as well as lost Icelandic works by **Ari Thorgilsson** and **Sæmund the Learned**.

ALCUIN OF YORK (*c.* 735–804). English cleric, scholar, and teacher, who was brought up and educated at **York** Minster in the kingdom of **Northumbria**. In 781, he was invited by the Frankish emperor **Charlemagne** to take up residence at his court in Aachen, where Alcuin remained until his elevation to the abbacy of Tours in 794. At court, he became the architect of the Carolingian Renaissance, reintroducing old texts and writing new ones, and attracting pupils from across Europe to his school; he reformed Latin pronunciation and laid down standards for the scriptoria; he helped draft royal policy; and he even negotiated between Charlemagne and the Mercian (*see* **Mercia**) king, Offa, during a prolonged stay in England 790–793. Alcuin was also the author of over 270 surviving letters, some of the most famous of which concern the Viking attack on the Northumbrian monastery of **Lindisfarne** in 793. In a letter to Æthelred, king of Northumbria, Alcuin described in vivid terms the attack of the pagan Northmen on the venerable church of St. Cuthbert's. In another letter, to Bishop Higebald and the congregation of St. Cuthbert at Lindisfarne, he attributed this attack to the sinfulness of the inhabitants of Britain, but he also offered the Lindisfarne congregation some small comfort by explaining the harshness of their "punishment" as reflecting God's greater love for them.

ALDEIGJUBORG. *See* STARAJA LADOGA.

ALFIVA. *See* ÆLFGIFU.

ALFRED THE GREAT (d. 899). King of **Wessex** 871–899. Details of Alfred's life and campaigns are primarily preserved in the *Anglo-Saxon Chronicle*, and in his *Life*, written by the Welsh monk, Asser. Alfred was the son of Æthelwulf of Wessex and succeeded his brother Æthelred at a time when England was under severe pressure from the attacks of the **Great Army** that had arrived in the country in 865. Alfred had married Eahlswith (d. 902), the daughter of a Mercian ealdorman, in 868, probably as part of a West-Saxon-Mercian alliance made in that year after the Danish occupation of Nottingham. In 871, the West-Saxon army fought the Great Army at Englefield, Reading, Ashdown, Basing, *Meretun* (after which Æthelred died), and Wilton, before making peace with the Viking army. After spending the winter of 874 at **Repton** in Derbyshire, this Great Army split into two: one half, under **Halfdan**, went north into **Northumbria**, where they settled in 876; the other half, under **Guthrum**, headed into Wessex. Following a surprise attack on his residence at Chippenham in 878, Alfred and a small force took refuge from continued Viking attacks in the marshes of Athelney, Somerset, where he built a fortification and waged a guerrilla war. According to later apocryphal tradition, this period of exile was when he burned the cakes a peasant woman had asked him to watch and when he was visited by a vision of St. Cuthbert. After rallying his army, Alfred won a great victory at **Edington** in 878 against Guthrum's army, which resulted in the establishment of a formal border between Wessex and Guthrum's kingdom in **East Anglia**. This agreement, known as the Treaty of **Wedmore**, was renewed in 886. The settlement also included the baptism of Guthrum and his Vikings, with Alfred standing as Guthrum's godfather.

Alfred used the time bought by the peace of Wedmore to fortify his kingdom against further Viking raids, establishing a series of strongholds (*burhs*) at key points in his kingdom, so that no place in Wessex was more than 32 kilometers from a *burh*; organizing a more effective militia; and developing a naval force. In 886, he drove the occupying Viking force out of **London**, formerly a Mercian possession, and received the submission of all the English people who were not under Danish control. His son-in-law, Æthelred of western **Mercia**, was put in control of the town, signaling a new and effective alliance between the two Anglo-Saxon kingdoms, which ultimately resulted in the emergence of a unified kingdom of England. In 892, a Viking army, led by **Hastein**, landed in Kent. However, Alfred's defensive measures proved effective: Hastein and part of his army was defeated at Benfleet by Alfred and his levies in 893; the garrison at Chichester put an army to flight in 894; and in 895 the Danes were forced to abandon a fort on the Lea after a river blockade was effected by the London garrison. The Danish army dispersed in 896, with individuals settling in East Anglia and Northumbria or sailing to **Frankia**.

Alfred was not only a great military leader; he was also concerned about the decline of Christian learning in his kingdom. He personally translated several important classical works, including Boethius's *De consolatione Philosophie*, Gregory the Great's *Regula pastoralis*, and St. Augustine's *Soliloquia*, into English, and he also commissioned the translation of other works. For example, Alfred had two accounts of Scandinavian geography by the merchants **Ohthere** and **Wulfstan** included in the translation of Orosius's *Seven Books of History against the Pagans* that he commissioned. The *Anglo-Saxon Chronicle* is essentially a record of Wessex's attempt to resist conquest by the Vikings for Alfred's reign and also appears to have been started upon Alfred's initiative. Alfred issued a new law-code, the first West-Saxon ruler to do so since the rule of Ine of Wessex (688–726), which was partially modeled on the eighth-century laws of Offa of Mercia and which aimed to unify the remaining Anglo-Saxon kingdoms.

Alfred died in October 899 and was buried at Winchester. His son, Edward the Elder, succeeded him. He only became known as "the Great" in the 16th century, and it seems that Anglo-Saxons regarded the achievements of his son and grandson, **Athelstan**, as more impressive than Alfred's. Alfred's reputation was first revived by the Anglo-Norman historian, William of Malmesbury.

AL-GHAZAL. Poet and ambassador from Andalusia in **Spain** sent by Abdurrhaman II, Moorish emir of Cordoba, to the court of the king of the **Majus** in the North. Al-Ghazal's journey is said to have taken place in 845, although the account of his diplomatic mission was only written down, by Ibn Dihya (d. 1235), in the 13th century. According to Ibn Dihya, the Majus king's court was situated on a great island in the ocean, three days' journey from the continent of

Europe, near to many other islands and a landmass that belonged to the Majus. On the basis of this description, it has been argued that Al-Ghazal visited either the Danish or Irish court. The account of Al-Ghazal's journey centers upon a poem he recited in praise of the Majus queen, Noud's, beauty, which he admits was a cynical gesture in order to win favor and concessions. The historicity of the whole account is dubious.

ALPHABET. *See* RUNE.

AL-TARTUSHI. *See* AT-TURTUSHI.

ALTHING (ON *Alþingi*). The national assembly of **Iceland** that, according to **Ari Thorgilsson**, was established in the year 930 (although most of what is known about its functioning postdates reforms made in the mid-960s), with a legal system modeled on that of Norway's **Gulathing**.

The Althing was held in the open air, on the plain known as **Thingvellir**, about 50 kilometers east of present-day Reykjavik in southwest Iceland. Proceedings were opened by the *allsherjargoði*, who was the holder of the chieftaincy established by Thorstein, son of **Ingolf Arnason**, who had played a key role in the establishment of the Althing. Every free man, except those excluded by outlawry, met at Thingvellir for two weeks at midsummer, and the most important legal decisions were made and disputes settled by the Althing, headed by the Law-Speaker (ON *lögsögumaðr*).

The Law-Speaker was elected for a three-year period by the *goðar* "chieftains" (*see* **goði**) and had to recite a third of the island's laws every year at the Law-Rock (ON *lögberg*) so that all of Iceland's laws were declared in the course of the Law-Speaker's three-year office. The first Law-Speaker was a man called Úlfljót, who was also responsible for drawing up Iceland's first law-code, *Úlfljótslög*. The Law-Speaker also presided over the legislative council of the Althing, the *lögrétta*, which consisted of all 36 *goðar* (39 after 965, and 48 after 1005) and, later, the two bishops of Iceland. In the 960s, this court was supplemented by four new courts, *fjórðungsdómr* "quarter courts," where cases from the newly established four quarters of Iceland (North, South, East, and West) were heard, if they could not be settled in their respective district **things**. Later, in 1005, a fifth court, *fimtardómr*, was set up in order to deal with cases that the quarter courts were unable to solve. In this court, a majority verdict was acceptable, in contrast to the quarter courts, where decisions had to be unanimous. After the conversion to **Christianity**, a decision taken by the Law-Speaker in 1000, a further court, *prestadómr* "the priests' court," was founded to administer Christian law.

The official end of each Althing was marked by the beating of **weapons**, *vápnatak*, a word that also appears to have given its name to the local administrative divisions of the **Danelaw**—**wapentakes**.

After the loss of Icelandic independence in 1262–64, the Althing lost much of its power: the *goðar* were replaced by royal officials; a new law code, modeled on Norwegian practice, was introduced in 1271; and the assembly met for just a few days each year and performed a largely judicial rather than legislative role. In 1798, when Iceland was under Danish control, the last session of the Althing was held at Thingvellir. For two years it was held instead in Reykjavik, but in 1800 the Danish king decided it should be replaced by a High Court in Reykjavik. The Althing was re-established, in Reykjavik, as a consultative assembly in 1843, although it did not meet for the first time until 1845. This new Althing consisted of 20 elected representatives: one from each county, one from Reykjavik, and six chosen by the king of Denmark. It met for four weeks every two years to discuss new bills that the Danish parliament had introduced and to draw up petitions on matters of particular importance. Although the new Althing could only offer the king of Denmark advice on financial and legal matters, its re-establishment was of great symbolic value to the Icelandic nationalist movement. The Icelandic parliament is today still called the Althing and claims to be the oldest parliament in the world.

AMERICA, NORTH, VIKINGS IN. The **Vinland** of Icelandic sagas is indisputably located in North America, although there is still considerable disagreement concerning the exact location of Vinland on that continent. Only one Scandinavian settlement site has been as yet excavated, that at **L'Anse aux Meadows** in Newfoundland, although genuine Scandinavian artifacts have been found from Ellesmere Island in the north to Maine in the south. Archaeological evidence from

L'Anse aux Meadows suggests that the Norse Greenlanders reached North America by around the year 1000, and although the occupation of that site was relatively short-lived, there is archaeological evidence which suggests that the Norse continued to visit parts of the North American continent and the Canadian Arctic islands in the far north.

Many objects of medieval Norse manufacture have been recently discovered during excavations on sites in Arctic Canada. Many of these come from Inuit dwelling sites on the Arctic mainland and neighboring islands and could have been acquired by trade, pillage, or chance discovery and recovery of discarded objects. In particular, a large number of artifacts have been recovered from the east coast of Ellesmere Island, which faces northern Greenland across Kane Bay, during excavations from the mid-1970s to the mid-1990s. For example, the finds from ancient Thule-culture houses on Skraeling Island, off the east coast of Ellesmere Island, include iron ship rivets, fragments of woolen cloth, a carpenter's plane, some fragments of chain mail, knife and spear blades, and a carved wooden figure whose features are non-Inuit in character. The majority of these finds from Arctic Canada can be dated to the 13th and 14th centuries.

Norse explorers encountered a number of different native peoples, whom they referred to as **skraelings**, an umbrella term that included both Paleo-Indian and Paleo-Inuit (Eskimo) peoples. The Dorset people, a Paleo-Inuit group, lived in the Canadian Arctic and northern Greenland, although their settlements started to contract around the year 1000, leaving Ellesmere Island and Greenland first. The Norse may have encountered them in Labrador, around the east coast of Hudson Bay, and on Baffin Island in the 13th century, but by the middle of the 15th century, the Dorset culture had disappeared from North America. Instead, from about 1200 onward, parts of Arctic Canada previously inhabited by the Dorset people were occupied by the ancestors of the modern Inuit, the so-called Thule people (named after a site in northern Greenland where their culture was first identified archaeologically). By the end of the 15th century, the continued expansion of Thule territory had led to the abandonment of Norse settlement sites in Greenland.

To date, the only genuine archaeological find from the area south of Newfoundland is a silver Norwegian penny from the reign of **Olaf**

the Peaceful of Norway, dated to between 1065 and 1080, which was found on an Indian settlement at Naskeag Harbor, Brooklin, in Maine in 1957. A small hole had been drilled into it, suggesting that it had been used as a pendant. A large number of stone artifacts from Newfoundland and Labrador have also been found on this site, which appears to have been the largest seasonal trading settlement in Maine, and the coin probably arrived here via trading connections with the Indian and Dorset peoples living in the north.

In addition to genuine Scandinavian artifacts, a number of other finds that are claimed to be relics of **Viking** voyages have been reported from North America. The most famous of these are the **Kensington Stone** and the **Vinland Map**, both of which have been rejected as fakes by the majority of serious scholars. *See also* HELLULAND; MARKLAND.

ANGANTYR. Also known as Ongendus. An early eighth-century king of Denmark who, according to **Alcuin's** *Life of St. Willibrord* (*see* **Willibrord, St.**), allowed Christian missionaries into Denmark and let the Anglo-Saxon missionary Willibrord take 30 young boys to train as Christian priests. However, he is also said to have refused to consider conversion himself. Although it is not clear how much of Denmark was ruled by Angantyr, he may have undertaken a number of significant building projects in Jutland. In particular, archaeological evidence reveals that the first phase of the **Danevirke** fortification across the base of the Jutland Peninsula, the construction of the **Kanhave Canal** on the island of Samsø, and the foundation of the town of **Ribe** were all begun in the early eighth century.

ANGLO-SAXON CHRONICLE. The *Anglo-Saxon Chronicle* is the name given to several closely related versions of a chronicle, compiled in various parts of England between the 9th and 12th centuries. Four vernacular chronicles, preserved in seven manuscripts, survive. However, only one contemporary copy of this compilation has been preserved, the so-called *Winchester* or *Parker Chronicle*, which is also known as the A redaction. All of the entries before 891 in the Winchester version were written by an unknown scribe at the Old Minster in Winchester. Several copies of the *Chronicle* were made in

892, and they may have been distributed, although to where is not clear. The other surviving versions of the *Chronicle* seem to be later copies, but all probably come from the same Alfredian archetype, produced somewhere in **Wessex** at the end of the ninth century. In this now-lost original compilation, all years from 756 to 842 appear to have been consistently two or three years in advance. The *Abingdon Chronicles*, B and C, begin with annals for 60 BC, but the other manuscripts start with the birth of Christ. Of the surviving manuscripts, the latest entry in the *Anglo-Saxon Chronicle* is the accession of Henry II in 1154 (the Peterborough or E version).

Although the different versions of the *Chronicles* were dispersed around the country, all but one of the manuscripts continued to be compiled in southern England (A in Winchester and Canterbury; B and C in Abingdon and Canterbury; E in Peterborough, where it was copied from an exemplar similar to D in 1121; and the bilingual Latin and Old English F, also in Canterbury). The exception is D, which was produced at Worcester in the Midlands during the middle of the 11th century, using, among other sources, a now-lost *Chronicle* that was probably written at York (the dioceses of York and Worcester were held by the same person between 972 and 1016). This lost *York Chronicle* is believed to have been written in the early 11th century using the Alfredian archetype and additional material derived from lost northern annals. The so-called *Worcester Chronicle* is therefore the best source for events in northern England, and it also displays some interest in Scottish affairs. It occasionally presents the Scandinavian raiders in a rather different light from the other versions of the *Chronicle*, as allies in local disputes, sometimes even forming alliances with churchmen.

For the reigns of King **Alfred** and King **Æthelred II**, the *Anglo-Saxon Chronicle* is an almost contemporary record, focusing on the **Viking** raids affecting southern England. The compiler of the *Chronicle*, writing around 892, seems to have had a fairly good and detailed knowledge of events since 865. For events before that date, he apparently had access to another chronicle that covered events up to 842, but between the years 842 and 865, it looks as though he had to rely upon memory. This is suggested by the simple frequency of accounts: in the 20 years before 842 there are annals for virtually every year (excluding 822, 826, 828), but between 842 and 865, there are only a total of five annals. Also suggestive of a change in source around 842 is the fact that the chronological dislocation of the dates ends in that year, and there is also a change in the date that the years begin at around the same time: in the second half of the century, they begin on 25 September, while the years in the earlier part of the ninth century begin on 25 December. The 892 chronicler was, to judge by his entries, almost totally preoccupied with the Viking armies and raids and Alfred's response to them. The secular focus of the chronicler is reinforced by the fact that, after 835, no mention is made of the plundering of monasteries and churches. After Alfred's death, the *Chronicle* continues its glorification of the West Saxon dynasty, with an account of the reconquest of the **Danelaw** by Alfred's children, Edward the Elder and Æthelflæd, Lady of the Mercians, before 920. However, for the 50 years or so following these campaigns, none of the Chronicles have very full information; there are gaps and there also appear to be some regional variations.

At the end of the 10th century, the *Chronicle* again becomes a detailed record, and the stimulus is apparently the same as that for the original compilation: the resumption of Viking raids. Several versions are almost identical between the years 983 to 1019. However, the focus of this compiler was not secular but ecclesiastical, and Æthelred II, king of the English, is singled out for criticism rather than praise.

Unfortunately, the *Anglo-Saxon Chronicle* provides little information about the Scandinavian settlements that took place in the ninth century, a development that fell outside the interests and purpose of the chronicler. There is even less about the 10th-century settlement of Vikings that took place in northwest England: the *Chronicle* is totally silent on this subject, and details of it have to be reconstructed principally on the evidence of place-names and oblique and scattered references in other sources. This example serves to demonstrate that although it provides a detailed account of some aspects of Viking activity in England, the *Chronicle* is not a full, reliable, or objective record of the Viking Age.

ANNALS OF FULDA. The *Annals of Fulda* take their name from the monk, Rudolf of Fulda, who is believed to have written one mid-ninth-century section of them on the basis of a marginal note in one of the manuscript groups (group 1). They cover the history of the part of the Frankish or **Carolingian** kingdom that lay to the east of the River Rhine and that later became Germany. There are three main manuscript traditions, which together cover the period from 714 to 901. Up until 830, the *Annals* appear to be a compilation using, among other sources, the *Royal Frankish Annals*, but after this date, they appear to be independent of all known written sources. The annals from 869 onward were apparently almost contemporaneous with the events that are recorded.

The *Annals of Fulda* mention a number of attacks by "Northmen": for example, in 845, one attack was recorded on Hamburg and three on **Frisia**, and the Vikings were paid off by **Charles the Bald** in the same year, after they sailed up the Seine to **Paris**; separate campaigns by a Northman called Rurik (*Roric*) and a duke of the Northmen called Godfred (*Godafrid*) are recorded in 850; in 882, Northmen set up camp at Asselt, 14 miles from the Rhine on the River Meuse, and suffered defeat at the hands of the Franks and the Bavarians; and in 891, another defeat was inflicted on the Northmen at their camp at Louvain on the River Dyle. Political deals, in which Scandinavians were granted land by various Frankish rulers, are also recorded (for example, in 850, when Charles the Bald is said to have granted land to Godfred in return for his support), and there is some reference to the political situation in Denmark (for example, in 854, the *Annals* refer to a civil war between **Horik**, king of the Danes, and his nephew, Guthorm [*Gudurm*]).

ANNALS OF ST-BERTIN. These annals are a continuation of the *Royal Frankish Annals*, and although they are named after the monastery of St-Bertin in present-day France, they were not composed there: the earliest and only complete manuscript of the *Annals* was preserved in this monastery. The *Annals of St-Bertin* begin in 830, following a rebellion against **Louis the Pious** and the removal of untrustworthy elements in Louis's entourage, and they continue up until 882. Although they resume where the *Royal Frankish Annals* finished, and were initially also composed by palace chaplains and archchaplains, it seems that, after 843, the author of the *Annals* was working at some distance from the royal household. The author of this section of the *Annals* was probably Prudentius, a Spanish chaplain at Louis's court, who was appointed to the bishopric of Troyes in 843. At around the same time, following the division of the **Carolingian Empire** at Verdun, the focus of the *Annals* narrows, dealing principally with events in the West Frankish kingdom and the affairs of its ruler, **Charles the Bald**. After Prudentius's death in 861, Archbishop Hincmar of Reims took over the writing of the *Annals of St-Bertin*, until his own death in 882.

Like the *Royal Frankish Annals* and the *Annals of Fulda*, the *Annals of St-Bertin* contain considerable information about Viking attacks on Frankish territory in the ninth century, about diplomatic dealings with the kings, princes, and leaders of the "Northmen" and "Danes," and they also provide a glimpse of the turbulent political conditions inside Denmark during this period.

ANNALS OF ULSTER. The *Annals of Ulster* survive in two manuscripts, *H* (in the library of Trinity College, Dublin) and *R* (in the Bodleian Library, Oxford), but they are not independent copies as *R* is a copy of *H* up until 1510, supplemented by some additional entries that cover the period to 1588. The bulk of both *H* (until 1489) and *R* (until 1510) were written for Cathal Mac Maghnusa and Ruadhrí Mac Craith respectively by Ruadhrí Ó Luinín, who died in 1528. The *Annals* proper begin in the year 431. The language of the *Annals* is Latin, apart from a very few exceptions, until 810, but after this date Irish becomes more common so that by the 830s about half of the entries are Irish. Irish seems to have been the preferred language for the more unusual entries, such as those relating to the **Vikings**. The forms of words and names reflect changes that took place in the pronunciation of Old Irish between the 7th and 10th centuries.

Despite the late date of these manuscripts, there is then a general consensus among scholars that the *Annals* are, for much of the Viking Age, a more or less contemporary record, based upon some other, now lost, set of annals. Indeed, other Irish annals, such as the *Annals of Tigernach*, appear to share the same source until 913, when they diverge. Up until 740, this shared source seems to have been a chronicle from the Scottish island of **Iona**; after this date, a source derived from the monastery at Clonard in Meath seems to have been used and continued to be important up until the mid-10th century. From the

11th century onward, the *Annals'* focus shifts to the north, and later on this northern source can be clearly linked to the Columban monastery of Derry.

The *Annals of Ulster* allow historians to follow Viking activity in **Ireland** in the 9th and 10th centuries more closely than in any other part of the British Isles. However, analyses of this activity have reached quite different conclusions: some scholars argue that the *Annals of Ulster*, together with other Irish annals, suggest that Viking attacks on churches were no more frequent than Irish attacks. However, a recent study has concluded that this view is too simplistic, and that in the first half of the ninth century at least, Viking attacks on churches far exceeded Irish attacks. The same study also points out the geographical bias of the *Annals*, which focuses on the east coast and the central eastern part of the country, at the expense of other areas in the ninth century. Similarly, there is evidence that the reduction of Viking attacks on churches, the so-called "forty years' rest," in the second half of the ninth century is accompanied by a more general reduction in the number of notices about ecclesiastical matters, excluding obits, and may therefore not solely represent a real decline in these attacks.

ANSGAR, ST. (c. 801–865). Known as the "Apostle of the North," Ansgar was the first archbishop of the newly established joint see of Hamburg-Bremen. The main source for his life and achievements is his biography, the *Life of St. Ansgar* (*Vita Anskarri*), which was written by his successor, Rimbert. This details Ansgar's role in the missions to convert pagan Scandinavia during the ninth century and was an important source for **Adam of Bremen's** *History of the Archbishops of Hamburg-Bremen*.

Ansgar, a monk from Corvey Abbey, Westphalia (present-day Germany), was first sent to Scandinavia by **Louis the Pious** in 826, following a request from the exiled Danish king, **Harald Klak**, that Christian missionaries be sent to Denmark. Harald Klak was once again driven into exile in 827, and Ansgar's work in Denmark was cut short. However, King **Björn** of the Svear (*see* **Svealand**) of eastern Sweden sent a request to Louis the Pious that a Christian missionary be sent to Sweden in 829. Ansgar traveled to Sweden with fine gifts from Louis the Pious, but pirates stole these and 40 religious books en route. However, some converts were made and the prefect of **Birka** built a church on his own land. Ansgar was recalled to the imperial court in 831 but later traveled to Rome where the Pope gave him the title of Papal Legate to Scandinavia and the Baltic and made him Archbishop of Hamburg (the see was amalgamated with that of Bremen and elevated to the archdiocese of Hamburg-Bremen, after its destruction by Vikings in 845). In the 850s, Ansgar returned to Scandinavia, building new churches in **Hedeby** and **Ribe** in Denmark (850 and 854 respectively), with the permission of its king, **Horik** I the Older, and in Birka in Sweden (852). *See also* CHRISTIANITY, CONVERSION TO.

ANSKAR, ST. *See* ANSGAR, ST.

ANUND JAKOB (d. *c.* 1050). King of the Svear (*see* **Svealand**) in the early 11th century, who succeeded his father, **Olof Skötkonung**, some time after Olof's death in 1022. Anund was the son of Olof by his wife, Estrith, and was the brother of Ingigerd, who married **Jaroslav the Wise** of **Kiev**, and Astrid, who married **Olaf Haraldsson**. Anund's coins, minted in **Sigtuna**, show that he had succeeded to the kingship of the Svear (*rex S[weonum]*) by 1026 and that he controlled Sigtuna until around 1030–1031. **Adam of Bremen** records that Anund lived until about 1050, information that seems to be derived from one of his main informants, **Svein Estrithsson** of Denmark, who spent some 12 years in exile in Sweden at Anund's court. Very little is known about Anund and his rule, but according to Adam, Svein Estrithsson fought for the Swedish king in Sweden, suggesting that his hold on the throne was not secure. Adam usually refers to Anund by his baptismal name, Jakob (or James), and his treatment of the Swedish king is very favorable, probably due to Anund's religious beliefs and his support for Olaf Haraldsson after **Cnut I the Great** drove Olaf out of Norway in 1028. Anund was succeeded by his brother, **Emund**, who, in contrast, Adam calls "the Bad" and "Gamular," probably "the Old" from ON *gamla*.

ARI THORGILSSON THE LEARNED (ON *Ari þorgilssonr inn fróði*) (1067/8–1148). The so-called "father of Icelandic history," Ari was the first Icelandic historian to write in the vernacular, using the earlier Latin history by **Sæmund the Learned** and the oral testimony of "wise" and "trusty" informants, such as his tutor, Teit Isleifsson; his uncle, Thorkel Gellison; and Thurid, daughter of Snorri *goði*. As well as writing the ***Book of the Icelanders***, it is also likely that Ari compiled the ***Book of Settlements***.

ARMY ROAD (Danish *hærvejen*). Prehistoric track that ran the length of the Jutland Peninsula, passing through the fortified line of the **Danevirke** in the south. This track was the main route for north-south travel in Viking-Age Denmark and is also sometimes known as the Ox Road.

ART. Viking art is generally applied art—art that was used to decorate a range of objects—rather than art for its own sake. Viking art is also generally characterized by zoomorphic designs—consisting of stylized animal ornament. Art historians normally divide Viking art up into six main styles, reflecting different but overlapping stages in its development, and these styles take their names from important artifacts that demonstrate the key features of each style. The earliest Viking art style is that found decorating the prow of the **Oseberg ship** and some of the animal-head posts found in the ship, while the latest is that named after the wooden carvings on the stave-church from **Urnes**, Norway.

In addition to animal ornamentation, stone sculpture also provides evidence of pictorial art. Many of these examples have **mythological** or heroic subject matter, such as the picture stones from **Gotland**, the rune-stone from **Ramsundberget** that depicts the legend of **Sigurd the Dragon-Slayer**, or the **Gosforth Cross** that shows scenes from **Ragnarok**. There are a few surviving fragments of tapestries, such as that from the Oseberg ship burial

During the 12th century, the European Romanesque style gradually replaced the Viking tradition. *See also* BORRE; BROA; JELLINGE; MAMMEN; RINGERIKE.

ASGARD. Asgard was the home and stronghold of the Æsir family of gods in Norse **mythology**. In *Gylfaginning*, **Snorri Sturluson** describes the construction of a fortification for the gods that is generally regarded as referring to the building of Asgard. As payment, the builder asked for the goddess **Freya**, as well as the sun and the moon, and the Æsir agreed to this on the condition that the work was completed by himself alone in just one winter, a period of time that they regarded as being impossibly short. However, at his request, **Loki** agreed that the builder's stallion, Svaðilfari, might help him. The horse worked so quickly that, three days before the deadline, Loki had to change into a mare in order to distract the stallion from its work and prevent the wall being completed. The result of this was that Loki gave birth to an eight-legged foal called **Sleipnir**.

ASHINGDON, BATTLE OF (OE *Assandun*). Battle fought by the English under **Edmund Ironside** against the **Viking** army of **Cnut I the Great** in Essex on 18 October 1016. The site of the battle is normally identified with Ashingdon in general works on the Vikings, although this identification is not certain, and a strong case can be made for Ashdon, also in Essex. Following the flight of Ealdorman Eadric Streona, with the troops from the Welsh marches, the English were defeated by the Vikings. Cnut commemorated the site of this battle in 1020 with a church dedicated to **St. Edmund** of **East Anglia**. Following *Assandun*, Edmund Ironside and Cnut met to discuss terms at Ola's Island in the River Severn, near present-day Deerhurst in Gloucestershire, and agreed to divide the country between them in the so-called Peace of Olney.

ÄSKESKÄRR SHIP. Merchant **ship** from the River Göta in western Sweden, built *c*. 980. The ship measures 16 meters long, 4.5 meters broad, and 2.5 meters deep, with a cargo capacity of 24 tons, and is one of the earliest examples of a Scandinavian trading vessel, a **knarr**.

ASSANDUN, BATTLE OF. *See* ASHINGDON, BATTLE OF.

ASTRID OLAFSDOTTIR (ON *Ástriðr Óláfsdóttir*). Daughter of the Swedish king, **Olof Skötkonung**, Astrid married **Olaf Haraldsson** of Norway in 1019. Astrid was Olaf's second choice, as he had first wanted to marry her sister, Ingigerd, who was, however, given in marriage to **Jaroslav the Wise** of **Kiev**.

ÁSYNJAR. *See* ÆSIR.

ATH CLIATH. *See* DUBLIN.

ATHELSTAN (d. 939). King of Anglo-Saxon England 924/5–39. Athelstan was the son of King Edward the Elder, but only succeeded to his throne after his half brother, Ælfward, died just one month after ascending the throne in July 924. Athelstan was formally crowned in September 925 and it is unclear why there was such a long gap between the death of his half brother and his coronation. The Anglo-Norman historian, William of Malmesbury, suggests that there was opposition to Athelstan because he had been raised at the Mercian (*see* **Mercia**), rather than the West-Saxon (*see* **Wessex**), court; certainly Ælfward also had a brother, Eadwine, who may have been preferred by the West-Saxon faction at court.

Athelstan's reign was marked by the extension of southern power into **Northumbria**, bringing him into conflict with the mixed Norse and Anglian population of Northumbria; the Scottish, under their king, Constantine III; the Welsh, and the Strathclyde Britons. Athelstan first received the submission of these various opponents at Eamont, near Penrith in the present-day northwestern county of **Cumbria**, in July 927, after the death of his Norse ally, **Sigtrygg Cáech** of **York**, prompted an expedition north. Although this control of the north was challenged, most famously in 937, at the Battle of **Brunanburh**, Athelstan still retained his overlordship of the region at the time of his death in October 939. Both his charters and his coins claim that he was king of the whole of Britain.

Athelstan's court was marked by a large number of foreign visitors, which included some from Scandinavia: **Hákon the Good**, son of King **Harald Fine-Hair** of Norway was fostered at his court, as was Alan II of **Brittany**, who had fled his duchy as it was overrun by **Vikings**; and the Icelandic poet, Egill Skallagrimsson (*see* **Egil's Saga**), also spent some time there.

AT-TURTUSHI. Ibrahim ibn Ya 'qub at-Turtushi was a Jewish merchant from Cordoba in southern **Spain** who visited the Danish town of **Hedeby** *c*. 950. He describes Hedeby as lying "at the very end of the world ocean." His account of the town provides information about the religious practices of its inhabitants, who he describes as worshippers of Sirius and a few Christians. He also discusses their lifestyles—they apparently ate a diet of fish and possessed little property or wealth—and their customs, which included the throwing of unwanted newborn babies into the sea.

AUD THE DEEP-MINDED (ON *Auðr in djúpúðga***).** Also known as Unn. Daughter of the most famous Norse Hebridean, **Ketill Flat-Nose**, and wife of **Olaf the White** of **Dublin**. Following the death of her father, husband, and her son, Thorstein the Red, Aud left the **Hebrides** for **Iceland**, where she established a family farm on Breiðafjörður. Her family came to be known by the name Laxdale and was the subject of a 13th-century saga, *Laxdœla Saga*.

– B –

BAFFIN ISLAND. *See* HELLULAND.

BALDER (ON *Baldr***).** God of the Æsir family. Balder was the son of **Odin** and **Frigg** and the husband of the goddess, Nanna. According to the *Prose Edda*, Balder was the wisest, friendliest, and best of the gods, praised by everyone and loved by everything; and "he is so fair in appearance and so bright that light shines from him." Balder lived in the heavens, in Breiðablik, where nothing impure could be found, and had a ship called Hringhorni and a ring called Draupnir.

Snorri's *Gylfaginning* contains a long section about Balder's death and his funeral. Following a series of dreams and premonitions that Balder had, in which his life was in danger, Frigg asked all **things** to swear a promise not to harm her son. Only mistletoe, which Frigg believed was too young to take an oath, was spared from this process, information that **Loki** then gained by tricking Frigg. He then persuaded Hod, a blind god, to throw the mistletoe at Balder, which resulted in his death. Balder's body was placed on his ship, and his broken-hearted wife, Nanna, collapsed and died; they were both burned in the funeral pyre that was lit on the ship, along with Balder's horse. Odin offered the goddess **Hel** a ransom for Balder and was told that Balder would be allowed to return to **Asgard** if all things wept for him. However, a giantess called Thanks (ON *Þökk*) refused, and Snorri claims that this was Loki in disguise. Loki was punished for Balder's death and for preventing his return by being bound to a rock, under the dripping fangs of a poisonous snake. According to the **Eddic** poem, *Balder's Dreams*, and **Saxo Grammaticus's** *History of the Danes*, Odin fathered a son (called Vali and Bous in the respective accounts) by a giantess called Rinda in order to avenge Balder's death. Saxo also describes Balder as an ancient Danish king, associated with the cult place at **Lejre**, and the same idea is also found in the poem *Bjarkamál*, which may, however, also owe much of its content to Saxo.

In both the *Prose Edda* and the Eddic poem, *Völuspá*, an account of **Ragnarök** immediately follows the details of Balder's death and Loki's punishment. Balder is one of the few gods who survived Ragnarök, along with his unwitting killer, Hod. This rebirth has been likened by some scholars to the resurrection of Christ, suggesting that the Balder myth was modified as a result of contact with Christianity.

BALLADOOLE. Site of a pagan Viking-Age **ship** burial from the northern parish of Jurby on the Isle of Man. The ship, measuring about 11 meters in length, had been placed in an early Christian graveyard, surrounded by stones set in the shape of a ship. It contained the remains of a man and woman, along with traditionally male grave goods that included horse-harnesses, stirrups, spurs, and a shield.

BALLATEARE. Site of a Viking-Age pagan burial from the southern parish of Arbory on the **Isle of Man**. The burial mound contained the remains of a man and a **woman**, although the grave goods were exclusively "male" in character consisting of, among other things, a sword in its scabbard, spears, knives, and the remains of a shield. The male skeleton, probably aged between 20 and 25, had been placed in a wooden coffin or a timber chamber, dressed in his cloak, which was then covered in soil and turf. The cremated remains of cattle, horse, sheep, and dogs were found near the top of the mound, along with a female skeleton, aged between 20 and 30, whose skull had been badly slashed as part of a ritual sacrifice.

BAYEUX TAPESTRY. The Bayeux Tapestry consists of eight separate pieces of linen, embroidered with wool of eight colors that have been joined together, giving a total length of 68.4 meters. The embroidery depicts some 79 different scenes concerning the events that led to the Battle of Hastings on 14 October 1066, when the English king, Harold Godwinsson, was killed by an invading Norman army under its duke, William II of **Normandy**. Above the scenes there are a number of Latin captions, explaining the sequence of events from when Harold said good-bye to Edward the Confessor, king of England, before setting sail to Normandy from his manor in Bosham *c.* 1063–64, until the flight of the defeated English from the battlefield in October 1066.

The tapestry is not mentioned in any written sources before 1476, when it appears in an inventory of Bayeux Cathedral's possessions, and then there is a further silence of some 250 years before part of it was sketched in 1724. The first complete picture of the tapestry was published in Montfaucon's *Monuments de la Monarchie Française* in 1728–1729. The work was very probably commissioned by a Norman; certainly it portrays events from a Norman point-of-view, although the workmanship appears to be English. An old French tradition claimed that it was embroidered by William's wife, Matilda, but most scholars have rejected this theory. A strong case has instead been made for Odo, Bishop of Bayeux and half brother of William the Conqueror, as the patron of the tapestry. It has been argued that the tapestry may have been produced in the English town of Canterbury, Kent (Odo was Earl of Kent 1067–1082), in the years immediately after the Conquest, and that it was first displayed in public at the dedication of Bayeux Cathedral in 1077. However, the Bayeux Tapestry is primarily a secular "document" and the connection with the Cathedral may be secondary.

The tapestry is of interest to historians of the **Vikings** because of the picture it gives of Norman **ships** and shipbuilding, **weapons** and warfare, some 150 years after **Rollo** established a Scandinavian colony in Normandy.

BELOOZERO. Town on the River Volga in **Russia** where, according to the ***Russian Primary Chronicle***, Sineus, Rurik's brother, settled following the episode known as "The Calling of the **Varangians**."

However, the figures of Sineus and Truvor, another so-called brother of Rurik, are probably later literary inventions by the author of the *Chronicle*, and so Beloozero's connection with Rurik's dynasty is of doubtful historicity.

BERGEN (ON *Björgvin* "pasture land by the mountain"). The western Norwegian town and port of Bergen is first mentioned in written sources in 1135, when the English monk Orderic Vitalis lists it in his *Historia Ecclesiastica* as the first of six *civitates* or towns lying on the Norwegian coast. Later sources date the town's foundation to *c*. 1070 in the reign of King **Olaf the Peaceful**, but while *Heimskringla* suggests that this was established on virgin land, *Morkinskinna* and *Flateyjarbók* imply that Olaf simply formalized arrangements, regulating a market place that was already in existence. Recent archaeological investigations around the harbor of Bergen have failed to reveal any artifacts or structures predating the 1130s, but this can be attributed to the fact that the Viking-Age shoreline lay approximately 140 meters behind the current harbor front. Current scholarly opinion favors the model of a gradual organic growth of settlement around Vågen, the inlet of the fjörd connecting Bergen to the North Sea, which was later formalized by Olaf.

Certainly the rapid rise to prominence that Bergen enjoyed after its "foundation" is suggestive of development before Olaf's time: by the 1130s, the social, economic, and topographic structures of Bergen were clearly those of a town; and the town seems to have played an important role in the Norwegian civil war that began around that time. There is also strong evidence for an earlier important royal estate at Alrekstad in Bergen, mentioned in the saga of **Harald Fine-Hair**, which is likely to have been an administrative, economic, and possibly market center during the Viking Age, particularly as Vågen was normally free of ice all year round.

We also know from *Heimskringla* that Olaf build a wooden church, Christchurch, at Holmen in Bergen and laid the foundations for the stone church that was to later become the cathedral; a list of bishoprics, compiled around 1120, includes Bergen, and it probably was derived from an earlier list dating to shortly after the year 1100. By 1240, Bergen had been declared the capital of Norway, replacing **Trondheim**, and King Hákon Hákonarson (d. 1263) built a royal hall (now called Håkonshallen) at the entrance to the town's harbor. Bergen thrived on the profits of exporting stockfish to England and the Low Countries, and the Hanseatic League established a "counting house" there in 1343. The German merchants of the Hanseatic League lived in a quarter of the town called Tyskebryggen "the German Wharf," and had soon assumed total control of the trade from Bergen. Excavations in and around Bryggen since the mid-1950s have uncovered, among other things, over 600 runic inscriptions (*see* **rune**) on wood and, to a lesser extent, bone and metal. These have revolutionized runic studies by revealing a much more casual use of the runic alphabet in everyday contexts than was previously known.

BERSERKER (ON *berserk*, **pl.** *berserkir* **"bear skin").** Name given to **Viking** warriors who fought so fiercely in battle that they did not need armor and did not feel pain. **Snorri Sturluson** describes this battle fury in *Ynglinga Saga*: "his [**Odin's**] men rushed forward without armor, were as mad as dogs or wolves, bit their shields, and were as strong as bears or wild bulls, and killed people at a blow, but neither fire nor iron told upon themselves" (ch. 6). Although Snorri Sturluson believed that the word was derived from ON *berr* "bare," meaning someone who fights without armor, it is more likely that a berserker means "person wearing a bear's skin," and who thus took on the characteristics of a bear in battle. In some sagas, such as the *Saga of Hrólfr Kraki*, the berserker is even said to have taken on the shape of a bear.

The earliest surviving reference to berserker is in *Haraldskvæði*, a **skaldic** poem composed by Thorbjörn *hornklofi* ("Horn-Cleaver" = raven) for the Norwegian king, **Harald Fine-Hair**, in the late ninth century and preserved in Snorri Sturluson's *Heimskringla*. In this poem, Harald is said to have had a troop of berserkers, who fought for him at the Battle of **Hafrsfjörd**, and they are also described as or linked with *Úlfheðnar* "men clad in wolf skins." This connection between wolf and bear is also apparent in other sources, such as *Egil's Saga*. Egil's grandfather was known as Kveld-Ulf ("evening wolf") and his father, Skalla-Grim was a berserker. Both father and grandfather are depicted as being uncontrollably violent at times: Kveld-Ulf's rage leads to his death, and Skalla-Grim almost kills his own son. The medieval Icelandic **law-code**

Grágás penalizes *berserkgangr* ("going berserk") with lesser outlawry, and those people present at the time received the same sentence unless they tried to restrain the man.

BIFROST (ON *bifröst*). Rainbow bridge that connects **Asgard**, the home of the gods, with **Midgard**, where humankind live. The red in the rainbow is said to be burning fire, to prevent unwanted visitors from crossing into the heavens. According to *Gylfaginning*, Bifrost is the most important bridge in the Norse cosmos. The etymology of the word *bifröst* is uncertain: it may be derived from the ON verb *bifa* "to sway, to shake," but the **Eddic** poems, *Grímnismál* and *Fáfnismál*, record the bridge's name as *bilröst*, which means "fleetingly glimpsed rainbow." The *Prose Edda* tells us that the bridge was also known as *ásbrú*, "bridge of the Æsir or gods," because they rode over it every day to their court at Unn's Well (ON *Urðarbrunnr*). The bridge was apparently built by the gods and its end in the heavens, at Himinbjörg, was guarded by the god **Heimdall**. At **Ragnarök**, the bridge is said to have collapsed as the sons of **Muspell**, probably giants, crossed the bridge to confront the gods.

BIRKA. Viking-Age town on the island of Björkö, Lake Mälaren, in the Swedish province of Uppland (to the north of the modern capital, Stockholm). Archaeological excavations suggest that the first inhabitants lived in Birka around the middle of the eighth century and that, at its peak, the town consisted of a population of about 900 people living in an area of *c*. 13 hectares. The town flourished until the end of the Viking Age, when **Sigtuna** became the most important town on Lake Mälaren. Birka was apparently abandoned toward the end of the 10th century, possibly due to the postglaciation rise in land levels in eastern Sweden, which made access to Lake Mälaren via a portage at Södertälje difficult.

Birka is one of the richest archaeological sites from Viking-Age Scandinavia. More than 3,000 burial mounds and graves, both pagan and Christian, have been found around the town. Excavations began back in the 17th century, although the first large-scale excavations took place in the 19th century, when over 1,000 burial mounds were investigated. The finds from these burials reveal that during the Viking Age, the town thrived on the profits of trade with the east, particularly with **Russia** and the Islamic world: northern furs were exchanged for silver and silks from the East. These burials also provide invaluable evidence of the transition from paganism to **Christianity** in eastern Sweden, suggesting that the process of conversion proceeded slowly and that pagans and Christians lived side-by-side for a considerable period of the town's history. Excavations begun in 1990 concentrated on the town's so-called "Black Earth" (this name is derived from rich organic waste that has made the soil darker than that elsewhere in the area). These excavations uncovered the town's regular grid plan, with plots divided by ditches and paths. The wealth of the town seems to have made it vulnerable to attack: in the ninth century, a hill fort, Borg, was built on the southern edges of the town, and in the following century, defensive walls were constructed around the town and a wooden palisade was built in the harbor.

Rimbert's *Life of St. Ansgar* provides us with some further details of Birka's history: the German missionary, **Ansgar**, visited the town in 829, when it was under the rule of a king called **Björn**. Ansgar stayed in the town for some 18 months, leaving a bishop and priests behind him to continue the mission after his return to Bremen. However, shortly after his departure, the clergy was driven out of Birka and at least one priest was killed. Although Ansgar did not return to the town until the 850s, when another church was built for the town, it is clear that Hamburg-Bremen continued missionary activity in Birka as Archbishop Unni of Bremen died in Birka *c*. 936.

BIRSAY, BROUGH OF. Tidal island off the northwest coast of mainland **Orkney**, **Scotland**, which was a center of political and ecclesiastical power in the Northern Isles during the late Viking Age. The place-name, Birsay, is derived from ON *Byrgisey*, "island of the *byrgi*," and *byrgi* is, in turn, a form of ON *borg* "enclosure." This word can also be used more specifically as "a place so shaped by nature that it can be easily shut off," thus a peninsula or narrow neck of land or even an islet. The *borg* referred to is presumably the Brough of Birsay, which can be reached by a causeway at low tide.

There have been extensive archaeological excavations on the Brough since the 1930s, revealing the remains of pre-Norse and Norse occupation. Although the island has often been associated with an early Christian monastic site, recent excavations have not been able to confirm this. Finds instead reveal that an important bronze-working industry was based on the Brough in the late eighth century, although structural evidence for a large Pictish population (*see* **Picts**) on the island is lacking. Three ogham inscriptions have been found on the Brough, two of which are casual graffiti dated to the ninth century. A fourth ogham inscription on a stone spindle whorl, dated to the eighth century, was found at the domestic settlement of Buckquoy, just across the bay from the Brough of Birsay. A unique symbol stone decorated with three warrior figures and two carved grave slabs have also been recovered from the Brough.

A complex of buildings, dated to the 10th and 11th centuries, has been excavated on the landward side of the Brough. These were originally identified as Earl **Sigurd the Stout's** and Earl **Thorfinn the Mighty's** "palaces" and are high-status constructions with complex drainage and heating systems and skillful masonry. More conventional Norse **longhouses**, occupied from the 9th into the 13th or 14th centuries, have been excavated on the slopes behind the church. The remains of what appears to be a Norse smithy, in use during the 10th and 11th centuries, were also found on this site.

The ruins of a church, incorporating the fragments of six Scandinavian runic inscriptions (*see* **rune**), also stands on the Brough. This church was previously believed to be the remains of Earl Thorfinn the Mighty's Christchurch. However, an early 12th-century date for the church is currently favored by scholars, andso this identification seems unlikely. Furthermore, it is uncertain if Thorfinn's church was actually located on the Brough, as *Orkneyinga Saga* only locates the church in the parish of *Byrgisherað*. The Brough church is recorded as being dedicated to either St. Peter or St. Colme, not Christ, and while the remains of an 11th-century church have not yet been identified in the locality of the village, the remains of a large and impressive 12th-century church have been excavated below the present parish church of **St. Magnus** in Birsay village, a suggestive dedication given that St. Magnus was initially buried in Thorfinn's church. The 16th-century Stewart earls' palace and bishops' palace are also situated in the modern village of Birsay, and recent excavations have uncovered a substantial 10th-century hall and later buildings in the village area, possibly the first seat of the **earls** of Orkney.

On the Brough, excavations have revealed an earlier church and graveyard underlying the 12th-century church and the graveyard on a slightly different alignment. Unfortunately these cannot be dated, but it is possible that the new 12th-century structures on the Brough are associated with the translation of Magnus's relics, some 20 years after his death, and a change in the status and function of the Brough community. The translation to Kirkwall certainly suggests a shift in the power base of the earldom to Kirkwall, and we find Bishop William increasingly associated with Egilsay and Kirkwall, rather than Birsay, in *Orkneyinga Saga*. Such a shift may have provided the backdrop to the incorporation of three rune-stones in the church on the Brough. The role of the Brough of Birsay complex after this shift in power is unclear, but the buildings associated and probably contemporary with the 12th-century church are likely to have been part of a monastic complex.

BJARKAMÁL ("The Lay of Bjarki"). Poem about the final battle of Bödvar Bjarki and Hjalti, **berserkers** of the heroic king of Denmark, **Hrólfr kraki**. According to Snorri's *Heimskringla*, this was recited by the skald Thormod Kolbrunarskald the night before the Battle of **Stiklestad** at the request of **Olaf Haraldsson**. Apparently, Olaf's sleeping army was roused and encouraged by the heroic poem. **Snorri Sturluson** includes a short quotation from the poem, and a further three excerpts—which contain terms for gold—are preserved in his *Prose Edda*.

However, the only complete version of the poem is found near the end of Book Two of **Saxo Grammaticus's *Gesta Danorum***. This account of the death of Hrólfr *kraki* and his men at **Lejre** at the hands of a Swedish army led by a witch called Skuld agrees in outline with that preserved in the later *Saga of Hrólfr Kraki*. However, Saxo's poem is in Latin and consists of 298 hexameters, presented as a dialogue between Bjarki and Hjalti, and Saxo concludes the poem with a statement that he "composed this set of admonitory speeches in meter because the same thoughts, arranged within the compass of a Danish poem, are recited from memory by many who are conversant with ancient deeds." Clearly there was a strong tradition relating to the events recounted in *Bjarkamál*, but the age of the poem, whether it was written down before Saxo and Snorri, and in what language it might have been composed, are questions that cannot be answered.

BJARKEYJARRÉTTR. Name given to the laws that applied in the trading centers or towns of Norway and Sweden and which were developed into separate municipal **law-codes** in the medieval period. The name is believed to be derived from **Birka**, Sweden's largest and most important Viking-Age trading center. The only town for which these laws (as opposed to later municipal codifications) survive is Lödöse in western Sweden, near present-day Gothenburg, although two fragments of the municipal code for **Trondheim**, known as the *Bjarkøyretten*, dated to *c*. 1250, survive for Norway.

BJARNI HERJÓLFSSON. According to the evidence of the *Saga of the Greenlanders*, Bjarni was probably the first European to sight **North America**. He was blown off course on a voyage from **Iceland** to **Greenland**, and as a result he sighted three new "countries": **Markland**, **Helluland**, and **Vinland**. Bjarni's parents had sailed to Greenland with **Erik the Red** in 985 and established a family farmstead at Herjolfsnes in the Eastern Settlement. The churchyard at Herjolfsnes, containing over 120 burials, was excavated in 1921. The teeth and bones of the skeletons show some evidence of a poor diet, and a unique collection of woolen clothing reveals that the inhabitants of Herjolfsnes in the first half of the 15th century wore woolen garments in European styles, rather than the furs worn by their Inuit neighbors.

BJÖRN IRONSIDE. Joint leader, with **Hastein**, of a **Viking** fleet of some 62 **ships** that looted around the Mediterranean between 859–862. According to **William of Jumièges**, Björn was the son of the legendary **Ragnar Loðbrók**, and his nickname was attributed to a spell of invulnerability that his mother had cast on him, which meant that he could not be hurt on the battlefield. Hastein (*Hasting*) is said to have been Björn's tutor and is characterized by William as a "very deceitful man." Together, they attacked the Spanish (*see* **Spain**), southern French, and North African coasts, and the Balearic Isles before reaching Italy, where they sacked Pisa. Finally they destroyed what they thought was Rome but which was in fact the town of Luna, some 300 kilometers to the north of Rome. They returned to their base on the Loire in France in 862, and Björn later died in **Frisia** after being shipwrecked off the English coast. Although the **Annals of St-Bertin** do mention a Viking leader called Björn, who swore an oath of fidelity to **Charles the Bald** in 858, William of Jumièges's account of Björn seems to owe more to fiction than to fact.

BJÖRN, KING. Rimbert's *Life of St. Ansgar* records that Björn was king of the Svear (*see* **Svealand**) in the late 820s and that he welcomed **Ansgar's** mission to **Birka**.

BLOOD-EAGLE (ON *blóðörn*). This gory rite is said to have been inflicted upon Ælla of **Northumbria** in 867 by the **Viking, Ivar the Boneless**, as revenge for Ælla killing his father, the legendary **Ragnar Loðbrók**. Descriptions of the blood-eagle are first found in the late 12th century and are associated with two historical figures (Ælla and **Halfdan**), as well as with two mythical figures (Lyngvi and Brusi). A recent suggestion that **St. Edmund** of **East Anglia** may have been the victim of the blood-eagle is unconvincing. Although there is some variation in the details, the "classic," most lurid, version of the blood-eagle involved the ribs being torn from the spine and the lungs being pulled out through an eagle-shaped cut on the victim's back.

The first extant reference to this ritual killing, and the only Viking-Age evidence for the blood-eagle, is a half stanza of the **skaldic** poem *Knútsdrápa*, composed by **Sighvatr Þórðarson**. This has been traditionally interpreted as: "Ivar had Ælla's back incised with an eagle" and seems to be the source of later Scandinavian accounts about the ritual. However, this interpretation has been challenged as a too literal interpretation of the poem, suggesting instead that Ælla's back was cut *by* an eagle, one of the carrion birds that circled battlefields; in other words, he was killed (in an otherwise unspecified manner). Certainly the highly elliptical nature of Sighvatr's poetry makes it open to misinterpretation.

BÓNDI (plural *bændr*). ON noun with the primary meaning of "head of the household." In the predominately agricultural and rural society of Viking-Age Scandinavia, this word is often used in the sense of "farmer, a person who owned a farm," but it is also frequently found on Viking-Age rune-stones (*see* **rune**) with the meaning of "husband." Later on, in the medieval period, with the development of towns and trade, the word also took on a more general meaning of "someone who owned land or property (in the town)," and thus "landlord" or "burgher." In the Icelandic **law-codes**, each *bóndi* was required to join the following of a chieftain (*see* **goði**) and to accompany him to the springtime assembly and to either pay a **thing**-attendance tax or to attend the **Althing** with their chieftain each summer. These laws also stated that a *bóndi* could choose which chieftain to follow and that he was allowed to change chieftains as often as once every year. The **Eddic** poem **Rígsþula** includes a reference to a man called Bóndi, who was one of the sons of the free farmer, Karl.

BOOK OF THE ICELANDERS (ON *Íslendingabók*). A short history of **Iceland**, from its settlement circa 870 until 1118, composed by **Ari Thorgilsson** between 1122 and 1132. This is the first extant history of Iceland and it is also significant as it is composed in Icelandic, not Latin. The *Book of Icelanders* records the settlement of Iceland; the establishment of the Icelandic national assembly, the **Althing**; the development of the Icelandic **law-codes** and administration; and the discovery and settlement of **Greenland**. However most space is devoted to a discussion of the conversion of Iceland to **Christianity** and the early history of the Icelandic church. Ari refers to a number of his sources, the majority of which are old and trustworthy people, such as Teit, Ari's foster-father and son of Bishop Isleif; Thorkel Gellison, Ari's uncle; and Thurid, daughter of Snorri **goði**.

BOOK OF THE MEASUREMENT OF THE EARTH (*Liber de mensura orbis terræ*). Latin work written by the Irish monk, Dicuil, in France *c*. 825. Dicuil writes that monks had visited and settled on various islands to the north and northwest of the British Isles, presumably in the North Atlantic. He provides brief descriptions of what appear to be the **Faroe Islands**, apparently inhabited by Irish hermits for about 100 years, and "Thule," which has been identified with **Iceland**. In his account of "Thule," Dicuil states explicitly that his source was the accounts of priests (*clerici*) who had lived there 30 years before he was writing.

Today, the *Book of Icelanders* survives in two 17th-century copies of a lost codex from *c*. 1200. According to his preface, Ari had written an earlier version of this work, and the version we have is his revised version, following suggestions by Bishop Thorlak of Skálholt (descended from **Aud the Deep-Minded**) and Bishop Ketill of Holar (descended from **Helgi the Lean**), and **Sæmund the Learned**.

BOOK OF SETTLEMENTS (**ON** *Landnámabók*). Probably compiled by **Ari Thorgilsson** in the early 12th century, this work includes a detailed account of the land taken by the original settlers of **Iceland**, organized topographically by the four quarters into which Iceland was divided, as well as comprehensive genealogies of these settlers. In all, some 430 different settlers, 3,500 personal names, and 1,500 farm names are recorded in this work, which made it an extremely useful source for later saga writers.

In total, there are five different redactions of *Landnámabók*: three were written or compiled in the medieval period and two were compiled in the 17th century. *Sturlubók* is attributed to Sturla Þórðarson (d. 1284) but the only extant version of this redaction is found in a 17th-century manuscript; *Hauksbók* is the work of Haukr Erlendson (d. 1334), written between 1306–1308, but it too is only found in a 17th-century manuscript. Haukr seems to have used *Sturlubók* and an older, now lost, version called *Styrmisbók*; *Melabók* was written at the beginning of the 14th century. This is actually preserved in the oldest manuscript, but it is unfortunately only fragmentary; *Skarðsárbók* is a 17th-century compilation based on *Hauksbók* and *Sturlubók*; and finally *Þórðarbók* is another 17th-century compilation, but based on *Skarðsárbók* and *Melabók*.

BORG. High-status settlement on the island of Vestvågøy, Lofoten, northern Norway. Although Borg lies well north of the Arctic Circle, archaeological work in the area has revealed that there was relatively dense settlement in the area during the Iron Age and Viking Age. In Lofoten, the climate was relatively mild, warmed by the Gulf Stream, and there was good fishing and good grazing for cattle. From the island of Vestvågøy alone, about 1,000 graves, 50 boathouses, and 18 farms are known from this period.

Borg itself enjoyed a protected harbor and a good view of the surrounding countryside. The Viking-Age structures from Borg include the remains of a chieftain's hall that was 83 meters long, dating to the eighth or ninth century, three boathouses, and a circular courtyard believed to have housed the chieftain's men. Luxury items from the site include pottery and glass from western Europe and two gold foil figures (Norwegian *gullgubbe*), believed to depict the god **Frey** and the giantess Gerd, that have a cultic significance. Finds of this nature are normally associated with Scandinavian trading centers, such as **Kaupang**, Helgö, **Birka**, and **Hedeby**. However, the majority of the finds were of an everyday character and suggest that farming and fishing were the most important economic activities at Borg.

BORNHOLM. Island in the Baltic Sea, which today is part of Denmark. However, an account of a journey from **Hedeby** to Truso by the English merchant, **Wulfstan**, preserved in King **Alfred the Great's** translation of Orosius' *Seven Books of History against the Pagans*, records that the island (*Burgenda land*) had its own king. Culturally, the island is distinct from Denmark in a number of ways: for example, Viking-Age rune-stones (*see* **rune**) continued to be raised on Bornholm after the custom ceased to be popular in Denmark at the end of the 10th century, and their design has more in common with Swedish rune-stones than Danish.

BORRE. Scandinavian **art** style that takes its name from the artifacts found in the burials at Borre, Vestfold, in southeast Norway. The cemetery at Borre contains nine large and a number of smaller burial mounds, and two cairns, making it the largest group of high-status burial mounds in Scandinavia. The burial mounds at Borre are believed to be those of the Viking-Age kings of Norway, and references in **skaldic poetry**, such as *Þjóðólfr* of Hvin's stanza quoted in *Ynglinga Saga*, substantiate the royal nature of the site. However, two of the large mounds have recently been given C14 dates in the seventh century, suggesting that the site was important before, as well as during, the Viking Age. The first mound was uncovered in the mid-19th century, when a gravel pit was dug. The remains of a **ship**, some 17 meters long, was found, along with a number of grave goods, the most important of which were the gilt-bronze harness mounts that gave the Borre art style its name.

The main characteristics of the Borre style are the so-called "gripping beast" motif and the ring-chain interlaced pattern. The Borre style was current from the mid-9th to the mid-10th century in Scandinavia, and is also found on artifacts from **Iceland**, the British Isles, **Ireland**, and **Russia**.

BRAAID, THE. Settlement in Marown parish on the **Isle of Man**, consisting of two **longhouses**, one of which measured a massive 21 meters by 9 meters and was constructed with large stone slabs. The smaller of the longhouses is interpreted as a stable or byre for livestock. The site is particularly interesting as a roundhouse. Built in the traditional Manx style, it stands adjacent to the typically "Scandinavian" longhouses. It is possible that the "Scandinavian" and "Manx" houses were occupied concurrently for a brief period, although the lack of diagnostic artifacts makes it impossible to discuss the question of interaction between Scandinavian and Manx cultures and populations on the site.

BRACTEATES. Disks of thin gold produced in Scandinavia during the fifth and sixth centuries that were originally imitations of Late Roman and Byzantine medallions showing the emperor's head. They were stamped with decoration, usually a central picture and surrounding patterns, on just one side, and had a loop so that they could be worn as pendants around the neck. Over 100 of these bracteates also have inscriptions in the older, 24-letter runic alphabet (*see* **runes**). Many of these runic letters are upside-down or backward facing, and although this has been traditionally interpreted as a sign of illiteracy among the gold-smiths who produced the bracteates, the problems of cutting an inscription in reverse in a die may account for a substantial number of these "mistakes." The well-known magical words *alu* "luck," *laukaR* "fertility, prosperity?" ("leek"), and *auja* "well-being" are the most commonly occurring words found in these bracteate inscriptions.

BRAGI. God of the Æsir who, according to the *Prose Edda*, was the god of poetry. He was married to the goddess, **Idun**, but otherwise very little is known about him and he is very rarely mentioned in **Eddic** or **skaldic** poetry. It seems likely that the god was in fact created by medieval writers from a historical figure, Bragi Boddason (also known as Bragi the Old), a ninth-century skald. In the medieval *Skáldatal* ("List of Skalds"), Bragi is said to have served at the court of the Swedish king **Björn**, who was visited by **St. Ansgar**. The *Prose Edda* contains some 20 stanzas of *Ragnarsdrápa*, a poem composed by Bragi that describes various **mythological** scenes that were depicted on a shield.

BRATTAHLÍÐ (Inuit *Qagssiarssuk*). Site on Eiriksfjörd, Eastern Settlement in **Greenland**, where **Erik the Red** built his farm at the end of the 10th century. In addition to being the political center of the Eastern Settlement, one of the earliest churches in Greenland was built at Brattahlíð by Erik's wife, Thjodhild. This turf structure and its associated graveyard, lying some distance from the 14th-century stone church that is visible today on the site, have been excavated by archaeologists. The graveyard contained an unusual mass grave near the south wall consisting of the disarticulated skeletons of some 13 males who had apparently been buried simultaneously. The remains of three different farms and a **thing** place can also still be seen at Brattahlíð. Brattahlíð is still one of the best locations for farming in Greenland.

BREVIS HISTORIA REGUM DACIE ("Short History of the Kings of Denmark"). Twelfth-century history of Denmark written by **Sven Aggesen**, possibly *c*. 1188, which begins with the first king of Denmark, Skjöld, and concludes in 1185, with the submission of Bugislav, prince of Pomerania, to Knut VI (d. 1202) of Denmark following the naval victory at Stralsund. As well as detailing the genealogy of the kings of Denmark and summarizing some 35 reigns, Sven's history incorporates longer sections of narrative that include two anti-German stories: the legend of Uffi, who defeated the Germans, and Queen **Thyre's** rejection of the German emperor, Otto. A lost genealogy, which Sven refers to, was originally appended to the *History*. Although Sven claims to have used old traditions and the stories of "aged men" in compiling his history, it seems that this was largely authorial rhetoric; certainly most of his information can be traced to written sources. As well as referring to the work of Icelanders, Sven was clearly versed in classical and biblical learning and cites, amongst others, Virgil, Ovid, and Lucan.

The *Short History* is preserved in two manuscript traditions (designated A and S), along with another of his works, the *Law of the Hird* (*see* **hird**) or *Vederlov*. Unfortunately, both traditions are problematic: A is an often unintelligible copy of a lost medieval manuscript made around 1570, and S is an amended copy of a lost medieval manuscript, made in the late 13th century; this 13th-century copy was in turn "corrected" by Stephan J. Stephanius for the first printed edition of Sven's works, made in the 17th century. Unfortunately, the 13th-century copy was destroyed in a fire in Copenhagen in 1728, and it is now impossible to separate Stephanius's amendments from those of the medieval scribe.

BRIAN BORU (Irish Brian *Bóraime* "of the tributes") (926–1014). High king of **Ireland** on his death at the Battle of **Clontarf** in 1014, Brian was the son of Cénneteig and the brother of King Mathgamain of the kingdom of Dál Cais (later known as Uí Briain). His family lands lay in Munster, western Ireland, along the lower reaches of the River Shannon, close to the **Viking** port of Limerick. Following the murder of Mathgamain in 976, Brian succeeded to his kingdom and immediately resumed Mathgamain's campaign against the Vikings of Limerick: he killed Ímar, king of Limerick, and his two sons in 977, and he defeated the Vikings of Limerick and their allies in battle in 978. Brian then set about extending his power in Ireland, actions that brought him into direct conflict with Máel Sechnaill II, high king of the Southern Uí Néill, who had himself waged war on the Norse (of **Dublin**). Following a series of territorial conquests by Brian, this struggle was resolved in 997, when Máel Sechnaill and Brian came to terms. As a result of this settlement, Máel Sechnaill received the northern half of Ireland and Brian the southern half. Brian thus became lord of Dublin and Leinster but was faced by a revolt in 999. However, the rebellion was soon quashed: the king of Leinster was held hostage until his submission, Dublin was burned, and its king, **Sigtrygg Silk-Beard** fled, before finally recognizing Brian's overlordship. With the troops, fleet and taxes of Dublin behind him, Brian felt confident enough to break his alliance with Máel Sechnaill. By 1005, Brian claimed to be high king of all Ireland, although in reality his effective control of northern Ireland should probably be dated to 1011. In Viking history, however, Brian is most famous for his part in the Battle of Clontarf, in which he was killed; a lost saga, *Brjáns Saga*, was later written about the king's death in this battle. Following the battle, Donnchad, Brian's son, led the remnants of his army home and Brian's body was taken to Armagh; Máel Sechnaill was restored as high king. Brian's posthumous reputation owes much to the 12th-century work of Uí Briain propaganda, *Cogadh Gaedhel re Gallaibh* the **"War of the Irish with the Foreigners."**

BRÍSINGAMEN. Necklace that belonged to the goddess **Freya**, but which was stolen from her by **Loki** according to Snorri's *Prose Edda* and the **skaldic** poem, *Húsdrápa* (which was one of Snorri's sources). According to *Húsdrápa*, Loki and **Heimdall** became seals and fought for the necklace at a place called Singasteinn. Otherwise very little is known about this myth, apart from a late 14th-century source, *Sörli þáttr*, the authenticity of which is doubtful. The Old English poem, *Beowulf*, refers to a necklace, *Brosinga mene*, which is said to have been stolen from Eormenric by Hama.

BRITTANY. The province of Brittany in the northwest of present-day France was inhabited by a Celtic population and was only incorporated into the **Carolingian Empire** at the very end of the eighth century. There were a number of Carolingian expeditions against the province in the early ninth century. **Louis the Pious** appointed a Breton called Nominoe to rule the province on his behalf, but after Louis's death in 840, Nominoe once more asserted Brittany's independence from the rulers of Frankia, sometimes siding with **Vikings** against the emperors. Nevertheless, the province suffered from Viking attacks from the beginning of the ninth century, and one of the most important Viking bases was situated on Breton territory, on the island of **Noirmoutier** at the mouth of the River Loire, near the provincial capital of Nantes. The monks who had inhabited this island constructed a fortification to defend themselves against raids, but finally left with the relics of their patron, St. Philibert, in 836 according to Ermentarius of Noirmoutier.

In 843 the so-called Loire Vikings started to overwinter on Noirmoutier, and there was an intensification of Viking activity in Brittany and Frankia in general. In 847, Nominoe appears to have paid off the Vikings, and their fleet moved south to raid Aquitaine. Shortly afterward, in 853, his son and successor, Erispoe, came to terms with a group of Vikings under Sidroc, and in the following year their combined forces attacked, unsuccessfully, the Danish army of Godfred that was encamped on the Ile de Bièce in the Loire. The second half of the ninth century saw more Breton alliances and deals with the Vikings, sometimes in opposition to the rulers of Frankia who sought to extend their own influence in Brittany and who also used Viking armies to help them in their campaigns. Civil war in Brittany after the death of its leader, Salomon, in 874, led to more alliances and counteralliances between different factions and to more Viking attacks. However, by 892, Alain of Vannes (also known as Alain the Great) had cleared the Viking armies from Brittany, and most of the **Great Army** left for England, signaling a period of peace for the province.

The death of Alain the Great in 907 marked the beginning of a yet more intensive period of Viking attacks on the province, at the same time as a Scandinavian colony was established in neighboring **Normandy**. Viking armies campaigned in Brittany from 912 and a Norwegian army led by Rögnvald took control of the province in 919, prompting many of its nobility and clergy to flee to the safety of the English court of **Athelstan**. Although Viking control of Brittany lasted over 20 years, virtually nothing is known about this period. There is no archaeological evidence that the warriors settled down and began to make their living from farming and trading, as was the case in the **Danelaw** and Normandy, and the capital, Nantes, appears to have fallen into ruin during the occupation. Indeed the limited archaeological evidence from the province suggests that the new overlords resolutely refused to change their Viking ways: four swords have been found, by chance, in the River Loire; two monasteries show evidence of 9th- or 10th-century destruction that is consistent with Viking attacks; there is a 10th-century pagan **ship** burial from the **Île de Groix**; a 10th-century fort from **Camp de Péran**; and a small number of other, unexcavated, earthworks that may represent Viking strongholds. A Breton rebellion was put down in 931, and shortly afterward, the grandson of Alain the Great, Alain Barbetorte, launched an English-backed invasion of Brittany in 936 and succeeded in restoring Breton control of the province three years later.

The **skaldic** poem, *Víkingavísur*, refers to two places in Brittany where **Olaf Haraldsson** is said to have been involved in fighting in the early 11th century: *Hringsfjörðr*, an unidentified location on the Breton coast; and *Hól*, the scene of a Viking stronghold, which is usually identified with present-day Dol in the northeastern part of the province.

BROA. Scandinavian **art** style that takes its name from the gilt-bronze bridle-mounts found in a burial at Broa on the Baltic island of **Gotland**, Sweden. The main characteristics of the Broa style are stylized animal decoration, including ribbon-like s-shaped animals, semi-naturalistic animals and birds, and the new motif known as the "gripping beast." The Broa style is generally dated from the second half of the eighth century to the early ninth century and is a precursor to Viking-Age art proper that begins with the **Oseberg** style. The burial at Broa also contained an iron sword with a cast-bronze hilt and a gilt pommel and grip, an amber bridge of a stringed instrument, two bronze buckles, a bronze strap-distributor, and 22 strap mounts of gilt-bronze.

BRUNANBURH, BATTLE OF. Battle fought by **Athelstan**, king of England, against an alliance of **Dublin Vikings**, Scots, and Strathclyde Britons that was led by Constantine II, king of Scotland, and Olaf Guthfrithsson of Dublin in 937. The *Anglo-Saxon Chronicle* entry for 937 records Athelstan's victory over "seamen and Scots" in the form of a heroic poem, and Celtic writers refer to the battle as "the great war." The location of *Brunanburh* is unknown, although many commentators favor a location in northern England. Place-name evidence suggests that it may well have been in Cheshire (present-day Bromborough), but this cannot be proven. Athelstan's victory renewed his authority in northern England.

BRYNHILD. *See* SIGURD THE DRAGON-SLAYER.

BUCKQUOY. Settlement site in the parish of **Birsay** and Harray, which lies in the northwest of mainland **Orkney**. Excavations at Buckquoy in the 1970s revealed that rectangular buildings, dated to the **Viking** period, succeeded cellular and figure-of-eight "Pictish" (*see* **Picts**) buildings. However, the break in **house** types is not reflected in the artifactual assemblage, which continued to be dominated by native Pictish-style products. The excavator argued on the basis of this evidence that there was some degree of social interaction between the native population and the incoming Norse settlers in the early Viking Age. Although this conclusion was called into question with the suggestion that the Pictish artifacts were found in Viking-Age deposits because of the site's disturbed stratigraphy, the absence of distinctive Norse-style artifacts from the rectangular structures supports the continued use of Pictish-style artifacts in the new houses.

The possibility that the rectangular buildings at Buckquoy were occupied by Picts rather than Vikings has been raised by the discovery of rectilinear buildings dated to the Pictish period at Skaill in Deerness on Orkney, although these were not known when Buckquoy was published in 1974. Nevertheless, other sites in the Bay of Birsay area share this lack of diagnostic Norse artifacts and the survival of earlier, native types in the early Viking Age. However, the survival of such artifacts does not necessarily presuppose a nonviolent confrontation. Even if the Pictish population had been wiped out, it seems unlikely that useful objects would be thrown away.

BURIALS. In the period before the Viking Age, cremation burial was the norm throughout Scandinavia. However, both cremation and inhumation burial were practiced in Viking-Age Scandinavia, and the latter became more and more common toward the end of the period following the **conversion to Christianity**. During the Viking Age, cremation nevertheless predominated throughout Norway and most of Sweden, while inhumation was already more common in Denmark (including the southern tip of Sweden, that was part of the medieval kingdom of Denmark) and the island of **Gotland** at the beginning of the period. The reason for this contrast is unknown, although it has been suggested that the early changeover to inhumation in Denmark might reflect closer links with Christian Europe.

In the countryside it appears that individuals were normally buried on the family farm, but in urban areas, burials were concentrated in cemeteries on the outskirts of towns. Extensive cemeteries, which have been partially excavated, surround the towns of **Birka** in

Sweden and **Hedeby** in Denmark. Before the conversion to Christianity, the deceased was usually dressed and accompanied by personal possessions, known as grave goods, with both forms of burial. These grave goods might vary from the everyday clothes and objects used by the individual to more lavish items, presumably intended for display. With cremation burials, these were all burned on a funeral pyre with the deceased, and the remains were then gathered and buried in a number of ways: the cremated bones may have been placed in a pot and buried in the ground; they may have been scattered in the grave itself; or all the remains from the pyre may have been put in a so-called cremation pit. Many cremation graves contain the burned bones of domestic animals, such as horses, dogs, pigs, cattle, sheep, and fowl. It was normal for cremation graves to be marked by a low burial mound or by stones, often arranged in the shape of a **ship** (known as a ship-setting). A large number of these stone-settings surround the cremations in the cemetery at **Lindholm Høje** in Denmark. **Ibn Fadlan** provides a famous account of a cremation burial involving a ship that took place on the River Volga in **Russia** during the early 10th century.

Burial in a ship (or a wagon or cart) and the use of ship-settings may suggest the belief that transportation was necessary to reach the next world, or possibly it was another way of emphasizing the high social status of the individual being buried. Similarly very large burial mounds, such as those found at **Jelling** in Denmark and **Borre** in Norway, have been interpreted as marking the burials of particularly wealthy and important individuals. One of the most famous examples of an inhumation burial in a ship is that from **Oseberg** in southwest Norway. Other forms of inhumation practiced during the Viking Age include elaborate chamber-graves, where the grave was lined with a wooden "house" with corner posts, floor, roof, and wall-paneling; simple coffin graves, where a simple coffin was placed in a grave; and, most basic of all, graves where the corpse was placed straight into the ground. Although some **rune-stones** are found in close proximity to stone-settings and burial mounds, rune-stones were not grave-stones, and they often appear to have been placed in prominent sites that would attract the attention of passers-by, such as roadsides, rather than in cemeteries or on graves.

Conversion to Christianity changed burial practices in Scandinavia: not only did inhumation become more common, the orientation of graves shifted from north-south to east-west, and the new religion discouraged the inclusion of grave goods in burials. Instead, the dead were usually placed in a shroud rather than their clothes and were buried in a simple wooden coffin that was placed in enclosed consecrated land, usually surrounding a church. Nevertheless, social distinctions remained in the Christian era: the upper classes were buried nearer the church than the lower classes, and priests and the very wealthy and important were buried inside the church, under the floor. Graves were probably marked above ground, with wooden markers or grave-stones, which provided a further opportunity to display social status.

BURRAY. One of the largest known Viking silver hoards in the British Isles was discovered at Burray on **Orkney, Scotland**. It consists of about a dozen coins, 26 pieces of **ring money** or plain silver arm rings, two small neck rings, and 111 pieces of **hacksilver** fragments, weighing some 2 kilograms in total. This hoard had been partly buried in a wooden container and then placed in a peat bog, and its burial is dated to between *c.* 997–1010.

BYZANTIUM (ON *Mikligarðr* **"great town").** City on the site of present-day Istanbul (Turkey) founded by the Roman emperor, Constantine, in AD 330. Byzantium was the capital of the eastern half of the Roman Empire and was still the center of a large eastern empire in the Viking Age. It was visited by Scandinavian raiders and traders who exchanged northern furs and **slaves** for luxury goods such as wines, spices, jewelry, and silks. Three trade treaties between the **Rus** of **Russia** and Byzantium, dating from 907, 912, and 945, are recorded in the *Russian Primary Chronicle*. This also records **Viking** attacks on the city: by Askold and Dir in 863–866 and by Oleg in 904–907. *The Homilies of Photius*, written by the patriarch of the city, also refer to the attacks by Askold and Dir. From the end of the 10th century, the emperor of Byzantium had a famous Scandinavian bodyguard, known as the **Varangian Guard**, which attracted mercenaries and warriors from all over northern Europe. Scandinavian **runes** have been found in Byzantium's Hagia Sofia church.

– C –

CAMP DE PÉRAN. Circular fortress on the northern coast of **Brittany** in present-day France. Excavations suggest that the **Vikings** and the Bretons (or French) fought a battle here in the early 10th century, although it is not clear if the Vikings were defending or attacking the fortress. The earth ramparts of the fort were burned and finds include a Viking sword; two spearheads; an ax; a silver penny, *c*. 905–925, from Anglo-Scandinavian **York**; a wool comb; and an iron pot. It has been suggested that the destruction of the fortress might be linked with the end of Viking rule in Brittany *c*. 936.

CANUTE. *See* CNUT I THE GREAT.

CAROLINGIAN EMPIRE. The Carolingian dynasty replaced that of the Merovingians and was established in 751, when Peppin II became king of the Franks. The Carolingian Empire was the creation of **Charlemagne** and included much of the former territory of the western part of the Roman Empire. It reached its greatest extent during the rule of Charlemagne's son, **Louis the Pious**, when the empire stretched from the Pyrenees and Italy in the south to the Low Countries (*see* **Frisia**) in the north. However, following Louis's death, the empire was divided among his three sons: **Lothar** received the Middle Kingdom of Lotharingia and Italy; **Louis the German**, the East Frankish kingdom, approximating to modern Germany and Austria, and **Charles the Bald**, the West Frankish kingdom, which later became France. This division, formalized in the Treaty of Verdun (843), initiated a period of civil war, which weakened effective resistance to **Viking** incursions.

The earliest Viking raids on the Carolingian Empire affected Frisia, including the important trading centers at **Dorestad** and **Quentovic**, at the very end of the eighth century. Charlemagne constructed coastal defenses that were temporarily effective at keeping the Vikings at bay. Some time around 838 the focus of Viking activity shifted west, and the Viking armies established raiding bases shortly afterward on islands in the rivers Seine and Loire. As well as enabling the Vikings to raid all year round, sailing up these rivers opened up the interior of the Carolingian Empire. Paris was attacked on at least three occasions, most famously in 885 (*see* **Paris, Siege of**), after which **Charles the Fat** was deposed for his failure to deal with these Vikings effectively. Grants of land were made to Scandinavians in the hope that they would limit further Viking incursions, the most famous of which was made by **Charles the Simple** in 911 to one **Rollo**, thus establishing the Duchy of **Normandy**. *See also ANNALS OF FULDA*; *ANNALS OF ST-BERTIN*; BRITTANY, VIKINGS IN; CHARLES THE BALD; NOIRMOUTIER, ERMENTARIUS OF; *ROYAL FRANKISH ANNALS*.

CHARLEMAGNE (742–814). King of the Franks 768–814 and emperor of the Frankish or **Carolingian Empire** 800–814. Much of Charlemagne's reign was spent in territorial conquest, which brought his empire to the southern border of Denmark at the very beginning of the Viking Age. Charlemagne waged war in the name of **Christianity**, suppressing paganism in Saxony and encouraging church reform and learning from his court at Aachen in present-day Holland. Charlemagne's response to early **Viking** raids was to order the fortification of bridges across major rivers so as to prevent Viking fleets from sailing upriver, and a system of coastguards at the mouths of rivers was established. These measures prevented serious Viking activity in Frankia until the 830s.

CHARLES II THE BALD (823–877). King of the West Franks 840–877 and emperor 875–877, Charles was grandson of **Charlemagne** and the youngest son of **Louis the Pious**. Charles's resistance to **Viking** raids was weakened by the threat of his rebellious brothers. From 845, Viking armies were frequently paid off, and, in 858, his siege of the Viking stronghold on the island of Oissel in the Seine was cut short by the rebellion of his brother, **Louis the German**. However, Charles did enjoy some success against Scandinavian armies, and in 873 he won a major victory over the Loire Vikings at Angers.

CHARLES III THE FAT (839–891). King of Alemannia 870, king and emperor in Italy 880, king of the East Franks 882, and king of the West Franks 884, Charles was the great-grandson of **Charlemagne** and the youngest son of **Louis the German**. Charles's most famous encounter with Scandinavian armies was his relief of their yearlong

siege of Paris in 886, after which he paid them tribute and allowed them to ravage Burgundy. Shortly afterward, in 887, he was deposed and replaced by Count Odo, the defender of Paris, and his own nephew Arnulf.

CHARLES IV THE SIMPLE (879–929). King of the West Franks 898–922, Charles was the grandson of **Charles II the Bald**. His most famous dealing with Scandinavian armies was the granting of land in Neustria (later known as **Normandy**) to a group of Vikings led by **Rollo**. According to **Dudo of St-Quentin**, this grant was confirmed in writing by a treaty signed at **St. Clair-sur-Epte** in 911. Charles was deposed and imprisoned in 922 and was murdered in 929.

CHRISTIANITY, CONVERSION TO. The first recorded Christian mission to Scandinavia took place before the beginning of the Viking Age, when **St. Willibrord** visited the kingdom of **Angantyr** of Denmark *c.* 700. According to the *Vita Willibrordi*, written by the Anglo-Saxon cleric **Alcuin**, the pagan Angantyr sold Willibrord some 30 boys to be trained as priests. Little else is known about Willibrord's mission.

In the early ninth century, another mission to Scandinavia was launched under the leadership of **Ansgar**, so-called Apostle of the North. The immediate impetus to this mission was political conditions in Denmark, where there was conflict between two rivals for the kingdom. One of the contenders for the Danish throne, **Harald Klak**, sought the assistance of the Frankish emperor, **Louis the Pious**, and he was baptized, along with his family and his retainers, at Ingelheim in 826. Following this episode, the emperor arranged for two churchmen, Ansgar and Autbert, to accompany Harald back to Denmark and provide spiritual guidance for him and his newly converted followers. Two principle sources record the events surrounding Harald's conversion: Rimbert's *Life of St. Ansgar* (*Vita Anskarri*) and Ermoldus Nigellus's *Carmen in honorem Hludowici*, but while Rimbert's account places the conversion in Frankia after the exile and highlights the importance of Louis and Ansgar in Harald's conversion, Ermoldus writes that Harald had already been virtually won over to the faith following the missionary work of Archbishop Ebo of Reims in Denmark in 823. Nevertheless, it is clear that following

Harald's baptism, Ansgar embarked upon the conversion of both Denmark and Sweden, visiting these kingdoms in the late 820s and again in the 850s. Churches were built in **Hedeby** and **Ribe** in Denmark and **Birka** in Sweden as a result of Ansgar's mission. However, these churches do not appear to have survived for very long, and, in the 10th century, another Hamburg-Bremen mission was launched by Archbishop Unni, who visited Denmark and Birka in Sweden in the 930s. At a synod called by Archbishop Adaldag in 948, Danish bishops from Ribe, Hedeby, and Århus attended, although it is not clear if they actually resided in these towns.

However, the official conversion of the individual Scandinavian countries followed the formal conversion of their rulers and these rulers' promotion of the new religion in their respective kingdoms. In Denmark, King **Harald Blue-Tooth** is generally credited with the establishment of Christianity as the national religion, following his own conversion by the German missionary Poppo *c.* 965. In Norway, three different kings embarked upon the sometimes forcible conversion of their people: **Hákon the Good** in the mid-10th century; **Olaf Tryggvason** at the end of the 10th century; and **Olaf Haraldsson**, later St. Olaf, during his reign in the early 11th century. All of these Norwegian kings had been converted abroad: Hákon was brought up at the court of King **Athelstan** in Wessex; the two Olafs were baptized while on Viking raids, Olaf Tryggvason at Andover in southern England (although **Snorri Sturluson** locates Olaf's baptism in the Scilly Isles, off the coast of Cornwall) and Olaf Haraldsson at Rouen in **Normandy**. Olaf Tryggvason was also responsible for the conversion of the Scandinavian colony in **Iceland** where, following his pressure, Christianity was accepted by the **Althing** in the year 1000. In Sweden, conversion to Christianity was apparently slower, probably due to the geopolitical fragmentation of the country and the relative weakness of its kings. At the end of the 10th century, a Christian king, **Olof Skötkonung**, tried to extend his power and to spread the new religion and is credited with establishing the first Swedish bishopric at Skara in Västergötland. Although a large number of 11th-century rune-stones (*see* **rune**) testify to the existence of Christians in eastern Sweden, paganism also persisted in parts of this area, around the cult center of **Gamla Uppsala**, until the early 12th century.

In many instances, the conversion of Scandinavians seems to have taken place as part of diplomatic and political deals. For example, in England, King **Alfred the Great** cemented the Treaty of **Wedmore** with the baptism of the Danish leader, **Guthrum**, and King **Æthelred II** was responsible for the conversion of Olaf Tryggvason of Norway. The conversion of the Danish king, Harald Blue-Tooth, was probably triggered less by the miracle performed by Poppo and more by the political threat posed by the German emperor, Otto I the Great, on Denmark's southern border.

CHRONICLE OF THE KINGS OF MAN AND THE ISLES (*Cronica Regum Manniae et Insularum*). Medieval Latin account of the Hiberno-Norse kings of the **Isle of Man** and the **Hebrides** from *c*. 1066 to 1266 and of Manx affairs and relations with other parts of the British Isles and Norway from *c*. 1016 to 1316. In addition, the work includes a catalog of all the bishops of Man and the Isles from *c*. 1060 to 1377. Before 1156, the dates of the *Chronicle* are unreliable; for example, the events of the year 1066 are given under 1047. Interestingly, the history makes no mention of Manx history or personalities before the year 1066 when it describes the visit of **Godred Crovan**, later king of Man, to the island. Before that date, the *Chronicle* mentions events in England, **Scotland**, **Wales**, and to a much lesser extent, Denmark and Norway.

This history was probably composed in the 13th century by monks at Rushen Abbey in the south of the island. It has been suggested that the *Chronicle* was begun following the dedication of St. Mary's Church in 1254, which is the date at which the first scribe broke off his work on the history, and that its purpose was to provide a record of the island since the days of the semilegendary king, Godred Crovan. Just one manuscript of the *Chronicle* is preserved (British Library Cotton Julius Avii), and the earliest hand seems to have copied or compiled the history around the year 1274; this scribe was responsible for the vast majority of the history proper. Several scribes then continued to work on the manuscript, largely on the section dealing with the bishops of Man and the Isles.

CLONTARF, BATTLE OF. Famous battle fought to the northeast of **Dublin** on Good Friday (23 April) 1014. The cause of the battle was the revolt of the Dublin Norse against the overlordship of **Brian Boru**, king of Munster and high king of **Ireland**. The Dublin Norse, under their king, **Sigtrygg Silk-Beard**, allied themselves with **Sigurd the Stout**, the **earl** of **Orkney**, and Máel Morda, king of Leinster, in opposition to Brian and his supporters, who included Máel Sechnaill, king of the Southern Uí Néill. The battle lasted all day and although the Dublin alliance was defeated, Brian was killed. The battle failed to alter the political landscape of Ireland: Dublin ultimately remained subject to increasingly powerful Irish kings and was never again to have the independence it had enjoyed in the 10th century. However, the significance of the battle was exaggerated by a later piece of propaganda, the *War of the Irish with the Foreigners*, in order to enhance the prestige of Brian's dynasty. In extant Norse literary sources (for example, *Njal's Saga*, based on a lost *Brian's Saga*), Brian is hailed as a holy saint.

CNUT I THE GREAT (ON *Knútr*) (*c*. 995?–1035). King of England, Denmark, and Norway during the early 11th century. Son of the Danish king, **Svein Forkbeard**, Cnut was with his father's army in England when his father died at Gainsborough in 1013, having just received the political submission of England. Cnut was chosen as leader by his father's army but was forced to leave England by the army of King **Æthelred II** of England. He returned in 1015, with **Thorkell the Tall** and Erik of **Lade**, and defeated the English at **Ashingdon** in Essex on 18 October 1016. Cnut later came to terms with Æthelred's son, **Edmund Ironside**, in a deal at **Olney**, which gave the English province of **Mercia** to Cnut. However, Edmund's death on 30 November meant Cnut was able to claim the English throne. He was probably crowned in London by Archbishop Lyfing early in 1017.

Cnut married Æthelred's widow, **Emma of Normandy** in July 1017, and their son, **Harthacnut**, was probably born in the following year. However, Cnut also had two sons called **Harold Harefoot** and **Svein Cnutsson** by his English consort, Ælfgifu, whom he had probably met during his father's English campaign, 1013–1014. Cnut's letters and his laws, which were drawn up by Archbishop Wulfstan of **York**, demonstrate his desire to be seen as an English king, and even **skaldic poetry** composed at his court, which must have been intended for a Scandinavian audience, emphasizes both his right to the English throne and his godliness (see, for example, Hallvarðr *háreksblesi*'s *Knútsdrápa*). In one of the few surviving images of Cnut, he and Emma are famously pictured presenting a gold cross to the New Minster in Winchester (*Liber Vitae*: New Minster Register, British Library, MS Stowe 944 f6r).

Cnut did not become king of Denmark until 1018/19, following the death of his older brother, Harald. While in Denmark at this time, Cnut composed the first of two known letters to his English subjects, in which he announced his intention to support the rights of the Church and to uphold just laws in his kingdom. He also explained that the purpose of his visit was to protect his English subjects from some unspecified danger. He returned to Denmark just a few years later, in 1022–1023, to deal with what was probably a challenge to his rule there. Certainly, in 1026, he faced and defeated a Danish-Swedish alliance in the Battle of **Holy River**. In 1027, Cnut attended the coronation of the Emperor Conrad II in Rome, and on his return journey, he sent a second letter to his English subjects, in which he claimed to be *rex totius Angliae et Denemarciae et Norreganorum et parties Suanorum* ("king of all England and Denmark, and the Norwegians and some of the Swedes"). Cnut's claim to be king of some of the Swedes is difficult to explain: coins minted in **Sigtuna**, with the legend CNUT REX SW, should be interpreted as copies of English coins rather than a genuine coinage recording Cnut's rule over the Svear (*see* **Svealand**)—for example, there are also dies from Sigtuna with the name of the English king, Æthelred II (ETHELRED REX ANGLORUM). However, a number of rune-stones (*see* **rune**) from central eastern Sweden do commemorate men who received Cnut's geld or payment in England, and the sort of overlordship Cnut was claiming would therefore seem to be a personal rather than a territorial one.

The letter of 1027 clearly demonstrates Cnut's belief that he was the rightful heir to the Norwegian throne, a claim presumably based on his grandfather's (**Harald Blue-Tooth**) overlordship, even though he as yet could not claim the kingdom was his. In the following year, however, Cnut won control of Norway, driving its king, **Olaf Haraldsson**, into exile. After Olaf Haraldsson's failed attempt to reclaim his throne at **Stiklestad**, Cnut appointed Ælfgifu and their son, Svein, as regents of Norway. Their rule was harsh and unpopular, and Cnut's rule of Norway probably came to an end before his death, when Ælfgifu and Svein were expelled by Olaf Haraldsson's son, **Magnus the Good**.

Cnut died at Shaftesbury, Dorset, in England on 12 November 1035, triggering a battle for power between his sons Harthacnut and Harold Harefoot in England and the disintegration of his North Sea empire. He was buried in the Old Minster at Winchester.

CODEX REGIUS. Manuscript copied by an unknown writer *c*. 1270 in **Iceland**. It was formerly kept in the Danish Royal Library, Copenhagen, but is now housed in the Árni Magnússon Institute, Reykjavik, Iceland. The fullest version of the *Elder* or **Poetic Edda** is preserved in this manuscript, although some leaves are missing from the cycle of **Sigurd the Dragon-Slayer**.

COGADH GAEDHEL RE GALLAIBH. *See* WAR OF THE IRISH WITH THE FOREIGNERS.

CONCERNING THE CUSTOMS AND DEEDS OF THE FIRST DUKES OF NORMANDY. *See* DUDO OF ST-QUENTIN.

CONSTANTINE VII PORPHYROGENITOS (905–959). Emperor of **Byzantium** and author of the *Administration of the Empire*. Constantine Porphyrogenitos ("born in the purple" = chamber of the Imperial Palace) was the son of Emperor Leo VI (d. 912) by Zoe Karvounospína ("coal-eyes"), who became Leo's wife in 906. Although Constantine was crowned coemperor with his father, probably in 908, he was unable to exert any real authority until 944. This was partly due to a religious conflict between Patriarch Efthýmios and Patriach Nikólaos, the latter of whom refused to recognize Leo's marriage to Zoe and thus Constantine's legitimacy. After this dispute was resolved in 920, through the offices of the Admiral of the Imperial Fleet, Rhomanós Lekapênós, Constantine was politically marginalized by Rhomanós, who installed members of his family in the Imperial Palace, married his daughter, Elénê, to Constantine, and had himself crowned as emperor in December 920. Rhomanós was overthrown by two of his sons, Stephanós and Constantine Lekapênoí in

944, but they in turn were deposed by Constantine, apparently at Elénê's prompting. Constantine Porphyrogenitos and Elénê had one son, Rhomanós II. Rhomanós and his second wife, Theophanó, made an unsuccessful attempt to poison Constantine, and it is possible that Constantine's death in 959 was the result of a second dose of poison administered by his son and daughter-in-law.

As well as the *Administration of the Empire*, Constantine Porphyrogenitos wrote a number of other works relating to, among other things, the provincial administration of the East Roman Empire (*De Thematibus*), and the protocol and ceremony of the East Roman Court (*De Caerimoniis Aulae Byzantinae*). He also wrote a biography of his grandfather, Emperor Basil I (d. 886), and commissioned 53 books of extracts from Hellenic literature, organized according to topics (two books survive, dealing with "embassies" and "virtues and vices" respectively).

CONSTANTINOPLE. *See* BYZANTIUM.

COPPERGATE. *See* YORK.

CORK. Town and port in southwest **Ireland**, at the mouth of the River Lee. Cork was the site of a monastery in the seventh century, and the *Annals of Ulster* record **Viking** raids there in 822 and 839. In 848, a Viking **longphort** was established, and we know the name of one of its leaders—Gnímbeolu—who was killed in 867. There were separate kings of Cork until 1174, but these kings acknowledged Irish overlordship as early as the eleventh century.

CRONICA REGUM MANNIAE ET INSULARUM. *See CHRONICLE OF THE KINGS OF MAN AND THE ISLES.*

CUERDALE HOARD. The largest **Viking** silver hoard known from Scandinavian settlements in the West. It was discovered on 15 May 1840 in the south bank of the River Ribble at Cuerdale, near Preston in Lancashire, England. Some of the hoard is now lost, but estimates suggest that it originally consisted of approximately 7,500 coins and 1,000 pieces of bullion (including ingots, jewelry, and **hacksilver**) and must have weighed around 44 kilograms. Of the coins, some

5,000 are contemporary Viking coins from **Northumbria**, including many from **York**, and **East Anglia**; about 1,000 are Anglo-Saxon coins from the reigns of **Alfred the Great** and his son, Edward the Elder; and the remaining 1,000 or so coins are predominantly continental, although there are about fifty Arabic coins, one Byzantine (*see* **Byzantium**), and four from **Hedeby**. Over fifty different mints are represented by the coins, ranging from Al-Andalus in the west to Al Banjhir in the east and from York in the north to Madinat al-Salam in the south. The date of the coins suggests that they were deposited *c*. 905, leading to speculation that it may be linked to the expulsion of the **Dublin** Norse in *c*. 902.

CUMBRIA, VIKINGS IN. Territory in northwestern England that had been partly and precariously brought under Northumbrian (*see* **Northumbria**) control before the Viking Age. This control was challenged in the Viking Age, not only by the **Vikings**, but also by the English kings to the south, the British kingdom of Strathclyde to its immediate north, and by the Scots, who absorbed Strathclyde at the beginning of the 11th century.

The Scandinavian settlement of Cumbria is not mentioned in any written sources. Indeed, contemporary written sources are almost entirely lacking for the area before the conquest of Carlisle by William Rufus in 1092. Although the raiding recorded in the Irish Sea region and the conquest of **York** in 876 probably impinged upon the northwest in some degree, for example, **Halfdan** is said to have made frequent raids against the **Picts** and Strathclyde Britons in the *Anglo-Saxon Chronicle* for 875, the fact that the community of St. Cuthbert left **Lindisfarne** in 875 for a refuge to the west of the Pennines suggests that northwest England was comparatively unaffected by Viking raids at this date. However, the expulsion of the **Dublin** Norse in 902 changed this. The Irish *Three Fragmentary Annals* records that Æthelflæd, Lady of the Mercians, granted land near Chester to a Scandinavian called Ingimundr in the first decade of the 10th century, and although the settlers appear to have started in a more or less peaceful manner, they attacked Chester shortly afterward. This episode is followed by indications of unrest in the northwest, such as the reference to Alfred son of Brihtwulf who fled east from *piratas c*. 915.

The establishment of a joint Norse kingdom of York and Dublin by **Ragnald** in the 920s enhanced the importance of the east–west routes in northern England and southern Britain, focusing attention on Cumbria. The English king, **Athelstan**, appears to have reconquered southern Lancashire in 934, purchasing land in Amounderness (north of the Ribble) from "the pagans" and granting it to Wulfstan, archbishop of York, apparently in an attempt to control one route to York. However, the English kings and English **earls** of Northumbria were not only concerned with Norse activities in the northwest: first the Cumbrians of Strathclyde and then the Scots started to expand south into the strategically important northwest, which controlled the York–Dublin axis *c*. 900. In 937, Athelstan and his brother, Edmund, fought and defeated a combined Norse, Scottish, and British army at **Brunanburh**, but the difficulties of control by a southern power were recognized by Edmund's grant of the kingdom of Strathclyde to the Scottish king, Malcolm, in 945. The northwest remained in a state of unrest: **Erik Blood-Ax** was killed at Stainmore, at the head of the Vale of Eden and gateway to the east-west pass over the Pennines to York, in 954; *Þored Gunneres sunu* ravaged Westmoreland in the south of Cumbria in 966; in 972, Kenneth II of **Scotland** ravaged Strathclyde to its southern boundary, said to be the River Dee in Cheshire; and **Æthelred II** of England harried Cumbria in 1000. However, the *Gospatric Writ* suggests that Earl Siward of Northumbria regained some control of Cumbria in the period 1041–1055. William the Conqueror's northern expedition certainly left the Normans in control of land below the River Ribble, for *Inter Ripaem aet Mersham* ("between the Ribble and Mersey") is appended to the Cheshire folios of *Domesday Book*. However, the lands north of the Ribble are not included in the survey, and the centuries following the Norman Conquest saw a continual tug-of-war between England and Scotland over this territory.

Although the documentary evidence paints a picture of disruption and raiding, place-name and sculptural evidence demonstrate that there was a substantial Scandinavian settlement in Cumbria and that there was sufficient wealth and stability in the region for people to commission stone sculpture from the middle of the 10th century onward. There are some 116 surviving pieces of Viking-Age sculpture distributed across 38 sites centered on Cumbria south of a line from Addingham to the River Ellen. Although the very act of commissioning stone sculpture was based upon English custom, there seems to have been a greater enthusiasm for such sculpture among a wider population than in the pre-Viking period. Some sculpture, such as the **Gosforth cross**, bears Scandinavian **art** styles or motifs, while ring-headed crosses and the **hogback** monuments testify to influence from **Ireland** on the new patrons of stone sculpture. Similarly, the forms of the Scandinavian place-names suggest that Danes, Norwegians, and Norsemen from Ireland and Scotland were involved in the settlement of Cumbria.

However, archaeological evidence for large-scale Scandinavian settlement in northwest England is lacking. Four certain pagan burials and a further five probable burials have been found in the region, along with 12 Viking-type hoards, including the large hoard from **Cuerdale**. A possible settlement site has been identified at **Ribblehead**, just outside the southeast boundary of Cumbria, in North Yorkshire. Bryant's Gill, Kentmere, in south Cumbria, appears to fit into the same class of settlement, but the archaeological evidence has not yet been fully examined and the cultural significance of the site is unclear.

– D –

DANEGELD. Name generally given to the payments made in England to the **Viking** armies during the reign of Æthelred II at the end of the 10th and the beginning of the 11th century. The *Anglo-Saxon Chronicle* records a series of such payments in the years 991, 994, 1002, 1007, 1008, and 1012, which ranged in value from 10,000 (991) to 48,000 pounds (1012) of silver. An extraordinary Danegeld was also levied by **Cnut I the Great** in 1018 to pay off his campaign army: 72,000 pounds was paid by England, excluding **London**, while London paid 10,500 pounds. Several thousand coins of Æthelred II have been found in Scandinavia and many more must have been melted down or spent.

However, the *Anglo-Saxon Chronicle* calls these payments *gafol* "tribute, tax"; the first occurrence of the term Danegeld is from the post-Conquest period, when it is used to describe the annual land tax

known as the *heregeld* that Æthelred introduced in order to pay for
the mercenary army of **Thorkell the Tall**, and which was revived by
Anglo-Norman kings. The modern usage of the term is thus rather
different from the original sense of Danegeld, and sometimes the
term is used even more generally to mean money or provisions given
to Viking armies in order for them to leave a town or region in peace,
a practice that seems to have been fairly common in western Europe.

DANELAW. The term Danelaw first occurs in two legal compilations
made by Archbishop Wulfstan of **York** during the reign of **Æthelred
II**. The so-called *Laws of Edward and Guthrum*, dated to between
1002 and 1008, refer to the compensation to be paid "*on Deone lag*"
if a **slave** was compelled to work on a church, while the law-code
known as VI Æthelred distinguishes between the legal penalties in
force in the districts under English law and those under Danish law.
The penalties in areas under Danish law were described simply as "in
accordance with their constitution." However, the earliest evidence
for the use of the term Danelaw clearly indicates that it was a legal
province of the kingdom of England, in spite of the emphasis on
"Danishness" in the term itself. Indeed, Æthelred II had apparently
extended English customs to the *Dena lage* in his law-codes, and
while his so-called Wantage Code, intended for circulation in the
Five Boroughs, allowed for differences of procedure, it did not permit different principles.

The first extant reference to the geographical extent of the
Danelaw was apparently recorded almost 40 years after the term first
occurs in Æthelred's laws. Later Anglo-Norman writers, such as
Simeon of Durham, also attempted to define the boundaries of the
Danelaw. The Danelaw of Anglo-Norman England was an extensive
region, consisting of some 15 shires (as opposed to the 9 shires of
West-Saxon (*see* **Wessex**) law and the 8 of Mercian (*see* **Mercia**)
law): Yorkshire, Nottinghamshire, Derbyshire, Leicestershire, Lincolnshire, Northamptonshire, Huntingdonshire, Cambridgeshire,
Bedfordshire, Norfolk, Suffolk, Essex, Hertfordshire, Middlesex, and
Buckinghamshire. This huge territory constituted approximately one-
third of the total area of the English kingdom at that time, and many
scholars are skeptical about the accuracy of these boundaries, especially given that evidence for Danish influence in this region varies

dramatically. Geographical definition of the Danelaw thus runs into problems from the very beginning, and these problems have been compounded by linking the term Danelaw with other aspects of Scandinavian influence in England. Often the Danelaw is simply and misleadingly identified with those areas of northern and eastern England that were settled by Scandinavians in the ninth century.

A further point of confusion is found in the treaty between **Alfred the Great** and **Guthrum** made at **Wedmore** in 886. This is sometimes regarded as formally establishing the Danelaw, by defining Danish and English spheres of control, along the following boundaries: "First as to the boundaries between us: up the Thames, and then up the Lea, and along the Lea to its source, then in a straight line to Bedford, then up the Ouse to Watling Street." However, while the old Roman road, **Watling Street**, is generally used by historians as a convenient border for delimiting the extent of ninth-century Danish settlement in England, and indeed, as the border between Danelaw and the rest of England, the treaty itself does not actually specify that the boundary ran along the whole length of Watling Street to Chester. Moreover, the Treaty of Wedmore itself was not, as is often implied, a treaty between the Danes and the English, it was simply one of a number of treaties made between the English and the **Viking** armies.

In summary, it seems extremely likely that the boundaries of the Danelaw were neither fixed nor clear-cut when referred to in Æthelred's law of 1008. Moreover, there is no straightforward relationship between the area described as the Danelaw by Anglo-Norman writers and the fluctuating area under Scandinavian control in the Viking Age. A final reminder is also needed about the status of northwest England, which is sometimes included in the Danelaw, as it lies north of Watling Street: Cheshire, Lancashire, and **Cumbria**, settled by Norwegians from **Ireland** and **Scotland** in the 10th century, were never included in the Danelaw, and formed a contested border zone between England and Scotland well into the post-Conquest period.

DANEVIRKE. A complex series of ramparts that together form a fortification which runs for some 30 kilometers along the base of the Jutland Peninsula, protecting Denmark's southern border (which ran along the River Eider, about 20 kilometers to the south). The earliest portions of the Danevirke were built around 737 and consisted of a 10-meter wide earth rampart, fronted by a ditch, that ran for 7 kilometers from the western end of the Schleifjörd in a southwesterly direction (constituting the so-called North Wall and part of the Main Wall). There were two principle phases of fortification during the Viking Age: the first under the rule of **Godfred** at the beginning of the 9th century and the second under King **Harald Blue-Tooth** in the middle of the 10th century. The ***Royal Frankish Annals*** record that Godfred extended the fortification in 808, although as yet this phase of work has not been identified archaeologically. The undated section of rampart known as Kovirke, broken only by the **Army Road**, might perhaps have been constructed by Godfred. A **dendrochronological** date of 968 suggests that Harald Blue-Tooth incorporated the defensive ramparts (the Semicircular and Fore Walls) around the town of **Hedeby** into the Danevirke, constructing a so-called Connecting Wall, and in the west, Harald also built an extension to the Danevirke, consisting of a 13-meter wide rampart known as the Crooked Wall. The fortification was subsequently maintained and extended well into the early 12th century when the Danish king Valdemar the Great (1157–1182) rebuilt some sections in brick. It was also refortified and used by the Danes in the 1864 war with Prussia and by the occupying German army in World War Two.

DE ADMINISTRANDO IMPERIO. *See* ADMINISTRATION OF THE EMPIRE.

DE MORIBUS ET ACTIS PRIMORUM NORMANNIAE DUCUM. *See* DUDO OF ST-QUENTIN.

DENDROCHRONOLOGY. Method of dating wooden objects based upon the growth rings of a tree. Trees have two growth rings per year and the width of these rings reflects the weather during the growing season—a narrow ring indicates poor weather and little growth, while a wide ring reflects considerable growth during favorable climatic conditions. Counting these rings reveals the age of the tree at the time it was felled, and the sequence of growth rings forms a pattern like a bar code. Another older sample of wood may have a sequence of growth rings that matches that of a younger tree, thus enabling archaeologists to move back their dating further into the past. Unfortunately, wood perishes very easily and is generally only preserved in either extremely arid or anaerobic archaeological environments. Within northern Europe and Scandinavia, bogs provide ideal conditions for the preservation of wood. Work on wood, such as oak, found in northern Europe has resulted in a dendrochronology that stretches back more than 7,000 years. Some of the most important Viking-Age artifacts that have been dated by dendrochronology include the **Oseberg ship** from Norway and the **Skuldelev ships** found in Roskilde Fjord, Denmark.

DICUIL. See *BOOK OF THE MEASUREMENT OF THE EARTH*.

DÍSIR. Female deities, whose qualities are difficult to define upon the extant written evidence. The ***Poetic Edda*** describes them both as dead **women** (*Atlamál*) and guardians of the dead (*Guðrúnarkviða*), and they are mentioned in numerous prose sagas too, most frequently appearing as ghost- or dream-like apparitions, but the word also seems to have been used in a more general sense to mean "woman." *Viga-Glum's Saga* and ***Egil's Saga*** mention a late autumn sacrifice, the *dísablót*, that took place in Norway, and **Snorri Sturluson** associates this with the pagan rituals performed at **Gamla Uppsala** in his ***Ynglinga Saga*** on the basis of the **skaldic** poem, ***Ynglingatal***. There are a number of Swedish and Norwegian place-names that include the word *dísir*, which may provide some support for the ritual worship of these deities.

DNEPR. See DNIEPER, RIVER.

DNIEPER, RIVER. Russian river linking the **Rus** settlement of **Gnezdovo** with the Black Sea. The Dnieper was the most important route for Scandinavians traveling east to **Byzantium** and could be reached either via Lake Ladoga (*see* **Staraja Ladoga**) and the rivers Lovat and Volkhov in the north or via the Baltic Sea in the east. The most important Scandinavian trading stations and settlements in **Russia** lay along the northern route: Staraja Ladoga, **Novgorod**, **Gorodišče**, Gnezdovo, and **Kiev**. The journey south to Byzantium, over the

Dnieper's rapids, is described in some detail by the emperor **Constantine II Porphyrogenitos** in his work the ***Administration of the Empire***.

DORESTAD. A major town and trading center in northwest Europe founded in the seventh century at the confluence of the rivers Lek and Rhine (near present-day Nijmegen in The Netherlands). Extensive archaeological excavations between 1967–1977 suggest that at its peak in the eighth century, the town had perhaps as many as 2,000 inhabitants living and working in an area of more than 60 hectares. A mint was established at Dorestad as early as 630, and other activities taking place in the Viking-Age town included metalworking, jewelry making, leather working, basket weaving, shipbuilding, bone working, and the manufacture of textiles. The size and wealth of the town made it a favorite target for **Viking** raiders after the first recorded raid in 834, and Frankish annals (*see **Annals of St-Bertin*** and ***Annals of Fulda***) contain frequent references to raids on Dorestad (in 835, 836, 837, 847, 857, and 863). Indeed, the town was apparently burned to the ground four times in the period 834–837. In 852, the Frankish emperor, **Lothar**, granted the town and other lands in **Frisia** to the Viking Rurik, in return for his protection of the coast against other Viking raids. However, Rurik's son, Godfred, used the town as a base for extensive raiding activity in the region. The town is not mentioned in written sources after 863, and no archaeological evidence has been uncovered for 10th-century occupation of the site. This may reflect a shift in the Rhine rather than the abandonment of the town because of the Viking raids.

DRENG (ON sg. *drengr* pl. *drengir*). ON word that means, in its simplest sense, "warrior" or "man," which is attested in both runic inscriptions (*see **rune***) and **skaldic poetry** from the Viking Age. **Snorri Sturluson** offers a definition of the word in ***Skáldskaparmál***: "Young men that have not settled down, while they are making their fortunes or reputation, are called *drengir*; they are called *fardrengir* who travel from land to land, king's *drengir* who are in the service of rulers, and they are also called *drengir* who are in the service of rich men or landowners. Manly and ambitious men are called *drengir*." There have been some attempts by historians to link drengs, along with **thegns**, to the growth of royal power and state formation in Scandinavia, arguing that the drengs named in runic inscriptions were exclusively in the service of kings. However, there is little definite support for this idea, which is essentially based upon the distribution of rune-stones that commemorate thegns and drengs. The evidence of the inscriptions does, however, support the idea that drengs were generally young warriors or travelers: they are usually commemorated by their comrades, parents or siblings, rather than by wives or children, and many of the inscriptions refer to the military or trading activities of the deceased dreng.

DRIMORE (MACHAIR). Norse settlement site on the island of South Uist in the Outer **Hebrides**, excavated in July 1956. Only a limited investigation of the site took place before construction work began on a missile range, but a rectangular **longhouse**, probably built of stone and turf, was uncovered from the sand that had protected and hidden it. Although the building and some of the artifacts are characterized as Norse, part of the walling is constructed in a typically pre-Viking fashion and a small silver plaque, decorated with ring-and-dot patterns, may also be Pictish (*see* **Picts**) rather than Norse. The discovery of an early Viking type antler comb suggests that the settlement must be dated to the Viking Age rather than the medieval period, and it appears that the occupation was fairly short-lived, although long enough for some modifications to be made in the longhouse. It is not clear if the site extended beyond this building, nor is it possible to clarify the relationship between the Norse building and possible earlier constructions.

DRÓTTKVÆTT ("court meter"). Highly complex metrical form used in the composition of **skaldic poetry**. *Dróttkvætt* is the meter used in the vast majority of surviving skaldic verse, preserved principally in the sagas of the Norwegian kings (e.g., ***Heimskringla***). It is characterized by stanzas of eight lines that are divided into two halves, known as *helmingar*, which usually form independent syntactical units. These halves are then further subdivided into two "long lines," which are linked by alliteration and stresses. The oldest known example of *dróttkvætt* is carved on the **Karlevi** rune-stone (*see* **rune**).

DUBLIN (ON *Dyflinn*). Dublin was one of the first permanent settlements established by the **Vikings** in **Ireland**, and the town grew out of the **longphort** or fortified camp established on the banks of the River Liffey, on the boundary of the kingdoms of Brega and Leinster, in 841. The site of this *longphort* has not yet been identified archaeologically, although nearby **Kilmainham** is a strong possibility. The so-called Dublin Norse were expelled from this settlement by an Irish alliance in 902, and when the town was re-established in 917, it was at a slightly different location, underneath the present-day city. Between 1961 and 1981, excavations in the Wood Quay area of the town, between the River Liffey and Christ Church Cathedral, revealed successive phases of settlement on this site. Regular plots, surrounded with earth banks, were laid out. The **houses** that the Scandinavian settlers built on these plots were not of characteristic Norse design and instead appear to represent an Irish-Sea tradition of building. The archaeological finds from Dublin are varied and of high quality, reflecting the town's powerful economic position from the end of the 10th century. A collection of some 12 runic inscriptions (*see* **rune**), carved on everyday objects of wood, a comb, and otherwise unworked pieces of bone and antler, have been discovered during excavations. These have been dated to the period *c*. 950–1125 and were probably carved by craftsmen working in the town. Various crafts flourished in Viking-Age Dublin—**ship**building (one of the **Skuldelev** longships was built here), comb making, shoe making, and wood and bone carving. The town also appears to have been a center for the export of **slaves**, textiles, and hides, while imports included silk, amber, walrus ivory, pottery, glass from England, the Continent, Scandinavia, and the East.

The Norse kings of Dublin were among the most significant political figures in the Scandinavian settlements of the British Isles during the 9th and 10th centuries. The first known king of Dublin was **Olaf the White**, who defeated his Danish rivals and won control of the town in 853. He was succeeded by his relative, Ivar (*Ímar*), whose rule was followed by a period of instability, civil war (893–894), and ultimately led to the expulsion of the Dublin Norse in 902. The zenith of Dublin's power came shortly after the recapture of the town by **Sigtrygg Cáech** in 917, when his kinsmen **Ragnald** also established Norse control of **York**. Dublin retained control of that city intermittently until 952, when **Erik Blood-Ax** of Norway seized control of York and by the end of the 10th century, Dublin's power and independence in Ireland was curtailed by the growing strength of the Irish kings. Scandinavian colonies in the **Isle of Man** and **Orkney** appear to have recognized the overlordship of Dublin for some time in the 10th century, but by the latter part of that century, the Norse **earls** of Orkney were extending their influence through the Northern and Western Isles of **Scotland**.

Although the last king of Dublin, Ansculf Torquilsson, only lost control of the town in 1169 (to an Anglo-Norman force), the Dublin Norse failed to recover their pre-eminence after defeat in a series of battles, most notably that fought at **Tara** in 980. By 997, Dublin acknowledged the overlordship of the king of Munster, **Brian Boru**, and even the alliance of its king, **Sigtrygg Silk-Beard**, with Leinster and Orkney failed to reap rewards — the Dublin Norse and their allies were defeated in battle at **Clontarf** in 1014.

DUDO OF ST-QUENTIN (*c.* 960–before 1043). Historian of the first dukes of **Normandy**, born in Picardy in present-day France. Dudo was a canon of St-Quentin, who was sent by the count of Vermandois to Rouen in 986 to secure Norman assistance against Hugh Capet, founder of the Capetian dynasty. Dudo spent some time at the court of Richard I, duke of Normandy, and was employed to write a history of the Norman dukes, which was finished between 1015 and 1026. This work, *De moribus et actis primorum Normanniae ducum* ("Concerning the Customs and Deeds of the First Dukes of the Normans"), was an apologetic for the Norman dukes. He also included details on pagan sacrificial rituals, including sacrifices to **Thor** and about how a pagan priest consulted the entrails of an ox in order to predict the outcome of the next Norman raid.

– E –

EARL (ON *jarl*). Title of the most prominent men below the kings in Viking-Age Scandinavia. An earl might be a royal official in control of a district or an independent ruler of a district. The most famous Scandinavian earls were the earls of **Lade**, who were extremely powerful in the 10th and 11th centuries and the earls of **Orkney** in **Scotland**. This word is the earliest recorded Scandinavian loanword into Irish, and it also superseded Old English *ealdorman* as the title of those men ruling districts of England under, and for, the king.

EAST ANGLIA, VIKINGS IN. Eastern English kingdom, consisting of the modern counties of Norfolk and Suffolk. The first **Viking** presence in East Anglia is recorded in the *Anglo-Saxon Chronicle* under the year 866: "a great raiding army came to the land of the English and took winter-quarters in East Anglia and were provided with horses there, and they [the East Anglians] made peace with them." Three years later, however, **Edmund**, the king of East Anglia, confronted the Viking army and was killed following a battle. **Guthrum**, the Viking leader of a section of the **Great Army**, used East Anglia as his winter base, from which attacks were launched against **Alfred the Great** of **Wessex**. Guthrum was formally granted the kingdom by Alfred in the Treaty of **Wedmore**. Following this, Guthrum's army is said to have shared out the land of East Anglia and to have settled there. However, Viking attacks did not stop, and the *Anglo-Saxon Chronicle* records that Alfred was involved in campaigns against Vikings from East Anglia in 885 and in 893; and that his son, Edward the Elder, came to terms at Tiddingford with the "raiding-army" of East Anglia, that had been incited to rebellion by Edward's cousin, Æthelwold, in 906. Following a prolonged campaign against the Viking armies of the **Danelaw**, Edward secured the final submission of East Anglia in 920.

In Norfolk, the Viking presence appears to have stimulated the growth of the towns of Thetford in the 10th century and Norwich in the 11th century. Thetford became the center of a pottery industry with finds widely distributed across the whole of the Danelaw, and Norwich emerged as a regional center following the establishment of a fortified *burh* there. Scandinavian street names in Norwich and church dedications to the Scandinavian saints, St. **Olaf Haraldsson** and St. Clement, testify to the impact of the Danish settlers. The Viking presence in rural East Anglia can also be traced in Scandinavian place-names, particularly in the Flegg area close to the present-day seaside resort of Great Yarmouth. In addition to this, metal-detector finds have, in recent years, added considerably to knowledge of Scandinavian material culture in East Anglia. In particular, finds of low-quality, mass-produced, and well-worn Viking-style jewelry and dress fittings suggest the Scandinavian settlers of the kingdom were generally poor and also confirm that the settlers probably included Scandinavian **women** (the *Anglo-Saxon Chronicle* entry for 893 records that the Viking army "secured their women and their ships and their money in East Anglia"). Other finds include Viking **weapons**, such as axes and a sword, stirrups and harness mounts, gaming pieces, and **Thor's** hammer amulets. Two pagan burials, dating to the late ninth or early 10th century, have been excavated in East Anglia, at Santon Down and Middle Harling. However, conversion to **Christianity** seems to have happened rapidly, as a mid-10th century fragment of a cross (the St. Vedast cross, Norwich Castle Museum) decorated in the **Mammen art** style testifies.

By the end of the 10th century, a fresh wave of Viking attacks led by **Svein Forkbeard** of Denmark and **Olaf Tryggvason** of Norway affected East Anglia and the kingdom of England as a whole. The English defeat in the battle at **Maldon** followed Olaf Tryggvason's raid on Ipswich, and the first **Danegeld** was paid to the victorious Viking army. The *Anglo-Saxon Chronicle* records attacks on both Norwich and Thetford in 1004, Thetford and Cambridge in 1010 (the same year that the Battle of **Ringmere** was fought in East Anglia), and by 1011 all of East Anglia was said to be overrun by Svein Forkbeard's army. Svein's son, **Cnut I the Great**, continued his father's campaign for the kingdom of England and in a piece of **skaldic poetry** (*Knútsdrápa*) is said to have "made corselets red in Norwich" during an attack in 1016. In the same year, Cnut defeated his rival for the English throne, **Edmund Ironside**, at **Ashingdon** in Essex, and he later commemorated his victory with a church dedicated to the East Anglian royal saint, Edmund. He also had Edmund's church at Bury rebuilt and Edmund's shrine placed in the care of Benedictine monks. Cnut appointed **Thorkell the Tall** as his **earl** in East Anglia in 1017. During Cnut's reign, the **Ringerike art** style was popular in southern and eastern England and is found decorating a number of horse harness and mounts from East Anglia. This was succeeded in the middle and end of the 11th century by the **Urnes** style, and a cathedral capital from Norwich Cathedral, dating to the early 12th century, testifies to continued Scandinavian influence in East Anglia after the Norman Conquest.

EASTERN SETTLEMENT. *See* GREENLAND.

EDDA. *See POETIC EDDA; PROSE EDDA.*

EDDIC POETRY. Name given to poetry on **mythological** or heroic themes. Most Eddic poetry is found in *Codex Regius*, although there are some examples in other manuscripts. In contrast to **skaldic poetry**, Eddic poetry is generally anonymous and has a simpler metrical form. The two most common meters are **fornyrðislag** and **ljóðaháttr**.

EDINGTON, BATTLE OF. Battle between **Alfred the Great** of **Wessex** and the **Viking** army of **Guthrum** fought near present-day Chippenham, Wiltshire, just after Easter in 878. It signaled the rise in fortunes of Alfred and Wessex, after a long series of defeats and Alfred's enforced exile in the marshes of Athelney in Somerset. Following this decisive victory, the Vikings granted Alfred hostages and took oaths, promising to leave Alfred's kingdom and consenting to the baptism of Guthrum. Three weeks later, Guthrum was baptized at Aller, near Athelney, and took the baptismal name Athelstan. Subsequently, Alfred and Guthrum made a peace treaty at **Wedmore**.

EDMUND IRONSIDE (d. 1016). King of England 24 April–30 November 1016. Edmund was the second son of **Æthelred II** by his first wife, Ælfgifu, although his claim to his father's throne seems to have been compromised by Æthelred's sons from his second marriage to **Emma of Normandy**. When Æthelred ordered the murder of Sigeferth and Morcar, two leading **thegns** of the **Danelaw**, in 1015, Edmund was moved to take action against his father—he married the widow of Sigeferth, claimed the property of her dead husband and brother, and declared himself ruler of the Danelaw. As such, he opposed **Cnut I the Great's** attempt to win control of the area, as a stepping-stone to claiming the English throne. Following his father's death in April 1016, Edmund was recognized as king and continued the English resistance to Cnut's invasion; Edmund fought six battles against the Scandinavians in the summer of 1016 alone. While he was victorious at Sherston, Cnut defeated him at **Ashingdon** and Edmund was forced to divide his kingdom in the subsequent settlement at Olney. Shortly afterward, Edmund died, apparently from wounds inflicted during battle, and his children were smuggled out of England for their own safety, leaving Cnut as king of England.

EDMUND, ST. (c. 841?–870). Last English king of **East Anglia** 855–869 who, according to the *Anglo-Saxon Chronicle*, was killed in battle by the so-called **Great Army** in 869 or 870 (versions E and A respectively). The F recension of the *Anglo-Saxon Chronicle* adds that the leaders of the men who killed Edmund were called Ivar (*Ingware*) (*see* **Ivar the Boneless**) and Ubba. Writing about a century later, however, Abbo of Fleury (see below) claimed that Edmund was captured but not killed in battle, and that he was then martyred for refusing to deny his Christian faith or to rule East Anglia as Ivar's puppet. According to Abbo, Edmund was tied to a tree, lashed with whips, then pierced with arrows until he looked like "a prickly hedgehog," and finally he was beheaded. A recent suggestion that St. Edmund of East Anglia may have been the victim of the **blood-eagle** is unconvincing.

By the end of the ninth century, Danish settlers in East Anglia were issuing a St. Edmund memorial coinage, inscribed with the Latin legend SCE EADMUND REX ("St. Edmund, King"), and the cult of Edmund was later promoted by the Danish king of England, **Cnut I the Great**. In the 930s, Edmund's armor-bearer related the story of his death to the English king, **Athelstan**; the audience at Athelstan's court included St. Dunstan, who in turn told the story to the Frankish scholar and cleric, Abbo of Fleury. At the end of the 10th century, Abbo of Fleury wrote his *Passio S. Eadmundi*, and it was later translated into English by Ælfric and incorporated into his *Lives of Saints*. According to Abbo, after his death, Edmund's head was hidden by the Vikings in the nearby wood of *Haglesdun* but was found by his countrymen, who were helped by the head calling out *hic*, *hic* (Latin "here"). The head, reunited with Edmund's body, was buried on the spot where it was found and a small chapel was built on the site, at which, some years later, miracles began to be reported. The location of Edmund's martyrdom has been linked to both Hellesdon, near Norwich, and Hoxne, in Suffolk. Hellesdon is similar to *Haglesdun*, but otherwise unlikely, while Hoxne is first mentioned in the foundation charter of the Abbey of Bury St. Edmunds, dated to 1101. However, a

slightly earlier account locates the martyrdom at Sutton, and recent research has discovered a series of place-names that seem to fit with
Abbo's account: six miles south of Bury St. Edmunds, an old field,
Hellesden, lies close to a place called Sutton Hall; to the north are
three names including the word king, Kingshall Farm, Kingshall
Street, and Kingshall Green—which would fit with Abbo's description of a royal estate lying close to the scene of Edmund's martyrdom.

Edmund's remains were translated to the monastery at
Bedricesweord—now known as Bury St. Edmunds, Suffolk—in the
10th century. The cult of St. Edmund became popular in **Ireland**, on
the European continent, and in Scandinavia. For example, **Ari
Thorgilsson**, writing in 12th-century **Iceland**, used the martyrdom of
Edmund as one of the key dates in his chronological framework.

EGIL'S SAGA (ON *Egils saga Skallagrímsonar*). One of the so-called
Family Sagas or **Sagas of Icelanders**, *Egil's Saga* was written in **Iceland** during the first half of the 13th century, *c.* 1230. It is preserved
in two vellum manuscripts (the version in *Möðruvallabók*, composed between 1320 and 1350, is used by most modern translators
and editors). It also survives in several paper manuscripts, the most
important of which is AM 453 quarto, as it contains the fullest text of
the saga. The saga's hero is the Icelandic warrior, merchant, farmer
and skald, Egil, and the events described took place across the western **Viking** world from the middle of the 9th to the end of the 10th
century. Its author is unknown, although many believe that this is the
work of **Snorri Sturluson**, who lived at Egil's farm in Borg from
1201–1206.

In the saga, Egil's father is said to have settled in Iceland to escape
a feud with the Norwegian king, **Harald Fine-Hair**, and already, at
the age of six, Egil appeared to be following in his father's footsteps:
he killed a boy with an ax because the boy beat Egil at a ball-game.
Like his father, Egil also made an enemy of the king of Norway, **Erik
Blood-Ax**, after killing one of his servants and then, later on, one of
his sons. Egil's travels took him to England, where he served King
Athelstan, fighting for him at **Brunanburh**; he was also baptized at
the king's request. It was on a further journey to England that Egil
was shipwrecked at the mouth of the **Humber** and ended up in the
kingdom of **Northumbria**, then ruled by his archenemy, Erik. His

meeting with Erik at **York** is one of the most famous episodes from the Icelandic sagas: Egil composed a praise poem in Erik's honor overnight, the so-called Head-Ransom poem (*Höfuðlausn*), with which he bought his life and freedom.

As well as this poem of 20 verses, the saga also contains a further 48 stanzas and five long poems that are attributed to Egil. His "Lament for My Sons" (*Sonatorrek*) is perhaps the greatest of these, describing his conflicting emotions through **Odin**, who is both god of the dead and of poetry: Odin has taken away his two sons but has given Egil the ability to cope with his grief through poetic expression. Egil finally retired to his farm at Borg in the west of Iceland, where he died of illness. He was buried as a pagan in a burial mound at Tjaldness, along with his clothes and **weapons**. However, the saga writer refers to a tradition that Egil's bones were transferred to the church at Mosfell, following the conversion of Iceland to **Christianity**. When a new church was being built at Mosfell, it is said that some very large human bones were found under the altar. The skull was "exceptionally large" and thick, and it is said to have withstood blows from an ax. These bones, believed to be Egil's, were re-interred at the edge of the graveyard at Mosfell. In recent years, it has been suggested that Egil may have suffered from Paget's disease, which is characterized by excessive bone growth.

EIRÍKS SAGA RAUÐA. *See ERIK THE RED, SAGA OF*.

EIRÍKSMÁL. Praise poem composed after the death of **Erik Blood-Ax** at the request of his queen, **Gunnhild**, which describes Erik's entry into **Valhalla**. The poem is now incomplete, with the fullest version preserved in chapter seven of the *Saga of Hákon the Good* (*see* **Hákon the Good**) in the manuscript *Fagrskinna*. However, **Snorri Sturluson** also quotes the first five lines of the poem in *Skáldskaparmál*.

ELDER EDDA. *See POETIC EDDA*.

EMMA OF NORMANDY (980/90–1052). Daughter of Richard I, Duke of **Normandy**, and his Danish wife, Gunnor. She married **Æthelred II** of England in 1002 (adopting the English name Ælfgifu) and, following his death, **Cnut I the Great** in 1017. She had five children, three by Æthelred and two by Cnut, and two of these (**Harthacnut** and Edward I the Confessor) became kings of England. During Cnut's reign, Emma seems to have enjoyed considerable status and power, appearing frequently in charter witness-lists, and she is famously depicted alongside Cnut, presenting a gold cross to the New Minster in Winchester, in the *Liber Vitae* (New Minster Register, British Library, MS Stowe 944 f6r). However, after Cnut's death and during the brief rule of **Harold Harefoot**, Emma was driven into exile in Flanders, under the protection of Count Baldwin. Harold's death in 1040 saw her return to England with her son, Harthacnut, now king of England, and for two years she enjoyed a similar degree of power and public prominence as she had under Cnut's rule. During this period she commissioned the **Encomium Emmae Reginae**, and an image in the only extant manuscript of this text shows her enthroned, receiving this work, with her sons Harthacnut and Edward I looking on. Despite the accession of another of her sons (Edward I the Confessor), upon Harthacnut's death in 1042, Emma's political career was at an end—Edward deprived her of her lands and treasure and she lived out her life in relative obscurity in Winchester. She was buried alongside Cnut, in the Old Minster, in Winchester.

EMUND. King of the Svear (*see* **Svealand**) in the second half of the 11th century. Emund was the son of **Olof Skötkonung** by a "concubine" according to **Adam of Bremen** and was the half brother of **Anund Jakob**, who he succeeded around the year 1050. Adam's attitude to Emund is hostile, describing him as "the Bad" (although sometimes also as "Gamular," meaning "the Old"). The reason for this probably lies in both Emund's birth and in his appointment of a bishop, Osmund, "of irregular status," a "vagabond" who did not recognize the primacy of the mission of Hamburg-Bremen. According to Adam, Emund was succeed by his nephew Stenkil.

ENCOMIUM EMMAE REGINAE. Work commissioned by **Emma of Normandy** in 1041–1042 after the death of her second husband, **Cnut I the Great**, and while her son, **Harthacnut**, was ruling as king of England. It survives in one mid-11th-century Latin manuscript (BL Additional 33241), written by two scribes, in which she is depicted enthroned with Harthacnut and Edward I standing beside her. *Encomium Emmae Reginae* was written by a monk in the monastery of St-Bertin (St-Omer), Flanders, as a history of Cnut's reign and his achievements, and is therefore also known as *Gesta Cnutonis Regis* "The Deeds of King Cnut." *Encomium Emmae Reginae* also describes Cnut and Emma's son, Harthacnut. Her earlier marriage to **Æthelred II** is not mentioned, nor are Emma's sons by Æthelred II, Alfred and Edward I the Confessor. Instead, the author (often called the Encomiast) focuses on the Scandinavian conquest of England in 1013–1016 by **Svein Forkbeard** and Cnut, on Cnut's reign, and on events following his death. In particular, the Encomiast is careful to clear Emma from any suspicion concerning the blinding of her son, the atheling (or prince) Alfred in 1036, and to place the blame on **Harold Harefoot**.

ENGLAND. *See* EAST ANGLIA; MERCIA; NORTHUMBRIA; WESSEX.

ERIK BLOOD-AX (*c.* 895/910–954) (ON *Eiríkr blóðöx*). Erik was one of **Harald Fine-Hair's** sons by his Danish queen, Ragnhild, and killed several of his brothers in his attempt to be recognized as sole king of Norway, hence the nickname "Blood-Ax." He ruled as king of Norway between *c.* 933–935, until he was deposed by his half brother, **Hákon the Good**, and driven into exile in England. He then briefly ruled as king of **York** from 947–948, until King Eadred of England (946–955) ended Erik's control of the Northumbrian (*see* **Northumbria**) capital. Following Erik's defeat, **Olaf Cúarán** of **Dublin** established himself as king of York, until Erik was able to reassert his control of the city in 952. He was killed shortly afterward, on Stainmore in North Yorkshire, after he had once more been defeated by the English and then betrayed by his followers. His death in 954 marked the end of Norse rule in York. One of the most famous saga accounts of Erik is preserved in *Egil's Saga*, when his sworn enemy, the Icelandic skald, Egil Skallagrimsson, composed the Head-Ransom poem (*Höfuðlausn*) in York, celebrating Erik's prowess as a warrior and a king. The poem, *Eiríksmál*, commissioned by his wife **Gunnhild** after his death also pays tribute to Erik's warrior qualities. Erik had many sons by Gunnhild, and the conflict between these sons and their rivals made Norway politically unstable for a generation.

ERIK THE RED (ON *Eiríkr inn rauða***) (d. c. 1002).** Founder of the Norse colony in **Greenland**, whose farm at **Brattahlíð** (present-day Qagssiarssuk) became the political center of the so-called Eastern Settlement. The details of Erik's discovery are preserved in two Icelandic sagas, the *Saga of Erik the Red* and the *Saga of the Greenlanders*. According to these sagas, Erik was born in Norway, but his family emigrated to **Iceland** in his childhood after his father, Thorvald, was outlawed for manslaughter. In 980, Erik himself was sentenced to outlawry by the Thórsnes assembly after a feud with one of his neighbors, and he subsequently set out to find the land that had been sighted some 60 years previously by **Gunnbjörn Ulf-Krakuson**. He returned to Iceland three years later and told of the "green land" that he had explored. On his return to Greenland with a group of Norse colonists, he established his farm, Brattahlíð, at the head of Eiriksfjörd on the western coast of Greenland. Today, the remains of three large farms and a **thing** place, dating from the 13th and 14th centuries, are visible at Brattahlíð, and the small turf church built by his wife, Thjodhild, has been uncovered by archaeological excavations. Erik and Thjodhild had two children and one of these, **Leif the Lucky**, is credited with the Norse discovery of **North America** c. 1000. According to the *Saga of the Greenlanders*, Erik refused to accompany his son on this voyage west because he fell from a horse while riding to the ship, which was considered a bad omen. In the same saga, Erik is said to have died shortly after Leif's return from **Vinland**, succumbing to a "serious disease" that reached Greenland via a Norwegian ship.

ERIK THE RED, SAGA OF (ON *Eiríks saga rauða***).** The *Saga of Erik the Red* is believed to have been written in Snæfellsnes, **Iceland**, shortly after 1264, and was written in part to glorify **Olaf Tryggvason**. It survives in two main manuscripts: *Hauksbók* is the oldest, a collection of sagas compiled in the early 14th century (written down before 1334), and *Skálholtsbók*, a collection from the late 15th century. Both of the extant versions of the saga derive from a common source, but there are many differences in style between them. *Hauks-*

bók is more polished, while the scribe of *Skálholtsbók* was often careless and made mistakes. However, in spite of this, textual analysis has demonstrated that *Hauksbók* was more extensively edited and altered, in order to give the saga a more classical tone. As the author of this work, Haukr Erlendsson, was related to **Thorfinn Karlsefni**, the first colonist, he also added extra family background in order to show the family in a favorable light. Therefore, while *Skálholtsbók* is longer and more garbled in places, it is believed to be closer to the original. However, the original beginning is lost and the first two chapters are taken from the **Book of the Settlements**. See also *VINLAND SAGAS*.

ERIK THE VICTORIOUS (ON *Eiríkr sígrsæll*) **(d. 995).** King of **Svealand** *c*. 980–95 and father of **Olof Skötkonung**. Erik allied himself with the Polish ruler, Boleslav, marrying his sister *c*. 992 and launching a joint attack on **Svein Forkbeard** of Denmark. Erik is supposed to have earned his nickname following his victory in the battle on the banks of the River Fyris, at Uppsala, fought some time between 980–990. This battle is probably that mentioned on runestones (*see* **rune**) from Hällestad and Sjörup in Skåne, southwestern Sweden, and the Högby stone from Östergötland clearly commemorates a warrior who fell in this battle. It is not clear who Erik defeated at Fyris River, although later Icelandic tradition recounts that it was Erik's nephew, Styrbjörn the Strong (*starki*), who had Danish backing (he was married to **Thyre**, daughter of **Harald Blue-Tooth**). The rune-stones from Skåne, which was then part of the Danish kingdom, support the idea of Danish involvement.

ERLING SKJALGSSON (*c*. 975–1028). Norwegian noble with his family seat at Sola, near present-day Stavanger. Erling Skjalgsson was married to Astrid, the sister of **Olaf Tryggvason**, and ruled an area of Norway that stretched from Lindesnes in the south to Sognfjörd, near **Bergen**. Erling is chiefly remembered for his enmity with **Olaf Haraldsson**. He fought against Olaf at the Battle of **Nesjar** in 1016 and was killed by Olaf's army at Boknafjörð in 1028.

EYRBYGGJA SAGA. One of the so-called *Family Sagas* or **Sagas of Icelanders**, *Eyrbyggja Saga* records the early history of the people of Eyrr, Thórsnes, and Álptafjörðr on the Snæfellsnes Peninsula in southwest **Iceland**. The author is unknown, although the saga was probably written at the Benedictine monastery of Helgafell *c*. 1250. The saga opens with the emigration of Þórólfr *mostrarskegg* to Iceland from Norway, on the advice of his god, **Thor**, and one of the most famous episodes in the saga is the account of how Þórólfr decided where to settle in Iceland. The family "temple" to Thor in Norway had been taken down and packed up with the emigrants and, on approaching Iceland, Þórólfr threw the posts of this temple overboard, saying he would settle wherever Thor directed him. The headland where they landed was thus named Thórsnes, and Þórólfr's farm, a new temple to Thor, and a **thing** place were built there. However, the central character in the saga is Snorri the Priest (963–1031) who, although a pagan "priest," persuaded the Icelanders to accept **Christianity** *c*. 1000. The saga ends with Snorri's death and a list of his descendants.

EYRIR. Scandinavian unit of weight that is equivalent to about 24 grams or one British ounce.

EYVINDR SKÁLDASPILLIR. Norwegian poet from Halogaland in north Norway, who served as a skald at the courts of **Hákon the Good**, **Harald Grey-Cloak**, and Earl **Hákon Jarl** of **Lade** in the 10th century. Two poems by Eyvindr, *Háleygjatal* and **Hákonarmál**, along with several single stanzas, survive. These suggest that Eyvindr's relationship with Harald Grey-Cloak was uneasy, as Harald was responsible for the defeat and death in battle of Eyvindr's earlier patron, Hákon the Good. Indeed, at the end of his life, Eyvindr is instead associated with the powerful **earls** of Lade, who had earlier supported Hákon the Good against Harald and the other sons of **Erik Blood-Ax**. Both *Háleygjatal* and *Hákonarmál* have been likened to other poems, *Ynglingatál* and *Eíríksmál* respectively, and Eyvindr's nickname of *skáldaspillir* has therefore been translated as "plagiarist" and "destroyer of skalds." However, it has been argued by some scholars that Eyvindr's work was the model for these poems, rather than being derived from them. Even if his work was later than these other poems, **skaldic poetry** was by its very nature a format with established traditions and rules, and Eyvindr's work should be seen in this light. It also seems likely that Eyvindr had strong political motives for modeling his poems on these earlier works, and his poetry thus had a particularly powerful resonance in the contemporary political climate.

– F –

FAFNIR. Name of the dragon that was killed by **Sigurd the Dragon-Slayer** in the Norse legend of *Völsunga Saga*.

FAGRSKINNA **("the fair parchment").** See *NÓREGS KONUNGA TAL*.

FAMILY SAGAS. See *SAGAS OF THE ICELANDERS*.

FAROE ISLANDS. Archipelago of some 22 islands in the North Atlantic. Writing about 825, the Irish monk Dicuil (*see Book of the Measurement of the Earth*) describes a group of islands north of **Scotland**, identified as the Faroe Islands, as being "full of innumerable sheep and a great many different kinds of sea fowl"; the name of the islands does indeed mean "Sheep Islands."

According to the *Saga of the Faroe Islands*, **Grim kamban** was the name of the first Norseman to have settled in the Faroe Islands, apparently in order to escape the increasing power of the Norwegian king, **Harald Fine-Hair**, during the late ninth century. However, Dicuil records that the hermits from Ireland, who had occupied these islands for about a hundred years, had fled at the time he was writing "because of Norse pirates." Although this evidence clearly places the Norse discovery of the Faroe Islands in the early part of the ninth century at the latest, archaeological excavations have as yet not recovered any artifacts that definitely predate *c*. 900. Nevertheless, the saga association of the first Faroese settlement with the activities of Harald Fine-Hair seems to be a later invention; certainly Grim's grandson is said, in the *Book of Settlements*, to have been among the first settlers in **Iceland**, which took place at the same time as Grim allegedly colonized the Faroe Islands. Grim's nickname, *kamban*, is of Scottish Gaelic origin, which also suggests that he did not leave Norway directly for the Faroe Islands, but instead spent some time in the Norwegian colonies of the Western Isles (*see* **Hebrides**).

We know very little about the Norse community of the Faroe Islands, mainly because the Faroe Islanders did not develop any tradition of writing histories, stories, and poems, in contrast to the Norse colony of Iceland. The only written account about the Faroe Islands is the *Saga of the Faroe Islands*, which was written in Iceland. One 11th-century runic inscription (*see* **rune**), from the bishop's seat at Kirkjubø, therefore constitutes the only written evidence produced in the islands during the Viking Age, but even the inscription on this stone is fragmentary and tells us little more than that runes were known and occasionally used on the islands in the Viking Age. There are also a handful of runic inscriptions, on stone and wood, which postdate the Viking Age. However, archaeological evidence provides some information about life on the islands in the Viking Age. An early Norse farmstead was excavated at **Kvívík** in 1942; two graveyards, near Tjørnuvík and at Sandur, are known, and excavations at the village of Leirvík have also uncovered some Viking-Age remains.

FAROE ISLANDERS, SAGA OF (ON *Færeyinga saga*). This saga was composed in **Iceland** *c.* 1220, although many of the events it relates are set in around 1000. No complete copy of the saga has survived; the fullest extant version is found in *Flateyjarbók*, in the sagas of **Olaf Tryggvason** and **Olaf Haraldsson**. The *Saga of the Faroe Islanders* records that **Grim kamban** was the first Scandinavian settler on the **Faroe Islands**, and that he arrived there during the reign of **Harald Fine-Hair** when "a great number of people fled [from Norway] because of his tyranny." However, there are problems with this chronology, and it seems that the islands were settled in some form or other before the end of the ninth century.

In addition to its account of the colonization of the Faroe Islands, the saga relates how the islanders were converted to **Christianity** by Sigmund Brestisson on behalf of the Norwegian king, including an account of the opposition to Sigmund from Thrand of Gate (ON *Þrándr ór Götu*); and it also discusses relations between the islanders and the kings of Norway. The prominence of the cunning pagan Thrand in the saga's narrative has led some translators and editors to add the subtitle, "The Story of Thrand of Gate," although in the end the saga's "hero" dies, and the islands are converted and brought into the Christian community of Europe.

FÉLAG. Cognate with the English word "fellowship," the term *félag* literally means the pooling of resources. Individuals in the fellowship were known as *félagi* (singular). This term is found on 22 Viking-Age rune-stones (*see* **rune**), such as the one from the island of Berezany in the Black Sea, with which **Grani** commemorated his *félagi*, Karl. Although the term implies an economic partnership, the runic evidence also suggests that the term was often used to describe men who fought alongside each other on Viking campaigns, presumably as they also shared their resources and booty. Indeed, later on it seems that the term came to refer to a more general kind of comradeship or friendship. All of the Viking-Age rune-stones that mention *félagi* were made by men for men, and many of them also describe their "partner" as a **dreng**.

FENRIR. The **mythological** wolf that was the offspring of **Loki**. The *Prose Edda* recounts how Fenrir could break free from any restraint, but that he was finally bound by the gods by a magic ribbon. This ribbon was made by dwarves from a cat's mew, a woman's beard, and the breath of a fish. The gods tricked Fenrir into being bound by daring him to prove his strength. Fenrir agreed to be bound on the condition that the god **Tyr** kept his hand in the wolf's mouth. When Fenrir found himself trapped, he bit off Tyr's hand. Fenrir killed and was killed by **Odin** at **Ragnarök**.

FITJAR, BATTLE OF. Fitjar was a royal estate on the island of Stord, just south of **Bergen** in western Norway. A sea battle was fought there *c*. 960 between King **Hákon the Good** of Norway and his nephew, **Harald Grey-Cloak**, the son of **Erik Blood-Ax**, following Harald's surprise attack on the island. Harald and his brothers, the so-called sons of Erik, had the support of the Danish king, **Harald Blue-Tooth**. Snorri's *Heimskringla* contains an account of the battle, which incorporates the **skaldic** verse of **Eyvindr skáldaspillir**. Hákon of Norway was killed at Fitjar, and Snorri concludes his saga of the Norwegian king with Eyvindr's memorial poem to Hákon, *Hákonarmál*.

FIVE BOROUGHS. The Five Boroughs of Derby, Leicester, Lincoln, Nottingham, and Stamford were part of eastern **Mercia** in the English East Midlands, settled by the Scandinavian army in 877. The five settlements were already local centers of some importance that were apparently reoccupied by Viking armies as fortified centers for their largely rural settlement. Both Derby and Leicester were recaptured by the English, under Æthelflæd, Lady of the Mercians, in 917–918, and it seems likely that the three other towns came under the control of the English at this time. Archaeologically, there is little clear evidence for a Scandinavian presence in these towns during the 9th and 10th centuries, although two pagan burials of warriors have been uncovered in Nottingham. Excavations in Lincoln have revealed evidence for the revitalization of the town, although much of this follows the English reconquest, and specifically Scandinavian artifacts include two runic inscriptions (*see* **rune**).

The term "the Five Boroughs" is first mentioned in the *Anglo-Saxon Chronicle* in 942 when the English king, Edmund, won back control of them from the Norse kings of **York**. The *Anglo-Saxon Chronicle* (recension E) also contains the only known reference to the Seven Boroughs in 1015. It has been suggested that Torksey in Lincolnshire and York may have been included alongside the five other towns.

FLATEYJARBÓK (**"Book of Flatey"**). Medieval Icelandic manuscript that was written by two priests, Jon Þórðarson and Magnus Þorhallsson, between 1387–1390. It consists of 225 large folio sheets, now bound in two volumes, and contains the largest collection of Icelandic sagas, compiled in order to create a continuous history of Norway. The four main sagas are the *Longest Saga of Olaf Tryggvason* (*see* **Olaf Tryggvason**), the *Separate Saga of St. Olaf* (*see* **Sagas of St. Olaf**), *Sverri's Saga,* and the *Saga of Hákon Hákonarson*, and these are supplemented by numerous other sagas, such as **Orkneyinga Saga** and **Saga of the Greenlanders**, *þættir* (short stories), *Nóregs konunga tal*; and the *Annals of Flatey*. In the second part of the 15th century, some 23 sheets containing, among other things, sagas of **Magnus the Good** and **Harald Hard-Ruler** were inserted into the manuscript, bringing it to its present-day total of 225 sheets. It has been estimated that the contents of *Flateyjarbók* must have been copied from at least 40 or 50 separate manuscripts, and much of its material is not found in any other extant sources.

The original owner and patron of *Flateyjarbók* is named in its preface: Jón Hákonarson, a wealthy farmer from Viðalstunga in northern **Iceland**. The manuscript's history is obscure until, in the 15th century, Þorleifur Björnsson, had the extra sheets added. After this the manuscript was owned by his descendants until it was given by Jón Finsson of Flatey (the island after which the manuscript is named) to the Icelandic bishop, Brynjólfur Sveinsson, in 1647. Shortly after it was gifted to the Danish king, Frederik III, and it remained in Copenhagen until 1971 when it was returned to Iceland. The manuscript is currently kept at the Árni Magnússon Institute in Reykjavik.

FORNAFN. This noun is only found in handbooks of grammar and poetics and may be modeled on the Latin *pronomen* "pronoun." **Snorri Sturluson** mentions *fornafn* in **Skáldskaparmál** and **Háttatal**. In *Skáldskaparmál*, Snorri divides *fornafn* up into two types: *viðrkenning* "circumlocution" and *sannkenning* "true description," both of which are used to refer to people without mentioning their names. A circumlocution would generally refer to a person by reference to their possessions or associates. For example, the god **Thor** could be called "the owner of the hammer **Mjöllnir**." An example of a true description is a descriptive word or phrase, like "the generous one," to refer to a king.

FORNALDARSÖGUR. See SAGAS OF ANCIENT TIMES.

FORNYRÐISLAG ("epic meter"). One of the principle meters of **Eddic poetry**, *fornyrðislag* consists of four line stanzas, with each line divided into two halves. These lines have two stresses and one alliterative syllable.

FORTIFICATIONS. *See* DANEVIRKE; TRELLEBORG FORTRESSES.

FRANKIA. *See* CAROLINGIAN EMPIRE.

FRANKISH ANNALS. See ROYAL FRANKISH ANNALS.

FREY (ON *Freyr*). God of the **Vanir** family, brother of **Freya**, and the son of **Niord**. According to **Adam of Bremen**, Frey was the third major god in the Scandinavian pantheon and was a fertility god. Frey was responsible for bringing the sun and rain that produced good harvests, and he was also the patron god of horses and horsemen. According to

Ynglinga Saga, the name of the Swedish Yngling dynasty was derived from the god Frey, who was also known as Yngvi-Frey. Although one of the Vanir, Frey lived in **Asgard** alongside the Æsir, where he had been brought as a hostage in the wars between the two races of gods.

FREYA (ON *Freyja*). Goddess of the **Vanir** family, sister of **Frey**, and daughter of **Niord**. Freya was the goddess of fertility and prosperity; she was also associated with physical beauty and sexual passion. According to Snorri's *Prose Edda*, she rode in a chariot pulled by cats. In *Lokasenna*, **Loki** accuses Freya of having numerous affairs with various male gods.

FRIBRØDRE RIVER. Site of a late Viking-Age shipyard on the island of Falster, eastern Denmark. Large quantities of fragmentary **ship** timbers and wood shavings found in the silted-up river suggest that old ships were wrecked here and new ones were constructed. Close to the south Baltic coast, finds of Slavic poetry and Slavonic elements in the local place-names suggest that this may have been in Wendish (*see* **Wends**) territory, under Danish control. Slavic influence is further suggested by the use of wooden dowels rather than iron clench nails to attach the strakes to the ship's frame.

FRIGG. Principal goddess of the Æsir, Frigg was the wife of **Odin** and the mother of **Balder**. In the *Prose Edda*, **Snorri Sturluson** describes how she asked every living thing to swear an oath not to harm Balder. According to *Lokasenna*, she slept with Odin's brothers, Vili and Vé. Her name is preserved in the name of the weekday, Friday (from OE *frigedæg*).

FRISIA. Area of northwest Europe, approximating to present-day Belgium and the Netherlands, which was part of the **Carolingian Empire** in the Viking Age. The Frisians were a Germanic people, living along the North Sea coast of Europe, between the mouths of the rivers Rhine and Ems, who were brought under Frankish control in 734. The region played an important role in trade between the Rhineland, the North Sea, and the Baltic, and the important trading towns of **Dorestad** and **Quentovic** were situated on Frisian territory. This, together with the geographical proximity of the coast to Denmark, made Frisia an obvious target for **Viking** raids. As early as the sixth century, the Danish king, Hygelac, is recorded as raiding in Frisia, although regular Viking raids only began *c*. 810, when the Danish king, **Godfred**, collected one hundred pounds of silver in tribute from the Frisians. As with the granting of **Normandy** to **Rollo**, Frankish leaders sought to limit Viking attacks through grants of lands to Viking leaders. In 841, **Lothar** granted the island of Walcheren and the neighboring area to "the pirate Harald." He also granted an area in southern Frisia to Harald's brother, Rurik, who had seized Dorestad in 850, in return for his agreeing to resist further Viking attacks on the area, an agreement that Rorik apparently kept. Following the Frankish siege of Asselt on the River Meuse, **Charles the Fat** granted territory in Frisia to Rurik's son, Godfred, in 882; and in return Godfred was baptized. However, Godfred allowed Viking armies to continue to pass through his territory and was murdered by the emperor's connivance in 885 after Godfred had been drawn into an alliance with Charles's cousin and rival, Hugh.

FRÖSÖ STONE. Viking-Age rune-stone (*see* **rune**) standing on the island of Frösö, near the present-day town of Östersund, Jämtland, in northwest Sweden. This is the only Viking-Age rune-stone found in this province, and it is also the northernmost of the Swedish rune-stones. Although Jämtland was part of Norway in the Viking Age, the rune-stone itself nevertheless belongs stylistically to the Swedish rather than the Norwegian tradition. The inscription has been compared to that on the Danish **Jelling** stone raised by **Harald Blue-Tooth**, as it commemorates the wholesale conversion to **Christianity** of the province and is the only Swedish rune-stone to directly refer to the conversion process: "Austmaðr, Guðfast's son, had this stone raised and this bridge built, and he had Jämtland Christianized. Ásbjörn made the bridge. Trjónn and Stæinn carved the runes." The stone is dated to the 11th century.

FULFORD (GATE), BATTLE OF. Battle fought outside **York** in northeast England on 20 September 1066 between a Norwegian army under **Harald Hard-Ruler** and a Northumbrian (*see* **Northumbria**) force under Earls (*see* **earl**) Edwin and Morcar. The Northumbrians were defeated and promised hostages to the Norwegians, who then encamped at nearby **Stamford Bridge**.

FUTHARK. *See* RUNES.

FYRIS RIVER, BATTLE OF. *See* ERIK THE VICTORIOUS.

FYRKAT. *See* TRELLEBORG FORTRESSES.

– G –

GALL-GAEDHIL. Ninth-century Irish annals mention *Gall-Gaedhil* or "Foreign Gael," who were involved in wars in **Ireland** (*Three Fragmentary Annals* 856; 858; 859; *Annals of Ulster* 856; 857). The precise meaning of this name is uncertain, but the *Gall-Gaedhil* appear to have been warriors of mixed Norse and Gaelic ancestry that had some connection with the **Hebrides** and southwest **Scotland**. The region of Galloway in southwest Scotland may even have derived its name from the link with the *Gall-Gaedhil*.

GAMLA UPPSALA. Literally Old Uppsala, located some 10 kilometers north of the modern town of Uppsala in central eastern Sweden. Gamla Uppsala seems to have been a religious and royal center from perhaps as early as the sixth century. Three great **burial** mounds, believed to contain the remains of three sixth-century kings of the Svear (*see* **Svealand**), are still visible. These mounds were excavated in the 19th century, revealing male cremation burials and a rich assortment of grave goods, which included gold Vendel-period jewelry. Three members of the Yngling (*see Ynglinga Saga; Ynglingatal*) dynasty—Egil, Aun, and Adils—mentioned in the 13th-century *Heimskringla* are traditionally believed to have been buried in these mounds, although there is no archaeological evidence to prove or disprove this identification. As well as the royal mounds, hundreds of smaller burial mounds can still be seen on the site, along with a **thing** or assembly mound and a 12th-century church. According to **Adam of Bremen**, however, a pagan temple "entirely decked out in gold" existed on the site possibly as late as the mid-11th century, and he described in some detail the pagan rituals performed at Gamla Uppsala every nine years. These included the worship of **Odin**, **Thor**, and **Frey**, and the ritual sacrifice of nine males of every living creature. His account was apparently based upon that of an eyewitness, although archaeologists have failed to uncover any evidence of the temple in excavations underneath the church.

GARDAR (ON *Garðar*). The episcopal see of **Greenland**, located in the so-called Eastern Settlement between Erik's Fjörd and Einar's Fjörd (present-day Tunnuliarfik and Igaliku Fjörd respectively) in the south of the country. The first bishop of Greenland was consecrated *c*. 1125 in **Lund**, present-day Sweden.

Gardar (present-day Igaliku) was the biggest Norse farm in Greenland and consisted of a church and churchyard, the bishop's residence, a large number of outbuildings (including cowsheds that could house more than one hundred animals), and a **thing** or assembly site. The church was excavated in 1926 and the remains of a 13th-century bishop, buried with a walrus-ivory crosier and a gold ring, were found buried in the northern chapel. The church ruins themselves also date to the 13th century, but at least two earlier phases lie underneath these.

GARÐARÍKI. *See* RUSSIA, VIKINGS IN.

GESTA DANORUM **("History of the Danes").** This is the first real history of Denmark, written in Latin by **Saxo Grammaticus**. According to Saxo's preface, the *Gesta Danorum* was written at the suggestion of Archbishop Absalon of Lund. It consists of 16 volumes and covers some 2,000 years of Danish history, beginning with the legendary King Dan (who it is claimed gave the country its name) and ending with the Danish conquest of Pomerania by Knut IV in 1185. The first nine books give an account of about 60 legendary Danish kings, including Amleth, believed to be the source of William Shakespeare's *Hamlet*. The last seven books contain Saxo's account of the historical period, but he achieves independent authority only when writing of events close to his own time. Saxo's aim in writing *Gesta Danorum* was to provide Denmark with a historical pedigree equal to that claimed by other western European countries. No alternative history was produced in Denmark before the Reformation, and Saxo's work later became a source of inspiration to many of the 19th-century Danish Romantic poets.

GESTA HAMMABURGENSIS ECCLESIAE PONTIFICUM. See ADAM OF BREMEN.

GESTA NORMANNORUM DUCUM. See WILLIAM OF JU-MIÈGES.

GESTA SWENOMAGNI REGIS ET FILIORUM EIUS ET PASSIO GLORIOSISSMI CANUTI REGIS ET MARTYRIS. See ÆL-NOTH; KNUT, ST.

GINNUNGAGAP (ON *Ginnungagap*). In Norse **mythology**, Ginnungagap was the void that existed before the world was created, separating the coldness of **Niflheim** in the north from the heat of Muspellsheim (*see* **Muspell**) in the south. Ginnungagap is described as a mild place in *Gylfaginning*, and when the ice and fire from Niflheim and Muspell met, life was created in the form of the giant Ymir and the cow Auðhumla. The precise meaning of the name Ginnungagap is uncertain; it has been translated as "the yawning void," "the mighty or deceptive void," and "the void filled with magical powers." **Adam of Bremen** glossed the Latin *immane baratrum abyssi* with "Ghinmendegop" in Book 4 of his *History of the Archbishops of Hamburg-Bremen*.

GNEZDOVO. Settlement located at the junction of the Rivers Lovat and **Dnieper** in present-day **Russia**. Gnezdovo consisted of a fortress, with a large settlement outside its walls and a huge cemetery with more than 3,000 **burial** mounds. Estimates put the maximum population of the town at *c.* 2,000, and excavations suggest a substantial and wealthy Scandinavian minority lived alongside the predominantly Slavic inhabitants of Gnezdovo. Finds include the largest Viking-Age silver hoard from Russia, found in 1868, which contained a number of Scandinavian artifacts. The site was abandoned at the end of the 10th century for a new settlement at present-day Smolensk.

GODFRED (d. 810). King of Denmark at the beginning of the ninth century. The *Royal Frankish Annals* first mention *Godofrid* in 804, when he failed to meet the Frankish emperor, **Charlemagne**, at **Hedeby**, following the Emperor's conquest of Saxony. Four years later, Godfred is recorded as attacking Charlemagne's allies, the **Abodrites**, burning the unidentified settlement at **Reric** and relocating the merchants of *Reric* to Hedeby, on Danish territory, as well as fortifying his southern border with the **Danevirke**. Godfred seems to have actively challenged Frankish control of **Frisia** and Saxony and in 810 attacked the coast of Frisia with a fleet of some 200 ships and imposed a tribute of 100 pounds of silver on its inhabitants. He apparently threatened to march on Charlemagne's capital, Aachen, but his ambitions were cut short by his murder in 810. His nephew Hemming (*see* **Harald Klak**) succeeded him and came to terms with the Franks.

GOÐI. A *goði* (plural *goðar*) was a man who held one of the 36 chieftaincies or *goðorð* (in 965, the number was increased to 39, and in 1005, to 48) in **Iceland**: there were nine each for the western, southern, and eastern quarters of the country, but the northern quarter had an extra three as it had an additional spring-time assembly. *Goðorð* could be inherited, bought, exchanged, or shared, although any **woman** who inherited a *goðorð* was required by law to give the position to a man.

Originally these chieftaincies were not linked to particular geographical territories, but were instead based on a client-patron relationship with his *þingmenn* "thing men," "followers," with all free men able to choose which *goði* to follow. The followers of different *goðar* might therefore live on neighboring farms. The followers of each *goði* had to accompany him to the local and national assemblies, or pay a tax to help cover the expenses of those who did go to the **thing**. Within each quarter, its *goðar* were responsible for calling the local springtime and fall assemblies, although the latter might be held for the followers of the individual *goði* rather than as an assembly for all the free men and *goðar* in the quarter. At the **Althing**, the *goðar* elected the Law-Speaker and constituted the legislative council, revising and making law, and determining punishments for breaches of the law. The free men and the *goðar* provided mutual support in the carrying out of their feuds and in protecting their interests at the local and national assemblies.

In the 12th and 13th centuries, these chieftaincies became associated with particular districts and were held by fewer and more powerful individuals and families, known as *stórgoðar* "large *goðar*." This process resulted in a destructive civil war between rival families and factions. Following Iceland's subjugation to the Norwegian crown in 1262–1264, the *goðorð* were abolished and replaced by *sýsla* or counties.

GOÐORÐ. *See* GOÐI.

GODRED CROVAN (ON *Guðroðr***; Old Irish** *crobh bhán* **"White-Hand") (d. 1095).** King of the **Isle of Man**, who is known as King Orry in Manx tradition. He is the first Scandinavian king of Man about whom any real details are known, and his descendants ruled the island until it was handed to England in the Treaty of Perth (1266). The most important written source for his rule, and that of his descendants, is the ***Chronicle of the Kings of Man and the Isles***.

Godred Crovan was probably born on the southern Hebridean island of Islay (where he also died), although he may have spent some of his childhood on Man. He fought alongside **Harald Hard-Ruler** at **Stamford Bridge** in 1066 and following the Norwegian defeat fled to Man and the protection of its king, Godred Sigtrygsson (d. 1070). He launched his own campaign for the kingship in 1079 and, following two defeats, was victorious in the Battle of **Skyhill**. During his sixteen years of power, Godred Crovan extended Manx influence north to the **Hebrides**, founding the so-called Kingdom of the Man and Isles, and he was also king of **Dublin** between 1091 and 1094.

GODS. *See* ÆSIR and VANIR.

GOKSTAD SHIP. Classic **Viking ship** discovered and excavated in Vestfold, southwest Norway in 1880. The ship was part of an elaborate **burial** and had been placed in a shallow trench and subsequently covered by an earth mound. The body of a man, aged 60–70 and apparently suffering from rheumatism, was placed under a specially constructed wooden chamber on the deck of the ship. His grave goods included a gaming board, 12 horses, 6 dogs, a peacock, several beds, a wooden sledge, 64 painted wooden shields, 3 small rowing boats, and various items of cooking equipment. The ship itself is made of oak and measures some 23.3 meters long x 5.2 meters broad x 2 meters deep. It is clinker-built, with 16 strakes or planks on each side and 16 pairs of oars, suggesting a double crew of 64. It had a single square sail and a big keel, giving it stability in deep water. **Dendrochronological** dating suggests that the timbers of the burial chamber itself were felled *c.* 900–905.

GÖNGU-HRÓLFR. *See GÖNGU-HROLF'S SAGA*; ROLLO.

GÖNGU-HROLFS SAGA (**"Saga of Hrolf the Walker"**). The *Saga of Hrolf the Walker* was written in **Iceland** in the 14th century. Its hero has been identified with the historical figure, **Rollo**, founder of the Duchy of **Normandy**, but the saga itself is a piece of romantic and fantastical fiction about Göngu-Hrolf's journey to **Russia** to court Princess Ingigerd on behalf of Earl Thorgny of Jutland. According to the saga, the hero earned his nickname because he was too heavy to be carried by a horse, and so he had to walk.

GORM THE OLD (d. 958–959). King of Denmark in the mid-10th century, whose rule inaugurated a new royal dynasty in Denmark. He was married to **Thyre**, whom he commemorated with a **rune-stone** raised at the new dynastic seat in **Jelling**, Jutland, Denmark. Very little is known about Gorm's life, but according to **Adam of Bremen** he was the son of *Hardegon* (Harthacnut?) and his family was from *Nortmannia* (variously identified as northern Jutland, Norway, and Normandy). *Hardegon* overthrew the Swedish dynasty of Olaf (*see* **Olaf dynasty**) who had been ruling in Denmark until *c.* 936, and while the full extent of his kingdom is unknown, it probably included the whole of the Jutland Peninsula.

A Christian mission (*see* **Christianity, Conversion to**), led by Archbishop Unni of Hamburg-Bremen, visited Denmark during the early years of Gorm's rule in the 930s, but nevertheless Gorm was apparently buried as a pagan in the north **burial** mound at Jelling on his death some 20 years later. His son, **Harald Blue-Tooth**, appears to have later disinterred him and to have had his body reburied in a grave under a newly erected church in Jelling, where he also commemorated both his parents with a Christian rune-stone. Excavations of the north mound in the 19th century revealed a wooden burial chamber, dated by **dendrochronology** to 958–959. A repaired hole in the roof of the burial chamber suggests that the mound had been entered previously, but with some care, rather than for the looting of the grave goods. Grave goods found by the excavators inside the chamber include a small silver cup decorated in the **Jellinge art** style, but no human bones were recovered. However, a disarticulated male skeleton, some 1.72 meters tall with arthritis in the lower back, believed to be that of Gorm, was excavated from underneath the church at Jelling in 1976–1979. Analysis of these bones, which had been wrapped together in a fine cloth, suggests that this man probably died in his 40s.

GORMLAITH (ON *Kormloð***) (d. 1030).** Daughter of Murchad mac Finn, king of Leinster (d. 972) in **Ireland**. Gormlaith was married three times and the complex family relationships that resulted from these marriages reflect the nature of Irish-Norse relations at the end of the 10th and beginning of the 11th century. Gormlaith's first husband was **Olaf Cúarán**, who she was probably married to in the 950s and by whom she had a son called **Sigtrygg Silk-Beard**; she then married and later divorced Máel Sechnaill (d. 1022), the Irish Uí Neíll rival to **Brian Boru**. Finally, Gormlaith married Brian Boru, Irish high king, and bore him a son called Donnchad, before apparently leaving Brian. At the Battle of **Clontarf**, her son Sigtrygg's **Dublin Vikings** and her brother, Máel Mórda of Leinster, fought against Brian Boru (although Sigtrygg himself was married to one of Brian's daughters, Sláine). In addition to these marriages, Gormlaith was apparently promised to **Sigurd the Stout** of **Orkney** and Brodir of the **Isle of Man** in the negotiations that surrounded Clontarf, with Dublin as her dowry.

GORODIŠČE (ON *Holmgárðr***).** Island south of the modern **Russian** city of **Novgorod**, on the northern edge of Lake Ilmen. It was here that Rurik (d. *c.* 879) settled, establishing **Rus** power in the mid-ninth century, and although his successor Oleg (d. 913) moved his capital to **Kiev**, *Holmgárðr* continued to be an important town. Excavations have revealed a defended market center that was occupied by a mixed Slavic and Scandinavian population in the 9th and 10th centuries. After the mid-10th century relocation of the settlement to the "new fortress" at Novgorod, some two kilometers away, Gorodišče became the residence of the princes of Novgorod and a military and administrative center. Scandinavian finds from the town include jewelry, such as an iron **Thor's** hammer ring; two rune-inscribed (*see* **rune**) bronze amulets; a pendant in the shape of a **woman**, that is possibly meant to be a **valkyrie**; and the head of a dress pin shaped like a dragon's head.

GOSFORTH CROSS. Tenth-century ring-headed cross standing on its original base in Gosforth churchyard, **Cumbria**, northwest England. The form of the monument is of Celtic origin, but the decoration is predominantly Norse with, for example, **Borre** style ring chain on the cross shaft. The cross is most famous, however, for the episodes of **Ragnarök**, the pagan Norse end of the world, which are depicted on the cross shaft alongside a crucifixion scene (at the bottom of the east side of the cross). The Ragnarök scenes include Viðarr's revenge on the wolf **Fenrir** who had killed his father, **Odin**; **Loki**, bound underneath the venomous jaws of a serpent, with his wife Sigyn holding a bowl to catch the venom before it fell on Loki; and the god **Heimdall**, identified by the horn he is holding, fending off a monster. A number of other warrior figures and monsters are shown on the north and south faces of the shaft, but these cannot be positively identified with any definite Ragnarök episode. It has been argued that the juxtaposition of Christian and pagan images may represent Christ's triumph over the devil, here represented by the old pagan gods, but this is not at all certain.

GÖTALAND. West Swedish kingdom, roughly approximating to the modern-day counties of Östergötland and Västergötland, around Lakes Vänern and Vättern. The inhabitants of this area were known as the Götar (ON *Gautar*), and they were separated from their Svear (*see* **Svealand**) neighbors to the northeast by a huge tract of impenetrable forest and marshland (Tiveden and Kolmården). Runic inscriptions (*see* **rune**) and place-names provide some evidence of cultural, and possibly political, contacts with the kingdom of Denmark (which also included part of southwest Sweden at this time)—quite natural given the importance of sea communications in this period and the difficulty of land communications—and Götaland was less remote from Europe than Svealand. Nevertheless, virtually nothing is know about the Götar in the Viking Age, and although they were apparently converted to **Christianity** before the Svear of east Sweden, the missionary **Ansgar**

did not visit them. The main source of written evidence for Götaland in the Viking Age is runic inscriptions carved on memorial stones. Among the rune-stones from the two provinces are the famous **Rök** and Sparlösa stones from Östergötland and Västergötland respectively.

The relative primacy of Svealand and Götaland has long been debated in Swedish historical scholarship. The traditional picture was of Svear dominance and conquest, but in recent years, many historians have argued for the primacy of the Götar. The first king known to have exercised power in both Svealand and Götaland is **Olof Skötkonung**, who was baptized at Husaby in Västergötland in 1010 (apparently by an English bishop, Sigfrid), but it was not until after the end of the Viking Age that a properly unified kingdom of Sweden emerged.

GÖTAR. *See* GÖTALAND.

GOTLAND. Swedish island in the Baltic, whose present-day capital, Visby, assumed its importance in the 11th century following the decline of its predecessor, **Paviken**. During the Viking and early medieval periods, Gotland was virtually independent of Sweden, and this independence is also reflected in its distinctive cultural artifacts, notably the Gotlandic picture stones that are decorated with **mythological** and heroic scenes. The limestone soils of the island provided abundant fertile land for both growing crops and grazing animals. Moreover, Gotland's position in the Baltic made it a convenient stepping stone on the sea routes from Scandinavia to the East and the South and an obvious distribution and market center for merchants. During the Viking Age, its closest relations seem to have been with the other Baltic island of Öland and the southeast Baltic coast. The wealth of the island can be clearly seen in its large number of coin hoards—over 700 Viking-Age hoards of silver are known from the island—although their deposition may also reflect the relative vulnerability of the island to piracy. Indeed, the remains of about one hundred forts (not all built in the Viking Age) have been found on Gotland. The largest of these, Torsburgen, built perhaps in the fourth century but still in use in the 10th century, covered an area of approximately 156 hectares. The **Broa art** style takes its name from the bronze mounts found on the island.

GRÁGÁS. *See* LAW-CODES, ICELANDIC.

GRANI. Sigurd the Dragon-Slayer's horse, which Sigurd loaded up with gold after killing the dragon, **Fafnir**.

GREAT ARMY (OE *micel here*). Viking army that, according to the *Anglo-Saxon Chronicle*, arrived in **East Anglia** in 866 and campaigned in England well into the 890s. The Great Army, or Great Heathen Army (OE *micel hæðen here*) as it is sometimes called, was at the time the largest Scandinavian force to have raided in England, and its arrival signified a shift from sporadic attacks to a long-term campaign that resulted in the permanent Scandinavian settlements of **Northumbria, Mercia,** and East Anglia. Following the settlement of East Anglia, much of the army seems to have crossed the North Sea and campaigned in the **Carolingian Empire**, returning when **Guthrum** broke the Treaty of **Wedmore** in 885.

Although the Chronicle refers to the army in the singular, it consisted of several distinct and shifting groups under a number of different leaders: **Halfdan** led the section of the army that settled in Northumbria in 875; Guthrum was the leader of the group that settled in East Anglia in 880; and the *Chronicle* also mentions leaders called *Ingware* (*see* **Ivar the Boneless**) and Ubba (869), Bagsecg (870), Oscytel and Anund (875), and **Hastein** (892, 893–894). Archaeological evidence for the presence of the Great Army has been recovered from **Repton** and, more recently, **Ingleby Heath**, both in the English Midlands. The contrast between these two sites, particularly in their respective forms of **burials**, has been interpreted as reflecting two distinct factions within the Great Army.

GREECE. *See* BYZANTIUM; GRIKKLAND.

GREENLAND. Large island in the North Atlantic. Some two-thirds of Greenland lies within the Arctic Circle and a vast ice sheet covers about 85 percent of its surface area. **Gunnbjörn Ulf-Krakuson** is believed to be the first European to have sighted Greenland. Both **Ari Thorgilsson** and **Adam of Bremen** refer to the establishment of the Norse colony of Greenland, but the so-called *Vinland Sagas* preserve more details about its discovery and colonization. It is attributed to

Erik the Red, who is said to have found the island some 14 or 15 years before the Icelanders were converted to **Christianity**. According to these sagas, Erik named the country Greenland so that it would attract colonists, but certainly there was relatively good pastureland along the fjörds. In *c*. 985, some 25 ships of colonists are said to have set out from **Iceland** to settle in Erik's Greenland, but only 14 of these arrived following a storm at sea.

The Norse colony of Greenland consisted of two main settlements on its southwestern coast: the Eastern Settlement (*Eystribyggð*) near the southern tip of the island and present-day Julianehåb; and 650 kilometers to its north, the Western Settlement (*Vestribyggð*), around the modern capital of Nuuk (Godthåb). The Eastern Settlement seems to have been the larger of the two with about 190 farmsteads, compared to about 90 in the Western Settlement. In addition to these, a group of about 20 farms located between the Eastern and Western Settlements was known as the Middle Settlement, near to present-day Ivigtut. The Norse population of Greenland has been estimated as between about 1,000 and 3,000 people in total, peaking around 1300.

Although the earliest settlers on Greenland were said to be pagan, as yet no pagan Scandinavian **burials** have been discovered there. Christianity is said to have reached Greenland through **Leif the Lucky**. Several churches and Christian graveyards dating to the Late Viking Age and medieval period have been identified on Greenland, including that at **Brattahlíð** on Erik the Red's farmstead. *Flateyjar-bók* lists some 12 churches in the Eastern Settlement and 3 in the Western Settlement. A Bishop of Greenland was appointed, based at **Gardar** in the Eastern Settlement, in 1126; an Augustinian monastery and a Benedictine monastery were also established in this Settlement. The Greenlanders modeled their society on that they had left behind in Iceland; for example, they too had an **Althing**, a constitution, and a **law-code**. Like Iceland too, they later surrendered their independence and recognized the Norwegian king (in 1261).

Cattle and sheep farming were the main economic activities of the colonists, supplemented with hunting and fishing. The hunting grounds around Disko Bay in the far north were known as *Norðsetr*. Confirmation of Norse exploration and activity in the north of Greenland is provided by the **Kingiktorssuaq stone**. The Greenlanders depended on imports for corn, timber, and luxuries, and in exchange exported furs, hides, walrus ivory, polar bears, and falcons. The colonists' way of life was essentially European, and when the climate of Greenland started to deteriorate in the Middle Ages (the so-called Little Ice Age), this led to problems. Excavations and analysis of skeletal and organic remains, such as those at Herjolfsnes (*see* **Bjarni Herjólfsson**) have demonstrated that Greenlanders wore woolen clothes rather than furs, like their Inuit neighbors, and their diet appears to have contained too little fat. This, rather than hostile relations with the Inuit (see **skraeling**), ultimately led to the extinction of the Norse colony of Greenland. The Western Settlement appears to have been abandoned by the middle of the 14th century, the Middle Settlement by the end of that century, and the Eastern Settlement by *c*. 1450. By the 15th century, contact between Greenland and her Scandinavian neighbors had been lost, and nobody was sure if descendants of the original settlers were still living on the island.

GREENLANDERS, SAGA OF **(ON *Grœnlendinga saga*).** This saga is believed to have been written in **Iceland** in about or just before 1200. The oldest surviving text is preserved in ***Flateyjarbók***, which was compiled in north Iceland between 1382–1395, and is therefore almost two centuries older than the original saga. In *Flateyjarbók*, the saga is incorporated into another saga, that of King **Olaf Tryggvason** of Norway. The beginning of the *Saga of the Greenlanders* was lost in this process, and its first chapter in modern editions and translations is a later addition, taken from a version of the ***Book of Settlements***. *See also VINLAND SAGAS.*

GRETTIR'S SAGA **(ON *Grettis saga*).** One of the so-called *Family Sagas* or **Sagas of the Icelanders**, *Grettir's Saga* was written in **Iceland** at the beginning of the 14th century. It survives in four complete manuscripts from the 15th and 16th centuries. The saga's hero is the Icelandic outlaw, Grettir Ásmundarson the Strong, who lived *c*. 996–1031. According to the saga, Grettir was outlawed for a killing and took refuge on the island of Drangey in Skagafjörður (north Iceland). The saga is unusual in the prominent role played by the supernatural, and there are some parallels with the Old English epic *Beowulf* (for example, Grettir's fight with the ghost, Glám). Glám's curse on Grettir ultimately led to his death.

GRIKKLAND. Old Norse name for the northeastern Mediterranean lands of the Byzantine Empire (*see* **Byzantium**). Viking-Age **rune-stones** from central eastern Sweden contain more references to *Grikkland* than to any other foreign country. The relative frequency of these references presumably reflects the opportunities there for acquiring wealth, whether it was in the form of trading, raiding, or military service (*see* **Varangian Guard**).

GRIM KAMBAN. According to the *Saga of the Faroe Islanders*, Grim *kamban* fled the tyranny of King **Harald Fine-Hair** of Norway and was the first Norse settler of the **Faroe Islands**. However, his Celtic nickname *kamban* suggests that he may also have spent time in **Ireland** or the **Hebrides**.

GROBIN. Fortified Viking-Age settlement in present-day Latvia, probably identical with the *Seeburg* in *Kurland* that is mentioned in the *Life of St. Ansgar* (*see* **Ansgar, St.**). According to this *Life*, the town was captured by the Svear (*see* **Svealand**) *c*. 850. Certainly there is considerable archaeological evidence for a Scandinavian presence in the town: grave goods with parallels in both central Sweden and **Gotland** have been discovered in the cemeteries around Grobin, and, more recently, a Gotlandic picture-stone has been found there.

GROIX, ISLE DE. Island off the south Breton (*see* **Brittany**) coast in present-day France. A **ship burial**, dating to the first half of the 10th century, was found on the island's headland. This is the only known male **Viking** burial in France. A longship (*see* **ships**) measuring some 14 meters in length, containing the bodies of an adult male and an adolescent, had been ritually burned and subsequently covered by an earth mound, with two parallel lines of standing stones marking the passage to the sea. Only metal fragments of the ship survived the funeral pyre—iron rivets, nails, and some fragments of iron decoration from the stern. The ship also contained a range of rich grave goods: **weapons** (swords, spearheads, shields, and an ax), riding gear, gold and silver jewelry, smith's tools, farming implements, and ivory gaming pieces.

GULATHING (ON *Gulaþing*). Legal province in western Norway, established *c*. 950. The law-code of the Gulathing is one of two surviv-

ing Norwegian **law-codes** and is preserved whole in a medieval manuscript, *Codex Rantzovianus*, dating to between 1250–1300, as well
as in a number of fragments.

GUNGNIR ("the swaying one"). The name of **Odin's** spear, which
was made by dwarves known as Ivaldi's sons according to Snorri's
Skáldskaparmál. According to the **Eddic** poem, *Sigrdrífumál*, **runes**
were carved into the point of the spear. Gungnir is one of Odin's main
attributes, and it was said that throwing a spear over opponents in battle dedicated them to Odin. Odin's self-sacrifice, as described in *Hávamál*, also refers to his being wounded by a spear.

GUNNBJÖRN ULF-KRAKUSON. According to the *Vinland Sagas*,
the first Norseman to sight **Greenland** when he was blown off course
on a voyage from Norway to **Iceland**, some 60 years before **Erik the
Red's** voyage to Greenland.

GUNNHILD (ON *Gunnhildr*). In *Heimskringla*, Gunnhild is said to
have been the daughter of Özurr Toti of Halogaland in northern
Norway. However, *Historia Norwegiae* provides the information
that she was the daughter of **Gorm the Old** and therefore the sister
of **Harald Blue-Tooth** of Denmark. Gunnhild is, however, chiefly
remembered as the wife of **Erik Blood-Ax** of Norway and the
mother of **Harald Grey-Cloak**. She ruled as Erik's queen in **York**
and returned to Norway after his murder. Following Erik's death,
she commissioned *Eiríksmál* in his memory. On her return to Norway Gunnhild supported Harald Grey-Cloak's and her other sons'
(there were six besides Harald) claims to the Norwegian throne, and
was therefore known as "the mother of kings" (ON *konungamóðir*).
She may be one of the few female poets of the Viking Age, although
just one half stanza is attributed to her, and this attribution is far
from certain. In the Icelandic sources, Gunnhild is depicted at best
as a manipulative and scheming **woman** (e.g., *Heimskringla*), and
at worst as a witch and a nymphomaniac (e.g., *Njal's Saga*
and *Egil's Saga*). Gunnhild and her sons left Norway for **Orkney**
after the death of Harald Grey-Cloak, and they are said to have harried in the west until the last of Gunnhild and Erik's sons, Guðrøðr,
died *c.* 999.

GUTHRUM (d. 890). Leader of the part of the **Great Army** that settled in **East Anglia**, eastern England. Guthrum joined the army in 871, was involved in the conquest of **Mercia**, and, in 875, led a section of the army to Cambridge, together with Oscytel and Anund. Guthrum's army systematically attacked the English kingdom of **Wessex** in 878, forcing its leader, **Alfred the Great** into temporary exile. However, Guthrum's subsequent defeat at **Edington** was followed by his baptism, alongside that of some of his men, and he adopted the English baptismal name of Athelstan, with Alfred standing as his godfather. The two leaders also signed a peace treaty at **Wedmore**, in which Alfred conceded East Anglia to the Scandinavian army. According to the ***Anglo-Saxon Chronicle***, Guthrum then went to **Frankia** and returned to England in 885, breaking the terms of the peace of Wedmore. However, upon his defeat by Alfred in 886, the treaty was renewed.

GYLFAGINNING (**"The tricking of Gylfi"**). Second part of Snorri's ***Prose Edda***. *Gylfaginning* is written in the form of a dialogue between Gylfi, a Swedish king disguised as a traveler called Gangleri, and three kings of the Æsir, named as High, Just-as-High, and Third. The purpose of the dialogue was a contest of wisdom, and in the course of Gylfi's questioning, the three kings provide what is probably the best account of Norse **mythology**, from the beginning of the world, through descriptions and stories of the gods, to the destruction of **Ragnarök**. Gylfi is prevented from winning the contest by the disappearance of the three kings and their hall at the end of the questions. However, the Æsir decide that they should continue the deception and adopt the names of the gods about whom they were talking, in order that they might be worshipped.

– H –

HACKSILVER. Name given to cut up pieces of silver coins, arm rings, and jewelry that is commonly found in Viking-Age hoards. The silver was cut up into pieces weighing standard amounts and was used instead of coinage.

HÆRVEJEN. *See* ARMY ROAD.

HAFRSFJÖRD, BATTLE OF (ON *Hafrsfjörðr*). Famous sea battle fought off the Norwegian coast, now Havsfjørd west of present-day Stavanger, by **Harald Fine-Hair** against an alliance of local chieftains and rulers. These included Erik, king of Hordaland; Sulki, king of Rogaland; Kjötvi the Rich, king of Agder, and his son, the **berserker**, Þórir Haklangr. An account of the battle is given in *Heimskringla*, where five stanzas of **skaldic poetry** composed by the poet, Thorbjörn *hornklofi* ("Horn-Cleaver" = raven), are quoted. These appear to be part of a longer poem of some 23 stanzas, generally called *Haraldskvæði*, about Harald Fine-Hair.

The date of the battle is uncertain. While later Icelandic writers, such as **Ari Thorgilsson**, date Hafrsfjörd to 870, modern historians prefer a date *c.* 885–890. According to later Icelandic tradition, Harald's victory made him the first king of a united Norway, triggering many Norwegians to seek out freedom from royal control in new lands in the North Atlantic. In reality it seems that Harald's kingdom did not extend north of present-day **Trondheim**.

HAITHABU. *See* HEDEBY.

HÁKON JARL SIGURDSSON (ON *Hákon jarl Sigurðarson*) (*c.* 940–995). Also known as Hákon the Great (ON *inn ríki*). **Earl** of **Lade** in Norway *c.* 963–995 and the last pagan ruler of that country *c.* 970–995. His father, Earl Sigurd, was murdered by **Harald Grey-Cloak**, whom Hákon Jarl drove into exile *c.* 968 with the support of the Danish king, **Harald Blue-Tooth**. Following the collapse of Harald Grey-Cloak's rule, Hákon Jarl and Harald Blue-Tooth shared power in Norway: Harald ruled the southern part of the country, nearest Denmark, while Hákon controlled the west coast as Harald's subordinate and Trøndelag in his own right. In *Heimskringla*, Hákon is said to have fought with Harald against the German emperor in 974 and to have been baptized following his defeat. Relations with the Danish king soured after Hákon renounced his new religion and Harald forcibly attempted to reconvert the earl. However, Hákon won control of the whole country following his victory against the **Jomsvikings** at the Battle of **Hjörungavágr**, and the

Danish kings were unable to reclaim their control or overlordship until *c*. 1000.

Hákon's rule is described in favorable terms in *Heimskringla*—the harvests were good, herring filled the fjörds, and there was peace throughout the country—but Hákon's attitude to **women** was described as "intemperate." He was married, but is said to have taken an unusually large number of concubines, sometimes for just a week or two at a time. He maintained a large number of skalds at his court, whose poetry (*see* **skaldic poetry**) provides important contemporary witness to his rule. Most notable is the poem, *Vellekla*, composed by the poet Einar Helgason, nicknamed *skálaglamm* ("scale-tinkle"). Hákon's reign was brought to an end by the arrival of **Olaf Tryggvason** in Norway in 995. Hákon fled to his mistress, Thora, who is said to have hidden him in a pigsty on her farm near Melhus, south Trøndelag (south of **Trondheim**). Shortly afterwards, Hákon was killed by his **slave**, Kark, in return for a reward by Olaf Tryggvason.

HÁKON THE GOOD (ON *Hákon góði*) (*c*. 920–960). King of Norway *c*. 935–960, Hákon was one of **Harald Fine-Hair's** sons and the half brother of **Erik Blood-Ax**. He became king of Norway after driving his half brother Erik out of the country with the support of **Earl** Sigurd of **Lade**; Earl Sigurd was rewarded by being allowed to retain control of Trøndelag. Hákon had been fostered and brought up, as a Christian, at the court of King **Athelstan** in England and is therefore also known as *Hákon Aðalsteinsfóstri* ("Athelstan's foster-son"). Hákon is credited with reforming the district **things**, establishing a naval force based on **leiðangr** and *skipreiður*, and developing a beacon system to warn of attacks. **Sighvatr Þórðarson's** *Bersöglisvísur* praises Hákon for his "just and kind" laws.

Hákon's nickname, "the Good," refers to his active support of **Christianity** in Norway: he invited missionaries (for example, the English bishop *Sigefridus* of Glastonbury) into his kingdom and had churches built. However, there was a pagan backlash against this attempt to convert his countrymen, and the churches were burned down and the missionary priests killed or driven from the country. In the mid-950s, the sons of Erik Blood-Ax revolted, with Danish support, against Hákon and he died, about five years later, from wounds sustained in battle against them at **Fitjar**. He was buried at Seim, north of present-day **Bergen**. Ironically, the **skaldic** poem, *Hákonarmál*, which was composed in Hákon's memory, is full of pagan imagery.

HÁKONARMÁL. Poem composed by **Eyvindr skáldaspillir**, which describes the last great battle of **Hákon the Good** of Norway, his conversation with **Odin's valkyries**, and his subsequent reception into the Norse pagan hall for warriors, **Valhalla**. The battle is recounted in the epic **fornyrðislag** meter, while the rest of the poem is composed in **ljóðaháttr**. *Hakonarmál* concludes with a sad reflection on the present enslavement of Norway at the hands of the sons of **Erik Blood-Ax** and the Danish king, **Harald Blue-Tooth**. The poem is preserved in *Heimskringla*.

HALFDAN (d. 877?). One of the leaders of the **Great Army** that arrived in England in 865. Halfdan is first named in the *Anglo-Saxon Chronicle* entry for 871, where he is said to have fought Æthelred of **Wessex** and his brother, **Alfred the Great**, at Ashdown. Halfdan and another "heathen king" called Bagsecg are there described as the leaders of one section of the **Viking** army. Halfdan is next mentioned in the *Chronicle* for 874, following the Great Army's split after **Repton**. He is said to have wintered on the River Tyne in **Northumbria** with a section of the army and to have raided among the **Picts** and Strathclyde Britons, who inhabited present-day **Scotland**. In 876, Halfdan and his men divided up Northumbria and settled down, "plowing and providing for themselves." Halfdan is not mentioned in the *Anglo-Saxon Chronicle* after this date. A brother of Halfdan, Ubba, is said in the *Chronicle* to have died in battle in Devon, Wessex, in 878, and the Anglo-Norman historian, Simeon of Durham, also claims that Halfdan and **Ivar the Boneless** were killed during this raid. However, Halfdan has been identified with the *Albann* who was killed at the Battle of Strangford Lough in Ireland in 877. In the later legendary tales about **Ragnar Loðbrók**, Halfdan is said to have invaded England with his brothers, Ivar the Boneless, Ubba, and **Björn Ironside** to avenge his father's death at the hands of Ælla of Northumbria.

HALFDAN THE BLACK (ON *Hálfdan svarti*) (d. 880?). Norwegian king whose saga is the second in Snorri's *Heimskringla*. Very little is known for certain about Halfdan and his reign, although he appears to have inherited control of the southern province of Agder at the age of 18 and to have acquired Vestfold, Romerike, Sogn, Hadeland by force. **Snorri Sturluson's** saga about Halfdan is short, includes many dreams and premonitions, and lacks any **skaldic** verse to substantiate the prose narrative. Halfdan is said to have had two wives called Ragnhild and two sons called Harald; the first of these sons died, but the second, **Harald Fine-Hair**, became king of Norway after his father's death. Halfdan is said to have died at the age of 40 and to have been buried in the province of Ringerike.

HAMBURG-BREMEN. *See* ADAM OF BREMEN; ANSGAR, ST.

HARALD BLUE-TOOTH (ON *Haraldr blátand*) (d. *c.* 987). King of Denmark and son of **Gorm the Old** and **Thyre**. Harald ruled from the dynastic seat his father had established in **Jelling**, Jutland, Denmark. On a **rune-stone** that Harald raised in Jelling, he claimed to have united Denmark under one king, to have converted the Danes to **Christianity**, and to have also won control of Norway (which he then ruled through his Norwegian ally, **Hákon Jarl** of **Lade**). **Widukind's** *Saxon Chronicle* preserves an account of Harald's conversion *c.* 965, attributing it to the German missionary, Poppo, who held a piece of red-hot iron in his hands to prove to Harald the superior power of his religion. However, there were also sound political reasons for Harald's conversion—not least, the German emperor, Otto I the Great, who threatened to launch a crusade against his northern neighbor. Following Otto's death in 973, the Danes raided across the German border, but the new emperor, Otto II, retaliated in 974 and captured the **Danevirke** and **Hedeby**, occupying them for some years. However, in 983, Harald attacked Germany with his **Abodrite** ally, Mistivoi, and recovered his earlier losses. This political alliance had been sealed with Harald's marriage to Tove, Mistivoi's daughter. Tove herself raised a rune-stone (*Danmarks Runeindskrifter* 55), which can now be found at the church of Sønder Vissing in north Jutland, to commemorate her mother. In the inscription, Tove describes herself as the daughter of Mistivoi and the wife of Harald the Good Gormsson.

Alongside his own rune-stone, Harald built a church at Jelling and apparently had his father's body removed from its pagan **burial** mound and reinterred underneath the church. Archaeological evidence suggests that a number of large-scale building projects were undertaken in Harald's reign: the so-called **Trelleborg fortresses**, an extension to the Danevirke, and a bridge at **Ravninge Enge**. However, it seems that this expansion of royal control was unpopular and Harald's rule was brought to an end by his son, **Svein Forkbeard**, although according to **Adam of Bremen** this was part of a pagan backlash against Harald's rule. Harald fled to *Jumne* (present-day **Wolin**) in Poland, where he died in *c.* 987. He was buried in the cathedral in Roskilde on the Danish island of Sjælland.

HARALD FAIR-HAIR. *See* HARALD FINE-HAIR.

HARALD FINE-HAIR (ON Haraldr hárfagri) (*c.* 850–*c.* 930). King of Norway from *c.* 885 to *c.* 930. Son of **Halfdan the Black**, Harald was apparently only 10 years old when his father died and he succeeded to the Norwegian kingdom of Vestfold. In medieval Icelandic historiography he is credited with the unification of Norway at the Battle of **Hafrsfjörd**. This is said to have prompted large-scale emigration from Norway to new lands in the North Atlantic by people who were unhappy with the new political state of affairs. According to **Snorri Sturluson**, Harald's ambition to become king of the whole of Norway was the result of an ultimatum from Gytha, the daughter of King Erik of the Norwegian province of Hordaland: she told Harald's messengers that she would only marry Harald if he was king of the whole of Norway. Despite his reputation as the first king of a united Norway, modern historians consider that Harald's kingdom was centered on Vestfold and southwest Norway and was, in fact, unlikely to have extended north of present-day **Trondheim**, where the **Earls** of **Lade** held power. The medieval Icelandic accounts of Harald's expedition to Norwegian colonies in **Scotland** and the Scottish Isles, apparently to bring "certain Vikings" under his control, are believed to be a later tradition, perhaps invented to explain the presence in **Iceland** of settlers from these areas of the British Isles.

Snorri's *Heimskringla* explains the origin of the nickname Fine-Hair: apparently Harald vowed not to cut his hair until he had won control of the whole of Norway, and was therefore called Harald Matted-Hair. However, after his victory at Hafrsfjörd, he had his hair

cut, thus earning his new nickname, Fine-Hair. Snorri also writes that
Harald left behind numerous children from his many wives and consorts, who included Gytha; Ragnhild of Denmark; Svanhild, daughter of Earl Eystein; and Áshild of Ringerike. Toward the end of his
life, he abdicated the throne of Norway in favor of his son, **Erik
Blood-Ax**.

HARALD GREY-CLOAK (ON *Haraldr gráfeldr*) (d. c. 970). Harald
was the eldest son of **Erik Blood-Ax** and **Gunnhild**. With the support of his mother and brothers, the so-called sons of Erik (also
known as the sons of Gunnhild), Harald overthrew his uncle, **Hákon
the Good** following the Battle of **Fitjar**. Harald succeeded to
Hákon's throne and ruled Norway for almost 10 years. *Heimskringla*
describes this as a time of bad harvests and poor weather, when farmers suffered as a result of their king's greed. There was also much political unrest, as Harald outlawed the worship of pagan gods and
attempted to bring the whole country under his control. Harald was
eventually killed in Denmark as a result of a plot between his one-
time ally, the Danish king, **Harald Blue-Tooth**, and the Norwegian
earl, **Hákon Jarl** of **Lade**.

HARALD HARD-RULER (ON *Haraldr harðráði*) (1015–1066).
King of Norway from 1046 to 1066, ruling jointly with his nephew
Magnus in 1046–1047. Son of Sigurd Syr, and half brother of **Olaf
Haraldsson,** Harald is one of the most famous **Viking** warriors and
kings. **Adam of Bremen** called him "The Thunderbolt of the North."
Aged 15, Harald fought with Olaf Haraldsson at **Stiklestad**, and, following defeat, he fled east, first to Sweden and then to the **Russian**
court of **Jaroslav the Wise** in **Kiev**. He later served as commander
of the **Varangian Guard** in **Byzantium** and campaigned extensively
in Sicily, Italy, and Bulgaria. His saga in *Heimskringla* claims that he
had an affair with the Empress Zoe, and that he helped in her suc-
cessful coup on the Byzantine throne. While Greek sources suggest
that the saga exaggerated his importance, he nevertheless made a
great reputation for himself in the East.

He was married to Elizabeth (Ellisif), daughter of Jaroslav the
Wise, on his return journey to Norway in 1044–1045. At the same
time, he also formed an alliance with the Danish king, **Svein Es-**

trithsson, in order to dislodge his nephew, **Magnus the Good Olafsson** from the Norwegian throne. However, on gaining power, at first as coruler with Magnus, Harald abandoned his Danish ally and spent almost 20 years of his rule challenging Svein's right to the Danish throne. In 1050, he burned the Danish town of **Hedeby**, but his war against Svein ended in stalemate in 1064. One of Harald's most famous expeditions was the invasion of England that he launched in 1066, in alliance with the **earls** of **Orkney** and Tosti, former earl of **Northumbria**. Harald's claim to the English throne was based on a treaty between **Harthacnut** and King Magnus the Good Olafsson of Norway, signed in 1036. A fleet of some 200 Norwegian ships sailed up the **Humber**, landing at Riccall on the River Ouse. Victory against the English at **Fulford** was, however, followed by defeat. Harald's invasion ended with his death in the Battle of **Stamford Bridge** in East Yorkshire on 21 September 1066, fighting against the English king, Harold Godwinsson. He was succeeded in Norway by his son, **Magnus II Haraldsson**.

HARALD KLAK (*Heriold* in the *Royal Frankish Annals*) (d. *c.* 852). King of Denmark who ruled for two separate periods (812–813 and 819–827) during the political unrest that followed the murder of King **Godfred** in 810. During 812–813, he seems to have shared power with his brother, Reginfred, and possibly his brother, Hemming, who was a vassal of the Frankish emperor, **Charlemagne**. According to the *Royal Frankish Annals*, the three brothers campaigned against rebels in Vestfold, Norway, which was then apparently part of the Danish kingdom. However, this first brief rule in Denmark was brought to an end by the revolt of **Horik** and his brothers, and, despite Frankish support, Harald and his brothers failed to win back power in 814. On Charlemagne's death, both Harald and Hemming entered the service of the new emperor, **Louis the Pious** (Reginfred was dead by this time), who negotiated peace between Harald and Horik, establishing their joint rule in 819. The *Royal Frankish Annals* report that Harald was back at Louis's court in 826, and that he and his household in exile were baptized by the Bishop of Mainz at Ingelheim in present-day Germany (*see* **Christianity, Conversion to**). Harald was granted **Frisia** by Louis, and he returned to Denmark in 827 with a Christian mission under **Ansgar**. However, he was unable to retain power on this occasion, nor, following a further visit to Louis's court, was he able to win back the Danish throne in 828. The next reference to Harald in the written sources comes some 24 years later, when the *Annals of Fulda* record his execution for treason in 852.

HAROLD HAREFOOT (*c*. **1015–1040**). Regent of England 1035–1037 and sole king of England from 1037 to 1040. He claimed to be the son of **Cnut I the Great** by his English consort, **Ælfgifu of Northampton**, although opponents suggested that Cnut was not his father. Upon Cnut's death in 1035, Harold's claim to his father's throne was supported by **Earl** Leofric of **Mercia**, while Earl Godwine of **Wessex** advanced **Harthacnut's** claim. However, Harthacnut's prolonged absence in Denmark allowed Harold to win the English throne, despite **Emma of Normandy's** attempt to have her eldest son, Edward, made king instead. Edward's plans for invasion were cut short by Godwine's shift of support to Harold, and in the political turmoil that followed, Edward's brother, the ætheling Alfred was captured and tortured to death. The *Encomium Emmae Reginae*, later commissioned by Emma, placed the blame for this squarely on Harold Harefoot. Following his coronation, Harold drove Emma into exile. His reign was brought to an end by illness, and Harold died in Oxford on 17 March 1040. He was buried at Westminster, but upon his accession to the English throne in 1040, Harthacnut had Harold's body dug up and unceremoniously thrown into a bog.

HARTHACNUT (*c*. **1020–1042**). King of Denmark from 1035–1042 and of England from 1040–1042. Harthacnut was the son of **Cnut I the Great** and **Emma of Normandy**. He was brought up in Denmark and was in that country when his father died. In Denmark, Harthacnut immediately faced an invasion by **Magnus the Good Olafsson**, who had ended Cnut's control of Norway shortly before his death in 1035. As a result, Harthacnut was forced to sign a peace treaty with Magnus in 1036. This recognized Magnus as king of Norway and made him Harthacnut's heir. It was this treaty that **Harald Hard-Ruler** later claimed gave him the right to the English throne.

Although he had the support of **Earl** Godwine of **Wessex** in England, Harthacnut's absence in Denmark meant that he was unable to press his claim to the throne over that of his half brother, **Harold**

Harefoot, and he only succeeded to the English throne following Harold's death. His rule there was short and unpopular: he levied a tax of 21,000 pounds of silver to pay for the expansion of his fleet from 16 to 62 warships; and he was accused of murdering Earl Eadulf of **Northumbria**. Harthacnut died at a wedding feast on 8 June in Lambeth (in present-day **London**) where, according to the *Anglo-Saxon Chronicle*, he was seized by convulsions as he drank. He was succeeded by his half brother, Edward the Confessor (d. 1065), the son of **Æthelred II** and Emma, who had apparently been invited back from **Normandy** to England before Harthacnut's death. Harthacnut was the last Danish king of England.

HASTEIN. Also known as Hasting, Hæsten, and Alstignus. Joint leader, with **Björn Ironside**, of a **Viking** fleet of some 62 **ships** that looted around the Mediterranean between 859–862, culminating in the destruction of Luna (instead of their intended target of Rome). The chief source of information about Hastein is the work of Norman historians, **Dudo of St-Quentin** and **William of Jumièges**. According to William, Hastein (*Hasting*) was Björn's tutor and was a "very deceitful man." Dudo of St-Quentin does not mention Björn, but his description of Hastein, who is said to be the leader of the Danish armies that attacked France, is vivid and condemning. William of Jumièges is the only source for the information that Hastein made peace with **Charles the Bald** and received the French town of Chartres, before selling it to a Frankish count, Theobald, after being warned of Charles's hostility.

After returning from Luna, Hastein continued to harry **Frankia**. Frankish sources (the *Annals of St-Bertin* and the *Chronicle of Regino de Prüm*) record that Hastein made peace with Salomon of **Brittany** in 869 and stopped raiding along the Loire in return for 500 cows. The final recorded chapter in Hastein's career comes from the *Anglo-Saxon Chronicle*, which records his arrival at the mouth of the River Thames with 80 ships in 892. Fortifications were built on opposite sides of the Thames at Milton Regis in Kent and Benfleet in Essex, but **Alfred the Great's** army succeeded in capturing the fort at Essex, along with Hastein's wife and two sons. These were, however, returned as one of the sons was Alfred's own godson and the other was the godson of Alfred's son-in-law. Hastein's army dispersed in 896, and it seems that Hastein may have returned to France where, William of Jumièges writes, he died in **Normandy**.

HÁTTATAL ("list of meters"). Final part of **Snorri Sturluson's *Prose Edda***. *Háttatal* consists of some 102 stanzas composed by Snorri in praise of the Norwegian king, Hákon Hákonarson (d. 1263) and Hákon's father-in-law, the Norwegian **earl**, Skuli Barðarson (d. 1240). Snorri probably wrote this poem soon after meeting Hákon and Skuli during his first visit to Norway in 1212–1220. The purpose of *Háttatal* is to demonstrate the various meters and verse forms a poet could use, and it is accompanied by a prose commentary that also discusses rhyme and alliteration.

HÁVAMÁL **("The Speech of the High One").** **Eddic** poem preserved in the 13th-century **Codex Regius**, although the original date of the poem is uncertain. Although *Hávamál* is preserved as one continuous poem of 164 stanzas, it is conventionally divided into six main sections. The first section (1–77 or 79), sometimes called the *Gnomic Poem*, consists of practical advice on conduct with values that are far from heroic, followed by more advice (81–94: things to do and beware of, especially (91–4) **women**). The remaining sections deal, for the most part, with **Odin** ("The High One"): Odin and *Billings mær* (95–102)—he was deceived by her; Odin and Gunnlöd (104–110)—he stole the mead of poetry from her giant father; *Loddfáfnismál* (112–137)—advice in the hall of Hávi (Odin); *Rúnatal* (138–145)—Odin's winning of runic (*see* **rune**) knowledge; *Ljóðatal* (146–163)—18 spells that the unnamed speaker (probably Odin) knew. While this collection is now known by the one name, *Hávamal*, which is written before the first stanza, it is therefore a very motley collection. It is a compilation of other poems and odd stanzas, which is varied in subject matter and verse forms, and which mixes didactic and secular matter with details about Odin and pagan beliefs.

HEAD-RANSON POEM. *See* EGIL'S SAGA.

HEBRIDES (ON *Suðreyjar*). Two distinct groups of islands, the Inner and the Outer Hebrides, lying off the west coast of **Scotland**, and thus also known as the Western Isles. Before the first **Viking** raids on the islands of Scotland, the Hebrides were part of two distinct regional kingdoms. The Outer Hebrides, along with **Orkney**, **Shetland**, and most of mainland Scotland north of the Clyde-Forth line, were inhabited by a Pictish population (*see* **Picts**). The Inner Hebrides were part of the Scottish kingdom of Dalriada, which also included western Argyll, and were inhabited by a Gaelic Celtic population.

The first recorded Viking raids on the Western Isles were the sacking of the monasteries on **Iona** and Skye in 795. Raids appear to have continued more or less regularly into the 830s: in 798 the Hebrides were plundered by Scandinavians (*do Lochlannaibh*) according to the *Annals of Inisfallen*, and Iona was revisited by Scandinavian pirates in 802; in 806, when 68 monks were killed; and in 825, when its prior, Blathmac, was killed for his failure to reveal the location of St. Columba's relics. However, by the ninth century, a mixed Norse-Gaelic community seems to have emerged in the Hebrides: the warriors known as the **Gall-Gaedhil**, who were involved in wars in **Ireland**, appear to have had their base there.

Politically, the Hebrides were dominated by their powerful neighbors: Ireland, Scotland, Orkney, and the **Isle of Man** all seem to have ruled the islands at different times in the Viking Age; Norway was too remote to ever exert any real control over its colonies. Irish influence in the Hebrides was strongest during the early Viking Age, but toward the end of the 10th century the Norse Earldom of Orkney emerged as the most powerful political force among the Norse colonies in the west. Earl **Sigurd the Stout** raided extensively in the west and his campaigns can probably be connected with the rash of attacks on the Hebrides and Man recorded in Irish annals. Sigurd's ambitions came to an end at the Battle of **Clontarf** when his army, assembled from the Northern and Western Isles, was defeated by **Brian Boru**, king of Munster. Sigurd died in battle and the Norse maritime dominion that he had created in the west crumbled, with his five sons dividing his apparently reduced territory.

Following Clontarf and the death of **Earl** Sigurd, the western seaboard of Scotland came under the influence of **Sigtrygg Silk-Beard** of **Dublin**, who was possibly supported by **Cnut I the Great** of England. However, the abdication of the former and the death of the latter in 1035 gave **Thorfinn the Mighty** the opportunity to reassert Orkney's power in the Hebrides. With his nephew, Rögnvaldr

Brúsasonr, Thorfinn raided in the Hebrides, Ireland, and a large area of western Scotland and fought a battle at *Vatsfjörðr* (possibly Loch Watten in Skye) in the Hebrides. ***Orkneyinga Saga*** claims that he won "all the Hebrides and a large realm in Ireland" (*allar Suðreyjar ok mikit ríki á Írlandi*). However, Orkney's control was relatively short-lived as in the late 11th century **Godred Crovan** laid the Western Isles under Man.

In 1098, the Norwegian king **Magnus Bare-Foot** attempted to assert Norwegian control over the Northern and Western Isles. He seized the earls of Orkney and set his son Sigurd over the islands, before sailing west, plundering the Hebrides and capturing the king of Man. A treaty was made with the king of Scotland, which conceded Bute, Arran, the Cumbraes, and Gigha in the Inner Hebrides to Norway. After Magnus's death in Ireland in 1103, Norwegian control seems to have been rather nominal, especially as civil war at home occupied the kings of Norway. From 1156, the Ardnamurchan Point, which divides the Western Isles and the Scottish coastal mainland into northern and southern spheres, became a political boundary, with the southern islands of Mull, Islay, and southern Argyll passing to the control of Sumarliði, a brother-in-law of Godred II of Man. The Manx kings continued to rule the Outer Hebrides until these were ceded to Scotland by the Norwegian crown in the Treaty of Perth, signed in 1266. The late 12th and 13th centuries were characterized by conflict in the Isles between the sons of Sumarliði, the Scottish king, and the Norwegian king, culminating in Hákon Hákonarsonr's expedition to the Isles, his defeat at Largs in 1263 and his death in Orkney. Although technically under the Scottish crown after the Treaty of Perth, descendants of Sumarliði (MacDougalls and later MacDonalds) remained as Lord of the Isles until 1493.

On the basis of the place-name evidence, the Outer Hebrides appear to have been more thoroughly scandinavianized than the Inner Hebrides. The Scandinavian linguistic evidence is particularly strong for the Isle of Lewis, where 99 of the 126 village names are purely Scandinavian. Norse loanwords are particularly frequent in the maritime vocabulary of the Outer Hebrides, especially Lewis, Uist, and Tiree. While there are fewer Scandinavian place-names in the southern islands, such as Arran, this linguistic impact is still generally greater than that found in the areas of England settled by Scandinavians, and has been estimated as much as 60 percent on Skye and about 30 percent on Islay. Apart from a few island names, none of the Gaelic place-names in the Isles can be proved to predate the Viking period. A total absence of documentary evidence makes it impossible to be sure if Gaelic survived in the islands or whether it was wiped out and reintroduced at a later date. However, literary and historical sources hint at intermarriage between Norse and native in the Hebrides. The survival of Gaelic seems likely given this factor and the lack of Gaelic place-names does not necessarily presuppose the absence of Gaelic speakers. Gaelic certainly seems to have enjoyed a resurgence in the 12th century, although it has been suggested that the Norse language did not totally drop out of use in the Hebrides until the early 16th century.

A number of Scandinavian runic inscriptions (*see* **rune**) have also been found in the Hebrides, on the islands of Iona and Barra in the Outer Hebrides and on the islands of Bute and Holy Island in the Inner Hebrides. The Holy Island inscriptions are graffiti inscribed by Norwegians on the walls of a hermit's cave in the 13th century, but the other three inscriptions reflect the integration of the Norsemen into the Celtic culture and population of the Hebrides: the form and decoration of the Kilbar (Barra) cross-slab and its use of the word "cross"; the word "cross" on the Inchmarnock (Bute) cross; and the decoration and form of the Iona slab, which apparently marked a Christian **burial**, all place these runic inscriptions in a Christian Celtic-Norse environment. Moreover, all of these inscriptions were found at churches. These inscriptions thus represent the adaptation of the Norse population of Scotland and the Isles to both Christian and Celtic customs.

While two settlement sites have been excavated at **the Udal**, North Uist and **Drimore**, South Uist, (and new excavations have taken place on Barra, at Bornish on South Uist, and at Bosta on Lewis) most of the archaeological evidence for Scandinavians in the Western Isles is limited to chance finds, particularly of graves. Some 30 or 40 pagan Norse grave finds have been recorded in the Western Isles, dating from as early as the second half of the ninth century. A large number of these **burials** were found in the southern islands of Colonsay, Oronsay, and Islay, and early references to a number of pagan burials indicate that there were probably pagan cemeteries at Cornaigbeg on Tiree and Ballinbay on Islay. Evidence also seems to be accumulating for a series of burials, including inhumations of a female and a child, at Valtos on Lewis. A number of rich boat burials, such as that found at Kiloran Bay, Colonsay, and other graves containing **weapons** and weighing scales have been excavated. Nevertheless, although many of the finds suggest that the Norse population of the Hebrides was principally made up of traders and warriors, there is some evidence of a more settled community: Of the 32 graves where it is possible to identify the sex of the interred, there are 14 female graves.

As well as the evidence of pagan graves, 15 silver hoards of Scandinavian type dating to the late 10th or early 11th century have been recovered from North Uist, Stornaway, Dibbadale, Tiree, Iona, Inch Kenneth, and Islay. The earliest of these is the mixed hoard of 111 Anglo-Saxon and Arabic coins and **hacksilver** from Storr Rock, Skye (*c.* 935), but many of the hoards were deposited around the year 1000 and have been linked with the political and military dominance of Earl Sigurd the Stout of Orkney in the Hebrides.

HEDEBY. Viking-Age town at the base of the Jutland Peninsula, just south of the modern town of Schleswig, on an inlet of the Schleifjörd known as Haddeby Noor. Today Hedeby lies within the borders of Germany, but in the Viking-Age it was a Danish settlement. The *Royal Frankish Annals* record that a town, *Sliesthorp*, was established in 808 by the Danish king, **Godfred**, and this is normally identified as Hedeby. However, excavations have revealed a settlement dating from the mid-eighth century, to the south of the area later enclosed by the town's ramparts. The Christian missionary, **Ansgar**, established a church in the town in the 820s, during his short-lived mission, and again when he returned in 854. A bishop of Hedeby was consecrated by Hamburg-Bremen *c.* 948. During the 10th century, Hedeby seems to have been ruled by a Swedish dynasty, known as the **Olaf dynasty**, whose names are preserved in two **rune-stones** from the town.

Only 5 percent of the area enclosed by the ramparts has as yet been excavated. The main settlement of Hedeby was centered on a stream running into Haddeby Noor. Rectangular **houses**, with two or three rooms, stood at the center of regular plots of land that were marked out by fences, ditches, or the stream. A reconstruction of a typical ninth-century Hedeby house stands at Moesgård museum, near Århus, Denmark. It is approximately 12 meters by 5 meters and is made of a wattle-and-daub infilling around vertical wooden posts. The outside of the house is supported by sloping timber posts. The main room, with a long hearth in the middle, is placed centrally in the building, with a further room at either end. Raised wooden platforms, used for sleeping, line the long walls of the main room.

Hedeby was perhaps the greatest of Viking-Age towns in Scandinavia, and at its peak it had perhaps as many as 1,500 permanent inhabitants. Its location meant that it was well placed for trading with eastern and southern Europe, via the Baltic Sea. In addition to the town, excavations have revealed extensive cemeteries surrounding it, consisting of perhaps as many as 7,000 **burials**, many of which contain lavish grave goods that reflect the wealth of the town. Its own silver coinage, modeled on Frisian (*see* **Frisia**) exemplars, was minted briefly in the early ninth century; and the town provides the only clear evidence for pottery making in Scandinavia.

However, Hedeby also suffered as a result of its location, straddling the contested border between Denmark and the expanding German empire and its wealth. The town was defended by a three-meter-high rampart, topped by a timber palisade, in the 10th century, and via the so-called Connecting Wall was incorporated into the **Danevirke**. These defenses were later extended and improved until the ramparts stood at 10 meters high, were 1,300 meters long, and enclosed an area of some 24 hectares. In addition to this, a hillfort (Hochburg) was constructed to the north of the town, and the town's harbor was protected by an underwater palisade. Nevertheless, Hedeby was burned to the ground on at least two occasions, including an assault by **Harald Hard-Ruler** in 1050, before its final destruction in 1066 by a Wendish (*see* **Wends**) force. A rune-stone from the town preserves a unique record of one such battle for Hedeby: it was raised by the Danish king, **Svein Forkbeard**, following his recapture of the town from an occupying force in the 11th century. One of his retainers, Skarði, was killed in the campaign, and Svein commemorated his bravery with a runic inscription. At the end of the 11th century, the town's role was taken over by nearby Schleswig, where the earliest medieval buildings to be excavated have been dated to 1071. *See also* AT-TURTUSHI.

HEIMDALL (ON *Heimdallr*). Norse god of the Æsir. Heimdall was the guardian of the gods and watched over the bridge **Bifrost**, to make sure that the giants did not cross it into the heavens. His hall, *Himinbjörg*, was near to the bridge. According to *Gylfaginning*, Heimdall was "great and holy," was known as the "White god," had golden teeth, did not need much sleep, could see things a long way away regardless of whether it was day or night, and was able to hear the grass growing. He is said to sound his horn (*Gjallarhorn*) at the beginning of **Ragnarök**, to warn the gods of the giants' approach. At Ragnarök, Heimdall and **Loki** are said to kill each other, and these two gods are also said to fight over **Freya's** necklace, **Brísingamen**. Heimdall seems to have been an important god, but much about him remains obscure. In *Völuspá* and *Rígsþula*, Heimdall is said to be the father of humankind. *Heimdali* and *Hallinskiði*, one of Heimdall's pseudonyms, are both given as poetic alternatives to the word "ram" in Snorri's *Skáldskaparmál*, and "Heimdall's sword" was another word for "head," as his sword was called *Höfuð* ("Head").

HEIMSKRINGLA ("Circle of the World"). A collection of sagas about the kings of Norway composed by the Icelandic chieftain, **Snorri Sturluson**, *c.* 1220 (although none of the existing medieval manuscripts name him as its author). The name *Heimskringla* is first recorded in the 17th century and is derived from the opening words of the first saga in the collection, *Ynglinga Saga*. Before this, Snorri's work seems to have been known by a number of different titles, including "The Book of Kings" (*Konunga bók*) or "The Book of Norwegian Kings" (*Nóregskonunga bók*).

After *Ynglinga Saga*, *Heimskringla* continues with 16 further sagas, covering the period from the beginning of the Viking Age under the semi-legendary **Halfdan the Black** to the reign of Magnus Erlingsson, who died in 1184. Approximately a third of the work is devoted to the 15-year reign of **Olaf Haraldsson**, the patron saint of Norway. This saga of St. Olaf (*Ólafs saga helga*), an adaptation of the *Separate Saga of St. Olaf* (*see* **Sagas of St. Olaf**), was apparently composed first and the rest of the sagas that make up *Heimskringla* written around it. The collection seems to have been extensively copied and used by later writers, and it survives in a number of medieval manuscripts and later paper copies. The oldest known manuscript, known as *Kringla* after the opening words *Kringla heimsins* ("Circle of the World"), was written some time before 1270, but only a single page of this has survived. There are, however, a number of good transcripts of *Kringla* that form the basis of most editions of *Heimskringla*.

The historical value of these **Kings' Sagas** is still debated. They were not written as modern analytical histories of the Norwegian kings but as dramatic narratives about key political players in Norway's past. Clearly the direct speech is not authentic, and there are references to magic, supernatural creatures, dreams, and premonitions. Character sketches and personal descriptions were used, as in other kinds of sagas, to illuminate the personality and motives of the individual. Nevertheless, Snorri did take a critical approach to his sources, placing most reliance on **skaldic poetry** that was generally composed for the kings and princes during their lifetimes. These poems were, he argued, trustworthy, as a poet would not dare to lie about a king's achievements in front of the whole court. Less is known about his prose sources, particularly as many of these have not survived or exist only in later versions that appear to differ from the texts that Snorri knew. At best, *Heimskringla* is a work that preserves historical fact alongside oral tradition and literary embellishment.

HEITI. Word meaning "name," and a technical term used by **Snorri Sturluson** to refer to the poetic synonyms used by **skaldic** poets. Today, an example of a *heiti* in English might be the use of the word "steed" for a horse. Snorri's examples in *Skáldskaparmál* include some of the *heiti* or synonyms for raven: crow, **Hugin**, **Munin**, early-flier, and flesh-marker; for bear: cub, grizzly, snarler, greedy-tooth, dark one, greedy one, forest-walker, and yellow bottom; and for the sun: day-star, disc, ever-glow, all bright seen, fair wheel, Dvalin's toy, and grace-shine.

HEL. The world of the dead in Norse **mythology** and the name of the goddess who inhabited it. Those who have died on land of old age or illness are said to go to Hel. However, in the later medieval period, Hel became associated with the Christian idea of hell, as a place of punishment, and in Snorri's *Prose Edda* is depicted as a cold, damp place in the north and a place of misery and suffering.

HELGI THE LEAN (ON *Helgi inn magri*). Son of Eyvind the East-
erner (so-called because he was brought up in Swedish **Götaland**)
and Rafarta, the daughter of the Irish king, Kjarval. Helgi was born
in the **Hebrides** and fostered there for two years before being sent to
Ireland. According to the *Book of Settlements*, his nickname was
given after his parents returned to the Hebrides to see how he
was; they "saw a boy there with fine eyes but no flesh on his bones,
for he was starved." Helgi married Thorunn Hyrna, one of the daughters of the famous chieftain **Ketill Flat-Nose**, and they had four children: Hrólfr, Ingvald, Ingunn, and Thorbjörg Holmasol.

The *Book of Settlements* contains a detailed account of the departure of Helgi and his family for **Iceland**. Particularly interesting is the
reference to Helgi's consultation of the god **Thor** as to where he
should go ashore. Helgi made landfall in the north of Iceland, claiming all of the district of Eyjafjörd between the headlands of Siglunes
and Reynisnes and, after several years, building a farmstead at
Kristnes ("Christ's headland"). The Christian place-name and the
reference to Thor provide an interesting insight to Helgi's religious
beliefs, and the *Book of Settlements* adds that although he believed in
Christ, he trusted Thor in all matters of seafaring and "for everything
that struck him as of real importance." These beliefs must reflect
Helgi's upbringing in the mixed Norse-Gaelic environment of the
western colonies in the ninth century.

Helgi and his family are also mentioned in a number of sagas, in-
cluding *Laxdæla Saga* and the *Saga of Erik the Red*. As well as
Helgi's own marriage into the family of Ketill Flat-Nose, his sister,
Thurid, was married to Ketill's grandson, Thorstein the Red (son of
Aud the Deep-Minded).

HELLULAND ("Stone- or Slab-Land"). Land sited by **Leif the
Lucky Eriksson** on his voyage to **Vinland**. According to the *Saga of
the Greenlanders*, Helluland was covered with glaciers, was barren,
and lay to the north of Vinland; the *Saga of Erik the Red* adds that
there were numerous foxes there. Following the discovery of Norse
artifacts at **L'Anse aux Meadows**, most scholars have identified Helluland with present-day Baffin Island off the coast of Canada.

HEMMING. *See* HARALD KLAK.

HERJOLFSNES. *See* BJARNI HERJÓLFSSON.

HILLERSJÖ. Famous **rune-stone** from the parish of Hillersjö in the central Swedish province of Uppland, about 20 kilometers south of **Sigtuna**. The rune-stone was raised by a **woman** called Gerlög in the 11th century. The inscription provides a brief history of Gerlög's family: her two husbands, Germund and Gudrik; her son, who is unnamed; her daughter, Inga, who married twice, to Ragnfast and to Erik; and her unnamed grandson. The purpose of this long and uniquely detailed inscription seems to be to record Gerlög's right to the property that she inherited. The inscription does not follow the usual Viking-Age commemorative formula and opens instead with an exhortation to passers-by to read the text: "Read! Germund took Gerlög, a maiden, as wife. Then they had a son before Germund was drowned and then the son died. Thereafter she had Gudrik as her husband . . . [the inscription is damaged at this point] . . . Then they had children but only one girl survived, her name was Inga. Ragnfast of Snottsta had her as his wife. Thereafter he died and then the son. And the mother (Inga) inherited from her son. Then she had Erik as her husband. Then she died. Then Gerlög inherited from Inga her daughter. Torbjörn skald carved the runes."

Gerlög's daughter, Inga, built a bridge and raised four rune-stones herself before her death, all of which commemorated her dead husband, Ragnfast. These rune-stones are found in the parish of Markim, about 20 kilometers east of Sigtuna, and testify to Inga's wealth as sole heiress of her father, Germund, and her son, Ragnfast's heir. The rules of inheritance outlined in this group of inscriptions are the same as those found in the Uppland Law, written down in 1296.

HIRD (ON *hirð* **from OE** *hired* **"household").** A hird was a retinue of warriors that followed a king, prince, or chieftain in Scandinavia, and which normally resided at the court of its king or lord. There is comparatively little information relating to the institution during the Viking Age; only two **rune-stones** from Denmark (DR 107 from Egå, north Jutland and DR 134 from Ravnkilde in north Jutland) mention men who were *landhirðir* and *hirðir* respectively, translated as "(land-)steward." Manne from Egå was explicitly said to be in the service of an otherwise unknown Norwegian called Ketill.

Most of the sources instead relate to the king's hird during the medieval period, particularly in Norway where the 13th-century texts, *Hirðskrá* and *Konungs skuggsjá* ("The King's Mirror"), provide considerable details about the structure of the hird. These suggest that the hird developed from a primarily military organization into the king's council. By around 1270, the Norwegian hird was a three-tier organization, consisting of *hirðmenn*, *gestir* ("guests") and *kertisveinar* ("pages"). The first of these groups also had several different subranks that approximate to barons (*lendir menn*), knights (*skutilsveinar*), and ordinary warriors (the *hirðmenn* proper). Although rather less is known about the Danish hird, the institution did exist there and a *Law of the Hird* (*Vederlov*) survives. This was written down *c*. 1080 at the request of Archbisop Absalon and King Knut VI, and it is claimed to derive from a law of **Cnut I the Great**. However, while some of the provisions may date to the 11th century, many do not, and this is probably an attempt to claim old authority for a largely new set of legal provisions. Versions of the *Vederlov* are found in the work of **Saxo Grammaticus** and **Sven Aggesen**. In the 12th and 13th centuries, members of the hird in Norway and Denmark started to move out of the king's court and into the countryside, as royal administrators, a process which ultimately led to the disappearance of the institution.

The institution of the hird was apparently unknown in Sweden. It only appeared in **Iceland** toward the middle of the 13th century, when the Norwegian king began to exert considerable influence on the power politics of the republic in the years before its submission to the Norwegian king in 1262–1264.

HISTORIA DE ANTIQUITATE REGUM NORWAGENSIUM ("History of the Ancient Kings of Norway"). A summary of Norwegian history from **Harald Fine-Hair** to Sigurd the Crusader (ON *Sigurðr Jórsalafari*, 1103–1130), although the last event mentioned took place in 1177. This work was composed by the monk, Theodoricus, who dedicated it to Archbishop Eysteinn Erlendsson of **Trondheim**. Archbishop Eysteinn died in 1188, so the history was presumably written between 1177 and 1188, which makes it one of the oldest Norwegian histories. However, very little is known about Theodoricus, although references to St. Hugh of the Parisian monastery of St-Victor may suggest that he studied there. Certainly, to judge from the sources he mentioned in his history, he had a sound classical education. He bemoaned the lack of written Norwegian history but mentions two sources by name: a life of **Olaf Haraldsson** and a now-lost *Catalogus regum Norwagiensium*, a catalog of the kings of Norway. To judge from his history, this catalog appears to have contained some details that differed from those given in Icelandic historical sources. Theodoricus also mentions the oral testimony of Icelanders among his sources, although it is not clear if he used the written histories of **Sæmund the Learned** and **Ari Thorgilsson**.

HISTORIA NORWEGIAE. An anonymous Latin history of Norway. The manuscript containing this account has been dated to around 1500, but the history itself appears to have been written rather earlier—it refers to a volcanic eruption and earthquake that happened in 1211 as being contemporary. It includes a geographical description of Norway and its North Atlantic colonies, as well as a history of the kings of Norway from their legendary forefathers, the *Ynglingar*, to **Olaf Haraldsson**. The manuscript in which the *Historia Norwegiae* is preserved is fragmentary and its ending is lost, but the third and final section of the history appears to have described the battle between paganism and **Christianity**. The author used a wide range of sources, classical and otherwise, which included **Adam of Bremen's** *History of the Archbishops of Hamburg-Bremen* and a lost Latin work on Norway, which the author of **Ágrip** also seems to have used.

HISTORIARUM ADVERSUM PAGANOS LIBRI SEPTEM. See *SEVEN BOOKS OF HISTORY AGAINST THE PAGANS.*

HISTORY OF THE ARCHBISHOPS OF HAMBURG-BREMEN. The *History of the Archbishops of Hamburg-Bremen* is a work of four volumes or books by the German cleric **Adam of Bremen**. The first three books cover the history of the archbishops from the eighth century, when they were involved in the conversion of the Saxons, right up to the death of Adam's patron, Archbishop Adalbart, in 1072. As one of the first official missions to convert the North was launched from the see of Hamburg-Bremen, this history includes important details about the archbishops' relationship with Scandinavia and its kings. In addition to this, the fourth and last book of Adam's history is essentially a geographical account of the Baltic, North Sea and North Atlantic regions, as background to Hamburg-Bremen's missions to convert the Scandinavian and Slavic peoples in these areas. This book in particular includes many interesting details about the society and economy of Viking-Age Scandinavia, as well as references to the discovery and settlement of **Vinland** and the Norse colonies of the North Atlantic (*see* **Iceland** and **Greenland**). However, Adam's vivid description of the sacrificial cult centered on a pagan temple at **Gamla Uppsala** in Sweden is perhaps the most famous part of his history.

Adam began work on his history after the death of his patron, Archbishop Adalbart, in 1072, and the work was finished some three or four years later when it was presented to Archbishop Liemar. However, Adam continued to revise and annotate his work, and most of the extant manuscripts of his history derive from this revised version. In all, some 141 additions were made by Adam, and 34 of these concern England, Denmark, Norway, **Russia**, and Sweden; 39 amendments were made to Book 4. No original manuscripts of Adam's history survive, but there are numerous copies. Three main manuscript traditions, known as A, B, and C, exist, with A representing the version closest to that presented to Archbishop Liemar (known as *a*), and thus generally lacking extensive annotations; and B and C containing more of the later annotations and revisions, although B has a number of errors introduced by a copyist who had difficulty in reading Adam's heavily annotated original (X), and the author of C has added some of his own material.

Throughout the Viking Age, Hamburg-Bremen fought to maintain its supremacy in Scandinavia against the threat of the English church, and, in particular, against the archbishop of **York**'s attempts to establish his dominance in the region. One of Adam's purposes in writing his history was probably therefore to provide written support for the claims of Hamburg-Bremen through recording the see's earlier missionary activity in the North. Indeed, in his prologue, Adam refers to the fact that "ancient and honorable prerogatives of your [Archbishop Liemar's] Church had been gravely diminished." Adam emphasizes the importance of oral sources in his history, and these included the Danish king, **Svein Estrithsson**, who Adam probably visited in Denmark *c*. 1068–1069. Other sources specified by Adam include the *Life of St. Ansgar* (*see* **Ansgar, St.**); classical writers and poets, such as Virgil, Horace, Ovid, Sallust, and Cicero; and papal letters and documents. *See also* CHRISTIANITY, CONVERSION TO.

HISTORY OF THE DANES. *See GESTA DANORUM*; SAXO GRAM-MATICUS.

HISTORY OF THE DUKES OF NORMANDY. *See* WILLIAM OF JUMIÈGES.

HJÖRUNGAVÁGR, BATTLE OF. Sea battle fought near present-day Ålesund, on the western coast of Norway, at the end of the 10th century. In this battle, the semilegendary **Jomsvikings** were defeated by **Hákon Jarl** of **Lade** and his son Erik. Accounts of the battle are preserved in **Snorri Sturluson's** *Heimskringla*, in *Jómsvíkinga Saga*, and in **Saxo Grammaticus's** *Gesta Danorum*. Although Snorri dated the battle to 994, Saxo writes that the attack was ordered by **Harald Blue-Tooth** of Denmark, which suggests a date before Harald's death *c*. 986; the battle is normally dated to the period 980–985 by modern historians.

HLAÐIR. *See* LADE, EARLS OF.

HNEFATAFL ("King's Table"). One of the most popular Viking-Age board games. Judging from the discovery of gaming pieces and boards, *hnefatafl* appears to have been known throughout Scandinavia and its colonies in the east and west. The rules of the game are not recorded, but it was a tactical game for two players.

HÖFUÐLAUSN. See EGIL'S SAGA.

HOGBACK. Viking-Age stone monuments that were probably placed over graves. Hogbacks are generally about 1.5 meters long and are shaped like contemporary **houses** and halls, with curving sides and a convex "roof" line, the latter from which they derive their name. Many hogbacks have architectural features, such as a shingled roof, and a large number also have three-dimensional beasts or bears that clutch both ends of the hogback. Some hogbacks, such as the so-called Giant's Grave from Penrith in **Cumbria**, appear to have been part of larger monumental arrangements involving hogbacks and crosses. The vast majority of the hogbacks seem, from their ornamentation, to date to the period *c.* 925–1000, although the example from Brechin, Tayside, **Scotland** has 11th-century features.

The distribution of the hogbacks is largely confined to northern England, with notable centers at Brompton and Lythe in North Yorkshire and Sockburn-on-Tees in County Durham. There is, however, a group of hogbacks from central Scotland, including a group of five from Govan (Glasgow), and single examples from **Wales** and **Ireland**. There are no Scandinavian hogbacks, and it appears that the monument may represent an adaptation of solid stone shrines known from the British Isles. The distribution of the hogbacks in northern England largely coincides with the distribution of Norwegian or Gaelic-Norse place-names, suggesting that Irish influence may be linked to the development of this "colonial" form of monument.

HOLMGÁRÐR. *See* NOVGOROD.

HOLY RIVER, BATTLE OF. Battle fought in 1026 in the province of Skåne in the southwest of present-day Sweden. **Cnut I the Great** was defeated in this battle by a Swedo-Norwegian alliance, led by King **Anund Jakob** of Sweden and King **Olaf Haraldsson** of Norway. An account of the battle, containing **skaldic** verse composed for Cnut by **Óttar the Black** and **Sighvatr Þórðarson**, is preserved in Snorri's *Heimskringla*. The *Anglo-Saxon Chronicle* also mentions Cnut's defeat in an entry for 1025, although it names his opponents as Ulf and Eilaf. **Earl Ulf** was probably Cnut's brother-in-law (and the uncle of Harold Godwinsson, future king of England) and is described as Cnut's "protector" of the Danish kingdom; he apparently championed the cause of Cnut's son, **Harthacnut**, in Denmark, and was frustrated by Cnut's long absences from Denmark. Eilaf may have been Ulf's brother. **Saxo Grammaticus's** account of the battle mentions a triple alliance between the Swedish and Norwegian kings and Earl Ulf. Despite Cnut's defeat, he was able to drive Olaf Haraldsson out of Norway and into exile just two years later.

HON HOARD. The Hon hoard is the largest Viking-Age gold hoard known from Scandinavia. It was discovered in a bog at Hon in Buskerud, Norway, during the 19th century, where it was probably deposited during the second half of the ninth century. The metalwork is of the highest quality and includes a gold trefoil brooch of **Carolingian** workmanship; a number of gold neck, arm, and finger rings of mixed provenance (including **Russian** and Anglo-Saxon pieces); several gold pendants inset with semiprecious stones; over 100 glass beads; and 20 gold or silver coins, all of which have had loops added to them for suspension. Very few of the objects are of Scandinavian workmanship. On the basis of the coins and the composition of the hoard, it has been suggested that this was part of the heavy ransom paid to Vikings in France for the return of Abbot Louis of St. Denis and his brother in 858.

HORIK. There were in fact two ninth-century kings of Denmark called Horik, generally known as Horik I the Older (d. 854) and Horik II the Younger (d. 864–873). Horik the Older was the son of the Danish king, **Godfred**, and according to the *Royal Frankish Annals*, he and three of his brothers seized power in 813, driving out **Harald Klak**. Frankish support for Harald Klak led to a brief period of shared power *c.* 819–826, but Horik forced Harald into exile once again in 826/7. By the 830s, all of Horik's brothers seem to have been dead, and Horik himself had come to some kind of agreement with the Frankish emperor, **Louis the Pious**. However, following Louis's death and the resulting battle for power between his sons, Horik sacked Hamburg and ignored Frankish demands to stop his subjects from raiding in **Frankia**. Horik apparently allowed the German missionary, **Ansgar**, to build churches in **Hedeby** and **Ribe** during the 850s. Around the year 850, he was forced to share the rule of his kingdom with two nephews. A third nephew, Guthorm (*Gudurm*), arrived in Denmark in 854, triggering a civil war between Horik and his nephews and resulting in Horik's death.

Little is known about Horik II the Younger, although in the *Annals of Fulda* he is described as a "small boy" and the only member of the royal family to have survived the civil war. He apparently refused to be baptized, but allowed missionary work to continue in his kingdom and sent gifts to Pope Nicholas II in 864. There is no further information about Horik II after this, and very little is known about conditions in Denmark in general for much of the following century.

HOUSECARL (ON *húskarl* **plural** *húskarlar***).** Name given to the household troops of the kings in England from 1016–1066 and, in the late 12th-century, it is found in the Danish *Vederlov* "Law of the **Hird**," which claims to go back to legal provisions made by **Cnut I the Great**. The earliest evidence for the use of the term comes from an account of the translation of the relics of Ælfheah of Canterbury in 1023. This late 11th-century account, by Osbern of Canterbury, records how the household troops ("called housecarls in the Danish tongue") of Cnut created disturbances to distract people's attention, guarded key points on the route the relics were transported, and accompanied the body itself in case there was any attempt to stop its movement from London to Canterbury. **Harthacnut** apparently used his housecarls to collect taxes in 1041, and when two were killed in Worcester, he sent an army and "almost all his housecarls" to punish the town. However, while it used to be believed that the housecarls performed a purely military role in the households of Cnut, Harthacnut, Edward the Confessor (d. 1065), and Harold Godwinsson (d. 1066), recent work has emphasized the nonmilitary contexts in which many housecarls appear. As well as collecting tax for Harthacnut, a number of housecarls, such as Bovi and Urk, appear in charters as both witnesses and as recipients of land grants. In *Domesday Book*, some people are described as both housecarls and **thegns** in different parts of the text, and both Bovi and Urk were also described as thegns (*ministri*). This evidence suggests that the housecarls were not a standing army of mercenaries but rather a group of retainers that followed and supported the king at court and in the countryside.

HOUSES. The houses built and inhabited by the Vikings varied across the Viking world, according to climate, available building materials, and function. The most common kind of house was a rectangular structure (often with curved side walls), which might measure some 5 to 7 meters in width and between 15 and 75 meters in length, depending on the status and wealth of the householder. This kind of dwelling is known as a longhouse and usually consisted of one main living room where all the inhabitants ate and slept and where household tasks such as cooking and weaving were performed. The two long walls of this room were generally lined with wall benches, built up with earth and lined with wood, upon which people sat, ate, and slept. Under the same roof, in rural communities, there was also a separate cattle byre (although toward the end of the Viking Age, animal houses and living quarters were often in separate buildings), and there may also have been a small room for storing foods and other goods. The longhouse was heated by a long hearth in the middle of the room, and smoke escaped from a small hole in the roof of the longhouse. Lighting was supplied by the fire, oil lamps (using herring or seal oil), and later on by wax candles. There were often no windows in the longhouse, although there might be some very small holes left in the walls, covered by a translucent material such as thin, scraped, and stretched animal skin, that let in a little light. The two exterior doors (to the byre and the main hall) were placed so as to minimize draughts, depending on the direction of the prevailing winds. The main longhouse might be surrounded by several separate buildings with specialized functions, such as a smithy, a dairy, servants' quarters, shelter for small animals, and a bathhouse.

In Sweden and Norway, where timber was in plentiful supply, these longhouses were generally of a solid blockhouse construction (horizontal logs with overlapping corners), using pine, and with a birch-bark and turf roof. However, in Denmark, where the climate was milder and where there was less timber, the walls of houses were frequently of wattle construction—clay plaster put on to a framework of upright wooden (usually oak) posts—with a roof of reeds or thatch. A reconstruction of a wattle-and-daub house from **Hedeby** can be found at the Moesgård Museum, near Århus in Denmark. In largely treeless Iceland, houses were built from turf, earth and stone, often partially sunken for insulation, and with walls measuring a meter or more in thickness. The **Stöng** farmhouse, preserved in volcanic debris, is a good illustration of an Icelandic longhouse.

HRÓLFR KRAKI, SAGA OF (ON *Hrólfs saga kraka*). One of the so-called *Sagas of Ancient Times*. It survives in some 44 manuscripts, the earliest of which dates to the 17th century. However, it is believed that the saga was probably composed in **Iceland** around 1400. Certainly, the Icelandic monastic library of Möðruvellir lists this saga among its collections in 1461. **Snorri Sturluson** refers to tales about Hrólfr in his *Skáldskaparmál* and **Saxo Grammaticus** also describes the exploits of Hrólfr in his translation of *Bjárkamál*, which suggests that stories about this heroic Danish king were popular well before 1461. Indeed, another reference to the king comes from the *Book of Settlements* where Hrólfr's sword, Skofnung, with which he was buried, is said to have been stolen by Skeggi of Midfjörd before he settled in Iceland. It was apparently passed down in the family until one of Skeggi's descendants, Gellir (d. *c*. 1073), was buried with the sword at Roskilde, near **Lejre**, in Denmark.

Hrólfr was king of Denmark in the sixth century, of the legendary Skjolding dynasty, with his seat at Lejre in Jutland. His nickname, *kraki* "pole-ladder," was derived from his stature, which was said to be tall, slim, and like a pole-ladder. The saga includes stories about Hrólfr's 12 champions and their role in Hrólfr's conflict with the Swedish king, Adils, which eventually brought about their and Hrólfr's death in battle. However, much of the material of the saga is clearly mythical and magical, and the saga narrative is constructed around sorcerers, trolls, elves, **berserkers**, and spells.

HRYNHENT ("accentuated verse"). Form of meter used in **skaldic poetry**. *Hrynhent* was the most important meter after **dróttkvætt**, and was particularly popular in the 14th century. *Hrynhenda*, composed by Arnórr Þórðarson jarlaskáld, is the first surviving praise poem in *hrynhent* and is actually named after the meter. It was composed in the mid-11th century in honor of **Magnus the Good Olafsson** of Norway.

HUGIN (ON Huginn "thought"). One of **Odin's** two ravens, the other being Munin (ON *Muninn* "the thought"). Hugin appears in the written sources, such as the *Poetic Edda* and **skaldic** verse, more frequently than Munin. In skaldic verse, the names Hugin and Munin are used to refer to ravens in general, usually in the context of battlefields where the fallen warriors are described as food for ravens. Odin was the god of warfare and the battlefield, and his ravens were the birds of the battlefield. Perhaps the most well-known reference to Hugin (and Munin) is in Snorri's

Gylfaginning, where it is said that the two birds fly around the world every morning, collecting information, and then fly back and sit on Odin's shoulders, whispering all that they have heard and seen. Ravens also appear to have been a popular motif for war banners: for example, *Orkneyinga Saga* (ch. 12) refers to a magic banner made for Earl **Sigurd the Stout** by his mother, which brought him victory.

HUMBER, RIVER. Major estuary in northeast England, which formed an important dividing line between the Anglo-Saxon kingdoms of **Northumbria** and Lindsey (northern Lincolnshire). Northumbria is derived from the OE *norð(an)hymbre* "the people living to the north of the Humber;" and the word, *suðhymbri* "the people living to the south of the Humber," is also found in, for example, the *Anglo-Saxon Chronicle*, where on two occasions (*s. a.* 697, 702) it appears to refer to **Mercia**. The annal for 827, however, talks of King Ecgberht's conquest of Mercia and "all that was south of the Humber."

The Humber was an important sea-route for **Viking** invaders and traders, connecting as it did with the Rivers Ouse and Trent. This allowed the Vikings to sail their ships up river to the Northumbrian capital, **York**, and down through the East Midlands to Nottingham, one of the so-called **Five Boroughs**. The *Anglo-Saxon Chronicle* mentions the Humber on eight occasions between 827 [829] and 1070. In 866, the **Great Army** is said to have crossed the mouth of the river on their way from **East Anglia** to York; in 942, the river is mentioned in a poem commemorating the conquests of King Edmund of England, where it is said to be one of the northern boundaries of the kingdom of **Wessex**; in 993, a Viking army is said to have raided at the mouth of the Humber; in 1013, **Svein Forkbeard** sailed north from Kent, past East Anglia, up the Humber and down the Trent to Gainsborough in Lincolnshire, where he received the submission of the northeast English; in 1066, the river was the scene of a confrontation between **Earl** Edwin of Mercia and Earl Tostig, renegade Earl of Northumbria and ally of **Harald Hard-Ruler** of Norway; in 1069, a fleet of rebellious northerners sailed from the Humber up to York as part of the uprising against Norman rule; and finally, in 1070, the invading fleet of King **Svein Estrithsson** of Denmark sailed up the Humber before receiving the submission of "local people."

HÚSDRÁPA ("House lay"). **Skaldic** poem composed in **Iceland** at the end of the 10th century by Ulf Uggason. The poem commemorates a new hall built by Olaf Peacock at Hjarðarholt and it describes the **mythological** scenes that decorated the wall panels of this splendid hall. The setting for Ulf's recital of the poem, a marriage feast for Olaf Peacock's daughter, Thurid, is described in *Laxdœla Saga*, although this saga does not contain any of the poem. However, **Snorri Sturluson** included 56 lines of the poem, mostly quoted in half-stanza chunks, in his *Prose Edda*. Three mythological subjects are mentioned in this *drápa*: **Balder's** death and funeral, **Thor's** encounter with the World Serpent (*see* **Midgard serpent**), and an otherwise unknown story of how the gods **Loki** and **Heimdall** took on the shape of seals and wrestled for the necklace, **Brísingamen**.

HVERGELMIR (ON *Hvergelmir*). Name of a spring, which may mean "the bubbling cauldron," in Norse **mythology**. *Gylfaginning* provides two conflicting accounts of exactly where Hvergelmir was located: in **Niflheim** and under the roots of **Yggdrasil**. **Eddic poetry** does not help to resolve this conflict; *Grímnismál* is the only poem to mention it, and this poem simply describes Hvergelmir as being filled from the antlers of a stag, Eikþyrnir, who stands on the roof of **Valhalla**. It also adds that all the rivers of the world had their source in Hvergelmir.

– I –

IBN FADLAN. Arabic diplomat—sent by the caliph al-Muqtadir in Baghdad on an embassy to the Bulghars—who lived on the River Volga. The king of the Bulghars had requested personal instruction in Islam from the Caliph and help in the construction of a mosque. Ahmad ibn-Fadlan ibn al-Abbas ibn Rashid ibn Hammad was the secretary and religious instructor of the delegation. His diplomatic log, *Risala*, famously describes a **Rus** community he encountered in an unnamed settlement on the Volga *c*. 922. This vivid eyewitness account, which forms about one-fifth of his report, provides considerable detail about the **burial** rituals and cremation in a **ship** of one of the Rus chieftains, which involved the ritual sacrifice of one of his **slave** girls. He also comments (positively) on the appearance and (negatively) on the hygiene of the Rus.

Part of Ibn Fadlan's account was included in a 13th-century geographical dictionary, *Mu'ajam al-Buldan*. An 11th-century copy of the complete text of the *Risala* was discovered in Meshed, Iran, in the early 20th century. A 16th-century geographer, Amin Razi, is believed to have had access to an even earlier copy of the diplomatic log.

ICELAND. The most important of the Scandinavian colonies in the North Atlantic, Iceland lies about 570 nautical miles west of Norway, touching the Arctic Circle in the north. Before the Viking colonization, the island seems only to have been populated by Irish hermits who, according to the ***Book of the Icelanders*** by **Ari Thorgilsson** "went away because they were not prepared to live here in company with heathen men." Little else is known about the island before the ninth century: Dicuil (*see* ***Book of the Measurement of the Earth***) may have been writing about Iceland when he described "Thule," where the sun stayed above the horizon all day and night in summer.

The traditional account of the Scandinavian settlement of Iceland is contained in a number of later, predominantly Icelandic, sources, such as the ***Book of Settlements*** and the *Book of the Icelanders*. While the latter attributes the colonization to "a Norwegian called Ingolf . . . settled south in Reykjavik," the *Book of Settlements* mentions three other **Vikings** who appear to have reached Iceland before **Ingolf Arnason**: two of these, Naddod and Gardar the Swede, were driven by storms toward the island, but a third, Floki Vilgerdarson from Rogaland in southwest Norway, apparently set out to settle the island, taking three hallowed ravens as his guides. He is said to have settled around Vatnsfjörd in the northwest, but the cold winter and spring destroyed the livestock he had brought with him, and, christening the island, Iceland, he decided to return to Norway.

Despite Floki's unfortunate experience of the Icelandic winter, colonization began in earnest. In fact, the new settlers found a country where the coastal climate was relatively mild because of the Gulf Stream, which warms the sea and the air around the western coast of Iceland. There was also fairly good land around the numerous fjörds and inlets, good enough to support livestock, and the sea too was also a valuable resource, providing fish, seals, walrus, whales, and sea birds. Although today Iceland is largely treeless, there were birch forests on the island in the Viking Age, which provided building material, and this could be supplemented with driftwood washed up on the shores.

The first settlement is dated by Ari to around the year 870, and the island is said to have been completely settled around sixty years later, by about the year 930. Ari and **Snorri Sturluson** both consider the desire to escape from the tyranny of King **Harald Fine-Hair** as the most important reason for this colonization process, but this is fairly certainly a later exaggeration covering more diverse and complex motives. The *Book of Settlements* lists some 430 separate settlements that were established by these colonists. As well as Norwegians, the settlers also included Scandinavians who had lived in Britain, especially in **Scotland** and **Hebrides**, and in **Ireland**. Consequently, some of the Norse settlers had Celtic wives or **slaves**, or Celtic names, such as the eponymous hero of *Njal's Saga*. Celtic names can also be found in some of the place-names of Iceland.

There is no evidence that any towns were established or developed on Iceland in the Viking Age. Icelanders instead traveled to Norway to buy and sell goods. Icelandic exports included walrus ivory, sealskin, and other products derived from marine mammals, such as walrus-hide rope. Icelandic wool was also an important export, and the basic unit of measurement, the *vaðmal*, was based upon a length of cloth. Reykjavik did not become the Icelandic capital until 1918, and for most of the Viking Age it appears to have been a predominantly rural settlement. Archaeological excavation has given us some idea of what Icelandic farms were like. In southern Iceland, in the Thjórsársalur valley, the eruption of the volcano, Mount Hekla, buried a number of Viking-Age buildings. One of the well-preserved farms was excavated out of the volcanic ash in 1939 at **Stöng**, and a reconstruction of what it must have originally looked like has been built.

As at home in Norway, the new society organized itself around local legal assemblies, called **things**. The country was divided into four, and each quarter had three or four things, under local chieftains, called **goði**. As well as providing secular leadership, people also gathered in the halls of their *goði* for feasts to mark the seasons and to worship their gods. There was also a national assembly called the **Althing** at which the most important legal decisions were made and disputes settled. It was at the Althing that **Christianity** was formally accepted *c*. 1000. With the advent of Christianity, churches were built and schools were founded for priests to study the new religion. It was these places that became the great literary centers of medieval Iceland, where large numbers of sagas, poems, and historical and religious writings were produced.

In keeping with the colonists' apparent desire to rule themselves, there were no kings of Iceland. Nevertheless, Iceland remained closely tied to Norway by bonds of family and by economics. Much of Iceland's trade was with the motherland, and the Norwegian royal court was the place for the young, ambitious Icelander to go. It was the Icelanders who wrote the history of the Norwegian kings (*see* **Kings' Sagas**) and much of the **skaldic poetry** about these kings. However, the Middle Ages saw the ideals of the free Icelandic republic collapse into civil war and politicking, and this lead ultimately to the republic's incorporation into the kingdom of Norway in 1262–1264.

IDUN (ON *Iðunn* "the rejuvenating one"). Goddess of the Æsir, who was married to **Bragi**, and whose main role it was to guard the apples of youth that the gods needed in order to stay young. Very little is known about this goddess, and **Snorri Sturluson** recounts just one myth involving Idun in his ***Prose Edda***. This relates how Idun and her apples were stolen by **Loki** and the giant, Þjazi. Loki was persuaded, on pain of death or torture, by the gods to bring her back, and rescued her in the form of a falcon (he borrowed this form from **Freya**). Pursued by Þjazi, in the shape of an eagle, Loki carried Idun back to **Asgard** in the form of a nut.

INGLEBY HEATH. Site of a group of some 60 **burial** mounds on the River Trent in Derbyshire, England, partially excavated in the 1850s, 1940s, 1950s, and which was investigated more recently in the 1980s. The men and **women** buried in these mounds had been cremated, making the Ingleby Heath burials the only definite examples of **Viking** cremations in England. The burials also contained the traces of burned animal bones and the remains of grave goods, including two swords, nails, and iron buckles. There were also some apparently empty mounds, interpreted as cenotaphs. The site at Heath Wood in Ingleby appears to have been in use for no longer than 20 or 30 years, and the excavators have drawn attention to both the similarities and the differences between Ingleby and the pagan burials at **Repton**, which lies just four kilometers to the southeast of Ingleby. It has been suggested that the two sites may physically represent the division of the **Great Army** that is recorded by the *Anglo-Saxon Chronicle*, and that at Ingleby the Vikings were making a clear statement of their religious and political affiliations in a hostile and unfamiliar landscape.

INGOLF ARNASON (ON *Ingólfr Arnason***).** According to **Ari Thorgilsson's** *Book of the Icelanders*, Ingolf was the first Norwegian to leave for **Iceland**, "when **Harald Fine-Hair** was sixteen years old," and he settled there following a second expedition a few years later. Ingolf is said to have made landfall at Ingólfshöfði and he claimed land for his possession at Ingólfsfell, but he finally settled at Reykjavik, the present-day capital in the southwest of the island. The *Book of Settlements* adds more details to the bare bones of this story, recounting how Ingolf and his foster brother, Leif (known as Hjorleif or "Sword-Leif") had to forfeit their estates to **Earl** Atli of Gaular as compensation for killing his two sons. Following this, they embarked on an expedition to find Iceland, previously sighted by Floki Vilgerdarson, spent one winter there reconnoitering the island and returned to Norway. In 874, they set out to settle Iceland, but were parted after sighting land. Hjorleif landed at Hjorleifshöfði, but he was killed by the Irish **slaves** he had brought with him, who were unhappy at his treatment of them. Ingolf cast his high-seat pillars overboard, vowing to settle where they landed, and he spent a number of years trying to locate them, during which time he also killed the Irish slaves responsible for Hjorleif's death. After discovering the pillars at Reykjavik, Ingolf took possession of the Reykjanes Peninsula, west of the river Oxára, as his land.

Ingolf married Hallveig Froðadóttir, and they had a son called Thorstein, who established the first **thing**-place, at Kjalarnes, before the institution of the **Althing**. Proceedings of the Althing were opened by the *allsherjargoði*, who was the holder of the chieftaincy established by Thorstein, son of Ingolf.

INGVAR THE FAR-TRAVELED (ON *Yngvarr inn víðförla*)

(d. 1041). Swedish leader of a fateful expedition to **Serkland** in the mid-11th century. Ingvar was said to be the son of Eymund and was of royal stock. His expedition is recorded in a group of about 25 runic inscriptions (*see* **rune**) from central eastern Sweden that commemorate those men who fell with Ingvar, as well as in an Icelandic saga, *Yngvars saga víðförla*, that was written down at the beginning of the 13th century. This saga is one of the so-called *Sagas of Ancient Times* or *fornaldarsögur*, and is based on an earlier, lost Latin *Life of Ingvar* by the monk Odd Snorrason, composed *c*. 1080. The text of the saga is preserved in two vellum manuscripts (A and B), which are both defective and which are both derived from the same lost original (X).

In *Yngvar's Saga*, the eponymous hero served the Swedish king, **Olof Skötkonung**, and "the king held him in higher respect than any other man." However, Olof refused to give Ingvar the title of king and so, according to the saga writer, the purpose of Ingvar's expedition was to find a kingdom for himself. It is claimed that his fleet amounted to some 30 ships. A small number of the Ingvar runestones certainly refer to men who "steered ships eastward with Ingvar," but it is impossible to be sure about the exact size of the expedition. After traveling through **Russia** and spending some three years at the court of **Jaroslav the Wise**, Ingvar's force headed east into unknown territory and increasingly fantastical adventures, with a romantic interlude in the form of Queen Silkisif of **Garðaríki**. According to this saga, the expedition was decimated by an unspecified sickness, probably around the Caspian Sea. Ingvar himself also died of this sickness, it is said, at the age of 25 in 1041, a date that agrees with the one recorded in Icelandic annals.

Most of the runic inscriptions, which offer contemporary evidence to support the often rather fantastical saga, are fairly terse, and simply state that the men accompanying Ingvar died in the east or the south. Some include short verses, such as the Gripsholm stone from the province of Södermanland (Sö 179). This was raised by Tola, mother of Ingvar's brother, Harald, who is described as Ingvar's brother, and describes the warriors as faring "like men / far after gold," before their death in *Serkland*. The wording of the inscription suggests that Tola was not Ingvar's mother; perhaps Harald was Ingvar's half brother, by a different mother, or perhaps the word "brother" was being used in the sense of comrade-in-arms. An extremely fragmentary rune-stone from Strängnäs (Sö 279) may offer some support for the saga's claim that Ingvar was the son of Eymund, for as well as echoing the Gripsholm stone's "southward in Serkland," it was apparently raised to commemorate men who are described as "sons of Eymund."

IONA. The island of St. Columba's church off the west coast of **Scotland** was a victim of the earliest recorded **Viking** attacks on Scotland at the end of the eighth and beginning of the ninth century. Further attacks are recorded in the 840s, and another is mentioned by Irish annals in 986. The hoard of some 350, predominantly English, coins discovered at the Abbey has been linked with this latter raid. Burned layers have been revealed by excavation, but it is not possible to determine if these represent Viking attacks rather than domestic accidents. However, the disruption caused by raiding is reflected in the transfer of St. Columba's relics to Scotland and then to **Ireland**.

However, the community on Iona survived. Sculpture continued to be produced on the island throughout the 9th and 10th centuries. Indeed, a 10th-century fragmentary cross or cross-slab carved in Scandinavian style and decorated with a Viking **ship** and what appears to be elements of the **Sigurd the Dragon-Slayer** legend has been found at Iona Abbey as well as another Scandinavian-style stone and an 11th-century rune-stone (*see* **rune**). The island became a place of pilgrimage and a center of Norse **Christianity**, with the Norse king of **Dublin, Olaf Cúarán**, retiring to the monastery in penitence and pilgrimage in 980. The mixed cultural influences of Iona are reflected in the local tradition that 48 Scottish kings, 8 Norwegian kings, and 4 Irish kings are interred on the island.

The earliest of the existing ecclesiastical buildings, St. Oran's chapel, is dated to *c*. 1080. Around the year 1200, Reginald, Lord of the Isles and son of Sumarliði, founded a Benedictine community on the island; a nunnery was established shortly afterward; and the cathedral, dedicated to Mary, was expanded and became the seat of the bishopric of Sodor and Man (until the abolition of episcopal sees in 1587). However, the late 12th- or early 13th-century parish church of St. Ronan demonstrates the presence of a secular population alongside the religious communities on the island.

IRELAND, VIKINGS IN. At the time of the first raids, Ireland was divided into several small kingdoms that frequently clashed in their bid for political and territorial dominance. Indeed, Irish annals record 25 monastic attacks by **Vikings** in the first 34 years of their operations, but 87 raids were carried out by various Irish factions in the same period. Another distinctive feature of Ireland at the time of the first Viking raids was the prominence of the Church and, in particular, the monasteries. There were no towns in Ireland, but the monasteries served as political and economic, as well as religious, centers. The abbots of the more important monasteries therefore wielded considerable secular power, and because of this, the destruction of monasteries was a feature of Irish warfare, even before the Vikings arrived, although it does appear to have increased as a result of Viking activity.

Viking activity in Ireland can be divided up into a number of distinct phases, beginning with hit-and-run raids, then escalating to more frequent and more widespread destruction, and culminating in the settlement of Vikings and their permanent presence on the Irish political scene. The Viking towns were, however, gradually brought under the control of the native Irish kings and by the end of the 10th century enjoyed little real political independence.

Attacks are first recorded in the ***Annals of Ulster***, which tells us that *Rechru* was burned by "the heathens" in 795. *Rechru* is usually identified with Rathlin Island, which lies off the northeast tip of Ireland. Inismurray and Inisboffin on the northwest coast also suffered in the same year. In 798, *Inis Pátraic*, St. Patrick's Island (off the east coast, north of **Dublin**) was burned by the Vikings and the shrine of St. Do Chonna was smashed. There were a series of intermittent attacks from this time into the 820s, but after 822 Viking attacks on Ireland became an annual occurrence. The monasteries on the north and east coasts of Ireland, such as Bangor, initially suffered most from this intensification. However, the next two decades, the 830s and 840s, saw several Viking fleets traveling inland along Ireland's rivers, extending the range of their raiding activities; Armagh, the most important monastery in northern Ireland, was attacked three times in 832 alone, and a further eight attacks on Armagh are recorded in the annals.

The character of most of the raids until this point was largely hit-and-run raids by small sea-borne forces that seldom strayed more than 30 kilometers from navigable water. However, after 836, the scale, frequency, and destructiveness of the raids intensified. The Vikings also seem to have begun one of their most profitable trades in Ireland, the **slave** trade, around this time. The raiders spent their first recorded winter in Ireland at Lough Neagh in the northeast in 840–841, and shortly after, in around 841, the first permanent Scandinavian settlements were established on the River Liffey at Dublin and on the River Boyne at Anagassan. These settlements are known as **longphorts** or **ship** camps and were followed by further settlements on the Shannon at Limerick, on the Barrow at Waterford, at Wexford, and at Cork (848). These bases allowed the Vikings to carry on their raids all around the year, rather than just confining them to the summer. However, the process of integration into the Irish political scene also appears to have begun in the late ninth century. There is the first evidence of intermarriage, conversion, as well as the participation in internal politics and conflicts as mercenaries, and also of the first defeats at the hands of Irish kings.

Irish annals record a new Viking threat around this time, the so-called dark heathens or Danes, who arrived in 849 and who were hostile to the Norwegian Viking fleets already operating in Ireland. For a short time there appears to have been considerable confusion and discord between rival Viking factions in Ireland, but this was resolved by the arrival of **Olaf the White** in 853, who asserted his overlordship over all the Scandinavians in Ireland. This signaled the beginning of two new developments: the rise of the Norse kingdom of Dublin and the Viking fleets' exchange of freelance raiding for employment as mercenaries by Irish kings vying for power. Olaf, together with his kinsmen, **Ivar** (*Ímar*) and Auðgisl (*Auisle*), ruled Dublin for the next 20 years and raided extensively in **Scotland** and the **Hebrides**. According to *War of the Irish against with Foreigners*, the death of Ivar in 873 marked the beginning of "forty years' rest" from large-scale Viking invasions. The 880s and 890s instead saw a series of dynastic feuds weaken the power of Dublin, and in 893 two distinct factions emerged, that of one of Ivar's sons and that of **Earl** Sigfrith.

In 902, there seems to have been a temporary truce between the various Irish kings, and the Dublin Norse were expelled from the country by an alliance led by the kings of Brega and Leinster. This resulted in the settlement of northwest England (*see* **Cumbria**) and the dispersal of Scandinavians around the Irish Sea area and as far afield as France. However, Vikings returned to Ireland under the leadership of the grandsons of **Ivar the Boneless** in 914. There appears to have been a clash between the Waterford Vikings (led by Barðr) and Ivar's Dublin dynasty (led by **Ragnald**), but Norse power in Dublin was re-established under Ragnald's kinsman, **Sigtrygg Cáech**, in 917, and Ragnald captured **York** in 919. In the 920s, Sigtrygg and Ragnald controlled the whole of the Irish Sea region from their strongholds in York and Dublin, and for some 20 years, Dublin's power in the Scandinavian colonies of the west was unrivalled. However, the power of the English kings was growing in northern England, and Olaf Guthfrithsson (d. 941) of Dublin was defeated at **Brunanburh**, along with the Scots and Strathclyde Britons. The last king of Dublin and York, **Olaf Cúarán**, was driven out of **Northumbria** in 949, and just a few years later, in 954, English control of the Northumbrian capital was reasserted. In the 940s, Dublin and other fortified towns in Ireland came under renewed pressure from the Irish, and the camps at Anagassan, Strangford, and Carlingford Loughs were evacuated during this period. The reign of Olaf Cúarán, baptized in England, saw the further integration of the Norse into the Irish political scene. This can be traced in the personal names of Norse dynasty (Olaf's daughter was called Maél Muire) and intermarriage with leading Irish families (Olaf was married to **Gormlaith**, daughter of the king of Leinster).

From 980, following a resounding defeat at the Battle of **Tara**, Dublin had to recognize the overlordship of Meath, and despite **Sigtrygg Silk-Beard's** attempts to resurrect the independence of Dublin (*see* **Clontarf, Battle of**), the Vikings in Ireland remained politically subservient to the high kings of Ireland. The 11th century saw the full integration of the Vikings into the Irish community, and the culture of the Scandinavian towns became Hiberno-Norse rather than simply Norse. The towns flourished, and Irish kings started to become involved with urban matters in order to harness the profits of the towns for their own ends: Limerick came under Irish control as early as 968, Waterford in 1035, and Dublin got its first Irish king in 1052. Apart from the period between 1078 and 1094, when Dublin was controlled by the kings of the **Isle of Man**, Dublin's rulers remained Irish until the Norman Conquest of Ireland in 1170.

The linguistic evidence for the Vikings in Ireland is comparatively small-scale; the surviving Old Norse contribution to Irish amounts to less than 50 words, many connected with shipping, trade, and warfare. The earliest loanword into Irish is *erell* from ON *jarl* "**earl**." Most of the Scandinavian place-names that resulted from the settlement are confined to the coasts, such as Dursey, Fastnet, Fota, and Waterford (ON *Veðrafjörðr*) on the south coast and Wexford (ON *Veigsfjörðr*), Wicklow (ON *Vikingaló*), Lambay, Skerries, Carlingford, and Strangford on the east coast. Outside of Dublin, just four runic inscriptions (*see* **rune**) are known from Ireland: from Greenmount (County Louth), Killaloe (County Clare), Beginish (County Kerry), and (just one rune from) Roosky (County Donegal). Although written in Old Norse and Scandinavian runes, both Greenmount and Killaloe demonstrate to some extent the mixing of Norse and Irish cultures in Ireland, the former in the Irish personal name *Domnall* and the latter in the ogham inscription that accompanies the runes. Nevertheless, despite cultural, social, and political interaction, it does appear that the Scandinavian towns of Ireland may have continued to be Norse-speaking communities, distinct from the hinterland, until perhaps the 13th century.

IRISH ANNALS. *See ANNALS OF ULSTER.*

ISLANDBRIDGE. *See* KILMAINHAM.

ÍSLENDINGABÓK. *See BOOK OF THE ICELANDERS.*

ÍSLENDINGASÖGUR. *See SAGAS OF THE ICELANDERS.*

ISTANBUL. *See* BYZANTIUM.

IVAR (Irish *Ímar*) (d. 973). *See* OLAF THE WHITE.

IVAR THE BONELESS. One of the sons of the legendary **Ragnar Loðbrók** who has been identified with the Ivar (*Ingware*) that is named by the *Anglo-Saxon Chronicle* as one of the leaders of the **Great Army** and also with the **Ivar** (*Ímar*) who is said to have ruled **Dublin** after the death of his brother, **Olaf the White**. It is generally accepted that Ivar the Boneless probably was the Ivar active in England with the Great Army in the mid-ninth century, who is said to have killed Ælla of **Northumbria** and **St. Edmund** of **East Anglia**. If he is also the Irish Ivar, he is said to have died in Dublin in 873. The nickname "Boneless" is not recorded until the 12th century, and its precise origins are obscure. However, it may be linked to a Faroese folktale that records the use of such a nickname to refer to the wind and ultimately to a capacity for battling the wind at sea.

– J –

JARL. *See* EARL.

JARLABANKI. Eleventh-century Swedish chieftain, who lived near Lake Vallentuna in the present-day province of Uppland. Jarlabanki had six **rune-stones** raised during his own lifetime, making him the most prolific sponsor of rune-stones in the province (U 127, 149, 164, 165, 212, and 261). Unusually, all of these stones were not raised in memory of one or more deceased relatives, but for Jarlabanki's own soul. Four of the rune-stones are practically identical and flank the ends of the causeway or "bridge," some 150 meters long, which Jarlabanki built in Täby. The building of bridges was associated with the Christian missionary church (*see* **Christianity, Conversion to**), a "good" work that helped people travel across the countryside to the new churches. On these four rune-stones, Jarlabanki states that he alone owned all of Täby. Another of his rune-stones, at Vallentuna (U 212, inscribed on both sides of the stone), tells us that he also made the (now-lost) assembly place at which the stone originally stood and adds that Jarlabanki owned the whole of the hundred (*Valænda hundare*), a medieval administrative division. Moreover, a further 12 inscriptions, possibly more, in the same district concern the Jarlabanki family, allowing scholars to construct a family tree. However, the traditional interpretation, in which Jarlabanki of Täby was seen as the grandson of Estrid and the father of Sven and Ingefast the younger, has been recently revised with Jarlabanki now being regarded as the father of Estrid and thus the great-great-grandfather of Sven and Ingefast.

JARLSHOF. Site of a Norse farmhouse on the southern tip of Mainland **Shetland**. The site was discovered after violent storms at the end of the 19th century, and subsequent excavations revealed a succession of **longhouses** and outbuildings on the site of an Iron-Age *broch* and roundhouse settlement, which was preceded by a Bronze-Age smithy. The primary longhouse and outbuildings appear to have been constructed at some time early in the ninth century, with a second longhouse being built shortly afterward and a third added in the 10th century. Modification, demolition, and construction on this site continued down to the 16th century when the New Hall was built, although a clear decline in the settlement took place in the 13th century. Most of the Norse finds come from the primary longhouse, a structure over 28.5 meters in length. These include combs, loomweights, hone-stones, spindle whorls, bone pins, playing pieces, pottery, and more than a hundred stone fragments with incised scratches and motifs. It has not been possible to determine if the site was still in occupation when the first Norse settlers arrived at Jarlshof as evidence is conflicting. However, many of the sketches and motif pieces found in the Norse longhouses are Pictish (*see* **Picts**) rather than Norse in character.

JAROSLAV THE WISE (980–1054). Also Yaroslav and Iaroslav. Grand Duke of **Kiev** 1019–1054, Jaroslav was the son of Vladimir I (d. 1015) of **Russia** and ruled **Novgorod** for his father. Following Vladimir's death, Jaroslav's brother Svyatopolk seized power in Kiev, and Jaroslav only succeeded in defeating and killing his brother in 1019 with the help of Scandinavian mercenaries. Jaroslav's rule is regarded as a cultural high point in the early history of the Russian state. He promoted **Christianity**, encouraged the translation of Greek texts into the Slavonic languages, had St. Sophia Cathedral built in Kiev, and codified the law (known as *Pravda*). Kiev thrived upon the trade passing along the River **Dnieper**, and the city was defended with a rampart during Jaroslav's reign.

Jaroslav maintained and developed Russian links with Scandinavia: he was married to Ingigerd, the daughter of the Swedish king **Olof Skötkonung**, and they had three daughters and five sons. Their daughter, Ellisif, was married to the Norwegian king, **Harald Hard-Ruler**; and Jaroslav's court appears to have had prominent Scandinavian visitors, such as the exiled **Olaf Haraldsson** and **Magnus I the Good** of Norway, and **Ingvar the Far-Traveled** of Sweden. Nevertheless, Jaroslav also made dynastic alliances outside Scandinavia, marrying other daughters to Andrew I of Hungary and Henry I of France, and four of his sons married into the **Byzantine** and German royal families. Despite the frequent references to Jaroslav in ***Heimskringla***, the language of Jaroslav's court, like the Church in Russia, was Slavonic, not Scandinavian, and Russia's foreign policy interests lay clearly and firmly in the east.

JELLING. Royal seat in north Jutland, Denmark. Today, a 12th-century church, two large **burial** mounds, and two **rune-stones** can be seen at Jelling. Jelling's fame owes much to King **Harald Blue-Tooth**, who built the first church at Jelling and raised the larger of the two rune-stones (Jelling II), commemorating his conversion of the Danes to **Christianity** and the unification of the country. His father, **Gorm the Old**, was buried in the north mound at Jelling but was apparently moved to a grave in the church, presumably by his son. The south burial mound at Jelling appears to have never contained a grave, although a pre-existing ship-setting was destroyed in the erection of this mound. Harald's own son, **Svein Forkbeard**, broke the dynastic connection with Jelling, and Harald himself was buried in Roskilde after being driven out of Denmark by Svein.

JELLINGE. Scandinavian **art** style, which takes its name from the silver cup found in the **burial** mound at **Jelling**, Jutland, Denmark. The style is conventionally spelled with an extra *e* on the end of Jelling, due to a misspelling in the first definitive English-language study of **Viking art** styles. The Jellinge style is characterized by fluid, ribbon-like creatures that have long pigtails on their heads. The Jellinge style was in use from the late 9th to the mid-10th century in Scandinavia and the British Isles. Confusingly, the **rune-stone** at Jelling is not decorated in the Jellinge style but in the later **Mammen** style.

JOMSVIKINGS (ON *Jómsvíkingar*). A legendary community of **Viking** warriors, which is said to have resided at *Jómsborg* (identified with **Wolin** in present-day Poland). The main source of information about the Jomsvikings comes from the *Saga of the Jomsvikings* (ON

Jómsvíkinga saga), which was written in **Iceland** *c.* 1200. Here, the community is said to have been founded by the Danish warrior, Pálnatóki, on the Baltic coast of Wendland (*see* **Wends**), and his successor was Sigvaldi Strút-Haraldsson. However, **Saxo Grammaticus** records an alternative tradition, in which **Harald Blue-Tooth** is said to have founded the fortress of *Jómsborg* as a base for piracy. Certainly Harald had links with Wendland; he was married to a Wendish princess and fled to the court of her father, Mistivoi, when driven into exile by his son **Svein Forkbeard**. However, Wolin is nevertheless known to have existed long before Harald's reign.

The Icelandic saga records that this community consisted of men between the ages of 18 and 50, who were employed as mercenaries. They had a reputation as bold and brave fighters and were bound by a strict code of honor. Most of the saga is set in the 9th and 10th centuries and concerns the Danish kings, Harald Blue-Tooth and Svein Forkbeard. The Jomsvikings are said to have fought for Harald at **Hjörungavágr**, where they were defeated by **Hákon Jarl**; and according to Snorri's *Heimskringla*, Sigvaldi is said to have betrayed **Olaf Tryggvason** at **Svöld**.

JÓRVIK. *See* YORK.

JUMNE. *See* WOLIN.

– K –

KANHAVE CANAL. This canal was constructed on the Danish island of Samsø, linking the natural harbor of Stavnsfjörd on the east coast with the sea to the west. The canal runs for about one kilometer and is some 11 kilometers wide, with a depth that would allow ships with a draft of up to 1.25 meters to pass through the canal. Its sloping sides were lined with wood, which has been dated by **dendrochronology** to *c.* 726. This date suggests that the canal may have been constructed for the eighth-century king of Denmark, **Angantyr**, possibly as a way of controlling traffic passing through the Storebælt to the Baltic Sea.

KARLEVI STONE. Rune-stone from the Baltic island of Öland, off Sweden's southeastern coast, which was raised around the year 1000 to commemorate a chieftain called Sibbe Foldarsson. The inscription on the Karlevi stone includes the only stanza of **skaldic poetry** composed in the **dróttkvætt** meter to be found on a runestone and therefore is the only known example of this genre preserved from the Viking Age: "Hidden lies the man whom the greatest virtues accompanied—most men knew that—*executor of the goddess of battles* (= warrior)—in this mound. A more honest *battle-strong god of the wagon of the mighty ground of the sea-king* (= captain) will not rule over land in Denmark."

KAUPANG. Viking-Age town on Viksfjörd in Vestfold, southern Norway. There is no clear reference to Kaupang in written sources, although it may possibly be identified with *Sciringesheal*, a trading town mentioned by the Norwegian chieftain, **Ohthere**. Excavations at Kaupang began in 1867, but the most extensive investigation to date of both the settlement and the surrounding cemeteries was undertaken between 1950–1970. Even so, less than 3 percent of the estimated 40,000 square meters that Kaupang occupied have been examined archaeologically. The earliest traces of settlement are dated to around 800 and the site was in use until the 10th century. It appears that Kaupang was never as large as **Birka** in Sweden or **Hedeby** in Denmark, being a small market center of local importance rather than an internationally significant town, and the **houses** excavated lacked hearths, suggesting only seasonal occupation. The town was abandoned by *c.* 900, perhaps because of a change in sea-levels or possibly due to a decline in links with Denmark (and Hedeby).

New excavations are currently ongoing in Kaupang to investigate the possibility that the town was more extensive or more permanently occupied than earlier investigations suggest. To date, these have revealed occupation dating back to the eighth century, with evidence of glass, amber, and textile production, the existence of regular plots of land, and the presence of buildings that were occupied during winter. No evidence suggesting a longer period of occupation has as yet been found. The preliminary results are expected to be processed and published by *c.* 2006.

KENNING. A form of **skaldic** diction, kennings are compounds that are essentially riddles. The solution to these riddles generally lies in Scandinavian heroic or **mythological** tales. For this reason, it can be hard for the modern reader to solve those kennings for which there are no contemporary explanations. In their simplest form, a kenning may consist of two words, such as "otter payment," meaning gold; "Ymir's blood," meaning the sea; or "wound-bee," meaning arrow. However, they may be more complex, although **Snorri Sturluson** stipulated in his *Prose Edda* that kennings within a kenning should not exceed five in number. The longest kenning on record was constructed by Þórðr Særeksson: "The sword-swinger in driven snow (= battle), with the troll of the shield (= ax), like a protective moon on the side of the steed of the boathouse (= **ship**)," which taken altogether means "man." Kennings were perhaps used by poets as a way of providing variety of expression within the strict metrical confines of the skaldic verse forms.

KENSINGTON STONE. The Kensington stone is a slab of greywacke, allegedly inscribed with **runes**, weighing 92 kilograms and measuring 76 × 40 × 15 centimeters, and is currently kept in the Alexandria Chamber of Commerce in Minnesota. It was found near Kensington, Douglas County, Minnesota in August 1898 by a Swedish immigrant farmer, Olof Ohman, from Forsa, Hälsingeland. The stone was apparently in the roots of an ash or poplar tree, estimated to be between 5 and 12 years old, that Ohman was grubbing up. The inscription reads: "8 Goths (or Götar [*see* **Götaland**]) and 22 Norwegians on an exploration journey from **Vinland** westward. We had our camp by 2 rocky islets one day's journey north of this stone. We were out fishing one day. When we came home we found 10 men red with blood and dead. AV[E] M[ARIA] save us from evil. We have 10 men by the sea to look after our ships, 14 days' journey from this island. Year 1362."

The first two scholars to examine the Kensington Stone, Professor Olaf Breda of Scandinavian Studies at the University of Minnesota and Professor George Curme in the Germanic Department at Northwestern University, both concluded that the inscription was modern. Leading Scandinavian runologists and philologists, such as Ludwig Wimmer of the National Museum of Denmark, also came to the same conclusion. However, the authenticity of the Kensington Stone was championed vigorously by Norwegian-born historian, Hjalmar R. Holand, from 1907 until his death in 1964. Holand linked the stone to a medieval expedition by the Norwegian Paul Knutson, basing his argument upon a confused Danish translation made in 1600 of a lost letter, dated to 1354. According to this, Knutson was sent to **Greenland** by King Magnus of Denmark and Norway in order to ensure that **Christianity** was being upheld in this North-Atlantic colony. Holand argued that upon finding Greenland's Western Settlement deserted, Knutson sailed west and south to **North America**, traveling to Rhode Island, Hudson Bay, up the Nelson River to Lake Winnipeg, and along the Red River into Minnesota in search of the missing Scandinavians. Following Holand's lectures and publications, the stone was exhibited at the Smithsonian Institute in Washington, D.C., from February 1948 to February 1949, when a cast replaced it and remained on exhibition until 1953. Among the converts won by Holand were Ole G. Landsverk and Alf Mongé, who went on to develop their own theory about the Kensington rune-stone. According to them, the text concealed a cryptic message, and they extended their theory to include many other Scandinavian runic inscriptions that are considered genuine.

However, Scandinavian philologists and runologists have continued to reject the stone as a fake for many reasons. The runes are relatively fresh, with little evidence of weathering considering they were supposedly carved in the medieval period, although this may be because the stone was buried. The Kensington rune-stone mixes rune-forms in use from the 9th to the 11th century in a random fashion, plus others that are otherwise unknown, but there are none of the later runes known from Scandinavia although the Kensington runes were supposedly carved in 1362. The date 1362 is written in Arabic numerals, but these were not known by Europeans until the 15th century. The language of the Kensington rune-stone is a mixture of modern Swedish and Norwegian with few out-of-place medievalisms and some otherwise unattested words.

KETILL FLAT-NOSE (ON *Ketill flatnefr*). The most famous of Norse Hebrideans, Ketill's settlement in the **Hebrides** is described in a number of Icelandic sources, such as the ***Book of Settlements*** and

Laxdœla Saga. In Icelandic tradition, this settlement is associated with **Harald Fine-Hair's** western expedition around 875, but although the historicity of this expedition is extremely doubtful, the strong saga tradition suggests that Ketill indeed had some control over the Hebrides around the middle of the ninth century. Ketill has been identified with the Ketill *find* (White), leader of the **Gall-Gaedhil**, who, according to the ***Annals of Ulster***, were defeated by **Olaf the White** in 857, and although the identification cannot be proven, it seems reasonable. Ketill and his family certainly personify the cultural and ethnic mixture of Norse and native populations in the Isles that is suggested by other written sources and by the place-name and archaeological evidence: one of his daughters, **Aud the Deep-Minded**, married Olaf the White of **Dublin**; another daughter, Thorunn, was married to **Helgi the Lean**, who was the son of a Swede and an Irish princess and who worshipped Christ and **Thor**. During the early 10th century, Ketill's family left the Hebrides to settle in **Iceland**, a move that may be linked to the revival in the fortunes of the Norse kings of Dublin *c.* 919.

KIEV. City in European **Russia** and seat of **Rus** power. Kiev is strategically located above the **Dneiper** rapids and on the important river route south to **Byzantium**. Following Rurik's establishment of Scandinavian power in **Novgorod**, Kiev is said in the ***Russian Primary Chronicle*** to have been seized by the warriors Askold and Dir. Rurik's successor, Oleg (d. *c.* 913), apparently captured the town from them *c.* 882, and Kiev became the center of Rus power. Excavations have revealed that a fortress, overlooking the Dnieper, was constructed around 900, and a market and craft quarter emerged in Podol on the riverbank below the fortress.

Kiev's influence grew further following the conversion of Vladimir I (d. 1015) to **Christianity** in 988. Churches, monasteries, and Russia's first cathedral, dedicated to St. Sophia, were built in the town during the rules of Vladimir and his son and successor, **Jaroslav the Wise**. These, in turn, contributed to a flowering of literature and historical writing (including the *Russian Primary Chronicle*) in the Slavonic language. Jaroslav formally organized the Church hierarchy, which was headed by the metropolitan of Kiev. However, following the death of Jaroslav, the political, religious, and economic significance of Kiev began to slowly decline as trade routes shifted and as the town was threatened by attacks from the east. In 1240, Kiev was sacked by the Mongols, and European Russia was controlled by the Mongol khans, based at Sarai on the Volga, for about two centuries afterward.

KILMAINHAM—ISLANDBRIDGE. Before the excavations at **Dublin**, the most significant finds from Viking-Age **Ireland** came from Kilmainham and Islandbridge on the River Liffey, approximately two and three kilometers respectively from the center of Dublin. Here, there appear to have been two mid-ninth-century cemeteries associated with the **longphort** of 841 and which were probably in use until the expulsion of the Dublin Norse in 902. The first finds were made at Kilmainham during the excavation of a rail cutting and were recognized as Scandinavian grave goods in 1846. Although the **burials** were not properly excavated, a watercolor painting, made in 1847, illustrates some of the Kilmainham finds, and the material found was also recorded in a series of catalogs. More burials were uncovered at Islandbridge in 1866 and 1869, but these were not fully recorded at the time. In 1933–1934, the first and only controlled excavation of two further accompanied burials at Islandbridge took place.

Although they are frequently treated as one enormous cemetery, Kilmainham and Islandbridge are quite separate. Together, they account for about 60 percent of all the known Viking graves in Ireland, with a further 20 percent of graves found within an eight-kilometer radius of the center of Dublin. Despite the imperfect record of the 19th-century finds, it seems that there are at least 43 individual accompanied burials from these two sites: 30 from Kilmainham (27 male and three female) and 13 from Islandbridge (10 male and three female). The finds include at least 40 swords, spears, axes, oval brooches, weighing scales, and lead weights. The two Islandbridge graves excavated in the 1930s also revealed animal remains: the jawbone of a cow, and two teeth, one of an ox and the other of a horse.

KINGIKTORSSUAQ STONE. Small **rune-stone** of phyllite discovered by a **Greenland** Inuit in a cairn on an island north of Disko Bay in 1824. Its inscription is dated to *c.* 1300 and records that "Erlingr

Sigvatsson, Bjarni Þórðarson and Endridi Oddson made this cairn the Saturday before Rogation Day [25 April] and . . ." The inscription concludes with six cryptic runes, which have not yet been interpreted, of a type found on the cross-slab known as Andreas V on the **Isle of Man**; in inscriptions from **Russia** and the Baltic island of Öland; and on the Norum font from the southern Swedish province of Bohuslän.

KINGS' SAGAS (ON *Konungasögur*). The so-called *Kings' Sagas* were, as their name suggests, written about Viking-Age and medieval kings and their contents span a period from about the 9th to the 13th century. The line between history and literature is extremely hard to draw with this type of saga. The vast majority of these sagas were written in **Iceland** in the 12th and 13th centuries, drawing on three main writing traditions: that of Latin chronicles, Latin legends of individual saints, and vernacular and Latin narrative histories. While most of the Kings' Sagas deal with the lives and rules of Norwegian kings, there are a couple of sagas that deal with kings of Denmark: **Knýtlinga Saga** and *Knúts saga helga* (*see* **Knut II Sveinsson, St.**). The kings of Sweden appear incidentally in some sagas, but the only saga to mention them in more detail is *Ynglinga Saga*, an almost **mythological** composition that traces the Norwegian royal line back to Swedish kings and that forms the opening chapter in the most important collection of *Kings' Sagas*, *Heimskringla*.

KLÅSTAD SHIP. Viking-Age trading vessel, or *knarr*, found at Klåstad, near **Kaupang**, in southwest Norway in 1893. The **ship**, measuring some 18 meters in length, was excavated in 1970, and it has been dated by **dendrochronology** to *c.* 990. The cargo of the ship included schist from a quarry at Eidsborg, Telemark, Norway, which had been cut into rough blocks for use as whetstones.

KNÚTR I. *See* CNUT THE GREAT.

KNUT II SVEINSSON, ST. (d. 1086). King of Denmark 1080–1086, Knut was one of the sons of Danish king, **Svein Estrithsson**, by an unknown mother. Before ascending to the throne, he spent time raiding in England between 1069–1070, when, according to the *Anglo-*

Saxon Chronicle, Danish armies plundered Peterborough and Ely; he returned to England in 1075, apparently in order to restore Danish control of the country, but despite attacking **York** Minster, Knut's army "dared not to join battle with King William," and decided instead to turn south to Flanders, seeking additional support against William the Conqueror. Knut later married Adela, the daughter of Count Robert I of Flanders. Knut continued to harbor ambitions of a Danish reconquest of England after he succeeded his elder brother, Harald Hén (r. 1074–1080), to the Danish throne in 1080, but became increasingly involved in the protection of Denmark's southern borders against the expansion of the German emperor, Henry IV.

At home, Knut introduced a number of financial measures to aid the clergy, the poor, and **women**, and he began the construction of a Romanesque cathedral in Odense, which was dedicated to him following his martyrdom on 10 July 1086 and subsequent canonization. Knut was killed in the church of St. Alban, containing relics of the saint that Knut had brought back with him from his raids in England. The rebels were those nobles and farmers who were involved in another expedition planned against England in 1085, who were annoyed at Knut's attempts to introduce higher taxation to finance the Danish Church and at his failure to join the fleet in Jutland. The Danish magnates involved in the murder of Knut promised to support his brother Olaf "Hunger" (r. 1086–1095), who in turn promised not to implement any of the financial and social reforms that Knut was threatening.

During Olaf's reign, however, there was famine and an epidemic, and the clergy claimed that God was expressing his anger with the Danes for killing their king, and the idea of Knut's sanctity started to grow. By 1095, the last year of Olaf's rule, Knut's remains were being credited with miracle cures. At the time of Knut's canonization in 1100, another of his brothers, Erik Ejegod (r. 1095–1103), was king of Denmark. Knut's saintly status was used as a tool by Erik and his brother and successor, Niels (r. 1104–1134), to establish their divine right to the throne of Denmark. Erik invited the Benedictine monastery of Evesham to set up a daughter priory, and one of its members, **Ælnoth**, wrote an account of Knut's *passio c.* 1122, promoting the dead king's cult. Erik was also responsible for the translation of Knut's relics to a new shrine on the altar of Odense's new cathedral.

KNÚTSDRÁPA ("Lay in Honor of Cnut"). Name of three **skaldic** poems, composed by **Óttarr the Black**, **Sighvatr Þórðarson,** and Hallfreðr háreksblesi respectively. Óttar's poem is preserved in *Knýtlinga Saga*. The poem deals with the military campaign of **Cnut I the Great** in England 1015–1016 and with the Battle of the **Holy River**. After reciting the poem at Cnut's court, Óttarr was apparently rewarded with a helmet full of silver. Sighvatr's poem was composed after Cnut's death and covers the king's pilgrimage to Rome in addition to the campaigns in England and at Holy River. Hallfreðr's poem emphasizes both Cnut's right to the English throne and his godliness.

KNÝTLINGA SAGA ("The Saga of the Knytlingar"). An Icelandic saga about the Danish kings who ruled from the 10th century until 1187. *Knýtlinga Saga* is believed to date from the middle of the 13th century and survives in two main manuscript traditions (designated A and B). The A group appears to be the oldest and was derived from a lost manuscript that was written *c*. 1300. The saga is particularly important for its **skaldic** verse, and some 50 of its 59 stanzas are not known from any other source. Like *Heimskringla*, which has the saga of the Norwegian royal martyr **Olaf Haraldsson** at its center, *Knýtlinga Saga* is dominated by the saga of **St. Knut II Sveinsson**. It has even been argued that the saga was composed by **Snorri Sturluson's** nephew, Óláfr Þórðarson hvítaskáld (d. 1259). The writer of the saga used Icelandic sources, such as *Heimskringla* and the *Saga of the Jomsvikings* (*see* **Jomsvikings**), and Danish sources, including **Ælnoth's** *Gesta Swenomagni*.

KONUNGASÖGUR. See KINGS' SAGAS.

KUFIC COINS. Silver coins frequently found in Viking-Age hoards in Scandinavia, which were produced from the mines at Transoxiana, central Asia, in the kingdom of the Muslim Arabs. The word "Kufic" is derived from the town of Kufah in present-day Iraq and was used to describe the script used on these coins. Until the middle of the 10th century, most of the silver reaching Scandinavia came from this source. However, after this date, the mines were exhausted and European sources of silver, notably German, replaced the Arabic.

KULI STONE. This is perhaps one of the most famous of Norwegian runic inscriptions (*see* **rune**) and can currently be found standing in the Vitenskapsmuseet, **Trondheim**. It was, however, originally set up on farmland on the remote island of Kuløy, which lies off the coast of the west Norwegian province of Møre and Romsdal, where a replica of the stone now stands. The top of the rune-stone is missing, and the fragmentary inscription has traditionally been read: "Thorir and Hallvard raised this stone in memory of Ulfljot [. . .] twelve winters had Christianity been (uirit ON *verit*) in Norway . . . "

The mention of a relative date ("twelve winters") in this inscription is unparalleled in any other Viking-Age runic inscription. However, unfortunately historians have problems in working out what the inscription meant by **Christianity** being in Norway. **Hákon the Good** had attempted to convert his subjects as early as the first half of the 10th century, although apparently with little success. Some scholars date the Christianization of Norway to the time of **Olav Tryggvason's** rule at the end of the 10th century, when he traveled around Norway using brute force to convert his subjects to Christianity and formally adopt it at their local assemblies, which might give a date of around 1008 for the raising of the Kuli stone. However, other scholars argue that the date from which the Kuli stone must be dated is the acceptance of Christian law at the national assembly in Moster in the 1020s, perhaps 1024, over which the later saint, **Olaf Haraldsson**, presided.

In 1984, archaeological excavations revealed that the stone had originally been placed at the end of the foundations of a wooden bridge that was laid over marshy ground. The most recent date for the Kuli stone is taken from the **dendrochronological** dating (counting of tree rings) of this bridge, which is 1034. This gives a date of 1022 for the acceptance of Christianity in Norway, which would fit well with the establishment of Christian law at the Moster **thing**.

The Kuli stone itself has been re-examined recently, using computerized micro-mapping, and a new reading based on this analysis by Jan Ragnar Hagland suggests that the traditional uirit is in fact um rit (ON *um rétt*) meaning "improved/corrected (things)," perhaps in terms of securing law and order.

KVÍVÍK. Site of a late 10th-century **longhouse** on the island of Streymoy, which is the best preserved Viking-Age farmstead on the **Faroe Islands**. Unfortunately, part of the site is now lost, having been eroded by the sea. A large rectangular house, some 20 meters long, with a central hearth and thick stone and turf walls stood at Kvívík, along with a byre that could house about 12 cattle in stone stalls. Finds from the site include a wooden toy horse. Kvívík provides some of the earliest evidence for Scandinavian settlement on the Faroe Islands.

– L –

LABRADOR. *See* MARKLAND.

LADBY SHIP. Ship burial discovered on a ridge overlooking Keterminde Fjord, northeast Fyn, Denmark, in the 1930s. Most of ship's hull has rotted away, but it has been possible to reconstruct it on the basis of the impression left in the ground and the positioning of the remaining iron rivets that fastened the planking to the hull. The ship was 20.6 meters long, 2.9 meters broad, and 0.7 meters deep, with 16 pairs of oars. It had first been covered by a wooden roof and then a mound had been constructed over it. A full-size reconstruction of the ship, *Imme Gran*, has been built and sailed successfully.

There was evidence that the grave had been disturbed and possibly robbed at some point. No body has been found and many of the grave goods are fragmented or dispersed over the stern section of the boat. However, some 6,000 articles or fragments of articles have been uncovered, and the number and character of these suggests a high-status burial. Finds include the remains of 11 horses, 4 dogs, decorated harnesses for the dogs and horses, a solid silver buckle of ninth-century Frankish (*see* **Carolingian**) workmanship, 45 arrowheads, and a wooden gaming board. The burial has been dated to the 10th century.

LADE (ON *Hlaðir*). Lade was the seat of a number of powerful Viking-Age **earls**, located on the outskirts of present-day **Trondheim** in Norway. It was the political and religious center of the Trøndelag region before being superseded by the town of Trondheim and before the power of its earls was eclipsed by the kings of Norway. Icelandic sources suggests that a now-lost saga about the Earls of Lade, *Hlaðajarla saga, may have existed. Certainly, the earls emerge as powerful political figures in Snorri's **Heimskringla** and are frequently cast in the role of kingmakers.

Hákon Grjótgarðsson is the first recorded earl of Lade, and he is said to have been allowed to retain his autonomy in Trøndelag in return for his support of **Harald Fine-Hair**. The most powerful of the earls was **Hákon Jarl** Sigurdsson, who overthrew **Harald Grey-Cloak** of Norway and cast off the overlordship of **Harald Blue-Tooth** of Denmark. Hákon Jarl's son, Erik, married **Svein Forkbeard's** daughter, Gytha, and campaigned in England with his brother-in-law, **Cnut I the Great**. Cnut appointed Erik as his first earl of **Northumbria** in 1017, but during Erik's absence in England, Erik's brother, Earl Svein, was driven out of Norway. The last earl of Lade, Hákon Eriksson, drowned in 1029.

LADOGA. *See* STARAJA LADOGA.

LANDNÁMABÓK. See BOOK OF SETTLEMENTS.

LANGBARÐALAND. Lombardy in northern Italy, but *Langbarða-land* was used by speakers of Old Norse to refer to Italy in general.

L'ANSE AUX MEADOWS. L'Anse aux Meadows on Epaves Bay in northeast Newfoundland is a Norse settlement site from around 1000, discovered in 1960 by Helge and Anne Stine Ingstad and subsequently excavated from 1961–1968. Further excavations were undertaken between 1973–1976 under Birgitta Wallace.

The site consists of eight buildings made of turf and wood, of which three were **longhouses** or halls, divided into three distinct complexes with one outlying building. Each of the halls had a smaller hut placed nearby, and one of the halls had two such huts; at least two of these four huts were probably workshops, but people may also have lived in them. The outlying eighth building was an isolated hut placed on the other side of the nearby Black Duck Brook, which contained a furnace for making iron from the bog iron ore found nearby. Finds from the buildings include iron rivets, a stone lamp, a soapstone spindle whorl, a bronze ring-headed cloak pin, and fire-starters made of jasper from **Iceland** and **Greenland**—all of which are paralleled on Norse sites in the North Atlantic and Scandinavia. In addition to this, some 30 pounds of iron and bronze slag, wooden objects worked by iron tools, and incinerated animal bones were recovered from the site. However, no evidence of cultivation nor any outbuildings for sheltering livestock has been found at L'Anse aux Meadows, indicating that its inhabitants were not self-sustaining farmers. The site was occupied for only a short time, but the buildings were solidly constructed, with permanent roofs, indicating that they were intended for year-round rather than seasonal use. Between 70 and 90 people could have lived in this settlement. The abandonment of the site was planned and orderly, with virtually all equipment taken with the inhabitants; the apparently deliberate burning of two of the emptied halls might have been done by the departing inhabitants or by the Native American population.

On the basis of the archaeological finds, Birgitta Wallace has suggested that it was a short-lived temporary base for a largely male group, who spent their summers exploring the lands further south. She draws parallels with the Leifsbuðir/Straumfjörd settlement in Vinland described in the *Saga of Erik the Red*. Proof of the southern voyages of the inhabitants of L'Anse aux Meadows has been found in the discovery of two butternuts during the excavations. These walnuts have never grown in Newfoundland, and the nearest location at which they can be found in the Saint Lawrence River valley in New Brunswick, east of present-day Quebec City.

L'Anse aux Meadows was the first and is still the only known Norse settlement site in **North America**. On the basis of the finds from the site, it has been identified as lying within the region known as **Vinland** in the Icelandic sagas. As L'Anse aux Meadows lies too far north for wild grapes to grow, Ingstad supported the suggestion that the name Vinland (ON *Vínland*) was in fact a mistranslation of

Old Norse *Vinland* meaning "land of meadows." This name would fit well with L'Anse aux Meadows, where there is a wide expanse of pastureland along Epaves Bay. However, the saga tradition is clear that Vinland was a "land of wine," and describes the discovery of grapes in considerable detail. Similarly, **Adam of Bremen's** 11th-century history refers to "Wineland."

Despite the finds at L'Anse aux Meadows, some scholars have doubted the equation of Newfoundland with Vinland, arguing that neither interpretation of the name Vinland would fit this location on Epaves Bay: it is too far north for grapes to grow (if Vinland is derived from ON *vin* "vine"); and although it is in an area of rich meadowland (if Vinland is derived from ON *vín* "meadow, pasture"), this place-name element was not current in West Norse place-names and, even if it was derived from East Norse usage, that word is normally only used as the second element in place-names. However, although grapes have never grown as far north as L'Anse aux Meadows, they do grow in New Brunswick, and this might perhaps be the location of the place called Hóp in the *Vinland Sagas*, which is described as lying to the south of the Norse base at Straumfjörd.

LAW-CODES, DANISH. The earliest attested Danish law-code, the *Vederlov* or "Law of the **Hird**," was written down *c*. 1180, although the authors claimed that its provisions dated from the reign of King **Cnut I the Great**. Between *c*. 1200–1241, the provincial laws of Jutland, Sjælland (Zealand), and Skåne (Scania) were compiled and copied, although none of the surviving manuscripts predate 1250.

LAW-CODES, ICELANDIC. The preserved Icelandic law-codes are known as *Grágás* "the Grey Goose." *Grágás* is essentially a mid-13th-century collection of old and new legal material that included an earlier tithe law of 1096 and the old Christian law, which was probably compiled in the 1140s. However, it is known from the *Book of the Icelanders* that Icelandic law-codes had been drawn up well before this, in the early Viking Age. The first code was apparently modeled on the Norwegian **Gulathing** law and was named Úlfljót's Law (*Úlfljótslög*) after its author, Úlfljót, who is said to have traveled to Norway in the early 10th century in order to find a model for the law of the newly established Icelandic commonwealth. The *Book of the*

Icelanders also records the decision to record laws in writing, which was taken at the **Althing** in 1117, and which resulted in the law-code known as *Hafliðaskrá*, named after Hafliði Másson, who was responsible for producing this first written copy of **Iceland's** laws.

LAW-CODES, NORWEGIAN. Norway had four legal provinces in the Viking Age: **Gulathing** (western Norway), *Frostuthing* (Trøndelag), *Eiðsifathing* (eastern Norway), and *Borgarthing* (Oslofjörd). In addition to these provincial law-codes, there was also the law of the towns, so-called **Bjarkeyjarréttr** or Bjarkøy laws. These laws were later revised and promulgated as a national law-code (*Landlög*) by King Magnus Erlingsson in the 1270s.

LAW-CODES, SWEDISH. Sweden's surviving law-codes are all medieval in date and there are no manuscripts that can be dated to before *c.* 1300. The provincial law-codes are generally divided into two main categories: the Svea Laws, which concerned the provinces of central eastern Sweden (*see* **Svealand**); and the Göta Laws, which applied to southern Sweden (*see* **Götaland**). In addition to this, there was a municipal law-code, Bjärkö Law (*Bjärköratten*), which applied originally to Stockholm. A new national law-code and municipal law-code was issued by King Magnus Eriksson around 1350.

LAW-ROCK. *See* ALTHING.

LAXDÆLA SAGA (**ON** *Laxdæla saga*). One of the greatest of the so-called *Sagas of Icelanders* written by an unknown author in **Iceland** around 1245 and preserved in six medieval manuscripts and fragments, the fullest of which is the 14th-century manuscript *Möðruvallabók*. It has been suggested that Óláfr Þórðarson hvítaskald (d. 1259) was the author, but others have argued that it was written by a **woman**, because of the unusual prominence of female characters in the saga.

The saga is essentially a dynastic chronicle of the Laxdale family, running from the settlement of their founding members, **Aud the Deep-Minded** and her brothers Björn and Helgi, in the Dales district of Breiðafjörður, western Iceland, in the late ninth century, up until the death of Gudrun Ósvífrsdóttir, a descendant of Björn, *c.* 1060. However, the saga is centered on Gudrun, her third (of four marriages) marriage to Bolli, one of Aud's descendants, and her tragic romance with Kjartan Olafsson, another of Aud's descendants. Gudrun, the great-grandmother of **Ari Thorgilsson**, persuaded Bolli to kill her former lover, Kjartan, triggering a blood feud between the two branches of the family that was only resolved by Snorri the Priest (d. 1031), another of Aud's descendants.

LEIF THE LUCKY ERIKSSON (*c.* 975–1020). Leif was the son of **Erik the Red** and, it is claimed, the first Scandinavian to set foot in **North America**. According to the *Saga of Erik the Red*, he was known as Leif the Lucky because of his rescue of a wrecked ship's crew and cargo. The account of Leif's discovery of **Vinland** is contained in the *Saga of the Greenlanders* and the *Saga of Erik the Red*. The more reliable *Saga of the Greenlanders* records that the Icelander **Bjarni Herjólfsson** was the first Scandinavian to sight land in North America, and that Leif bought Bjarni's ship and retraced his route; while the *Saga of Erik the Red*, which generally emphasizes the importance of Erik's descendants, claims that Leif actually discovered the "lands whose existence he had never suspected."

LEIÐANGR (Danish *leding*, Swedish *ledung*). The name of the **ship** levy used to raise fleets for the defense of medieval kingdoms of Scandinavia. **Snorri Sturluson** attributes the establishment of this institution in Norway to **Hákon the Good**, who is said to have divided the country's coastal districts into *skipreiður* that were each responsible for providing and equipping a longship. However, although Hákon probably reorganized Norway's coastal defenses, the system Snorri describes appears to be that known in Norway during his own lifetime and there is no contemporary evidence for its existence in the Viking Age. Similarly, although it has been claimed that the *leding* system in Denmark dates from the reigns of **Svein Forkbeard** and **Cnut I the Great**, there is no evidence for its existence there until the very end of the Viking Age, during the reign of **St. Knut II Sveinsson**. The first Swedish evidence for the *ledung* comes from the medieval period.

LEJRE. Royal seat and cult site located on the Danish island of Sjælland, south of present-day Roskilde, which has been identified with the legendary *Hleiðargarð* in the ***Saga of Hrólfr Kraki*** from as early as the twelfth century. According to this saga, Lejre was the seat of the Skjoldung dynasty, and it has also been identified with the royal hall, *Heorot*, in the Anglo-Saxon epic poem, *Beowulf*.

Excavations at Lejre in the mid-1980s uncovered the remains of a massive hall, measuring 48.3 meters by 11.5 meters, dated to the mid-ninth century. This hall, the largest yet known from Scandinavia, overlay a similar construction dating to the mid-seventh century. The nearby princely **burial** mound, *Grydehøj*, which is dated to the mid-sixth century, further testifies to Lejre's importance in the Migration Age. An 80-meter-long ship-setting provides some evidence of the religious and cultic functions of the site. Thietmar of Merseburg, writing in the early 11th century, also records a ritual sacrifice at Lejre, which is described as the capital of Denmark. This rite seems to offer a Danish parallel to that held in Swedish **Gamla Uppsala**; it took place every nine years, in January, and involved the sacrifice of 99 men, and the same number of horses, as well as dogs and cocks. Thietmar's description is apparently based on information obtained in 934, when the German Emperor, Henry I, invaded Denmark.

LEWIS CHESSMEN. A collection of some 78 chessmen, along with 14 plain counters (for another board game, the predecessor of checkers) and a belt-buckle, were discovered in a drystone chamber in the sand dunes of Uig Bay on the island of Lewis in the Outer **Hebrides** in 1831. Most of the chessmen are carved from walrus ivory, although a few may be made from whale's teeth. Some of the pieces may be unfinished. The hoard may have belonged to a merchant traveling along the sea route from Scandinavia to the Norse colonies in the West, or perhaps to a walrus-ivory carver.

The chessmen comprise almost four complete chess sets, with 8 kings, 8 queens, 16 bishops, 15 knights, 12 warders (castles or rooks), and 19 pawns. The kings and queens sit on thrones and are wearing crowns; the kings hold a sword across their knees, and the queens are holding the right side of their faces with their right hands. All of the bishops have miters and crosiers, and some also have a book or hold their right hands up in a blessing. The knights are armed with shield, spear, and sword and are wearing conical helmets. The warders are depicted as helmeted foot soldiers, armed with sword and shields (one of the warders is shown biting his shield). The pawns are abstract and are not depicted as human.

The ornamentation and details of **weapons** and dress on these beautifully detailed minisculptures suggest a date in the second half of the 12th century. Research by staff from the British Museum has drawn attention to parallels in the foliage ornament on the back of the thrones with that on some early stave-church portals in western Norway, and on some stone sculpture in **Trondheim**, and suggests that they may have been produced in Trondheim, where a similar and now-lost queen was also discovered in the 1880s, during excavations of St. Olaf's Church, underneath the present-day Public Library.

LIBER DE MENSURA ORBIS TERRÆ. *See BOOK OF THE MEA-SUREMENT OF THE EARTH*.

LIÐ. Old Norse word for the men following a particular lord, generally used in the sense of a group of warriors or an army. Individual members of the *lið* were known as *félagi* (*see* **félag**), who appear to have been bound to each other and their lord by an unwritten code of honor and loyalty. A *lið* might vary in size from just a few men to sufficient warriors to man a large fleet.

LINDHOLM HØJE. Site of a large Viking-Age cemetery near Limfjörd in northern Jutland, Denmark. Most of the 700 or so **burials** are cremations, and about 200 of these are marked by stones set in the shapes of ships, squares, triangles, and circles. The earliest burials date to the sixth century and the cemetery finally appears to have gone out of use around the year 1100, when the associated settlement was abandoned because of drifting sand dunes. In addition to the cemetery, excavations of the village in the 1950s revealed a Viking-Age field, some 30 meters by 40 meters, which had been "fossilized" by a thick layer of sand blown over it in a storm some time during the 11th century. As well as the long furrows that had been ploughed, footprints and wheel tracks across the field were also preserved.

LINDISFARNE. Tidal island off the Northumbrian coast, also known as Holy Island, which was an important and early center of **Christianity** in northern England. A monastery was founded by St. Aidan of **Iona** on the site given him by King Oswald of **Northumbria** in 635. However, the monastery is most closely associated with St. Cuthbert, who was a member of the Lindisfarne community and whose body was buried to the right of St. Peter's altar in March 687. When, some 11 years later, the monks dug up Cuthbert's body in order to place it in a small casket, they apparently found that his body was completely uncorrupted. Cuthbert's shrine became the most important cult center in the English kingdom of Northumbria, and the *Lindisfarne Gospels* reflect the wealth of the community as well as its technical expertise in the late seventh and eighth centuries. However, this fame and wealth also seems to have had some undesirable side effects: frequent visits from members of royalty and nobility must have interfered with religious life and to have perhaps provided temptations of the flesh that were hard to resist. Both Bede, in his *Ecclesiastical History of the English People*, and **Alcuin** of **York** hint that monastic observance was not as it should be in the monastery of St. Cuthbert.

The community on Lindisfarne was attacked by **Vikings** in June 793, perhaps the single most famous Viking raid in western Europe. Details of the attack were later recorded in the ***Anglo-Saxon Chronicle***, which mentions "terrible portents" that preceded the raid: "fiery dragons," perhaps comets, in the sky, lightning and famine. Letters from Alcuin of York, written from the court of **Charlemagne** in Aachen, also discuss the attack, interpreting it as God's divine judgment on a sinful Northumbria. Although the *Chronicle* mentions "looting and slaughter," the community nevertheless survived the attack. However, some years later, the threat of further attack forced the monks to leave the island, taking with them Cuthbert's relics and those of other saints, and even dismantling the timber church of St. Peter to take with them. Nevertheless, stone sculpture dating from the ninth to the 11th centuries suggest that some kind of religious activity continued on the island. Interestingly, one piece, dating to *c*. 900, shows scenes associated with Doomsday: on the one side of the grave marker is a cross, flanked by the sun and the moon, and on the other, an army of warriors with axes and swords held above their heads, a scene that has generally been interpreted as a Viking army.

The community of St. Cuthbert found two temporary resting places, at Norham on Tweed, which they left at the end of the ninth century, and at Chester-le-Street, where they spent 112 years, before moving to Durham in or around 995. Benedictine monks from Durham recolonized the island in the 1090s, but Cuthbert's relics are today still in Durham, in the Norman Cathedral there. No visible remains of the Anglo-Saxon monastery can today be seen on the island; the ruins that are still standing there are of the later Benedictine abbey.

LJÓÐAHÁTTR ("song meter"). One of the principal meters of **Eddic poetry**, a *ljóðaháttr* stanza consists of two long lines with four stresses and two alliterative syllables, and two half lines with two stresses and two alliterative syllables. These are arranged alternatively so that the stanza begins with a long line, followed by a short line, the second long line, and the second short line.

LÖGBERG. *See* ALTHING.

LOKASENNA ("Loki's blasphemies"). One of the poems of the *Poetic Edda* in which **Loki** throws insults and accusations at all the major gods and goddesses. The reason for this outburst is Loki's exclusion from a feast in Ægir's hall, because he had killed one of Ægir's servants. Among his insults, he accuses **Idun**, **Freya**, and **Frigg** of infidelity and promiscuity; **Bragi** of cowardice; **Odin** of sorcery; **Niord** of being a hostage, whose mouth was used as a urinal by the daughters of giants; and **Tyr** of allowing Loki to have a child with his wife without seeking compensation. Only **Thor** is able to silence him, by threatening him with **Mjöllnir**, his hammer, but not before Loki has also accused him of cowardice.

LOKI. Although a god of the **Æsir**, Loki is a puzzling figure in Norse **mythology**. In the *Prose Edda*, he is said to be the son of a giant called Farbauti by the giant's wife, Laufey or Nal; with the giantess, Angrboda, Loki had three offspring: the goddess **Hel** and two mythical beasts, the **Midgard serpent** and the wolf **Fenrir**. He had the ability to change shape and, as a mare, Loki gave birth to **Odin's** horse, **Sleipnir**; he is also recorded as taking on the form of an otter and a salmon.

In the numerous mythological sources that mention Loki, he acts both for and against the gods of the Æsir. For example, one of the stories in the *Prose Edda* in which he plays a role, that of the abduction of the goddess **Idun**, sees him handing over Idun to the giant Þjazi but then helping the Æsir to rescue her and the apples of youth that she guarded. Similarly, when **Thor** lost his hammer to the giants, he was accompanied by Loki on his journey to Jotunheim, and Loki helped him to win it back (*see* **Þrymskviða**). He also helped the gods get the better of the giant who built the wall around **Asgard**.

On the negative side, Loki was responsible for the death of **Balder** and, as punishment, was bound by the gods to a rock under dripping poison. The fetters with which he was bound are said to be the intestines of his son Vali, who had been turned into a wolf that then devoured Loki's other son, Narfi. Loki was only saved from death by his wife, Sigyn, who held a bowl to catch the poison. When Loki finally broke free from these fetters, he led his offspring monsters and the inhabitants of Hel, from the helm of his ship Naglfar, against the gods in the final battle of **Ragnarök**. He and **Heimdall** kill each other in this battle.

One of the most famous episodes from the *Poetic Edda* that concerns Loki is found in the mythological poem, ***Lokasenna***, which records his verbal lambasting of virtually all of the Norse pagan deities.

LONDON. The Anglo-Saxon settlement and port of *Lundenwic* was located to the east of the city's Roman walls, near the present-day Strand. It was not until the late ninth century that post-Roman settlement in the walled area of London appears to have begun in earnest, and at the same time the undefended *Lundenwic* was abandoned. This renewed activity within the city walls, initially in the western part of the city near the cathedral, may be associated with the "refoundation" of London by **Alfred the Great** in 886. Certainly the **Viking** attacks that are recorded in written sources of the period would have made the protection offered by the city walls an important and attractive factor in any settlement. The inhabitants of London had already suffered a number of attacks: the first of these was in 842, which was shortly afterward followed by the arrival of 350 **ships** on the Thames in 851 (although doubt has been cast on the accuracy of this figure of 350, as it is exactly 10 times the size of the fleet mentioned in the years 843 and 836). The ***Anglo-Saxon Chronicle*** mentions that the

Viking armies also wintered in London in 872, and the entry for 886 suggests that the city may have been in the hands of the Danes before Alfred occupied the town in this year.

There is little written evidence for London in the 10th century. However, by the second quarter of the 10th century, London was among the most important mints in the country, with eight moneyers. During the 10th and early 11th century, the city emerged as the most important mint and the most important seat of Æthelred II's government. Excavations have confirmed the rapid expansion of settlement inside the walls following about 950. Toward the end of the 10th century Viking raids recommenced, and London's status seems to have made it a favorite target. In 992, the English fleet gathered in London in an unsuccessful attempt to counter the renewed Viking threat. In 994, an army led by **Olaf Tryggvason** and **Svein Forkbeard** attacked the city, and the *Anglo-Saxon Chronicle* entry for 1009 claims that although London was frequently attacked by the Vikings, it had survived these attacks "untouched." However, after Æthelred's death in 1016, there was much activity in and around London by the Scandinavian army of **Cnut I the Great**, and the *Anglo-Saxon Chronicle* reports that Vikings overwintered in the city in 1016, before Cnut succeeded to the English throne in 1017. This intense military action is reflected in the large numbers of Scandinavian-type swords, spearheads, axes, and stirrups that have been found in London, particularly near the Thames.

It is noticeable that the majority of the noncombative "Scandinavian" objects discovered in London are decorated in the early 11th-century **Ringerike** style, and can therefore probably be associated with the reigns of Cnut and his sons. As the culture of king and noble, Scandinavian culture was certainly raised in prestige and was probably favored by a wider circle of non-Scandinavians, who wished to emulate the fashions of the court. The Ringerike-style artifacts from London include two stone fragments from the City of London; a fragmentary slab from All-Hallows-by-the-Tower, Barking; a bone pin from the Thames; bronze plates from Smithfield, London, and the splendid **rune-stone** found in the graveyard of St. Paul's Cathedral.

Scandinavian influence in London is suggested by a variety of other sources. The church of St. Clement, later called St. Clement

Danes, served a mid-11th-century Danish suburb between Westminster and Fleet Street. There were several churches dedicated to the Scandinavian saints, **St. Olaf Haraldsson** and **St. Magnus**, although it is not certain whether the Magnus dedication is the patron saint of Norse Orkney or a more obscure figure. The church of St. Nicholas Acon, founded at some point after *c*. 1040, owes the second element of its name to a man bearing the Scandinavian name Hákon.

LONGHOUSE. *See* HOUSES.

LONGPHORT. Irish Gaelic term used to describe the first permanent bases of the **Viking** armies in **Ireland**, essentially fortified harbors that protected the **ships** of the armies. According to the *Annals of Ulster*, the first *longphort* was established in **Dublin** in 841 and others were subsequently built at Waterford, Wexford, **Cork**, and Limerick. Many of these *longphorts* developed into towns and trading centers.

LONGSHIPS. *See* SHIPS.

LOTHAR (d. 855). King of the so-called Middle Kingdom of Lotharingia and Italy after the Treaty of Verdun (843), Lothar was the eldest son of **Louis the Pious**. He had been made coemperor of the **Carolingian Empire** and heir in 817, but later rebelled against Louis following the birth of his half brother **Charles the Bald**. Lothar is said to have granted Walcheren in **Frisia** to a **Viking** called Harald in 841, in return for his support in the rebellion against Louis the Pious. After Lothar's death in 855, his territory was subdivided between his three sons (Louis II, Charles, and Lothar II), and following the deaths of Charles and Lothar II, Lothar's brothers, **Louis the German** and **Charles the Bald**, divided Lotharingia between them.

LOUIS THE GERMAN (d. 876). King of the so-called Eastern Kingdom after the Treaty of Verdun (843), Louis was the son of **Louis the Pious** and the father of **Charles the Fat**. His kingdom was partitioned between his three sons in 864 (Charles the Fat, Carloman, and Louis the Younger), a division that was confirmed on his death.

LOUIS THE PIOUS (778–840). Emperor of the Franks 814–840, Louis was the only surviving son of **Charlemagne** and the father of **Lothar**, **Louis the German**, Pippin, and **Charles the Bald**. Lothar was appointed co-emperor and heir in 817, and Pippin and Louis the German were given their own subkingdoms. However, this arrangement was upset by Louis's marriage to Judith of Bavaria in 819 and the birth of their son, Charles the Bald, in 823. Charles was granted his own subkingdom in 829, provoking rebellion on the part of his three elder sons, led by Lothar. Louis was deposed 829–830 and 833–834, and his death in 840 was followed by civil war between his three surviving sons Lothar, Louis, and Charles that was only resolved in the division of the **Carolingian Empire** at Verdun. The conflict that characterized the 830s coincided with or resulted in a serious escalation of **Viking** activity. Louis tried to counter this with new fortifications on the Rhine in 835 and 837 and through diplomatic means: he supported the Danish king **Harald Klak** in his bid for power and initiated **Ansgar's** mission to convert the Danes to **Christianity**.

LUND. Town in Skåne, present-day Sweden, which belonged to Denmark during the Viking Age. It has been suggested that the name Lund was modeled on that of **London**, the seat of **Cnut I the Great**, who is said to have played a significant role in founding the town. However, archaeological excavations suggest that the town's foundation predates Cnut's reign, and that the earliest settlement took place in the late 10th century. Nevertheless, the town thrived on its connections with the royal court and with the Church. Cnut is known to have established a mint in the town, and by the middle of the 11th century Lund had some five churches. Although there is evidence for craft production in the town, particularly leather working, trade was much less important than in the early Viking-Age trading centers and towns of Scandinavia. Around 1060, a bishopric was founded in Lund, and the town became the ecclesiastical center of Scandinavia in 1104 with its elevation to the status of an archbishopric. Work on a Romanesque cathedral began shortly afterward in the 1120s.

– M –

MAGNUS III BARE-FOOT OLAFSSON (ON *Magnús berfœttr*) (1073–1103). King of Norway from 1093 until his death. Son of **Olaf the Peaceful**, Magnus ruled with his cousin Hákon Magnússon for the first two years following his father's death. He is particularly remembered for his campaign to tie the western colonies closer to Norway and to assert Norwegian royal control over these settlements. During his first expedition westward in 1098, he succeeded in installing his own son, Sigurd, as ruler of the earldom of **Orkney**, in subjugating the **Hebrides** and the **Isle of Man**, and in winning control of the island of Anglesey, off the north coast of **Wales**. As *Heimskringla* records, this latter conquest was the southernmost area in the British Isles over which a Norwegian king had ever ruled. Magnus's expedition was concluded with a treaty with King Edgar of **Scotland**, which recognized Magnus's sovereignty over the southern Hebrides.

Magnus launched a second western expedition in 1102, spending the winter at the court of the Irish high king after capturing **Dublin**. He was killed while campaigning in Ulster, northern **Ireland**, during the following summer. The Irish ambushed his army as it scouted for food to take on the voyage back to Norway. His successors were unable to maintain his achievements in the west, and Norwegian authority gave way to Scottish and Anglo-Norman primacy.

MAGNUS BARE-LEGS. *See* MAGNUS BARE-FOOT.

MAGNUS II HARALDSSON (d. 1069). King of Norway 1066–1069. Eldest son of **Harald Hard-Ruler** and Þóra Þorbergsdottir, Magnus was appointed regent by his father before Harald left for England in 1066. Following Harald's death at **Stamford Bridge**, Magnus ruled the whole of Norway for one winter, and then he and his brother, **Olaf the Peaceful**, divided their father's kingdom between them. According to Snorri's *Heimskringla*, Magnus ruled over the northern part of the country, and Olaf the eastern part. Magnus is said to have fallen ill and to have died from ergotism in 1069. He was buried in **Trondheim**, and his brother succeeded to the whole kingdom of Norway.

MAGNUS I THE GOOD OLAFSSON (ON *Magnús goði Óláfsson*)
(*c.* **1024–1047).** King of Norway 1035–1047, Magnus was the son of
Olaf Haraldsson by Alfhild, one of Olaf's servants. He spent his
childhood in exile at the court of **Jaroslav the Wise** in **Russia**, and
only became king of Norway after driving out **Ælfgifu of
Northampton** and **Svein Cnutsson**, who held power in the name
of **Cnut I the Great** from *c.* 1028. Following Cnut's death in 1035,
Magnus took advantage of Danish weakness and launched an attack
against **Harthacnut**, which resulted in the signing of a treaty that
recognized Magnus as king of Norway and named Magnus as
Harthacnut's successor in Denmark. Magnus ruled as king of Denmark from 1042 until his death, when Cnut's nephew, **Svein Estrithsson**, reclaimed the Danish throne. For the last year of his reign
in Norway, Magnus was forced to rule jointly with his uncle, **Harald
Hard-Ruler**, who had otherwise threatened to oust Magnus with the
support of Svein Estrithsson. Magnus was succeeded as king of Norway by his uncle.

MAGNUS, ST. (d. 1117). Earl of **Orkney** *c.* 1105–1115, Magnus was
the son of Erlend II, who ruled Orkney together with his brother
Paul after the death of their father, **Thorfinn the Mighty**, in 1065.
Orkneyinga Saga presents the joint rule of Erlend and Paul as both
a harmonious and a relatively peaceful period in the island's history,
but there was considerable hostility between their sons. During Erlend's and Paul's lifetimes, the islands were divided into two separate earldoms in order to minimize conflict between Magnus,
Erlend's son and Hákon, Paul's son. As Paul was the oldest brother,
he received the West Mainland, including the prestigious center at
Birsay and the southern Isles of Orkney; Erlend received the East
Mainland and the northern Isles of Orkney.

The division in Orkney politics persisted for over a century, and
both factions called on external support to bolster their positions:
Hákon, the great-grandson of the Norwegian king, **Magnus I the
Good Olafsson**, looked to Norway, while on the other hand, Magnus
commanded considerable support in **Scotland** and **Shetland**. Hákon
hoped that **Magnus Bare-Foot** of Norway would back his claim to
be sole ruler of Orkney during his western expedition of 1098, but instead King Magnus deposed Hákon's father, Paul, and Erlend, and

sent them back to Norway (where they both died that winter) and set up his own son, Sigurd, to rule Orkney with the help of a council. Both Hákon and Magnus accompanied Magnus Bare-Foot on his journey south to the **Hebrides**, the Irish Sea, and the Menai Straits, where Magnus Bare-Foot fought against the Normans for control of Anglesey, possibly with the aim of restoring the native Welsh ruler, Gruffydd ap Cynan, as a Norse puppet king (*see* **Wales**). Here, Magnus of Orkney refused to fight, a decision that Magnus Bare-Foot attributed to cowardice but which *Orkneyinga Saga* ascribed to his piety. After the battle, Magnus of Orkney managed to escape and took refuge with King Edgar of Scotland, who helped Magnus to become earl of Caithness, as a preliminary to reclaiming his half of Orkney.

The death of Magnus Bare-Foot led to his son, Sigurd, being recalled from Orkney in 1102 and in 1104, Hákon was named earl of Orkney once more. Magnus returned to Orkney to contest Hákon's position, and it was agreed that he should visit Norway to obtain the royal verdict on his claim. As a result, Hákon and Magnus shared the earldom from about 1105 to 1114, during which time Magnus married a **woman** from "the noblest family there in Scotland." However, after Magnus left Orkney to take part in a campaign against the Welsh with Henry I of England and Alexander I of Scotland, Hákon took over the rule of the whole earldom. On Magnus's return, the two earls and their armed followers met at a **thing**, or assembly place, and a temporary peace was negotiated, before they agreed to meet on the small island of Egilsay during Easter week to finalize the terms of their treaty. It was here that Magnus met his death, killed by Hákon's cook following a decision by the thing men. Magnus's skull, discovered in a pillar in the Cathedral at Kirkwall in 1919, shows that he was probably killed by a blow to his forehead.

Hákon went on a pilgrimage to Rome and Jerusalem following the murder of Magnus, receiving absolution from the pope, and he arranged for Magnus to be buried in Christchurch in Birsay. However, miracles began to be reported at Magnus's grave. This cult was strongly encouraged by his nephew, Rögnvald Kali Kolsson (d. 1158), in his bid for the earldom of Orkney, and he was responsible for the building of St. Magnus Cathedral in Kirkwall (*c.* 1136–1137), where Magnus's body was moved.

MAJUS. Arabic word meaning "heathens" that was originally applied to those who believed in Zoroastrianism. It came to be used by all unbelievers and acquired new associations with fire worship, incest, and warlocks. This word was used by the Muslims in **Spain** to refer to the **Vikings**, who they believed to be fire worshippers.

MALDON, BATTLE OF. Maldon lies on the River Blackwater in Essex and was the site of a battle fought by the English, under Ealdorman Byrhtnoth of Essex, against a **Viking** fleet commanded by **Olaf Tryggvason** of Norway on either 10 or 11 August 991 (although the A version of the *Anglo-Saxon Chronicle* dates it to 993). The *Anglo-Saxon Chronicle* contains a brief reference to the battle and to the first payment of **Danegeld**, which followed the English defeat. But a fragmentary Old English poem, known as *The Battle of Maldon*, preserves a fuller and more famous account of the battle in 325 lines of alliterative verse. The manuscript that contained this poem was burned in 1731, and all modern editions of it are based upon a written transcript of the text made by David Casley shortly before the fire. According to this poem, the battle saw the English literally snatching defeat from the jaws of victory after Byrthnoth's ill-advised decision to allow the Vikings to cross a narrow causeway across the river to meet the English army. The poem's main theme is loyalty, particularly the loyalty of those who fought heroically to avenge the death of their lord, Byrhtnoth, despite the inevitable loss of their own lives.

MAMMEN. Scandinavian **art** style that takes its name from an axhead discovered in a grave at Mammen, Jutland, Denmark. The Mammen style succeeded the earlier **Jellinge** style and is characterized by more solid looking beasts whose bodies are decorated with pelleting. The Mammen style was current during the second half of the 10th century. Most examples of this style are found in Scandinavia, but there are some insular examples from the **Isle of Man** and **Orkney**. It has recently been argued that the Mammen style may in fact have originated in the British Isles.

MAN, ISLE OF, VIKINGS IN. Island in the Irish Sea. As elsewhere in the British Isles, the Scandinavian settlement of Man was probably preceded by raiding, and it is unlikely that the raids recorded in the Irish Sea region at the beginning of the ninth century did not also affect Man. There are no written references to the Scandinavian settlement of Man, so archaeological, place-name, epigraphic, and sculptural evidence must be used when trying to reconstruct the details of the Norse colonization.

Extensive archaeological evidence for a Scandinavian presence on the island exists in the form of pagan graves and settlement sites. The earliest evidence is provided by a number of rich pagan **burials**, from the late-ninth and early-10th century, which have been excavated around the island's coast. These include the **ship** burials at Knock-y-Doonee and **Balladoole** and the burial mound at **Ballateare**. A pagan cemetery, closely associated with a pre-existing Christian cemetery at Peel Castle, has recently been excavated, revealing the richest pagan female burial from this period in the British Isles. This is also the only pagan female burial to be found on Man, a fact that has led some scholars to suggest that the Norse settlement was primarily that of a male warrior class, which subsequently intermarried with native Celtic **women**. There is some support for this in the 35 runic inscriptions (*see* **rune**) on stone crosses found on the island, a unique collection of Scandinavian memorial stones from the British Isles, that commemorate people with both Norse and Celtic names. Nine settlement sites from the Norse period have been identified and excavated on the island. There are five small promontory fortifications, two shielings (hillside buildings, used in the summer when sheep and cattle grazed in the mountains), and two farmsteads, including the well-known settlement at **Braaid**. Dating these sites is difficult, as associated artifacts are frequently not found.

The Isle of Man became the center of the Norse kingdom of the southern **Hebrides** in the later part of the 11th century under its king, **Godred Crovan**. Prior to this the island had fallen under the control of the Norse kingdom of **Dublin** and the Norse **earls** of **Orkney** at different periods in the Viking Age. When the joint kingdom of **York** and Dublin was established under **Ragnald** in the 920s, Man was dominated by Dublin and was indeed centrally placed to take advantage of trading connections between Ireland and England. During the latter part of the 10th century, Earl **Sigurd the Stout** of Orkney is said to have defeated Godred Haraldsson, king of Man, and to have incorporated the island into the Norse earldom. **Olaf Tryggvason** also fought in Man according to *Heimskringla*. Manx armies probably fought and were defeated at **Tara** and **Clontarf**, following which the island and Manx fleet were heavily attacked. The island may have remained under Orkney until about the time of the death of Earl **Thorfinn the Mighty** in 1065, but on the basis of numismatic evidence, which shows close connections with Dublin, it has been suggested that the Dublin Norse may have gained control of Man after Clontarf. The island was certainly in the hands of a king with Dublin connections in 1066. Godred Crovan established an independent Manx kingship following his victory at **Skyhill** in 1079.

In 1098 and 1102, **Magnus Bare-Foot** attempted to assert Norwegian sovereignty over the Northern and Western Isles with two expeditions, but his death in 1102 was followed by the return of Olaf Godredsson to Man. In 1156, Godred II of Man and Sumarliði of Argyll partitioned the Western Isles, with the Manx king keeping the Outer Hebrides and Man and Sumarliði taking the islands south of the Ardnamurchan Point. Godred Crovan's descendants continued to rule the island until 1266, when, following the defeat of Norway and the Manx king at Largs in 1263, the Scots and Norwegians signed the Treaty of Perth, and Scotland purchased Man and the Western Isles from Norway.

The linguistic evidence for Scandinavian influence on Man is rich but problematic. The island's place-names have a strong Norse flavor, and only three Gaelic place-names (Douglas, Rushen, and Man itself) can be shown to predate Norse settlement. On the basis of this it has been argued that Norse was the dominant language between *c*. 900–*c*. 1300 and Gaelic probably died out during the period of Norse hegemony. However, this argument has been rejected by some scholars, who point to Celtic influence on smaller administrative divisions on the island, to Celtic patronymics in Manx runic inscriptions and the Celtic nicknames of the Crovan dynasty, and to Gaelic alternatives to Norse place-names that are known from some sources. It is argued that the written evidence for place-names is biased in favor of the aristocratic, Norse names, which were later anglicized and preserved. This school of thought sees the Norse settlement of Man as a small-scale aristocratic take-over, with the vast majority of people continuing to speak Gaelic.

The most important feature of the island's administration was the assembly place at **Tynwald**, where the 48 (reduced to 36 when the Inner

Hebrides were conceded to Sumarliði in 1156) representatives of the **Suðreyar** met. The continuity of this assembly down to the present day is unique in the context of Scandinavian colonies in the west and testifies to the impact of Scandinavian settlement on Man.

MARKLAND ("Land of Forest"). Land to the north of **Vinland** that was first sighted by **Bjarni Herjólfsson** according to the *Saga of the Greenlanders*, although according to the *Saga of Erik the Red*, **Leif the Lucky** was the first to discover Markland. Markland is described as a heavily forested land, which was a good source of timber for the inhabitants of treeless **Greenland**, and it has been identified with Labrador.

MERCIA, VIKINGS IN. Anglo-Saxon kingdom in the English Midlands, which rose to prominence in the eighth century under its king, Offa (757–796). The territorial boundaries of this kingdom appear to have fluctuated, but at its greatest extent in the century before Viking raids began, Mercia stretched from the Welsh borders in the west to the kingdom of **East Anglia** in the east, and from the **Humber** in the north to the Rivers Thames and Avon in the south, embracing a number of distinct peoples.

Beorhtwulf, king of Mercia, is recorded as unsuccessfully confronting a large Viking fleet around Canterbury and **London** in the *Anglo-Saxon Chronicle* for 851. Just two years later, Mercia was forced to ask for West Saxon help (against the Welsh), an alliance that was confirmed by the marriage of Mercia's new king, Burgred (852–874), to the daughter of Æthelwulf, king of **Wessex**. The kingdom of Mercia suffered its first real taste of **Viking** attacks following the arrival of the **Great Army** in 865, and these fatally weakened the kingdom and ultimately brought it under the leadership of the West Saxon kings. In 867, the Viking army attacked Nottingham; even with the support of Æthelred of Wessex and his brother, **Alfred the Great**, Burgred was forced to come to terms with the Vikings. Further deals with the Vikings were struck in 871 and 872, but following the occupation of **Repton**, the Viking army drove Burgred out of his kingdom and into exile. He was replaced by Ceolwulf II (874–879), who is described in the *Anglo-Saxon Chronicle* as a Viking puppet ruler and characterized as a "foolish king's **thegn**." In 877, the

Chronicle records that the Scandinavians settled part of Mercia and granted part of it to Ceolwulf. The Scandinavian part of Mercia, roughly corresponding to the East Midlands, lay in the area that became known as the **Danelaw**, while the English part of Mercia, or the West Midlands, briefly preserved a degree of independence under Æthelred (d. 911), "Lord of the Mercians," who succeeded Ceolwulf and who was married to Alfred's daughter, Æthelflæd (known as "Lady of the Mercians") in around 886. Following the death of Æthelflæd in 918, control of Mercia passed to Alfred's son, Edward the Elder of Wessex, who deprived Ælfwynn, the daughter of Æthelred and Æthelflæd, of power and took her to Wessex.

By the time of the death of Æthelflæd, Scandinavian control of the East Midlands was largely ended: a series of campaigns by Edward and Æthelflæd had led to the recapture of Viking strongholds at Northampton in 914, and Derby, Leicester, Nottingham, and Stamford in 917 and 918. However, in 942, King Edmund is said to have won Mercia and the **Five Boroughs** back from the Norse (*Norðmannum*), suggesting that **Dublin-York** kings, Olaf Guthfrithsson and **Olaf Cúarán**, had held power in the region for a time. Nevertheless, the power of the Scandinavian kings of York was curtailed during the reign of **Athelstan** and ended for good in 954.

Lasting evidence of the Scandinavian settlement of this region can, however, be traced in the many Scandinavian place-names ending in *by* and *thorp*. The eastern county of Lincolnshire has the highest density of Scandinavian place-names in England, with approximately 50 percent of village names in its northern part being of Scandinavian origin, and field names show that this Norse influence extended to the lowest level. The coinage from Lincoln between the years 973 and 1016 reveals almost 50 percent of moneyers' names to be Scandinavian, and the variety and number of Scandinavian personal names recorded in Lincolnshire source material down until the end of the 13th century is impressive. The Domesday population of sokemen or freemen was the largest in England (*c.* 1,100 individuals), rarely falling below 40 percent of total population in all of Lincolnshire's 33 **wapentakes**. These sokemen were once believed to be the descendants of free Danish settlers as they are found in their largest numbers in Danelaw, and while this view is no longer accepted, the difference in the social composition of the population may possibly be attributed to the effects of the Danish settlement.

Svein Forkbeard of Denmark received the submission of Lindsey (north Lincolnshire) and the Five Boroughs in 1013. Æthelred II of England subsequently punished the region by harrying Lindsey in 1014. When **Cnut I the Great** returned from Denmark in 1015, he won the support of the treacherous ealdorman of Mercia, Eadric Streona. Following Cnut's defeat of **Edmund Ironside** at **Ashingdon** in 1016, Cnut himself was recognized by Edmund as king of Mercia in the Treaty of **Olney**. However, Edmund's death on 30 November 1016 cleared the way for Cnut to be declared king of England in 1017. Eadric Streona was given the earldom of Mercia, until his murder at Cnut's Christmas court of 1017.

MICEL HERE. *See* GREAT ARMY.

MIDDLETON CROSS. The remains of at least seven stone crosses, dating from the 10th century, have been found in and around St. Andrew's church in Middleton, North Yorkshire, England. The most famous of these is Middleton 2, a ring-headed cross that was removed from the walls of the church in 1948. This shows a seated human figure wearing a conical helmet and a sheathed knife on his belt. The warrior is surrounded by his **weapons**: a spear, sword, and shield. The reverse of the cross-shaft shows a ribbonlike beast in profile, which has been regarded as an incompetent attempt at the Scandinavian **Jellinge** style. Three of the other cross fragments depict similar warrior figures, and one is also decorated with a Jellinge-like beast.

The warrior figure on the Middleton cross has been the subject of much debate. Traditionally, it was seen as showing a Viking warrior, lying in a grave surrounded by his weapons, as one would expect a pagan to be buried. However, more recent interpretations have instead regarded it as depicting a Viking lord, seated on a throne, which would account for the warrior's short legs and for two otherwise unexplained circular pellets above the warrior's shoulders (interpreted as the top of the throne). The juxtaposition of a Viking warrior with a Christian cross has made the Middleton cross a favorite illustration in works on the Vikings in England and neatly demonstrates the rapid conversion of Scandinavian settlers to **Christianity** and the fusing of cultures that took place in northern England after the ninth-century settlement.

MIDGARD (ON *Miðgarðr*). Midgard, "middle enclosure," was the world of humankind in Norse **mythology**. According to Snorri's *Gylfaginning*, Midgard was the name of the wall or rampart that was created from the giant Ymir's eyelashes, which protected the earth's inhabitants from the giants. However, elsewhere in the *Prose Edda*, Midgard is used as a name for the world in which humans and gods lived. Midgard was surrounded by an ocean, in which the **Midgard serpent** lived.

MIDGARD SERPENT (ON *Miðgarðsormr* **"world serpent").** Mythical beast living in the ocean around **Midgard**, the home of humankind. The serpent is said to be the offspring of **Loki** and a giantess called Angrboda and is also known by the name Jörmungandr. In *Hymiskviða*, one of the poems in the *Poetic Edda*, **Thor** is said to have gone fishing for the Midgard serpent, using an ox's head for bait. He caught it, but Hymir, the giant whose boat he was in, cut through the line. This scene is shown on a number of **rune-stones**, such as the one from Alstad, in Uppland, Sweden. At **Ragnarök**, Thor and the serpent kill each other.

MIKLIGARÐR. *See* BYZANTIUM.

MJÖLLNIR. Hammer belonging to the god **Thor** that, according to *Skáldskaparmál*, was made by the dwarfs, Brokk and Eitri, sons of Ivaldi, as part of a bet with **Loki**. When thrown, Mjöllnir made thunder and lightning and returned like a boomerang to Thor's hand. The theft of Mjöllnir by the giant Þrymr is the subject of the comical poem *Þrymskviða*.

MÖÐRUVALLABÓK. Icelandic manuscript written by a single, unknown scribe in northern **Iceland** in the middle of the 14th century, which contains the most important and comprehensive collection of the so-called *Sagas of the Icelanders*. Its name is derived from the farm, Möðruvellir, in Eyjafjörður, because the 17th-century owner of the farm, the lawman Magnús Björnsson, wrote his name in the manuscript in 1628. The sagas contained in the manuscript are ordered geographically, from south to east, like the *Book of Settlements*, starting with *Njal's Saga* and ending with *Fóstbrœðra saga*. Other sagas found in the manuscript include *Egil's Saga*, *Bandamanna saga*, and *Laxdœla Saga*.

MORKINSKINNA ("the rotten parchment"). Manuscript produced in **Iceland** *c.* 1275, which includes sagas of the kings of Norway from the beginning of the reign of **Magnus the Good Olafsson** in 1035 until the mid-12th century. It is believed that it ended, like *Heimskringla*, with the Battle of Ré (1177), just before Sverrir Sigurdsson became king. However, the end of the manuscript is missing. Several gaps in the earlier part of *Morkinskinna* can be supplied from *Flateyjarbók*. As well as the *Kings' Sagas*, *Morkinskinna* also contains a large number of *þættir* (short stories) about Icelanders and some extracts from **Ágrip**. An earlier version of *Morkinskinna*, known as the *Oldest Morkinskinna*, is believed to have been written in the early 13th century and to have been used in the writing of *Fagrskinna* and *Heimskringla*.

MUNIN. *See* HUGIN.

MUSPELL. According to Snorri's *Prose Edda*, Muspell was a land of fire, found in the south and defended by the giant Surt, who would burn the world at **Ragnarök**. **Ginnungagap** arose where the heat of Muspell met the chill of **Niflheim**. Elsewhere in the *Prose Edda*, there are references to Muspell's sons or people who, led by Surt and **Loki**, confront the gods at Ragnarök.

MYTHOLOGY. Scandinavian mythology was polytheistic, centered upon the struggle between the gods (*see* **Æsir**) and the giants, and consisted of myths of origin, destruction (*see* **Ragnarok**), and ultimately rebirth. The two warring factions who confronted each other at the end of the world were, however, also intimately linked in the creation of the world, for the gods are said to have created the Norse mythological universe from the body of Ymir, the ancestor of the giants. The figure of **Loki** is a further link between the gods and giants, for while he is said to be descended from giants, he also appears to spend much of his time living with and even helping the gods. Although two gods, **Balder** and his half brother Hod, survive Ragnarok, no giants are said to have been part of the new mythological order. In addition to the conflict between the gods and giants, there is also said to have been war between two different groups or tribes of gods, the Æsir, the most important of which appear to have been **Odin** and **Thor** and the **Vanir**, which consisted of **Niord**, **Frey**, and **Freya**.

This mythology is preserved in largely medieval sources, the most important of which are the *Prose Edda* and the *Poetic Edda*. Both of these works are characterized by an effort to systemize their source material, and the extent to which they accurately reflect pre-Christian beliefs is hotly debated. Certainly Snorri's *Edda* is prefaced by his claim that the gods were in fact human and had tricked **humankind** into believing that they were divine beings. This same argument is also found in *Ynglinga Saga*, the first, largely mythological, saga in Snorri's history of the kings of Norway, *Heimskringla*. Apart from these sources, there are some **skaldic poems** that deal with largely mythological subject matter, such as **Bragi** Boddason's *Ragnarsdrápa*, which includes the important myth about Thor and the **Midgard Serpent**, and Ulf Uggason's *Húsdrápa*, which also refers to this encounter, as well as describing Balder's funeral, and Loki and **Heimdall's** conflict over the necklace **Brísingamen**. Place-names incorporating the names of gods also provide some evidence about the distribution and popularity of their cults, as do archaeological finds such as amulets and images of gods.

– N –

NESJAR, BATTLE OF. Sea battle fought near the mouth of Oslofjörd in southern Norway on Palm Sunday (26 March) in 1016. *Nesjar* means "of the headlands" and probably refers to present-day Brunlanes on the coast between Langesundfjörd and Oslofjörd. In this battle, King **Olaf Haraldsson** of Norway defeated an alliance of powerful Norwegian rivals, including Einar þambarskelfir (Tambarskelve) and possibly Erlingr Skjálgsson (although **skaldic** support for his role is lacking), led by **Earl** Svein Hákonsson of **Lade**. Olaf's victory at

Nesjar is the subject of a series of verses, *Nesjavísur,* composed by the skald, **Sighvatr Þórðarson**, and quoted extensively in Snorri's *Heimskringla*. Following his defeat, Svein of Lade first fled to his brother-in-law, **Olof Skötkonung**, in Sweden and then to **Russia**, where he seems to have died.

NESTOR'S CHRONICLE. *See RUSSIAN PRIMARY CHRONICLE.*

NEWFOUNDLAND. *See* L'ANSE AUX MEADOWS.

NIDAROS/NIÐARÓSS. *See* TRONDHEIM.

NIDHOGG (ON *Níðhöggr*). Name of the dragon that, according to the **Eddic** poem, *Grímnismál*, lives in and gnaws at the roots of **Yggdrasil**. However, another Eddic poem, *Völuspá*, describes Nidhogg ("the one very full of hatred") as living in the north at *Niðavellir* "the dark plains" and *Niðafjöll* "the dark hills," where it collects and sucks the blood from corpses. The final verse of *Völuspá* is about Nidhogg, who is apparently the only creature to have survived **Ragnarök**. In his **Gylfaginning**, **Snorri Sturluson** describes Nidhogg as both inhabiting the roots of Yggdrasil and as tormenting the dead, but, in contrast to the information from *Völuspá*, Snorri says that Nidhogg tormented the dead in the spring known as **Hvergelmir**.

NIFLHEIM (ON *Niflheim*). In *Gylfaginning*, **Snorri Sturluson's** account of Norse **mythology**, Niflheim "the dark or misty world," is identified with **Hel** and Niflhel, where the "wicked" go after their deaths. However, later on in the same work, it is also said to be the place where those who die of sickness or old age are sent. Snorri also writes that Niflheim, cold and grim, is older than the world and was separated from the heat of **Muspell** by **Ginnungagap**. One of the roots of **Yggdrasil** is said by Snorri to have reached down into Niflheim, with the spring, **Hvergelmir**, underneath the root.

NIORD (ON *Njörðr*). God of the **Vanir** tribe and father of the twins **Frey** and **Freya**. According to *Gylfaginning* and *Lokasenna*, Niord was sent to the Æsir as a hostage. He is said to control wind, fire, and the sea, but very little else is known about him. Niord was married to Skaði, the daughter of a giant, but the marriage was unhappy as Niord wanted to live in his hall Nóatún, which was by the sea, while Skaði preferred the mountains.

NJAL'S SAGA (ON *Brennu-Njáls saga*). One of the most famous and popular of the so-called *Sagas of the Icelanders*. *Njal's Saga* was written in **Iceland** by an unknown author at the end of the 13th century, probably between 1275–1285. Twenty-four manuscripts and fragments containing all or part of the saga have survived, the earliest of which dates to *c.* 1300.

The saga is set in the 10th and early 11th centuries and, as its name suggests, is centered on the figure of Njal Thorgeirsson, a farmer from Bergthorsknoll, and a series of feuds that, in spite of his own wisdom and generosity, led to his and his family's death. In addition to this story, the saga also includes accounts of two key historical events: the conversion of Iceland to **Christianity** and the Battle of **Clontarf**. The first section of the saga concerns the actions of Hall-gerð, the wife of Njal's friend, Gunnar, which bring about the exile, outlawry, and death of her husband; then Njal's own sons bring about their own and their father's death after slaying Þraín and his son, Höskuld—their kinsman, Flosi, then burns them in their **house**; the final chapter of the saga concerns the reconciliation of Kári, Njal's son-in-law, and Flosi.

NOIRMOUTIER, ERMENTARIUS OF. Noirmoutier, an island at the mouth of the River Loire in **Brittany**, present-day France, was the site of a monastery dedicated to St-Philibert. Ermentarius was a member of this island community in the early ninth century and describes, in his *De Translationibus et Miraculis Sancti Filiberti*, how from 819 the monks spent their summers on the mainland because of the threat of **Viking** raids, before deciding to abandon the monastery altogether in 836, as the threats grew worse. Together with the relics of their saint, the community sought refuge in the interior of the country, finally settling at Tournus, Burgundy, some 40 years later in 875.

The Vikings started overwintering in **Frankia** in 843, using the island of Noirmoutier as their first semipermanent base. Writing around 960, Ermentarius recorded in vivid prose a long list of Viking atrocities, which included the destruction of numerous towns—Angers, Tours, Orléans, and Rouen—and the capture of many others—including Bordeaux, Limoges, Toulouse, and Paris. However, Ermentarius's writings are characterized by a strong sense of Christian outrage at the suffering inflicted by pagan peoples, and his account is therefore not entirely trustworthy.

NONNEBAKKEN. *See* TRELLEBORG FORTRESSES.

NÓREGS KONUNGA TAL **("Catalog of the Kings of Norway").** Anonymous history of the kings of Norway from the time of **Halfdan the Black**, to the early 9th century, to the Battle of Ré in 1177, when King Magnus Erlingsson defeated his rival, Eystein Eysteinsson. *Sverri's Saga* begins at the point where both this history and *Heimskringla* end. Since the 17th century, this history has been known as *Fagrskinna* "the fair parchment," but it is now only preserved in paper copies. Two manuscripts of *Nóregs konunga tal* were lost in the fire at the Royal Library in Copenhagen in 1728, one dating from the middle of the 13th century and one from the beginning of the 14th century. However, it is believed that this history was first written down in the early 13th century, probably in or around **Trondheim** in Norway. Although there are a number of similarities with *Heimskringla*, it is likely that this stems from the author's use of some of the same sources as **Snorri Sturluson** later used. It has been suggested that *Nóregs konunga tal* may have been commissioned by King Hákon Hákonarson (d. 1263) of Norway.

NORMANDY, VIKINGS IN. Area of northern France that was granted to Scandinavians in the early 10th century and that had developed into a powerful and virtually independent duchy by the 11th century. Initially, territory around Rouen and the mouth of the River Seine, formerly known as Neustria, was given to the **Viking** leader, **Rollo**, by **Charles the Simple**, on the condition that Rollo and his army would defend it against other Viking armies. **Dudo of St-Quentin** says that this settlement was the result of a deal that was formally acknowledged in the Treaty of **St. Clair-sur-Epte** in 911. Rollo's son and later successors to the dukedom of Normandy extended the region under their control by a series of wars. Already, by 924, when Rollo died, the territory had been extended to the River Vire in the west, and under his son, **William Longsword**, the areas of the Cotentin and Avranches were acquired (933). However, William's territorial ambitions brought him into conflict with Arnulf I of Flanders, and he was murdered in 942. Nevertheless, the Normans retained their new acquisitions, which gave them a territory approximately three times the size of their original grant. Scandinavian place-names reflect the distribution of this settlement.

However, it seems that the Normans were rapidly being integrated into French society and politics, adopting the language and religion of France. William Longsword himself married the Frankish princess, Liégeard, and his son and successor, Richard, had to be sent to Bayeux for a Norse education, as Rouen was French-speaking by that time. Richard too married a Frankish princess. The duchy of Normandy therefore appears to have been a very much Christian, feudal French society, with the dukes appearing as patrons of monasteries and involving themselves in the secular politics of France.

From their settlements in Normandy, the Normans embarked on several other major campaigns in Europe. The most important of these was the invasion of England in 1066 by Duke William of Normandy, the so-called Conqueror and Bastard, who became king of England following his victory at Hastings. In addition to this, Norman adventurers traveled south to southern Italy and Sicily, where they served the local nobility as mercenaries fighting the Arabs and the Byzantines (*see* **Byzantium**), and where they ultimately established small kingdoms of their own. Most notably, the sons of Tancred de Hauteville established their rule over the southern Italian regions of Calabria and Puglia (Apulia) in the 1050s and over Sicily in the following decades. Roger II, a grandson of Tancred, brought these Norman possessions together into the kingdom of Sicily in the early 12th century.

NORMANIST CONTROVERSY. The Normanist controversy centers upon the question of whether or not the founders of the early Russian state were Scandinavian or Slavonic. The whole question of Scandinavian influence and presence in **Russia** was dominated by this controversy for much of the 18th, 19th, and 20th centuries. Fierce debate was first provoked by the claims of German historians, Gottlieb Siegfried Bayer (1694–1738) and August Ludwig von Schlözer (1735–1809), that before the advent of the **Vikings**, the Slavs of Russia lived like savages. In turn, Russian and Soviet historians retaliated by downplaying or denying the Scandinavian contribution to the Russian state.

The Normanist school believed the **Rus** to be Scandinavian Vikings, who founded the first consolidated Russian state among the eastern Slavs, centered on **Kiev**. However, the anti-Normanists argued that the Slavs had established their own state, which was then attacked and briefly ruled by Scandinavians in the 10th century. The debate was often characterized by extreme racial hatred—for example, Adolf Hitler supported the argument that the Slavs had lived like savages before the "civilizing" influence of the Scandinavians. As a consequence, the view that the Russian state was established by Scandinavians was banned in the Union of Soviet Socialist Republics in 1949.

However, the current scholarly consensus is that the Rus probably was a largely Scandinavian people. Certainly there is philological support for the Normanist view in the place-names around **Novgorod**, and the Scandinavian character of the names of various early rulers of Russia, given in the ***Russian Primary Chronicle***, as well as in contemporary identifications of the Rus with Scandinavia. Archaeological excavations in Russia have also revealed a significant, if small-scale, Scandinavian presence in some of Russia's earliest towns and trading centers. However, this archaeological evidence also clearly indicates that the Scandinavians only ever formed a minority population in the Russian towns, that the native peoples of Russia were not in need of "civilization," and that the Rus were soon slavicized, adopting the customs and dress of their new country.

NORN (from ON *norrænn* "Norwegian, Norse"). Name given to the form of the Scandinavian language spoken on the Northern Isles of **Orkney** and **Shetland** for some 800 or more years. There is little written evidence for this language, and before *c.* 1300, the only texts known to have been written in the Northern Isles are some 60 runic inscriptions (*see* **rune**), a large proportion of which appear to have been carved by Scandinavian visitors to the islands. During the 18th century, some efforts were made to collect and preserve elements of this West Norse dialect, most notably the Lord's Prayer from Shetland recorded by George Low. However, by the time that a systematic attempt to record the language of the Northern Isles was made, at the end of the 19th and the beginning of the 20th century, Norn was largely a dead language overtaken by Scots and English. Indeed, Scots appears to have replaced Norn as the language of prestige in Orkney before the Reformation. The last Norse manuscript from Orkney was written in 1426, while the last from Shetland is dated to 1607. The last native speakers of Orkney Norn probably died in the middle of the 18th century and those of Shetland Norn *c.* 1800.

NORNS (ON plural *nornar*). Mythological females who control the fate of people. **Snorri Sturluson** mentions three norns by name in *Gylfaginning*: Urd ("happened, became," i.e., past), Verdandi ("happening, becoming," i.e., present), and Skuld ("become," i.e., future), who are said to live by a spring under **Yggdrasil**. However, he also writes that there were other norns, both good and bad, who visit everyone at their birth in order to determine their lives.

NORTH AMERICA. *See* AMERICA, NORTH.

NORTHUMBRIA, VIKINGS IN. Anglo-Saxon kingdom in northeastern England, which stretched from the River **Humber** in the south to the Firth of Forth in the north. The kingdom was formed *c.* 600 and consisted of the two previously independent kingdoms of Deira (between the Humber and the Tees) and Bernicia (between the Tees and the Firth of Forth); parts of northwestern England were later incorporated into this kingdom (*see* **Cumbria**). The kingdom enjoyed its "golden age" in the two centuries preceding the arrival of the **Vikings** at **Lindisfarne** in 793. Important monasteries at Whitby, Jarrow, and Lindisfarne became European cultural, as well as religious, centers, as demonstrated by, for example, Bede's *Ecclesiastical History of the English People* and the *Lindisfarne Gospels*. These undefended monasteries along the northeast coast were also, however, among the Vikings' favorite targets.

The arrival of the **Great Army** in the kingdom of Northumbria coincided with a battle for power at **York** between Ælla and Osberht.

The Vikings, under their leaders, **Halfdan** and **Ivar the Boneless**, captured the town in 866 and both Ælla and Osberht were killed trying to retake it in the following year. Just 10 years later the *Anglo-Saxon Chronicle* records that Halfdan's army had settled in Northumbria and that "they were plowing and were providing for themselves." This settlement resulted in the redistribution of land, the renaming of old settlements, and the establishment of new settlements, a process that can be traced in the large numbers of Scandinavian place-names in Northumbria. In Yorkshire, more than 700 place-names are of Scandinavian origin, accounting for about 48 percent of names in East Yorkshire, 45 percent in North Yorkshire, and 31 percent in West Yorkshire. However, the Viking kingdom of Northumbria, centered on York, does not appear to have controlled Bernicia, which retained its own rulers based at Bamburgh. The place-name evidence for a Scandinavian presence in this region is correspondingly sparser than for Yorkshire, apart from a concentration of names south of Durham.

The politics of Northumbria during the late ninth and 10th centuries are shadowy and have to be pieced together from Irish, Scottish, and English chronicles. However, it is clear that during the early 10th century, following the conquest of York by **Ragnald** in 919, the kingdom was controlled by the Norse kings of **Dublin**. This control was challenged by the English kings and, in 927, **Athelstan** succeeded in expelling its king, Guthfrith, from York. At around the same time, Ealdred of Bernicia recognized Athelstan's overlordship. Athelstan subsequently minted coins in his name at York, but his death in 939 allowed the Norse of Dublin to once more challenge English control of Northumbria. Athelstan's successors, Edmund and Eadred, both claimed to rule Northumbria, but their control seems to have been shaky and intermittent. Nevertheless, by 954, the last Scandinavian king of Northumbria, **Erik Blood-Ax**, was driven out of York and killed, and Northumbria was entrusted to Earl Oswulf. When Edgar came to the throne in 959, he succeeded to the kingdoms of Essex, **Mercia**, and Northumbria. However, English rule was enforced through a series of earls, and it appears that the old division between Deira and Bernicia persisted in these appointments. For example, Earl Oswulf appears to have renounced control of York in 966, retaining control of northern Northumbria while an earl called

Oslac ruled the kingdom of York until around 975. However, in 1006, Earl Uhtred's rule of Bernicia was extended south by Æthelred II to include the earldom of York, thus unifying Northumbria.

Archaeologically, the Scandinavian presence in Northumbria has not left much trace outside York: modest Viking-Age farms at **Ribblehead** in North Yorkshire and Simy Folds in County Durham lack distinctly Scandinavian artifacts; there are accompanied **burials** from Kildale (North Yorkshire), Wensley, Camphill (North Yorkshire), and Cambois (Northumberland); and the isolated discovery of a pair of oval brooches from Bedale in North Yorkshire may also have come from a grave. The largest single source of artifactual evidence is provided by stone sculpture—some 400 pieces of Viking-Age sculpture have been discovered in Yorkshire, and there appear to have been important production centers in the Vale of York and the Vale of Pickering (see, for example, the **Middleton cross**). Although no inscriptions in Scandinavian **runes** have yet been found in Viking York, one fragmentary sundial, inscribed with Anglo-Saxon capitals and runes, is known from Skelton-in-Cleveland on the northeast coast. Moreover, some inscriptions in Anglo-Saxon capitals, such as the Kirkdale sundial from the Vale of Pickering, include Scandinavian names and display possible traces of Scandinavian influence in their grammar and vocabulary.

Northumbria appears to have hardly suffered when Viking raids resumed at the end of the 10th century. Although the *Anglo-Saxon Chronicle* refers to the destruction of Bamburgh in 993, the kingdom is not mentioned again until the submission of "Earl Uhtred and all Northumbria" to **Svein Forkbeard** in 1013. However, there are hints at unrest in the area: the community of St. Cuthbert at Chester-le-Street (*see* **Lindisfarne**) was forced to flee, settled briefly at Ripon, before moving to Durham. The disruption that this implies may, however, reflect Scottish cross-border raiding that was taking place at this time (and which continued to take place well into the Anglo-Norman period and beyond). In 1016, Uhtred appears to have sided with **Edmund Ironside** against Svein's son, **Cnut I the Great**, before Cnut advanced on his kingdom and threatened York. Uhtred then hastily submitted to the Danish leader, but was nevertheless killed. Cnut now appointed Erik of **Lade** as his **earl** in Northumbria, but the native Anglian earls at Bamburgh appear to have continued to govern the northern part of the earldom: Uhtred's brother, Eadwulf *Cudel*, ruled the area north of the Tees briefly, and he was succeeded by Uhtred's sons, Ealdred and Eadulf. However, the absence of their names from witness lists in charters suggests that they were in fact in revolt against Cnut. Siward, who was appointed Earl of Northumbria at York in 1033, had to invade and harry the area north of the Tees in 1042 or 1043, after which date Northumbria was once again a single earldom.

The appointment of Tostig as earl of Northumbria in 1055 brought direct West-Saxon (*see* **Wessex**) rule to Northumbria for the first time, with disastrous consequences. He appears to have overtaxed his earldom, to have failed to protect it against the growing power of the Scottish kings, and, in 1064, Tostig killed Cospatric, the eldest son of Uhtred of Bamburgh, and two other prominent **thegns**. The result was that Northumbria rose in revolt, and chose an outsider, Earl Morcar of Mercia, as their new ruler. King Edward the Confessor was forced to recognize this appointment, and he exiled Tostig. However, Tostig returned just a year later, with the support of the Norwegian king, **Harald Hard-Ruler**, and confronted the king of England in the Battle of **Stamford Bridge**. The Norwegian invasion failed, but shortly afterward, the Norman invasion of southern England succeeded. In 1069, **Svein Estrithsson** of Denmark launched an invasion, which was welcomed by the Northumbrians who are described in the *Anglo-Saxon Chronicle* as "greatly rejoicing." The Danes and Northumbrians attacked York and destroyed the new Norman castle. Royal authority, which had totally collapsed in Northumbria, was only reasserted by the brutal "Harrying of the North" that William the Conqueror undertook in 1069. A subsequent invasion of Northumbria was launched by **Knut II Sveinsson** in 1075, but Knut "dared not join battle" with William. The last recorded plan for a Scandinavian invasion of Northumbria was by Knut II in 1085. However, he was prevented from launching his invasion by unrest at home.

NOVGOROD (ON *Holmgárðr* "settlement on the island"). The defended **Viking** settlement of *Holmgárðr* was located on Lake Ilmen on the River **Dnieper** at **Gorodišče**, some two kilometers south of the center of present-day Novgorod in **Russia**. Novgorod ("the new town") was founded on the River Volkhov at the beginning of the 10th century and by the end of that century had become the most important **Rus** settlement in the north, eclipsing **Staraja Ladoga** and Gorodišče.

The town is bisected by the Volkhov, with the so-called Merchants' Bank on the east bank of the river and the Sofia Bank (named after the 11th-century cathedral) on the west. The residence of the Rus' rulers, a defended citadel or kremlin, also lay on the Sofia Bank. Excavations have uncovered entire streets of buildings, and the waterlogged conditions have preserved large quantities of organic material. These include a large collection of letters written on birch bark, children's toys, clothes, and musical instruments. *Holmgárðr* is named on a number of 11th-century **rune-stones** from Sweden, one of which (from Sjusta in Uppland) mentions a church dedicated to the Norwegian royal martyr, St. **Olaf Haraldsson**, in the town.

– O –

OBODRITES. *See* ABODRITES.

ODIN (ON *Óðinn*). Chief god in the Norse pantheon, according to most sources, and ruler of **Asgard**. Odin was also known by many other names, including the All-Father, the High One, and the Hooded One, which are listed in the *Prose Edda*. Odin was the god of the battlefield; fallen warriors, who had died heroically, would be taken by **valkyries** to Odin's hall, **Valhalla**, to feast and drink until they were required to fight against the gods' enemies at **Ragnarök**. Odin was also associated with knowledge, particularly of **runes** and poetry. His wisdom was gained by hanging for nine days and nine nights from the world tree, **Yggdrasil**, and he sacrificed one of his eyes in order to learn the secrets of runes. Odin was married to the goddess **Frigg** and together they had a son called **Balder**, the purest and most beautiful of the gods. In *Gylfaginning*, Odin is also said to be the father of **Thor**. He rode a magical eight-legged horse called **Sleipnir** and was frequently accompanied by two ravens, **Hugin** and **Munin**, who reported all that they saw to Odin. In literature and **art**, Odin is often depicted with a spear, **Gungnir**, which he is said to

have thrown over a battlefield to indicate which warriors would join
him in Valhalla.

OHTHERE (ON *Óttar*)**.** Norwegian merchant from Halogaland in
northern Norway. Ohthere is known from his account of Scandinavian geography that was incorporated into the Old English translation
of Paulus Orosius's *Seven Books of History against the Pagans*.
This revised translation of Orosius was commissioned by **Alfred the
Great** at the end of the ninth century, who also supplemented it with
a geography of northern Europe, derived from, among others,
Ohthere and **Wulfstan**.

Ohthere's account appears to be a written record of an interview he
had with King Alfred, who he calls his lord (*hlaford*), at Alfred's
court in the English kingdom of **Wessex** *c*. 890. The Norwegian recounts several journeys he had made in order to gather tribute from
Lappish and Finnish tribes, to sell his goods at the Scandinavian market towns of **Hedeby** and *Sciringesheal* (*see* **Kaupang**) and to satisfy
his own curiosity about what lands lay to the north of his own home.
He also includes details of sailing times between the different places.
Exactly where Ohthere lived in Halogaland is unknown—most of the
province lies to the north of the Arctic Circle, and it has been suggested that he may have lived near to present-day Tromsø, where
archaeological excavations have revealed a number of Viking-Age
settlements including, for example, those at Senja and Kvaløya.

The name *Ohthere* is an anglicized version of Old Norse *Óttar*, and
there is no evidence to connect him with the Jarl Ohtor mentioned in
the A redaction of the *Anglo-Saxon Chronicle* for 918 or with the
hero of *Orvar-Odds Saga*.

OLAF CÚARÁN (ON *Óláfr kváran* "sandal;" **Old Irish** *Amlaíb
Cúarán*) **(d. 981).** King of **Dublin** 945–980 and of **York** 941–944;
949–952. Olaf was the son of **Sigtrygg Cáech** of Dublin and York,
and was married to the Irish princess, **Gormlaith**, by whom he had a
son, **Sigtrygg Silk-Beard**. His Irish nickname may be connected to
the idea of the sandal as an emblem of kingship.

The *Anglo-Saxon Chronicle* preserves some sparse details relating to Olaf's campaigns in York, recording the Northumbrians' acceptance of Olaf from **Ireland** as their king in 941; Olaf's submission

to King Edmund (d. 946) of England and his subsequent baptism; and the flight of Olaf Sigtrygsson from York and **Northumbria** in 944. The entries for 949 and 952 simply and tersely recount Olaf Cúarán's arrival in Northumbria and his expulsion at the hands of **Erik Blood-Ax**.

Olaf is the only Norse king for whom Irish praise poetry survives, and it is argued that his rule of Dublin saw an inspired blend of Irish and Norse, and Christian and pagan, cultures. Moreover, the newly established town center flourished during Olaf's reign. However, politically the end of Olaf's rule of Dublin is associated with the end of Viking independence in Dublin and the re-emergence of Irish overlordship. The crushing defeat that Olaf suffered at the Battle of **Tara** in 980 was a crucial turning point in the fortunes of the Norse in Ireland. Olaf himself subsequently retired to **Iona**, where he died in 981.

OLAF DYNASTY. Name given to the Swedish kings who ruled Denmark during the first half of the 10th century. Very little is known about these kings, for whom **Adam of Bremen** is the principal source. The dynasty was apparently founded by Olaf, who conquered Denmark after the death of the otherwise unknown King Helgi; his sons Gnupa (*Chnob*) and *Gurd* ruled with him or succeeded him; and then Sigtrygg (*Sigeric*), Gnupa's son, became king. **Widukind** provides some support for Adam, as he refers to a king *Chnuba* who was forcibly baptized following Henry I of Germany's invasion of Denmark in 934. Further support is provided by two **rune-stones** from **Hedeby**, which were raised by Ásfriðr in memory of Sigtrygg, her and Gnupa's son. Adam writes that Sigtrygg was overthrown by one Harthacnut (*Hardegon*) from *Nortmannia* (Norway or Normandy?), who may have been the father of **Gorm the Old**. Indeed, Adam once refers to Gorm as *Hardecnudth Vurm* and it has been suggested that this was an error for *Hardecnudth filius Vurm* "Gorm, son of Harthacnut."

OLAF HARALDSSON, ST. (ON Óláfr Haraldsson; *Óláfr inn helga* "the Holy"; *Óláfr inn digri* "the Stout") (995–1030). King of Norway 1015–1028. Son of Harald the Greenlandish (*inn grenski*), a local king in southeastern Norway, but brought up by a foster father, Sigurd Sow (*sýr*), in the district of Ringerike, north of present-day Oslo. He embarked on his first **Viking** expedition at the age of 12. Skaldic poetry by Olaf's poets, **Sighvatr Þórðarson** (*see* **Víkingavísur**) and **Óttar the Black** (*Höfuðlausn*), are the most valuable sources for Olaf Haraldsson's career as a Viking. Olaf was converted to **Christianity** at Rouen in 1014 while campaigning in **Normandy** in the service of the exiled king of England, **Æthelred II**. He returned to Norway shortly afterward and was recognized as king in **Trondheim** in 1015. However, he soon made a number of powerful enemies, following a ruthless campaign to convert all of his countrymen and to establish churches throughout Norway. Opponents to his rule were supported by **Cnut I the Great** through his vassal, **Earl** Hákon Eriksson of **Lade**, and in 1028 Olaf was forced into exile in **Russia**, staying with his kinsman **Jaroslav the Wise**. On his return to Norway in 1030, following the death of Earl Hákon, Olaf and his army encountered an army of peasant farmers from Trøndelag who had the backing of Cnut. In the resulting battle at **Stiklestad**, Olaf was killed. His body was buried on the banks of the River Nid in Trondheim.

Following his death and the imposition of Danish rule under Cnut the Great's son and regent, **Svein Cnutsson**, miracles began to be reported around Olaf's grave in Trondheim. According to Snorri's ***Heimskringla***, his coffin was reopened by Bishop Grímkell, one of Olaf's English advisors, and it was found that the king's hair and nails were still growing. Olaf was declared a saint and his bones were translated to a shrine near the high altar of St. Clement's church in Trondheim. During the reign of **Olaf the Peaceful**, his relics were moved to Christ Church, on the site of the present-day cathedral. During the medieval period, Olaf's shrine became one of the most important centers of pilgrimage in northern Europe. He was worshipped as Norway's patron saint, although he was never formally canonized. His feast day is celebrated on the anniversary of the Battle of Stiklestad, 29 July. Churches dedicated to Olaf are recorded in Russia (*see* **Novgorod**), the British Isles, and throughout Scandinavia. Olaf's life and career are recorded in several different sagas (*see **Sagas of St. Olaf***), as well as in *Heimskringla*.

OLAF THE PEACEFUL (ON *Óláfr kyrri*; also known as *Óláfr búandi* "the farmer"; and according to the *Anglo-Saxon Chronicle*, *mundus* "the elegant"?) (1046–1093). King of Norway

1066–1093. Son of **Harald Hard-Ruler** and Þóra Þorbergsdóttir, Olaf ruled jointly with his older brother **Magnus II Haraldsson** between 1067 and 1069. Olaf accompanied his father on his ill-fated expedition to England in 1066, and following Harald's death in the Battle of **Stamford Bridge**, Olaf traveled to the Norse earldom of **Orkney** before returning to Norway the following year. His nickname stems from the peaceful conditions that prevailed in Norway during his reign. He is said to have built a new church, Christ Church, for the relics of St. **Olaf Haraldsson** in **Trondheim**, and was considered by **Snorri Sturluson** to be the founder of **Bergen**, but the short saga in *Heimskringla* provides little more information than this. He died of sickness and was buried in Christ Church, Trondheim.

OLAF THE WHITE (ON *Óláfr inn hvíti*; **Irish** *Amlaíb, mac righ Laithlinde* **"son of the king of** *Laithlinde***").** In Icelandic saga tradition, Olaf the White was the husband of **Aud the Deep-Minded** and father of Thorstein the Red. In *Laxdœla Saga*, he is said to be the son of Ingjald, who was in turn the son of King Frodi the Valiant. Olaf is usually identified with the *Amlaíb* that is the first recorded king of the **Vikings** in **Ireland**. According to the *Annals of Ulster*, *Amlaíb* arrived in Ireland in 853, ended the conflict between the Danish and Norwegian Vikings, and took tribute from the Irish. In 859, the *Annals of Ulster* record that he invaded the kingdom of Meath with his companion Ivar (*Ímar*; **Ivar the Boneless?**) and an Irish king, Cerball mac Dúnlainge. In 863, with Ivar and another Norse king, Auðgisl (*Auisle*), Olaf plundered **burial** mounds on the River Boyne.

Olaf apparently ruled from **Dublin**, although he is recorded as raiding "all the land of the **Picts**" in central Scotland, with his brother Auðgisl and a band of "foreigners" from Ireland and **Scotland** in 866. The British stronghold of Dumbarton Rock in Scotland was besieged for four months in 870 and subsequently plundered and destroyed by the Norse, under Olaf and Ivar; Auðgisl's death, at the hands of "kinsmen," was recorded in 867. In 871, Olaf and Ivar returned to Dublin with 200 **ships** that were carrying "a great prey" of Angles, Britons, and Picts. Olaf disappears from contemporary historical records after this, and when Ivar died in 873, he is recorded as being "king of the Norsemen of all Ireland and Britain."

OLAF TRYGGVASON (968–1000). King of Norway 995–999/1000, renowned for his fierce advocacy of **Christianity**. Olaf claimed the Norwegian throne as the great-grandson of **Harald Fine-Hair**. His mother, Astrid, fled Norway just after Olaf was born and he spent his childhood in Estonia and **Russia** at the court of Vladimir I (d. 1015). Olaf later embarked upon a career as a **Viking** and is recorded raiding in England by the *Anglo-Saxon Chronicle* in 991. He fought at the Battle of **Maldon** and was subsequently paid a large **Danegeld**, before being converted to Christianity in 994. Olaf returned to Norway in 995 and seized the throne following a rebellion against the pagan **Hákon Jarl** of **Lade**. According to **Snorri Sturluson**, Olaf founded the Norwegian town of **Trondheim** as a center of royal power. He then proceeded to forcibly convert Norway, the Northern Isles, and **Iceland**. According to both Snorri and **Saxo Grammaticus**, Olaf proposed to **Sigrid the Proud** and subsequently rejected her in favor of Thyre, the daughter of **Svein Forkbeard**. Svein subsequently married Sigrid and, according to Snorri, both Sigrid and Thyre urged their respective husbands to wage war on each other in order to avenge insults they had suffered. The result was the confrontation at **Svöld**, when Olaf was killed fighting a combined Danish and Swedish army. His **ship**, the Long Serpent, in which he fought this battle, is one of the most famous of Viking-Age ships, and his saga in *Heimskringla* includes a long description of it, its construction, and its crew. Following Olaf's death, Norway was carved up by the victors of Svöld.

ÓLÁFS SAGA HELGA. See SAGAS OF ST. OLAF.

OLOF SKÖTKONUNG (d. c. 1022). King of Sweden c. 995–1022. Olof was the son of King **Erik the Victorious** and his mother is said to have been **Sigrid the Proud**. He ruled from the newly founded royal town of **Sigtuna**, where he issued the first royal coinage of Sweden. Although these coins proclaim him as king of the Svear (*see* **Svealand**), he had strong links with **Götaland**, founded Sweden's first bishopric at Skara in Västergötland, and was called "ruler of the Götar" and "prince of the Svear" by a contemporary poet. The nickname Skötkonung ("tribute king") suggests that he recognized another king as his overlord, probably **Svein Forkbeard** of Denmark.

Certainly, Olof fought alongside Svein at the Battle of **Svöld**, which resulted in the defeat and death of King **Olaf Tryggvason** of Norway. He was rewarded with land and tribute in Norway, but these were disputed following **Olaf Haraldsson's** return to Norway. Eventually terms were agreed between the Swedish and Norwegian kings, and their treaty was sealed with the marriage of **Astrid**, Olof's daughter, to Olaf. His other daughter, Ingigerd, was married to **Jaroslav the Wise** of **Russia**. Olof was succeeded as king by his son, **Anund Jakob**.

ORKNEY. Southern group of islands in the so-called Northern Isles of Orkney and **Shetland**. Orkney lies just 10 kilometers north of the north coast of **Scotland**. The traditional story concerning the beginning of Scandinavian settlement in the Northern Isles is given in the 12th-century *Orkneyinga Saga*, which claims that **Harald Fine-Hair** of Norway sailed to the Northern Isles in order to put a stop to the raiding of "certain **Vikings**" who used the islands as their base. Harald's western expedition is said to have taken place after his victory at the Battle of **Hafrsfjörd**. However, this date seems rather late, given indirect references in Irish annals to Viking raids in the region and, more particularly, archaeological material from Orkney, both of which suggest Viking activity began around 800. Moreover, the historicity of Harald's western expedition is doubtful, as it seems unlikely that his position in Norway was sufficiently secure to permit such a venture. The current consensus seems to be that the islands were probably raiding bases for perhaps up to half a century and were settled by a Scandinavian population during the ninth century.

It is not clear whether the islands were rapidly settled, like **Iceland**, with insignificant numbers of new settlers in the subsequent years and centuries, or whether settlement was a more or less continuous process over a century or more. This question has been overshadowed by the debate on the relationship between incoming Norse settlers and the native population. In the course of the Scandinavian settlement, the native population of **Picts** disappeared from the historical, archaeological, and linguistic record, a disappearing act that is so complete that some scholars have argued for the wholesale and deliberate elimination of the Picts on Orkney by incoming Scandinavians. However, archaeological evidence from a number of sites hints at some kind of continuity in artifactual assemblages from the Pictish period through to the early Viking Age, and on the basis of this evidence, a number of scholars have argued for a degree of social integration between the Pictish and Norse populations of Orkney in the ninth, and perhaps 10th, century. Certainly the Norse community on the **Brough of Birsay** had access to Pictish artifacts, which might have been obtained through trade or through the subjugation of the Pictish population. Nevertheless, it certainly seems that incoming Scandinavian settlers had more or less obliterated the culture of the pre-existing Pictish population by the end of the 10th century. Place-name evidence (some 99 percent of Orkney's place-names are of Norse origin) and the survival of the Norse language, **Norn**, down to the 18th century clearly demonstrate the thorough "scandinavianization" of the islands.

Several Scandinavian settlement sites have been identified on Orkney by excavation: the Brough of Birsay; **Buckquoy** in Birsay; Skaill in Deerness; the Brough of Deerness; Orphir; Pool on Sanday; **Westness** on Rousay; and Tuquoy on Westray. The majority of these appear to have been high-status Norse sites and most date from the 12th century.

Approximately 40 pagan **burials** have been uncovered on Orkney, with a roughly equal number of male and female burials. In particular, a ninth-century female grave and six possible Viking-Age graves have been found at the Broch of Gurness; a boat-burial was discovered at **Scar** on Sanday; and cemeteries have been recorded at Westness on Rousay and Pierowall on Westray. The large number of pagan burials on Orkney contrasts sharply with the evidence from its northern neighbor, Shetland. Saga tradition credits **Olaf Tryggvason** with the wholesale conversion of Orkney in 995. It is unlikely that this event, if it occurred, had an immediate significant effect on the beliefs of the wider population. Earl **Sigurd the Stout's** own acceptance of **Christianity** seems to have been a political expedient and he died at **Clontarf** carrying **Odin's** raven banner. However, this cannot have been the first time the **earls** and the Orkney population came into contact with Christianity: The Christian Pictish population may have played some part in the conversion of Norse settlers, although this is much debated. Place-names in Old Norse *papa* "priest, monk" seem to indicate Norse recognition of Christian communities and it is suggested that some Pictish religious sites continued to be used by the Scandinavian population. However, the two main contenders for such continuity, the Brough of Birsay and the Brough of Deerness, have not yielded any archaeological evidence for Pictish-period churches.

In the 10th century, Orkney became the base of a powerful earldom that later, particularly during the 11th-century rule of Earl **Thorfinn the Mighty**, exercised considerable power over other Norse colonies in the **Hebrides** and **Ireland**. The most important archaeological site on Orkney is the Brough of Birsay, Thorfinn's seat and where he established the first fixed bishop's see in Orkney c. 1050. **Adam of Bremen** writes that Archbishop Adalbert of Hamburg-Bremen consecrated one Þórólfr to Orkney, an appointment probably connected with Thorfinn's pilgrimage to Rome, and two successors to Þórólfr, John and Adalbert, are named. However, Adam's purpose was to emphasize the power of Adalbert and Hamburg-Bremen in the North, and he may therefore be claiming more legitimate authority for Adalbert than was actually the case. Indeed, in 1072–1073, Earl Páll Þorfinnssonr received a **York** appointee, Ralph, as bishop. The first native Bishop of Orkney, William the Old, was appointed in 1102. His long tenure (until 1168) saw the death and canonization of Earl **Magnus**; the building of St. Magnus Cathedral in Kirkwall (c. 1136–1137); the removal of the bishop's see to Kirkwall; and the transference of Orkney to the diocese of **Lund** in 1112 and to **Trondheim** in 1153.

Two characters stand out in 12th-century Orkney: Earl Rögnvald Kali and Svein Ásleifarson. Svein Ásleifarson, whose career is recounted in some detail in *Orkneyinga Saga*, has been described as the "ultimate Viking," and his death in **Dublin** c. 1171 in many ways symbolizes the end of the Norse era. His contemporary, Rögnvald, was the nephew of the martyred St. Magnus and founded the Cathedral dedicated to Magnus's memory. He ruled as earl between 1136 and 1158 and was canonized himself after his death. Although his rule saw what is generally described as an Old Norse renaissance in Orkney, paradoxically the earldom was open to increasing influence from the wider Christian world. The Cathedral of St. Magnus, the very symbol of the Norse earldom, was based on models from England (Durham) and Scotland (Dunfermline). Scottish earls held the

earldom from 1231 and, following the Treaty of Perth (*see* **Hebrides;
Isle of Man**) in 1266, Orkney became potentially vulnerable to Scottish takeover. There were Scottish bishops and clergy from the 14th century and by the 15th century the clergy appear to have been entirely Scottish. The arrival of a considerable number of settlers from Scotland, particularly in the 14th and 15th centuries, and the growing trade with Scotland, accelerated "scottification." The language of government, religion, and trade increasingly became Scots, and the last extant document in the Scandinavian language is dated to *c*. 1426. Scandinavian ownership of the islands was formally surrendered to Scotland in 1468, shortly afterward followed by the transfer of the bishopric to the jurisdiction of St. Andrews.

ORKNEYINGA SAGA. One of the so-called *Kings' Sagas*, covering events in **Orkney** from the 9th century to the end of the 12th century. *Orkneyinga Saga* was probably written in **Iceland** around the year 1200 by an Icelandic author, possibly a member of the Oddi family from southern Iceland or the Hvassfell family from northern Iceland. Its text is now found in three fragments *c*. 1300 and in a fuller version preserved in *Flateyjarbók* from the end of the 14th century; a further manuscript was destroyed in the fire at the Royal Library in Copenhagen in 1728.

The saga originally appears to have begun with the rule of the sons of **Rögnvald of Møre** and to have ended with the death of Svein Ásleifarson (*c*. 1171). This original compilation was apparently used by **Snorri Sturluson** as one of the sources for his saga of St. **Olaf Haraldsson** of Norway. In the early 13th century, *c*. 1230, a new version of the saga was produced, under the influence of Snorri's *Heimskringla*, which added a legendary introduction, as well as details of miracles associated with **St. Magnus** of Orkney and of the Norse settlements in Caithness, northeast **Scotland**. While the 11th-century rule of Earl **Thorfinn the Mighty** is treated in some detail in the saga, some two-thirds of its narrative concerns the Orcadian political scene from *c*. 1090, with particular emphasis on the contemporaries Earl Rögnvald Kali and Svein Ásleifarson.

OROSIUS. *See SEVEN BOOKS OF HISTORY AGAINST THE PAGANS.*

OSEBERG, SHIP AND ART STYLE. The Oseburg ship is one of the most famous Viking **ships** to have been discovered although, paradoxically, reconstructions have shown that this particular ship did not handle well in open water and that it was probably a *karfi* (leisure ship) designed for coastal sailing. The ship was excavated in 1904 in the province of Vestfold, southeast Norway. It had been buried in a mound of blue clay that provided excellent preservation conditions. **Dendrochronology** puts the date of the ship's construction at *c*. 820, and the **burial** itself is dated to around 834. The ship is 21.6 meters long, 5 meters wide, and 1.6 meters deep, and it had 15 pairs of oars. On board the ship, two females had been laid out in a small hut structure and the bodies of the **women** were accompanied by a wealth of grave goods. These included 5 richly decorated animal-head posts, a wagon, 4 sledges, 5 beds, a tent, storage chests, a wall-hanging, a bucket filled with apples, 12 horses, an ox, and various household and farming utensils. It appears that the mound had been broken into at an earlier date, and it is possible that jewelry and other valuables may have been robbed. One of the women buried in the ship was some 50 or 60 years old and appeared to have suffered from rheumatism. Two pairs of shoes, tailored to fit her swollen feet, were found in the burial. The other woman seems to have been much younger, at some 20 or 30 years old. There has been much speculation about the identity of the two women and their relationship. It has been claimed that the burial was that of Queen Ása, the mother of **Harald Fine-Hair**, and one of her maids, and although this is unlikely on chronological grounds, it probably was the grave of a member of the royal house of Vestfold. The ship and the grave goods are currently on display at the Viking Ship Museum in Oslo, Norway.

The Oseberg **art** style, generally dated 750–840, takes its name from the burial, particularly the beautifully decorated prows of the ship and the intricate and accomplished wooden carving found on the wagon, sledges, bedstead, and animal-head posts. The carver of one of the animal-head posts has been nicknamed the Academician because his work was so accomplished. The main feature of this earliest Viking-Age art style is the animal ornamentation, with the animals' bodies twisted and distorted into fluid patterns that are virtually unidentifiable as animals. Some of the Oseberg pieces also have the motif known as the "gripping beast," which is a key element of the **Borre** style. The more or less contemporary **Broa** style is extremely similar to the Oseberg style.

OSLO. Town located at the top of the Oslofjörd in southeastern Norway. The earliest mention of Oslo in *Heimskringla* is in the saga of **Harald Hard-Ruler**. According to Snorri, Harald established a market place there and he often resided there, because the town was well supplied by the extensive arable lands surrounding it, and because it was a convenient base both for attacking Denmark and defending southern Norway from Danish attacks. Archaeological excavation has, however, revealed that occupation on the site began somewhat earlier than the second half of the 11th century, perhaps *c*. 1000. Harald's contribution to the development of Oslo can probably be compared with **Olaf the Peaceful's** formalization of the status of **Bergen**, encouraging the development of an existing market place, through the provision of protection, the building of churches, and the increased demand occasioned by the presence of the king's court. Oslo, however, remained less important than either **Trondheim** or Bergen throughout the Middle Ages.

OSTMEN. Name for the Norse settlers in Irish towns, especially **Dublin**, that was first used in the 11th century. These Norsemen became increasingly hard to distinguish from the native Irish: they were Christian, spoke a Norse dialect that had been heavily influenced by Gaelic syntax and vocabulary, and, in some instances, spoke Gaelic. However, the Ostmen were recognized as a separate ethnic group following the English conquest of Ireland in 1171 and were granted the same rights as English settlers. In practice, however, these rights were often not recognized, as the Ostmen could not be easily distinguished from their Irish neighbors.

ÓTTAR. *See* OHTHERE.

ÓTTAR THE BLACK (ON *Óttar svarti*). Icelandic skald (*see* **skaldic poetry**), who was the nephew of **Sighvatr Þórðarson**. Óttar served at the courts of the Danish king, **Svein Forkbeard**, the Swedish king, **Olof Skötkonung**, and the Norwegian king, **Olaf Haraldsson**. One of the most valuable sources for Olaf Haraldsson's career as a **Viking** is

Óttar's poem, *Höfuðlausn* "Head Ransom." This was composed after Óttar is said to have offended the Norwegian king by reciting a romantic poem about Olaf's wife, **Astrid** (the daughter of Olof Skötkonung). Shortly afterward, Óttar moved to the court of Olaf's enemy, **Cnut I the Great**, in England. His *Knútsdrápa* records Cnut's campaigns in England and his confrontation at **Holy River** and won him rich reward in the form of a helmet full of silver pennies.

OX ROAD. *See* ARMY ROAD.

– P –

PARIS, SIEGE OF. Viking attacks on Paris were recorded four times: in 845, when a Viking fleet of 120 **ships** sailed up the Seine and was only prevented from looting the town by the payment of a huge tribute of 7,000 pounds of silver and gold coin and bullion; in 856, when the town was said to have been attacked and burned on 28 December; in 861, when it was burned again; and, most famously, in 885-886, when the town was besieged by Scandinavians for over a year.

At this time, Paris was not the capital of **Frankia** and the settlement was confined to an island in the Seine, Île de la Cité. It was joined to both riverbanks by two defended bridges, the stone *Grand Pont* and the wooden *Petit Pont*. A Viking fleet, under Sigfrid, attempted to negotiate passage upstream, past Paris, with Joscelin the Bishop of Paris. When refused, his army attacked the defended towers on the bridges but with no success, and so his army began its siege of the settlement in late November 885. One bridge was destroyed by floods in February, and Sigfrid offered to lift the siege for a mere 60 pounds of silver. This offer was refused by the Parisians. Following the death of Bishop Joscelin in April, Count Odo managed to leave Paris in order to urge **Charles the Fat** to come to the town's rescue. Charles eventually succeeded in relieving the town and its starving inhabitants, but he allowed the Vikings free passage up the Seine and gave them 700 pounds of silver. He was not forgiven for this and was deposed in 887. Odo was then crowned king of the West Franks, and he succeeded in driving the Vikings from the region in a series of campaigns over the following two years. A vivid account of the siege was written by a monk, Abbo, who was in Paris, recounting the glorious resistance of the two hundred French, under Count Odo, against what he extravagantly claimed was an army of 40,000 Vikings.

PAVIKEN. Small seasonal market town on the west coast of **Gotland**, the archaeology of which suggests it was one of the richest trading centers on the island. No traces of permanent occupation have been found during excavations, but there is clear evidence of trade and craft activities. Artifacts found include Arabic coins and weights, and glass *tesserae* from northern Italy; and ship-repairs and substantial fishing activity took place in the town.

PICTS. Name given to the indigenous inhabitants of northern **Scotland** (north of the Forth and Clyde estuaries), the Outer **Hebrides**, and the Northern Isles of **Orkney** and **Shetland**. The various tribal confederations in Pictland, recorded by Roman authors, were probably given the label *Picti*, "the painted ones," by the Roman garrison in northern Britain in the third century. They were described as tattooed barbarians by classical authors, as immigrants from Scythia by Bede in his eighth-century *Ecclesiastical History of the English Church*, and as pygmies who lost their strength at midday and hid underground by the 12th-century author of the ***Historia Norwegiae***. While it is possible that the Picts painted or tattooed their bodies, they were certainly not recent immigrants to Scotland, and **burial** evidence has conclusively demonstrated that they were no shorter than other inhabitants of the British Isles. Souterrains or underground "houses" are known from Pictland, but these were storehouses and refuges rather than living quarters and appear to have largely gone out of use by the end of the second century. Bede describes Pictish society as matrilinear, with inheritance rights and the right to the throne passing down the female rather than the male line. However, this claim is disputed by many modern historians.

The Picts are a rather shadowy people, largely due to the almost complete absence of written sources from Pictland, and to their total disappearance from the historical record during the ninth century, when they were absorbed into the expanding kingdom of Scotland on the mainland and overwhelmed by **Viking** settlers on the Scottish isles. The only surviving Pictish documents are copies of lists of kings, written in Latin, which cover the period from the mid-sixth century onward. By around the year 600, it appears that Pictland was undergoing conversion to Christianity. According to Bede, the Pictish king Nechton sent a request for advice on religious matters to Ceolfrid, abbot of the Northumbrian monasteries of Monkwearmouth and Jarrow in 710. This advice, when received by Nechton, was duly translated into Pictish for the king and then "sent out [. . .] to all the provinces of the Picts to be copied, learned, and adopted." Nevertheless, nothing is known about the work, writings, and even locations of the religious houses of Pictland. The "mystery" of the Picts has been further increased by more than 200 surviving stone monuments from Scotland and the Isles, decorated with a range of symbols. These same symbols are used across Pictland from the mid-sixth century onward, suggesting that they functioned as a means of communication for the Picts, but their meaning is unfortunately lost to modern scholars. From the eighth century onward, Pictish stone sculpture often incorporates a cross as a central element in its decorative scheme. Irish missionaries are also credited with introducing the ogham alphabet to Pictland in the seventh century, but although ogham inscriptions are found on a number of stone monuments and smaller objects, many texts are unintelligible, leading to considerable debate about whether or not the Pictish language was in fact a Celtic language, related to Gaelic.

PIRAEUS LION. Marble lion that stood in the harbor of Athens, Porto Leone. It was decorated with a **rune-inscribed** serpent, in the classic Swedish style, during the late Viking Age. Unfortunately, much of the inscription is now illegible due to weathering and damage. The lion presently stands in Venice, where it was taken after a Venetian victory in Athens in 1687.

POETIC EDDA. Collection of poems on **mythological** and heroic subjects that is preserved in the ***Codex Regius***. Most of the poems found in this manuscript are known only in this form. Although the *Codex Regius* is some 50 years younger than **Snorri Sturluson's *Prose Edda***, it is believed that the poems are older than the 13th century, hence the collection is also known as the *Elder Edda*. The manuscript is divided into two sections, the first of which deals with mythological material and the second, with poetry about heroic figures. Some of the most well-known mythological poems within the *Poetic Edda* are **Völuspá**, **Hávamál**, **Rígsþula**, **Lokasenna**, and **Þrymskviða**. The heroic section includes 16 poems about **Sigurd the Dragon-Slayer**, as well as poems about the Norse heroes, Helgi Hundingsbani and Helgi Hjörvarðsson. The *Poetic Edda* is one of the most important sources for Norse mythology and cosmology and has given its name to the genre known as **Eddic poetry**.

PROSE EDDA. Also known as *Snorra Edda* or the *Younger Edda*, the *Prose Edda* is a handbook for those wanting to compose skaldic poetry written by **Snorri Sturluson**. Together with the **Poetic Edda**, it is one of the most important sources for Norse **mythology** and cosmology. The *Prose Edda* was composed around 1220, and consists of three main parts: *Gylfaginning*, *Skáldskaparmál*, and *Háttatal*, which are preceded by a prologue. The prologue describes how **Odin** and a great following of people left their home in Troy, Asia, and settled briefly in Saxony, before moving north to Scandinavia. His descendants, the men of Asia, or **Æsir**, spread throughout the northern countries of Denmark, Sweden, and Norway, marrying and having children. *Gylfaginning*, the following section, describes how these Æsir came to be worshipped as gods and is the most important part of the *Prose Edda* for the study of Norse mythology. The other two sections, *Skaldskáparmál* and *Háttatal*, include lists of **kennings**, **heiti**, and rules for the composition of poetry, all of which contain a good deal of material relating to various myths about the pagan gods of Scandinavia.

– Q –

QUENTOVIC. Important trading center in **Frisia**, located on the River Canche, near Étaples in present-day France. Occupation on the site dates back to the late sixth century, when a mint was established there, and the settlement later expanded to cover an area of approximately 45 hectares at its maximum extent. As well as being a center of cross-Channel trade, craft activities such as iron smelting, pottery making, and weaving took place in the town. Like nearby **Dorestad**,

Quentovic suffered a number of **Viking** attacks, including that of 842, when many of its inhabitants were killed or taken prisoner. The town was apparently abandoned in the 10th century, probably due to the silting up of the river that made access from the sea difficult.

– R –

RAGNALD (d. 920–921). **Viking** king of **York** *c.* 914 (or earlier) and 919–921. Ragnald was one of the grandsons of **Ivar** (*Ímar*) of **Dublin** and may have been among those expelled from Dublin in 902. Following this expulsion, there were raids on Dunkeld (903) and in Fortriu (904) in southeast **Scotland**, and one of Ragnald's brothers, Ivar, is said to have died in the latter attack. It is therefore possible that Ragnald himself was involved in this campaign, particularly given other references to the activities of the sons of Ivar in Scotland around this time. According to the *History of St. Cuthbert*, Ragnald won a victory against the **Northumbrians** and Constantine, king of the Scots, at Corbridge in 914, and he apparently plundered Strathclyde in the same year, before defeating a Norse rival, Bárðr Óttarson, in a sea battle off the **Isle of Man**. It is possible that Ragnald was already king of York at around this time, and the Anglo-Norman historian, Simeon of Durham, certainly suggests that this was the case. Moreover, the York St. Peter's coinage underwent a change around 915, becoming heavier and bearing the symbols of a sword (found on the coins of Ragnald's brother and successor, **Sigtrygg Cáech**) and a **Thor's** hammer. A new secular coinage from York, bearing the name RAIENALT, has also been dated to the period *c.* 910–915 and can probably be associated with Ragnald's first period of rule at York.

In 917, Ragnald is reported to have arrived at Waterford in **Ireland** with a fleet and campaigned in Munster. However, the following year saw him returning to Scotland and confronting the Scots in the second, inconclusive, Battle of Corbridge. In 919, Ragnald recaptured York (wrongly dated to 923 in the *Anglo-Saxon Chronicle*), and he is said to have submitted to Edward the Elder of England in the following year at Bakewell. The *Annals of Ulster* record his death in 921, and he was succeeded in York by his brother, Sigtrygg Cáech. As Sigtrygg left Dublin in 920 and as Guthfrith, another of his kinsmen, arrived in Dublin from York in 921, it is likely, however, that Ragnald did in fact die in 920.

RAGNAR LOÐBRÓK (Ragnar "Shaggy-Breeches"). Legendary **Viking**, whose nickname was derived from the trousers he wore in order to protect himself during a battle with two giant serpents. In **William of Jumièges**, the first writer to mention *Lothbroc*, he is said to have been an Anglo-Scandinavian king and the father of **Björn Ironside**, who forced Björn into exile and thus into a life of raiding and pillaging. Book nine of **Saxo Grammaticus's** *History of the Danes* describes Ragnar as a relative of the ninth-century Danish king, **Godfred**, who became king himself and made heroic conquests across the Viking world. His first wife was said to be Laðgerða, but he later divorced her and married a Swedish princess, Þóra, whose father wished to reward him for killing two giant serpents. However, the 13th-century Icelandic *Saga of Ragnar Loðbrók* names his father as Sigurd *hringr*, another Danish king, and he is said to have married the daughter of **Sigurd the Dragon-Slayer** and the **valkyrie** Brynhild after Þóra had died. According to tradition, Ragnar was killed by the Anglo-Saxon king of **York**, Ælla, who threw him into a snake pit. His sons, **Ivar the Boneless**, **Björn Ironside**, **Halfdan**, and Ubba are said to have invaded England and to have killed Ælla with the gory ritual of **blood-eagle** to avenge their father's death. Although his sons are historical figures, there is no evidence that Ragnar himself ever lived, and he seems to be an amalgam of several different historical figures and pure literary invention.

RAGNARÖK. Ragnarök, or "the twilight of the gods," was the name given to the final apocalyptic battle between the gods and the giants in Norse **mythology**, which led to the destruction of the earth. In the course of this battle all of the major gods died while killing their enemies: **Odin** was swallowed by the wolf **Fenrir**; **Thor** was poisoned by the venom of the **Midgard serpent**; **Frey** was killed by the giant, Surt; **Tyr** by the hound Garm; and **Heimdall** by **Loki**. However, the earth and several gods, including **Balder**, were reborn, but so too was the corpse-eating dragon, **Nidhogg**. This story of resurrection has led some scholars to question the influence of Christian cosmology in the story as preserved in the *Prose Edda* and *Poetic Edda*.

The most important descriptions of Ragnarök come from these two later written sources, particularly *Gylfaginning* and *Völuspá*. Viking-Age stone sculpture, such as the **Gosforth cross** from northwest England, provides some contemporary evidence for these Ragnarök myths.

RAMSUNDBERGET. Flat outcrop of granite in the central Swedish province of Södermanland, which is decorated with an 11th-century rune-inscribed dragon and carvings that depict the story of the Norse legendary hero, **Sigurd the Dragon-Slayer**. The Ramsundberget carvings are perhaps the clearest and single most famous illustration of the Sigurd legend. Sigurd is shown twice, killing the dragon, whose body is inscribed with **runes**, and sucking his thumb after burning it on the dragon's heart that he was then roasting. **Regin**, the beheaded smith, with his tools, is also shown, as are the birds that warned Sigurd of Regin's treachery; the dead otter, whose death started the fateful cycle; and Sigurd's horse, **Grani**, which is loaded up with the gold Sigurd had taken from the dragon's cave. Sigrid, "mother of Alrik, daughter of Orm," commissioned the runic inscription in memory of her husband, Holmger, "father of Sigröd." Sigrid also had a now-lost bridge made for Holmger's soul—this sort of "good work" is believed to have been encouraged by the missionary church in Scandinavia (*see* **Christianity, Conversion to**).

RATATOSK. According to *Gylfaginning* and the **Eddic** poem, *Grímnismál*, Ratatosk ("Drill-Tooth") was the name of the squirrel that ran up and down the trunk of **Yggdrasil**, carrying messages between the eagle sitting in the branches of the World Ash and the dragon, **Nidhogg**, lying at the roots of the tree.

RAVNINGE ENGE. Located some 10 kilometers south of **Jelling** in Denmark, Ravninge Enge is the site of a wooden bridge over marshy land that has been **dendrochronologically** dated to *c*. 980. The bridge measures about 700 meters in length, 5 meters in width, and, with more than a thousand supporting oak posts, could carry weights of up to about 5 tons. The construction of the bridge has been linked to the rule of **Harald Blue-Tooth**, as it improved and enhanced the status of the roads leading to and from his dynastic seat at Jelling.

REGIN (ON *Reginn*). The dwarf smith, who was **Sigurd the Dragon-Slayer's** foster father and **Fafnir** the dragon's brother. Regin encouraged Sigurd to steal the gold that Fafnir guarded and forged him a special sword called *Gramr* for the task. Regin and Sigurd planned to share the gold equally, however, Regin secretly plotted to kill Sigurd and to take all the gold for himself. After being warned by some birds of Regin's plans, Sigurd beheaded his foster father. *See also* RAMSUNDBERGET.

REPTON. Site of **Viking** winter camp and mass **burial** on the River Trent in Derbyshire, England. Repton is mentioned in the ***Anglo-Saxon Chronicle*** entries for 874 and 875 (referring to 873 and 874 respectively), where it is stated that the **Great Army** took winter quarters there before splitting up into two factions: **Halfdan** led a section of the army north into **Northumbria**, while **Guthrum**, Oscytel, and Anund headed to Cambridge. The remains of a D-shaped ditch and earth rampart about 200 meters long have been found at Repton, and excavations on the site of a former mortuary chapel of the Anglo-Saxon church of St. Wystan have revealed a mass grave that was covered by a mound. This contained the disarticulated remains of approximately 250 people, placed around a separate high-status male burial. About 80 percent of the bodies found in the grave were male, between the ages of 15 and 45. As the bones do not show much evidence of battle wounds, it has been suggested that the people buried were killed by disease rather than in battle. In addition to the mass grave, a number of burials were found close to the church, and coins found in the excavations of these have been dated to 873–874. One of these graves contained a man, aged 35–40, who had been buried with a **Thor's** hammer amulet, his sword and scabbard, and two knives. He had been killed by a large blow to his groin and was apparently castrated; the tusk of a wild boar had been placed in between his legs when he was buried. The excavators interpret the burials as the remains of some of the Great Army, although other scholars have suggested that these may in fact rather be the remains of the victims of the Great Army. Just four kilometers from Repton is another site with a large number of Viking burials, **Ingleby Heath**.

RERIC. Town on the Baltic coast of present-day Germany belonging to the Slavic **Abodrites**, the exact location of which is unknown. *Reric* is mentioned in the *Royal Frankish Annals* under the year 808, when the town was apparently destroyed and its merchants forcibly relocated to **Hedeby** by the Danish king, **Godred**. In the following year, an Abodrite leader was murdered at *Reric*. A number of possible contenders for *Reric* have been suggested: Old Lübeck, Mecklenburg, and Dierkow. Of these, Mecklenburg, near Wismar, seems most likely as there are early ninth-century finds that include Arabic coins, although Dierkow, near Rostock, has also yielded evidence of occupation, with a harbor, cemeteries, and a number of Scandinavian artifacts excavated there. There is, however, no archaeological evidence for settlement at Old Lübeck before 817.

REYKJAVIK. *See* ICELAND.

RIBBLEHEAD. Site of Viking-Age rural settlement in North Yorkshire, England. The farm consists of a **longhouse**, bakery, and smithy placed around a central courtyard in the classic Norse fashion, and is dated to the ninth century on the basis of coin finds, which include a bronze *styca* of Archbishop Wulfhere of **York** from around 862. Very few artifacts were otherwise found, and those that were, such as a bronze bell and quernstone, are not particularly Scandinavian in character. Ribblehead is therefore normally characterized as an Anglo-Scandinavian, rather than **Viking**, settlement site.

RIBE. Viking-Age town on the north bank of the River Ribe in Jutland, Denmark. Ribe was founded around 705, when an enormous layer of sand was put down and a series of plots were laid out in a grid along the riverbank. This organized "foundation" suggests that it was the initiative of someone with considerable economic and political power, such as the Danish king **Angantyr**. The discovery of some 150 silver coins, known as *sceattas*, decorated with pictures of **Odin** and a backward-facing animal, in the eighth-century deposits at Ribe suggests that coins may even have been minted in the new market place by this king. Craft activities in the town included the working of amber, bone and antler, leather, and iron. It appears that at this early stage Ribe was a seasonal market place for itinerant traders rather than a permanent settlement. However, to the southeast of the town was a small collection of buildings that seem to have been occupied all year round, and nearby some 30 pagan graves (largely cremations) from the eighth century have been excavated.

Ribe, lying just five kilometers from the North Sea, was very well placed for trade with the Low Countries and England, but it also had important links with **Frankia**, to the immediate south, and Norway to the north. The largest group of artifacts found during the excavations at Ribe was glass drinking vessels and pottery, imported from the Rhineland. Thick and widespread layers of manure suggest that Ribe may have been an important cattle market for the region.

Around 800, the market place at Ribe appears to have been made more permanent, and an area of about 10 hectares was enclosed by a semicircular ditch. During the ninth century, Ribe was mentioned in written sources for the first time, when it is said that the missionary **Ansgar** visited the town and was granted permission by King **Horik** the Younger to build a church there. The next mention of Ribe concerns its first bishop, Leofdag, who is said to have participated in a church synod at Ingelheim in Germany, along with the bishops of **Hedeby** and Århus. The Archbishop of Hamburg-Bremen, Adaldag, probably appointed them to their sees on this occasion. However, the names of the bishops are not Danish, and it is not clear if they actually resided at their sees; they may have been appointed to reinforce Hamburg-Bremen's claims to religious primacy in Denmark.

In the second half of the 10th century, the three towns of Ribe, Hedeby, and Århus were fortified. The shallow ditch around Ribe was replaced by a new ditch, some 8 meters in width and 1 meter in depth, which was fronted by an earth rampart. This fortification has been linked to **Harald Blue-Tooth's** German wars of 974 and 983. As the town grew in the 11th century, this ditch in turn was filled in and built upon, and a new ditch and rampart, topped with a timber palisade was built to the east of the old ditch.

By the end of the Viking Age, Ribe was the center of a bishopric that appears to have controlled the whole of the Jutland Peninsula. It was also an important mint, named on the coins of **Cnut I the Great**, **Harthacnut**, and **Svein Estrithsson**. The town continued to expand and spread to the opposite, southern bank of the River Ribe in the 12th century. A stone cathedral and a royal castle were built on the south side of the river, and the center of Ribe shifted here, to where the present-day city center lies.

RÍGSÞULA ("The Lay of Rig"). **Eddic** poem that tells of the journey of "the wise god" Ríg to the **houses** of three different families. In a short prose introduction to the poem, Ríg is said to be the god **Heimdall**. The three families Ríg visits represent three different social classes: slaves, free farmers, and nobility. Following Ríg's visit, each of the couples have a child that personifies the social class to which they belong: Ái and Edda (great-grandfather and great-grandmother) had a son called Þræll ("slave, laborer"); Afi and Amma (grandfather and grandmother) had a son called Karl ("free man, farmer"); and Faðir and Móðir (father and mother) have a son called Jarl ("earl, lord"). In turn, each of the three sons marry and have their own children: Þræll married Þír ("maid") and they had several children, whose names include Drumbr ("rotten log") and Kleggi ("horse-fly"); Karl married Snør ("string") and their children include Bóndi ("yeoman, farmer") and Smíðr ("craftsman, smith"); and Jarl married Erna ("the capable one") and their children included Aðal ("noble") and Konr ungr ("young descendant"?). The name of this latter child is clearly a pun on the Old Norse *konungr* "king," and indeed Konr ungr grows up to be a wise and mighty man, taking over the name Ríg (which is also another word for king, derived from Irish *rí*).

Although *Rígsþula* is usually linked with the poems of the *Poetic Edda*, it is found in *Codex Wormianus*, a 14th-century manuscript containing Snorri's *Prose Edda*. The poem of 48 stanzas is apparently incomplete, with the end missing. There is no scholarly consensus as to its dating, with suggested dates ranging from the 9th to the mid-13th century.

RINGERIKE. Scandinavian **art** style that takes its name from a region in central Norway, where several raised stones are decorated in this style. The main motif found in the Ringerike style is the so-called "great beast." This beast is characteristically embellished with thick tendrils and pear-shaped lobes. The Ringerike style was popular during the first half of the 11th century and some of the most famous examples of the style, such as the **rune-stone** from St. Paul's Cathedral in **London**, come from southeast England, where **Cnut I the Great** was king at this time.

RINGMERE HEATH, BATTLE OF. Battle fought to the immediate north of Thetford in Norfolk, England, on 5 May 1010. The **Viking** army of **Olaf Haraldsson** confronted the English army of Ulfcytel "Snilling," **Earl** of **East Anglia**. Although Ulfcytel's Cambridgeshire forces stood firm, the East Anglians are said in the *Anglo-Saxon Chronicle* to have fled from a Viking known as Thurcytel "Mare's Head" and from the battlefield. The English consequently suffered a disastrous defeat that allowed the Vikings to harry the region for three months and to burn down Thetford and Cambridge. The English dead included Athelstan, the brother- or father-in-law of King **Æthelred II**, Athelstan's son, Oswy, and "many other good **thegns** and countless people." Two **skaldic** verses, composed by **Sighvatr** Þórðarson and **Óttar the Black**, commemorate Olaf's victory in the battle, and are preserved in Snorri's *Heimskringla*. However, in these sources the battle at Ringmere Heath, along with others fought by Olaf at this time, is presented as part of a campaign by Olaf to assist the English king Æthelred II against the Danes, under **Svein Forkbeard**.

RING-MONEY. Silver arm rings of a standard weight that were used as currency by Scandinavians before they started to mint their own coins.

RIURIKOVO GORODISHCHE. *See* GORODIŠČE.

RÖGNVALD EYSTEINSSON OF MØRE (ON *Rögnvaldr Eysteinsson*). Norwegian **earl** and ally of **Harald Fine-Hair**. According to *Heimskringla* and *Orkneyinga Saga*, Harald made Rögnvald ruler of North Møre, South Møre, and Romsdal on the western coast of Norway in return for his support in Harald's campaign to win control of the whole of Norway. Rögnvald is said to have had six children, two (Hrolf [*see* **Rollo**] and Thorir) by his wife Hild (Ragnhild in *Orkneyinga Saga*) and three (Hallad, Hrollaug, and Torf-Einar) by consorts. The mother of his sixth child, a son called Ivar, is unknown. Ivar is said to have been killed during Harald's western expedition (the historicity of this expedition is dubious), and Rögnvald was apparently given control of **Orkney** and **Shetland** by Harald as compensation for his loss. However, he immediately handed over the islands to his brother, **Sigurd the Powerful**. Sigurd was briefly succeeded by Rögnvald's son, Hallad, and then by Torf-Einar ("Turf-Einar"), who is said to have been the first man to use peat for fuel on the islands. Rögnvald was burned to death in his **house** by two sons of Harald Fine-Hair, who apparently resented the earl's power and their father's reluctance to grant them control of any part of his kingdom. Thorir, another of Rögnvald's son, inherited his father's position and was married to one of Harald Fine-Hair's daughters.

RÖK STONE. Rune-stone standing in the cemetery of Rök parish, Östergötland, southeast Sweden. The stone itself is 4 meters high, 1.5 meters wide and 0.5 meters thick, and runes are carved on all four sides and the top of it. The order in which the different lines of text should be read is unclear. The inscription consists of 750 characters, making it the longest, as well as the most complex, of Scandinavian runic inscriptions. It is carved mainly in short-twig runes, but there are also some runes from older *futhark* and some cryptic runes. The meaning of the inscription is not always clear, but it was apparently a memorial stone raised for Væmoð by his father, Varin. In addition to this, it contains heroic, legendary, and historical references to Theodoric; to 20 kings lying on a battlefield; to 20 kings with only four names (i.e., five kings each had the same name), who were the sons of four sons; to **Thor**; to Sibbi, who at the age of 90 fostered or begot a son. The Rök inscription also includes the oldest verse of **fornyrðislag** meter, an epic form of **Eddic poetry**.

ROLLO (ON *Hrólfr* **French** *Rollon***) (c. 860–932).** Scandinavian founder of the duchy of **Normandy**. There has been considerable debate about Rollo's nationality. In French sources, he is called a Dane, but according to *Heimskringla*, Rollo was the son of **Rögnvald of Møre** and is said to have left Norway after being outlawed by King **Harald Fine-Hair**. In support of his account, **Snorri Sturluson** quotes a verse composed by Rollo's mother, Hild, lamenting his outlawry. While most historians accept that Rollo probably was a Norwegian, it is clear from place-names in Normandy that his army must have consisted of Danes and **Vikings** from the Norse colonies in the West too. After leaving Norway, Rollo then apparently proceeded to raid in the **Hebrides**, England, the Low Countries, and France, before establishing himself in an area along the Seine River. According to Norman annals, based on the accounts of **Dudo of St-Quentin** and **William of Jumièges**, he arrived in this region in 876, but modern historians prefer a date nearer to the year 900.

Charles III the Simple granted Rouen and the surrounding area to Rollo sometime after 911 and, in return, Rollo agreed to end his attacks on Charles's kingdom. Rollo was also baptized and he married Gisla, the daughter of Charles the Simple. After Gisla's death, he is said to have married Popa, daughter of Berengar of Bayeux. However, despite the treaty, conversion, and marriage, Rollo continued to raid in the region, and both he and his son, **William I Longsword**, considerably extended their territory in northern France: by 924, Rollo had expanded his control to the River Vire, incorporating Bayeux. He is then said by Dudo to have abdicated in favor of William *c*. 925. *See also GÖNGU-HRÓLFR'S SAGA*; ST. CLAIR-SUR-EPTE, TREATY OF.

ROSKILDE FJORD. *See* SKULDELEV.

ROYAL FRANKISH ANNALS (*Annales regni Francorum*). Annals composed at the royal court of **Charlemagne**, king of the Franks. They cover the period 741 to 829, at which point the *Annals of St-Bertin* begin. Conventionally, the *Royal Frankish Annals* are divided into three parts, covering the periods 741–795, 795–807, and 808–829, on the basis of differences in language and style. Although the *Annals* were clearly written by more than one person, the authors are unknown. Einhard, author of the *Life of Charlemagne*, has been suggested as one possibility, but although there is some resemblance, this appears to be mainly due to the fact that Einhard used these annals himself. The oldest manuscript of the *Annals* was found in the monastery of Lorsch, near Worms, but their content clearly demonstrates they were written at the royal court.

The *Annals* were begun at some point between 787 and 793, by the first author, on the basis of some now-lost annals. The first section is therefore not a contemporary record, unlike the second and third sections. The reason for writing the *Annals* is unknown. Charlemagne promoted the writing of history at his court, but it is unclear whether or not he ordered the writing of the *Royal Frankish Annals*. It certainly seems quite likely that he was involved, as the *Annals* essentially present a record of his achievements and those of his son and successor, **Louis the Pious**. Moreover, the chronicler keeps quiet about disasters in the field and about internal troubles during the first section; and he also seems to have intimate knowledge of the affairs he was writing about—the campaigns, the composition of armies, and the purpose of the military action.

These *Annals* include many details about the relationship between the Danes and the Franks in the late eighth and early ninth century, at a time when Charlemagne was expanding his empire. Denmark is first mentioned in 777 when the Saxon chieftain, Widukind, sought refuge with King Sigifrid in Denmark; in 782 King Sigifrid sent ambassadors to the Frankish court; and **Viking** activity is recorded in 800 and again in 810 and 820. The *Royal Frankish Annals* also constitute a key source for the study of early Danish history, being the only source to record the names of Danish kings of the late eighth and early ninth centuries, although the form of these differs from the Scandinavian versions: for example, *Heriold* is **Harald Klak**, *Godofrid* is **Godfred**, and *Sigifrid* is Sigfred. The *Annals* are particularly useful for tracing the dynastic conflicts in early-ninth-century Denmark: Louis the Pious supported Harald against the sons of Godfred; but one of these sons, **Horik**, won the Danish throne in 827 and held it until his death in 854. The *Annals* also record the conversion of the Danish king, Harald Klak, and the subsequent launch of **Ansgar's** mission to convert the Danes and Swedes to **Christianity**. However, these missionary efforts by the Franks failed, and in 845 Horik attacked and burned Ansgar's cathedral in Hamburg.

RUNE. Character in the alphabet used by Scandinavians during the period *c*. 200–*c*. 1400, before the Roman alphabet became the dominant script. This runic alphabet, known as the *fuþark* or *futhark* after its first six letters, originally consisted of 24 characters, but at the beginning of the ninth century, it was reduced to just 16 characters in Scandinavia. There were two main versions of this 16-rune, or younger, *futhark*: short-twig runes and long-twig runes. The forms of the short-twig runes were simpler than those of the long-twig *futhark*. Both of these younger *futharks* were, however, insufficient for representing all the sounds of the Old Scandinavian language, and in the period after the 10th century, new "dotted" versions of some of these runes appeared, which helped to distinguish between different sounds, for example, *k* and *g*, *d* and *t*, *e*, and *i*. The *futhark* used in the medieval period was a mix of short-twig and long-twig forms, augmented with several of these "dotted" runes.

During the Viking Age, the runic alphabet was used primarily on memorial stones. Some 3,000 rune-stones have survived from this period, the vast majority in Sweden. In the eastern Swedish province of Uppland, about 1,800 rune-stones commemorate people who had died, both at home and abroad, although occasionally, rune-stones record the deeds of people who were still alive. Most of these Viking-Age rune-stones are inscribed with the same formulaic commemorative text: "X (person) raised this stone in memory of Y (another person), his or her Z (relationship between X and Y)." A Christian prayer, the signature of the rune-carver, or a brief description of the status or achievements of Y, and sometimes X, may follow this commemorative formula.

Scholars are still uncertain as to why so many rune-stones were raised in Scandinavia during this brief period. Older theories linked them to **Viking** raids and to **burial** customs in the transitional period between pagan and Christian beliefs. However, these theories do not account for either the small number of stones that commemorate people who died away from home (*c.* 10 percent of the total) or the fact that rune-stones generally do not seem to be associated with burials. Current scholarship regards the rune-stones as a product of a complex mix of social and economic factors, which varied according to time and place.

Runes are often assumed to be a magical script used by non-Christians, and it is therefore frequently believed that their use was opposed by the Christian church. However, the *futhark* was a practical alphabet, used in the Germanic world in the period before the Roman alphabet became dominant. The spread of **Christianity** was certainly important in establishing the dominance of the Roman script. However, extant inscriptions from Scandinavia show that runes were used much more commonly for Christian texts and messages than for other non-Christian religious and magical purposes in the Viking Age.

RUS. The name **Russia** is derived from the word Rus, found in the Slavonic languages, and paralleled by Rhos in Latin, 'Rös in Greek, and Rüs in Arabic. Rus was, along with **Varangian**, one of the words used to describe the Scandinavians active in Russia and the East. The etymology of this word is usually explained as Finnish *ruotsi* "Swede," which is derived in turn from the Swedish word for "rower" and which is found in the name Roslagen, the legal area around Stockholm. However, an alternative derivation may be from Greek *rusioi* "blondes."

Although some Soviet historians argued that the Rus were Slavs rather than Scandinavians (*see* **Normanist Controversy**), there is contemporary evidence to support the Scandinavian origin of the Rus. The *Annals of St-Bertin* record that some envoys of the prince of Rhos (sent by Emperor Theophilus of **Byzantium**) visited the Frankish court of **Louis the Pious** in 839, and it identifies them as being of Swedish origin (*gentis Sueonum*). Bishop Liutprand of Cremona identified the Rhos with Northmen in 968: "There is a people dwelling in the north whom for some bodily quality the Greeks call Rus, we, however, by reason of their homeland call them *Nordmannos*." The Rus names for the rapids on the River **Dnieper**, given in the 10th-century *Administration of the Empire*, also appear to be of Scandinavian origin and are certainly distinguished from the Slavonic names by **Constantine II Porphyrogenitos**. However, by the 11th century, the Rus had largely been assimilated among the Slavonic population.

RUSSIA, VIKINGS IN. Scandinavians called Russia either *Svíþjóð hinn mikla* ("Sweden the Great" or "Greater Sweden") or *Garðaríki* ("Kingdom of Towns"). **Viking** activity in European Russia (between the Arctic and Black Seas in the north and south respectively, and between Poland in the west and the Urals in the east) is traditionally said to have begun in the mid-ninth century, with the arrival of the **Rus** leader, Rurik (d. *c*. 879), as recorded in the *Russian Primary Chronicle*. However, archaeological evidence suggests that Scandinavian, and particularly Swedish, merchants were active in the region considerably earlier than this, in the mid-eighth century. They reached Russia by a number of routes, and the Rivers **Dnieper** and Volga opened up Russia to them. From the Dnieper, they could sail into the Black Sea and then to **Byzantium**, the capital of the Byzantine Empire (*Grikkland*). An 11th-century Scandinavian runic (*see* **rune**) inscription, raised in memory of a man called Karl by his business partner (*see* **félag**), Grani, was found on the island Berezany in the Dnieper outlet to the Black Sea. From the Volga, the Vikings could sail down to the Caspian Sea and reach the Middle East (*Serkland*). The Arabic writer and diplomat, **Ibn Fadlan**, gives a vivid picture of a Rus community on the Volga in the 920s.

The Scandinavians did not only develop trading routes through Russia, traveling onto destinations in the south and east. There is also archaeological evidence that they settled in Russia. Scandinavians established trading centers in order to take advantage of the region's wealth, settling in towns such as **Staraja Ladoga**, **Gorodišče**, **Novgorod**, and **Kiev**. The extent of this wealth can be traced in the huge number of Arabic dirhams (silver coins) that have been found in Sweden, particularly Gotland. These were received in exchange for, among other things, northern furs, slaves, and amber. This trade with the Arabic world appears to have increased in the mid-ninth century, reaching a peak by about 950. It subsequently declined following the exhaustion of the silver mines in Asia and the collapse of the Samanid state, and Russian trade was reoriented westward to the Baltic.

Scandinavians encountered a number of distinct and different people during their travels in European Russia: Finns and Balts in the northwest, Bulghars in the northeast, Khazars in the south, and East Slavs in western Russia. The *Russian Primary Chronicle* emphasizes the political and economic overlordship that the Scandinavians enjoyed in Novgorod and Kiev, but it seems that the Scandinavian rulers were rapidly assimilated to the Slavic population of Russia. This can be traced in the names of the Rus dynasty; Svyatoslav I (d. 978) was the first to have a Slavonic name, and he gave a Slavonic name to his son, Vladimir I (d. 1015), who adopted Eastern Orthodox **Christianity** as the "state" religion in 988. While Vladimir employed Scandinavian mercenaries or **Varangians** to help him in his campaign for control of Kiev, he dismissed most of them from his service following his victory as they posed a potential threat to his position in Russia. Nevertheless, links with Scandinavia appear to have thrived during the reign of **Jaroslav the Wise**. He was married to Ingigerd, the daughter of the Swedish king **Olof Skötkonung**; his daughter, Ellisif, was married to the Norwegian king, **Harald Hard-Ruler**; and Jaroslav's court appears to have had prominent Scandinavian visitors, such as **Olaf Haraldsson** and **Magnus I the Good** of Norway and **Ingvar the Far-Traveled** of Sweden.

RUSSIAN PRIMARY CHRONICLE. Also known as _Nestor's Chronicle_, from the name of the monk Nestor, who was once believed to have written the _Chronicle_ in **Kiev** around 1100. In Slavonic, the _Chronicle_ is usually called _Povest'_ from the first words of its title, meaning "The Narrative (of Past Times)." The work survives in two major versions: the so-called Laurentian version, named after the 14th-century copyist, Laurence; and the 15th-century Hypatian version, named after the monastery where it was found. These versions are both based upon a 12th-century compilation, probably made in Kiev, and this 12th-century compilation in turn seems to have used largely 11th-century material. The monk Nestor is believed to have been one of the compilers involved in this work.

The _Chronicle_ takes the form of an annalistic account, a year-by-year record of events between 852 and 1110, centered on the Kiev dynasty. However, it is essentially an attempt by a converted people to interpret their past: there are long biblical sections and the _Chronicle_ is rich in legend and myth. One of the most important of these myths for historians of the **Vikings** is the episode known as "The Calling of the Varangians," which describes how warring Slavic peoples decided to ask the **Varangians** to come and rule over them in 862, as they could not decide who among them should be king. This episode forms the center of the so-called **Normanist Controversy** over who founded the **Russian** state: Scandinavians or Slavs, and many of the details are suspect. The whole episode is rather reminiscent of other legends of origin, and while Rurik is known from other sources, his brothers—Sineus and Truvor—may be literary creations to explain later Scandinavian presence in a number of urban centers in Russia. The chronology is also problematic, as we know from archaeology that there were Scandinavians in Russia in the early ninth century, and that by 860 they were organized enough to attack **Byzantium** from their bases in Russia.

Nevertheless, the *Chronicle* does contain some useful details about the activities of the **Rus** in the 9th and 10th centuries in the areas that are now Russia, Byelorussia, and the Ukraine, including a number of journeys from their base in Kiev to Byzantium. The *Russian Primary Chronicle* also contains details about a number of treaties signed by the Rus and the Byzantine Greeks in 907, 912, 945 and lists the names of the Rus negotiators; most of these names appear to be Scandinavian names that have been slavonicized to some degree.

– S –

SÆMUND THE LEARNED (ON *Sæmundr inn fróði Sigfússon*) (1056–1133). Icelandic priest and scholar, Sæmund was the son of a priest and his family lived at Oddi, **Iceland's** principal cultural and religious center in the south of the island. He studied for a number of years in France and returned to Iceland around 1076. He built a new church at Oddi and was instrumental in establishing tithe laws on the island in 1096. Sæmund married and had three sons and a daughter; his grandson, Jón Lóptsson, was **Snorri Sturluson's** foster father, and the so-called *Oddaverjar* became one of the most influential and important families in the late Icelandic republic. Sæmund is most famous, however, for his historical writing. Although none of his work has survived, it is referred to by several later writers, including **Ari Thorgilsson** and the author of *Nóregs konunga tal*. It appears that Sæmund wrote a short chronological history of Norwegian kings, probably in Latin (Snorri names Ari Thorgilsson as the first writer of history in Icelandic). The ***Poetic Edda*** was once believed to have been the work of Sæmund and was known for a time as *Sæmundar Edda*.

***SAGAS OF ANCIENT TIMES* (ON *Fornaldarsögur*).** The so-called *Sagas of Ancient Times* are not, as their name suggests, historical accounts, but rather heroic legends and adventure tales that were, for the most part, written in 14th-century **Iceland**. Although they often took historical figures as their subject, the story that was built around these characters lacked historical foundation. For example, one of the most famous of these sagas, *Göngu-Hrolfs Saga*, is about the founder of the Norse colony in **Normandy**, more usually known as **Rollo**. However, the fantastical story recounted in this saga is clearly just that, a story or fairy tale. There are about 30 surviving examples of *Sagas of Ancient Times*, and the most well known of these are *Völsunga Saga* and the *Saga of Hrólfr Kraki*.

SAGAS OF THE ICELANDERS (ON *Íslendingasögur*). The so-called *Sagas of the Icelanders* or *Family Sagas* are perhaps the best known of the sagas and include such classics as *Egil's Saga* and *Njal's Saga*. Most of them, as their names suggests, are set in **Iceland**, and they concern the lives of Icelandic farmers and chieftains in the period 870–1050. There is a preoccupation with representing Iceland as a bastion of freedom, centered on the heroic farmer who had no need of king or state. About 40 of this type of saga are preserved, and the majority date to the 13th century. Although the sagas are usually set in the past, these sagas are more literary creations than historical works, and they are romance-like in their structure. Unlike *Kings' Sagas*, the vast majority of these sagas are also anonymous.

SAGAS OF ST. OLAF. As well as the saga of **Olaf Haraldsson** found in Snorri's *Heimskringla*, a number of other sagas about the Norwegian martyr king are known. The oldest of these is the *Oldest Saga of St. Olaf* that was written at the end of the 12th century, and which survives in just six fragments. Although the language of these fragments is Icelandic, the author is unknown. A Norwegian revision of this saga, known as the *Legendary Saga of St. Olaf*, was composed in the Trøndelag region of Norway in the mid-13th century; this survives in just one manuscript and includes considerable detail about his miracles in order to demonstrate his spiritual significance. **Snorri Sturluson's** *Separate Saga of St. Olaf*, which was revised for inclusion in his *Heimskringla*, appears to have been partially based upon a biography of the king and saint that was written by Styrmir Kárason around 1220. Parts of this biography are found in *Flateyjarbók*. This *Separate Saga* was, in turn, adapted and augmented by new material in the 14th century.

ST. ANSGAR. *See* ANSGAR, ST.

ST. BRICE'S DAY MASSACRE. Massacre of "all the Danish men who were among the English race" that was ordered to take place on St. Brice's day (13 November) 1002 by **Æthelred II**. According to the ***Anglo-Saxon Chronicle***, the massacre was ordered because of the king's suspicions of a Danish plot to kill him and claim his kingdom. The victims may have included Gunnhild, the sister of **Svein Forkbeard** of Denmark, and her husband, Pallig. A charter of Æthelred, made some two years later, also refers to this massacre with reference to St. Frideswide's Minster in Oxford. This charter compensated St. Frideswide's, which had been burned down by local residents because some Danes were inside, seeking sanctuary.

ST. CLAIR-SUR-EPTE, TREATY OF. This is said to be the name of an agreement signed by **Rollo** and **Charles the Simple** in 911, in which Rollo was granted the territory of Neustria, which formed the core of the later duchy of **Normandy**. However, while it seems that Rollo and Charles did come to some kind of deal, this treaty and the date 911 may be a later invention or tradition. From contemporary sources, we know that Rollo and his Danish army besieged Chartres in 911, but that they were defeated. The next time Rollo is mentioned in written sources is sometime between 913–918, when he appears as a Christian leader, with full authority over Rouen. In a royal charter of 918, Charles the Simple refers to some kind of deal with Rollo, by which Rollo was given land in return for defending Charles's kingdom. This charter suggests that the agreement with Rollo was made sometime between 911 and 918, and probably 911–913, but at what point is unknown, and whether there ever was a Treaty of St. Clair-sur-Epte is also unclear. Certainly the royal charter of 918 does not specify the area that Rollo was given, although it appears to have been upper Normandy (the eastern part of the later Duchy).

ST. OLAF. *See* OLAF HARALDSSON, ST.

SAXO GRAMMATICUS (*c.* 1150–*c.* 1220). Twelfth-century Danish writer, whose nickname Grammaticus comes from the elaborate Latin prose of his great historical work, ***History of the Danes***. Little is known about Saxo's life except that he was probably from the island of Sjælland and that he came from a family of warriors. He was probably a clerk in the service of Absalon, who was bishop of Roskilde from 1158–1192 and archbishop of **Lund** from 1178 to 1201. Saxo is first mentioned in **Sven Aggesen's** *Historia Regum Danicae compendiosa*, where he is described as writing the history of the Danish kings of the 11th century.

SCAR BOAT BURIAL. The boat (*see* **ships**) **burial** at Scar on the beach of the **Orkney** island of Sanday was discovered in September 1991 and subsequently excavated during storms in November and December 1991. The boat was clinker-built with oak planks and measured about 7 meters in length, with space for perhaps six oars. A simple burial chamber had been created by filling the east end of the boat with stones, which was then separated from the rest of the boat with a large upright slab. In the remaining space, three bodies had been laid out: in the central part of the boat, a **woman** in her 70s and a child of about 10 or 11 were placed lying on their backs; and in the more cramped west end of the boat, a man in his early 30s, who was about 1.8 meters tall, had been placed on his back, with his legs bent up to fit into the space. This west end of the burial had been partly destroyed by high tides and sea erosion, and there had also been some damage to the skeleton of the woman, caused by an otter's nest that had been built there. The remaining grave goods consisted of, for the man, a broken sword in its scabbard, a quiver of eight arrows, 22 whalebone gaming pieces, a comb, two lead weights, and possibly a shield; and for the woman, a spectacular and highly unusual whalebone plaque, believed to be used for smoothing linen, a gilt-bronze equal-armed brooch, an antler comb, two spindle-whorls, an iron weaving-batten, shears, a needle-case containing two needles and thread, a sickle, and a maplewood box. Both the plaque and brooch have close parallels in northern Norway, and it has been suggested that this woman may have been among the early Norwegian settlers of Orkney. The burial is dated to the end of the ninth century.

SCOTLAND, VIKINGS IN. Before the first **Viking** raids on the islands and coast of Scotland, the modern country of Scotland was a collection of regional kingdoms rather than a single political unit.

The Outer **Hebrides**, **Orkney**, **Shetland**, and most of the mainland north of the Clyde-Forth line were inhabited by a **Pictish** population. The Scottish kingdom of Dalriada included western Argyll and the Inner Hebrides as far north as Skye. The British kingdom of Strathclyde, centered on Dumbarton Rock, lay to the southwest of the Clyde-Forth boundary. An Anglian population had also settled in southern Scotland, and Irish settlers inhabited the Rhins of Galloway. This political geography was radically altered as a consequence of Scandinavian raids and settlements. By the mid-ninth century the Scots, under pressure from Scandinavians in the west, had taken advantage of Pictish weakness in the east and under their king, Kenneth mac Alpin, had taken political control of Pictland. In the 10th century, Strathclyde was added, and the Scots fought the **Northumbrians** for control of what is now northwest England well into the medieval period.

The first recorded Viking raids on mainland Scotland followed almost 40 years of raids on its islands and **Ireland**. By this time, Scandinavians seem to have been actively involved in the political conflicts of Scotland (and Ireland). In 836, a chieftain of apparently mixed Norse and Gaelic ancestry from northern Ireland, Guðifreyr mac Fergus, went to fight on the side of Kenneth mac Alpin in Dalriada, and the *Annals of Ulster* record that "heathens" fought a battle against the men of Fortriu in central Pictland in 839. The **Gall-Gaedhil** mentioned in Irish annals may have been based in the Hebrides and southwest Scotland, and it is also argued that **Olaf the White** of **Dublin** may have been linked to this area. The establishment of a powerful Norse kingdom in Dublin in 853 was followed by extensive campaigning in mainland Scotland by Olaf and his kinsmen, and again after the expulsion of the Dublin Norse in 902, there seems to have been a concerted, if ultimately unsuccessful, attempt to win land and power in Scotland.

Following the re-establishment of the Norse in Dublin in 917 and their subsequent conquest of **York**, there was renewed interest in the routes east from Ireland. However, the 10th century also saw the emergence of another Norse threat to mainland Scotland, the growing power of the **earls** of **Orkney**. *Orkneyinga Saga* suggests that Vikings from the islands had raided Caithness in northeast Scotland from the early Viking Age. However, Earl **Sigurd the Powerful** is recorded as conquering the whole of Caithness, as well as much of Argyll, Moray, and Ross, in the mid-10th century. *Orkneyinga Saga* also mentions Sigurd's building of a stronghold in the south of Moray, tentatively identified as Burghead. There seems to have been recurrent fighting with the rulers (known as mormaers) of Moray over control of Caithness in the first century or so of the earldom, and later there was conflict with the burgeoning power of the Scottish kings.

The role of the Scottish kings in the fortunes of the Norse earls of Orkney remained important throughout the Viking and Norse periods, as rival claimants to the earldom could be made earl by the Scottish king, as well as the Norwegian king. The importance of the Scottish connection is clearly visible in the marriage alliances made by the earls, with the Scottish royal house and with the rulers of Caithness. **Sigurd the Stout** strengthened his hand in Scottish politics by marrying the daughter of Malcolm, king of the Scots. Earl **Thorfinn the Mighty** is said to have been given Caithness and Sutherland (northeast Scotland) and the title of earl by his grandfather, the Scottish king, Malcolm II. Although conflict over Caithness with the mysterious Karl Hundison, ruler of Moray, dominated the early years of Thorfinn's rule, *Orkneyinga Saga* records that Thorfinn "won for himself nine Scottish earldoms," as well as territory in the Scottish islands. Although the precise significance of the nine Scottish earldoms is uncertain, Thorfinn's substantial gains in Scotland, and elsewhere, seem to be clear, and he is credited with subjecting the mainland as far south as Fife. It is possible that the Scottish gains may have been given in return for support of the Scottish kings against the mormaers of Moray. Hinting at such an alliance is Thorfinn's half-Scottish ancestry and the marriage of Ingebjorg, either Thorfinn's daughter or widow, to Malcolm III Canmore of Scotland. Certainly after his rule, Caithness seems to have been an integral part of the Norse earldom of Orkney, with the earls residing at Duncansby, the former seat of the local rulers.

The place-names of Caithness are dominated by Scandinavian names, with virtually all of the settlement names in the region of Scandinavian origin. Sutherland, to the east, displays a mixture of Norse and Gaelic names, similar to that found in the Hebrides. A range of archaeological evidence relating to the Viking Age and Late

Norse period has been found in the modern county of Caithness, including two runic inscriptions (*see* **rune**) from Thurso. Settlement sites have been identified at Freswick Links (south of Duncansby Head on the east coast), Robertshaven (close to Duncansby Head on the north coast) and Huna (near to Robertshaven), and another possible but as yet unexcavated habitative site may exist at Reay (on the north coast, west of Thurso). Graves of a Scandinavian type have been found at Castletown (female skeleton, a pair of oval brooches, a jet arm ring, and a bone bodkin); Westerseat near Wick (two dissimilar oval brooches); Mill of Watten (skeleton in cist, iron spearhead); Haimar (Scandinavian **weapons**); Huna (possible boat **burial**); Reay (pagan cemetery); and Harrow (penannular brooch).

There is some evidence for Scandinavian settlement in mainland Scotland south of Caithness. There are a number of Scandinavian place-names on the western mainland, but these are topographical (describing natural features) rather than habitative (describing settlements) place-names. Scandinavian place-names are generally few and far between in southeast Scotland, with perhaps just 10 purely Scandinavian names found in the region. Although there are a number of place-names containing Scandinavian personal names, these are compounded with English words and were almost certainly not given by Scandinavian speakers. Archaeological evidence for a Scandinavian presence in mainland Scotland outside the northeast is similarly sparse. There are two runic inscriptions: a brooch from Hunterston, Strathclyde in the southwest, and a now-lost bronze crescent-shaped plaque from Laws in the southeast. There is a pagan female grave from near Perth and a lost coin hoard, deposited *c*. 1025–1032, from Lindores, near Newburgh. A number of **hogback** monuments are known from the southeast, although their distribution suggests a layer of Anglo-Scandinavian influence from northern England, corresponding to the place-names of southeast Scotland.

In 1098, the Norwegian king **Magnus Bare-Foot** attempted to assert Norwegian control over the Northern and Western Isles, which brought him into some conflict with the Scottish kings. A treaty was made with Edgar, the king of Scotland, which conceded Bute, Arran, the Cumbraes, and Gigha to Norway (*Heimskringla* describes the treaty terms: all the islands off the west coast separated by water navigable by a ship with its rudder set), while Kintyre on the mainland remained in Scottish hands. After Magnus's death in Ireland in 1103, the kings of Norway appear to have had little authority in the Scottish islands, leaving them vulnerable to takeover by Scotland. The late 12th and 13th centuries saw intensified conflict in the Isles between the sons of Sumarliði, King of the Isles, the Scottish king, and the Norwegian king. This culminated in Hákon Hákonarson of Norway's ill-fated expedition to the Isles, his defeat by the Scots at Largs in 1263, and his death in Orkney.

SERKLAND. Old Norse word for the Muslim lands in the Middle East, with their capital at Baghdad in present-day Iraq. *Serkland* is mentioned on a number of Viking-Age **rune-stones** from Sweden, such as those that describe the ill-fated expedition of **Ingvar the Far-Traveled**. The name is either derived from the word "Saracen," used to describe Muslims, or from Latin *sericum*, meaning "silk."

SEVEN BOOKS OF HISTORY AGAINST THE PAGANS (*Historiarum adversum Paganos Libri Septem*). History written by the Spanish churchman, Paulus Orosius, with the encouragement of Bishop Augustine of Hippo. Orosius's history originally covered the period from the Creation until AD 417, and was essentially a catalog of all the disasters that had afflicted the world and which the ancient pagan gods had been powerless to prevent, designed to refute claims that Rome's collapse under barbarian attacks was the revenge of the ancient gods for the recent adoption of **Christianity** as the religion of the Empire (AD 380). The history began with a geographical survey of "the world," which, however, excluded much of Europe north of the Alps. A geography of northern Europe, including parts of Scandinavia, was added in the ninth-century Old English translation of Orosius commissioned by **Alfred I the Great**. *See also* OHTHERE; WULFSTAN.

SHETLAND, VIKINGS IN. Northern group of islands in the so-called Northern Isles (ON *Norðreyjar*) of **Orkney** and Shetland. The Shetland archipelago lies some 80 kilometers north of Orkney's most northerly island and some 320 kilometers west of **Bergen** on the Norwegian coast. There are even fewer written sources for the Viking-Age history of Shetland than there are for its southern neighbor, Orkney. For example, ***Orkneyinga Saga*** mentions Shetland and Shetlanders only infrequently, mostly referring to Shetland's role as a port of call on the way to Orkney; as a base for attacks on Orkney; as a source of manpower for these attacks; and as a place of temporary refuge for people from their enemies in Orkney.

Despite the lack of written evidence, raids on the islands are believed to have begun at the end of the eighth century and archaeological evidence suggests that settlement began in the ninth century. Place-names indicate that the islands were completely scandinavianized in the course of the Viking Age. However, relatively little Viking-Age archaeological material has been found on Shetland. In particular, only two pagan graves, both apparently female as they contain bronze oval or "tortoise" brooches, have been found on the islands, both on Unst. Indeed, despite the thorough Scandinavianization of Shetland suggested by its place-names, there are indications of continuity from the pre–Norse period. In particular, carved stones in the Christian **Pictish** tradition continued to be produced in Shetland after Norse raids and settlement had commenced, while such sculpture ceases at the end of the eighth century in Orkney. It has been suggested that the continuing production of sculpture on Shetland and the lack of such sculpture on Orkney reflects differences in the scale of early Norse settlement, with more colonists being initially attracted by fertile Orkney. Such a difference in the density of Scandinavian settlement would have presumably also facilitated Pictish survival.

Jarlshof, at the southern tip of Mainland, is the classic, but exceptional, example of a Viking-Age farmstead in the Northern Isles. However, Norse **longhouses** have also been excavated at da Biggins, Papa Stour; Underhoull, Unst; and Sandwick, Unst. Both da Biggins and Sandwick appear to post date the Viking-Age, while the simple farmstead at Underhoull seems to have been occupied from the late 9th to the early 11th century. An Iron-Age complex of hut circles, workshop and souterrain preceded the Norse settlement at Underhoull, but the site was certainly deserted when the first Norse settlers arrived. Only two Viking-Age hoards of Scandinavian character have been recovered from the islands, both from southern Mainland, at Quendale and Dunrossness. The Quendale hoard was discovered in 1830 and consists of some **ring-money** and Anglo-Saxon coins of Æthelred II, **Athelstan**, and Edgar (d. 975), suggesting a deposition date of *c*. 1000. Only one coin, a penny of **Harald Hard-Ruler**, remains of the 1844 find at Dunrossness, but it is said to have been found with several similar coins and some cut up silver arm rings. The most famous of Shetland's archaeological treasures, the St. Ninian's Isle hoard, was buried *c*. 800 and consists of 28 pieces of Pictish ornamental silver. The hoard was buried beneath the floor of an early church on the site of a later, now ruined, church.

SHIPS. The classic symbol of the **Vikings** is their ships. These ships made raiding, trading, colonization, and, therefore, the Viking Age possible. Viking ships were clinker-built (with overlapping planks), steered by a rudder on the right-hand side of the ship, and were propelled by oars or a square sail affixed to a single mast. Planks were split from logs and were not sawed, which resulted in a strong and flexible hull. The classic Viking warship or longship is represented by **Skuldelev** 2 from Denmark, with some 30 pairs of oars, which is the largest longship yet excavated. Ships of this size were sometimes also known as *drakkar* "dragons." Famous *drakkar* include **Olaf Tryggvason's** *Long Serpent* and **Olaf Haraldsson's** *Visunden* ("The Ox," so-called because its prow was decorated with the head of an ox). Longships tended to have a shallow draught, which allowed them to beach easily and to travel through relatively shallow inland waters, as well as at sea.

Although the Vikings are popularly associated with warships, archaeological excavations have revealed a range of different Viking ships, adapted to the conditions and environment in which they were used. Trading vessels were generally broader than longships, with deeper drafts, more storage space, and fewer oars, and were known as *knarr*. One of the largest known *knarrs* (from Hedeby) measured 25 meters in length, compared to the 28 meters of Skuldelev 2, and had a capacity of 38 tons. This type of ship is likely to have been used for the Viking colonization of the North Atlantic. There were also leisure ships, known as *karfi*, such as those from **Oseberg** and **Gokstad**. These had more oars than a *knarr*, but were wider and deeper than the longships, with space to carry all the luxuries required by a chieftain or king on a voyage.

SIGHVATR ÞÓRÐARSON (d. c. 1043). Poet (*see* **skaldic poetry**) at the court of **Olaf Haraldsson**, who fought alongside Olaf at the Battle of **Nesjar** and composed *Nesjavísur* in honor of Olaf's victory. One of his most famous, and earliest, pieces of work was *Víkingavísur*, which catalogs Olaf's earlier expeditions in England, France, **Spain**, and the Baltic. Sighvatr was sent by Olaf to Earl Rögnvald of Västergötland, Sweden, in 1017–1018 (his embassy is described in *Austrfaravísur* "Verses on an Eastern Journey") and then, in 1020, to England to see what plans **Cnut I the Great** had for Norway (resulting in *Vestrfararvísur* "Verses on a Western Journey"). Following Olaf's exile in 1028, Sighvatr went on pilgrimage to Rome and was there at the time of Olaf's final battle at **Stiklestad**. He remained with **Astrid**, Olaf's widow, in exile in Sweden and only returned to Norway when the Norwegian royal line was restored with the crowning of Olaf's son, Magnus, in 1035. He then served **Magnus I the Good**, and composed one of his most famous poems, *Bersöglisvísur* "The Plain-Speaking Verses," as a warning to Magnus against taking revenge against opponents of his father. In this poem, he also defined the qualities of a good king. No complete example of his poems has survived (*Bersöglisvísur* is the best preserved), but Sighvatr was quoted extensively in **Snorri Sturluson's** saga about St. Olaf (*see* **Sagas of St. Olaf**) and over 160 stanzas of his poetry still survive. *See also KNÚTSDRÁPA.*

SIGRID THE PROUD (ON *Sigriðr in stórráða***).** In *Heimskringla*, Snorri writes that Sigrid was the daughter of the prominent Swedish chieftain and warrior, Sköglar-Tosti, the widow of **Erik the Victorious**, the second wife of **Svein Forkbeard**, and the mother of **Olof Skötkonung**. However, in **Adam of Bremen**, Svein is said to have only one (unnamed) wife, who combined characteristics of Sigrid with those of Svein's first wife, Gunnhild—she was the widow of Erik, the mother of Olof, and the sister of Boleslav of Poland. According to both **Snorri Sturluson** and **Saxo Grammaticus**, Sigrid was also proposed to by **Olaf Tryggvason** of Norway before her marriage to Svein, and both also recount (different) stories of how Olaf subsequently shamed and offended her. The result of this enmity between Sigrid and Olaf was that Svein Forkbeard and Olof of Sweden formed an alliance against Norway that ultimately led to Olaf's death at **Svöld**. There is considerable doubt over whether Sigrid ever actually existed, although a **rune-stone** from Yttergärde, Uppland, Sweden, may refer to her father. It commemorates a Swedish **Viking** who was paid **Danegeld** by a leader called Tosti, as well as by **Thorkell the Tall**, and **Cnut I the Great**. This Tosti has been identified with Snorri's *Sköglar-Tosti* ("Battle-Tosti").

SIGTRYGG CÁECH (ON *Sigtryggr* **Irish** *cáech* **"squinty")** **(d. 927).** Sometimes Sihtric Caoch. Norse king of **Dublin** 917–921 and of **York** 921–927. Sigtrygg was the grandson of **Ivar** (*Ímar*) of Dublin and, with his brother **Ragnald**, re-established Norse power in **Ireland** and Dublin 914–917. In 919, the *Annals of Ulster* recorded a Norse victory (under Sigtrygg) at Dublin, which led to the death of the high king, Níall Glúndub, five other Irish kings, and many nobles. This event is also recorded in the *Anglo-Saxon Chronicle* for 921, although it mistakenly describes Níall as Sigtrygg's brother; The *Annals of Ulster* record that Sigfrith, Sigtrygg's brother, was killed by a "kinsman" in 888, and the English version of events seems to represent a confusion of the events of 888 and 919. In 920, Sigtrygg is said to have abandoned Dublin, but the following year saw the arrival of his brother, Guthfrith, another grandson of Ivar (*Ímar*) in that town, and the death of another of Sigtrygg's brothers, Ragnald (although the *Anglo-Saxon Chronicle* confusingly records that Ragnald won York in 923).

Sigtrygg appears to have succeeded Ragnald as king of York sometime around 921, and in the *Chronicle* for 925 (correctly 926) is described as king of **Northumbria**. In the same year, he came to terms with the English king, **Athelstan**, at Tamworth, was baptized, and married Athelstan's sister, Eadgyth. However, the Anglo-Norman historian, Roger of Wendover, writes that shortly afterward he renounced both his new faith and his bride. Sigtrygg died the following year (correctly 927, "at an immature age," according to the Irish annals), and was succeeded in York by Guthfrith, his brother. A number of coins, minted at York and inscribed with the legend SITRIC REX, survive.

SIGTRYGG SILK-BEARD (ON *Sigtryggr silkiskegg*) **(d. 1042).** Also appears as Sihtric Silkenbeard in some English-language scholarship.

King of **Dublin** 989–1036, Sigtrygg was the son of **Olaf Cúarán** of Dublin and **York** by his Irish-born wife, **Gormlaith**. Sigtrygg's autonomy as king of Dublin was limited by two successive Irish high-kings, firstly Máel Sechnaill II of Meath and then, after 997, **Brian Boru** of Munster. Sigtrygg allied himself with the king of Leinster and rebelled against Brian's overlordship of Dublin in 999 but was soon forced to submit to the Irish king (who was also his stepfather) and he married Brian's daughter, Sláine, in the settlement that followed. However, some years later, in 1012, Sigtrygg once again used Leinster support to challenge Brian's overlordship, and he helped to forge the anti-Brian coalition that faced the Irish high king at **Clontarf** in 1014.

Njal's Saga includes a praise poem, *Darraðarljóð*, which describes the victory in battle of a young king over the Irish. The saga writer identifies this young king, rather dubiously, with Sigtrygg. Sigtrygg himself did not fight at Clontarf, and *Orkneyinga Saga* claims that he actually ran away from the battle. The Dublin Vikings were instead led by his brother, Dubhgall. Although Brian was killed, his old rival, Máel Sechnaill, simply reclaimed his control of Dublin, so that Sigtrygg's position remained essentially unaltered. He abdicated in 1036, and Sigtrygg's nephew Echmarcach mac Ragnaill became king of a Dublin that was much reduced in its political, if not its economic, power.

During his reign, the first Hiberno-Norse coinage was struck at Dublin (*c.* 995–1020). Sigtrygg's coins were closely related to the contemporary coinage of King **Æthelred II** of England, and some of them were more or less straightforward copies. Others, however, bear the legend SIHTRC REX or occasionally SIHTRC CVNVNC (from ON *konungr* "king"), alongside the Dublin mint-signature. Sigtrygg was a Christian (*see* **Christianity, Conversion to**) king and undertook two pilgrimages to Rome in 1028 and 1042 respectively; he also founded Dublin's Christ Church Cathedral *c.* 1030. He was murdered on his second journey to Rome.

SIGTUNA. Viking-Age town situated at the mouth of the River Fyris on Lake Mälaren in Uppland, Sweden. Sigtuna was probably founded around the year 975 by the Swedish king, **Erik the Victorious**, and was laid out on a regular grid plan. During the rule of **Olof Skötko-**

nung, the first Swedish royal coinage was issued from the town. Unlike its predecessor, **Birka**, Sigtuna never appears to have been a significant trading center. Indeed, recent excavations have revealed only small-scale crafting activity, and it is probable that the town was just a local market center. The town's importance lay in the fact that it was an administrative and religious center for the growing power of the Swedish king. A large number of Viking-Age **rune-stones** were raised around the town, and it has been suggested that these reflect territorial and political statements by those who were affected by the extension of royal power.

SIGURD THE DRAGON-SLAYER (ON *Siguròr fáfnisbani*). Heroic figure who features prominently in Old Norse literature (for example, the *Prose Edda*, *Poetic Edda*, and *Völsunga Saga*) and **art** (for example, 10th-century stone crosses from northern England and the **Isle of Man** and the 12th-century wooden portals from Hylestad stavechurch in Norway). The German *Nibelungenlied* epic, the basis for Richard Wagner's *Ring*, and its hero, Siegfried, parallel the Scandinavian legends about Sigurd.

According to Old Norse literature, Sigurd was the son of a dead hero, Sigmund, and was brought up by the smith, **Regin**. Regin had a brother, who had been turned into a dragon and who guarded an immense but cursed treasure of gold. This gold had originally belonged to a dwarf, Andvari. Sigurd was encouraged by Regin to steal this treasure, and the smith gave him a specially forged sword that incorporated part of Sigmund's sword to help him. Following Regin's advice, Sigurd dug a pit, hid in it, and when the dragon passed over the pit on its way to drink at a nearby pool, Sigurd stabbed and killed it, and could thus take the unguarded treasure. Sigurd cut out the dragon's heart and roasted it as Regin had requested, but he burned his thumb while doing so. As he sucked his thumb to cool it, he tasted the dragon's blood, which gave him the ability to understand the speech of birds. These promptly informed Sigurd that his foster father, Regin, was going to betray and kill him and take the treasure for himself. Sigurd preempted this by beheading Regin, and then proceeded to load up his horse, **Grani** (son of **Sleipnir**), with the treasure. This part of the Sigurd legend is shown very clearly on the rune-inscribed rock, **Ramsundberget**, and episodes of it occur on other pieces of stone sculpture.

The next part of Sigurd's story concerns his love affairs with Bryn-hild and Gudrun. After exchanging rings and vows of fidelity with the **valkyrie** Brynhild, Sigurd traveled to the court of a king, Giuki, who had three sons: Gunnar, Hogni, and Guttorm, and one daughter: Gu-drun. Sigurd was given a love potion by Gudrun's mother, which made him forget Brynhild and fall in love with Gudrun. They were married and Sigurd became blood brothers with Gunnar and Hogni. Gunnar then sought Sigurd's assistance to win the affections of Bryn-hild. Brynhild lived in a hall surrounded by a barrier of fire and swore that she would only marry the man who could ride through the flames. Gunnar was unable to do this, but Sigurd agreed to pretend to be Gun-nar and to win Brynhild for his blood brother. Brynhild and Gunnar were thus married and came to live at Giuki's court, but Sigurd then remembered his love for Brynhild. His wife, Gudrun, and Brynhild quarreled over whose husband was the best, and Gudrun revealed the deception to Brynhild. Brynhild, in turn, confronted Gunnar and said that she had slept with Sigurd (she did not mention that he had in fact placed a sword between them). Thus incited to revenge, Gunnar asked his brother Guttorm, who was not a blood brother of Sigurd, to kill Sigurd. Both Sigurd and Guttorm died in this confrontation. Shortly afterward, Brynhild killed herself and asked to be burned on the pyre, next to Sigurd, with a sword placed between them.

SIGURD THE POWERFUL (ON *Sigurðr inn ríki*) (**d.** *c.* **870).** First **Earl** of **Orkney** *c.* 850–870, Sigurd was given the title by his brother, **Rögnvald of Møre**. He is said to have won the whole of Caithness and Sutherland in northeastern **Scotland** in alliance with Thorstein the Red, the son of **Aud the Deep-Minded**. They also conquered further Scot-tish territory in Argyll, Moray, and Ross, building a stronghold at Burghead. According to *Orkneyinga Saga*, Sigurd killed a Scottish earl called Máelbrigte "Tooth" during one of these Scottish campaigns, but after cutting off Máelbrigte's head and hanging it on his saddle, Sigurd grazed his leg on one of the earl's teeth. This is said to have turned septic, and the Orcadian earl apparently died from the wound. Sigurd was buried in Sutherland, on the banks of the River Oykel.

SIGURD THE STOUT (ON *Sigurðr inn digri*) (**d. 1014).** **Earl** of **Orkney** *c.* 985–1014, Sigurd was the son of Earl Hlöðvir of Orkney and an Irish princess, Eithne. He married the daughter of Malcolm, a Scottish king, and they had a son, Hvelp. According to *Orkneyinga Saga*, during **Olaf Tryggvason**'s visit to Orkney in 995, Sigurd was forcibly baptized and made to surrender Hvelp to the Norwegian king as a hostage. When Hvelp died in Norway shortly afterward, Sigurd renounced his allegiance to Olaf and, it is assumed, his new religion too.

Sigurd's power extended well beyond the Northern Isles of Orkney and **Shetland**; he is said to have ruled territory in **Scotland** (Ross and Moray, Sutherland and the (?Caithness) Dales—Sigurd is certainly recorded as winning a victory over a Scottish ruler, Finnleik, at Skitten Myre, near Duncansby, in Caithness). He also appears to have been recognized as overlord of the **Hebrides** as far south as the **Isle of Man** and ruled these islands through his brother-in-law, Gilli. Sigurd was killed in the Battle of **Clontarf**, and *Njal's Saga* claims that he fell wrapped in the magical raven banner that his mother had woven in order to bring Sigurd a victory.

SKALDIC POETRY. Derived from the Old Norse word *skald* "poet," essentially this was praise poetry that was usually composed by known authors in the service of Scandinavian kings, princes, and **earls**. This differentiates it from anonymous **Eddic poetry**, which is normally **mythological** and legendary in its subject matter. Skaldic poetry was composed orally and recited in front of its subject in public performances. Most of the known skalds appear to be Icelanders, such as Egill Skallagrimsson (*see* ***Egil's Saga***) and **Sighvatr Þórðarson**.

Skaldic poetry was normally composed in stanzas of eight lines, and is characterized by complex structures and cryptic vocabulary. Several subgenres of skaldic verse are known, such as panegyrics, funeral lays, shield poems (describing pictures on decorated shields), and occasional verses (*lausavísur*). A variety of different meters could also be used, but **dróttkvætt** is the most well known of the skaldic meters. **Snorri Sturluson's** *Prose Edda* was written as a handbook for those wishing to compose skaldic poetry.

Although believed to have been composed in the Viking Age, most skaldic poetry is preserved in medieval manuscripts, especially those of the ***Kings' Sagas***, where they are used to lend authority to the prose text. Indeed, in his prologue to **Heimskringla**, Snorri states that skaldic poetry was an important historical source because although it was praise poetry, to recite false praise in front of an audience would be "mockery, not praise." Very few poems are quoted in full—usually a verse or two would be given to support the prose. The late preservation of this poetry has led to much discussion about its authenticity and reliability. It is generally argued that the complex rhythmical and alliterative rules helped the poems to retain their original form, in spite of the problems normally associated with oral transmission of texts. Only one *dróttkvætt* poem survives in a contemporary "document"—that carved in **runes** on the **Karlevi** stone—although there are other skaldic verse forms found occasionally on other rune-stones, particularly from the central eastern Swedish provinces of Uppland and Södermanland. *See also* HEITI; KENNINGS.

SKÁLDSKAPARMÁL (**"The language of poetry"**). Third part of Snorri's **Prose Edda**, which includes a list of **kennings** and **heiti**, as well as number of prose narratives that explain the origin of some of these poetic circumlocutions. Interestingly, a list of kennings for Christ is included as well as those for the Norse pagan gods. This list is preceded by a dialogue between the god of poetry, **Bragi**, and Ægir, who is said to be skilled in magic and to have lived on an island called Hlesey; and by an exhortation to use this book in a spirit of "scholarly enquiry and entertainment," while remembering that Christians should not believe in heathen gods. As proof of the latter, there is a section describing how the gods of the Æsir were people from Troy in Asia who deliberately distorted events in order that they should be regarded as gods.

SKIPREIÐUR. *See* LEIÐANG.

SKRAELING. Derogatory Old Norse name given to the native inhabitants of **Greenland** and **North America**, whom Scandinavians encountered during their exploration and colonization of the North Atlantic. The meaning and etymology of the word is uncertain. It has been suggested that it may be connected to either Norwegian *skræla* "to scream" or Icelandic *skrælna* "to shrink," although in these languages today the word *skræling* means "coarse fellow" and "weakling" respectively.

Although the Norse sources use this word to describe all the non-European peoples they came across in these places, Scandinavians must have encountered several different and quite distinct aboriginal peoples, including people of the Dorset and Thule cultures, the latter of which were the ancestors of the Inuit of Greenland, and a number of Indian peoples, probably including ancestors of the Newfoundland Beothuk and the Labrador Innu.

The word *skraeling* is first recorded in **Ari Thorgilsson's** *Book of the Icelanders*, where he likens the houses, skin boats, and stone artifacts found in Greenland with those used by the people "whom the Greenlanders call *skraeling*" living in **Vinland**. *Historia Norwegiae* also mentions the *skraelings*, recording that they lived in the north of Greenland, that their flesh wounds went white and did not bleed, and that they used walrus tusks and sharp stones for fighting. This suggests that Scandinavian encounters with the Dorset and Thule peoples were not friendly, and certainly, the *Icelandic Annals* entry for 1379 records a *skraeling* attack on the Greenlanders, in which 18 men were killed and two boys were taken as **slaves**. However, archaeological finds suggest that there may also have been some more peaceful trading between the Scandinavians and the native peoples of Greenland. While it used to be believed that the Norse colonies in Greenland died out as a result of Inuit aggression, archaeological analysis of Scandinavian and Inuit lifestyles suggests that the Norse failure to adapt their European way of life to the demands of the deteriorating climate in Greenland played a significant role in the demise of the Scandinavian population of the island.

SKULDELEV SHIPS. Five Viking **ships** were discovered at Skuldelev in Roskildefjörd, Denmark, during the 1960s. They had been deliberately sunk to partially block the fjörd, presumably for defensive purposes, in the 11th century. The finds from Skuldelev revealed for the first time the variety of Viking ships: two longships, two *knarrs*, and one all-purpose vessel were recovered, and there were also differences between ships of the same type. For example, although Skuldelev 2 and 5 are both longships, Skuldelev 2 measured some 28 meters by 4.5 meters and had 30 pairs of oars; but Skuldelev

5 was just 18 meters by 2.6 meters and had only 12 or 13 pairs of oars. An analysis of the wood of Skuldelev 2 has shown that it was made from oak that had grown in eastern Ireland, although it had been repaired with Danish oak, and that it was constructed *c*. 1060. It is the largest known longship to have been excavated and appears to belong to the *drakkar* class of longships.

SKYHILL, BATTLE OF. Battle fought in 1079, near Ramsey in the north of the **Isle of Man**. In this battle, **Godred Crovan** defeated the Manxmen, whose ruler is not known, and established his own ruling dynasty on the islands. According to the ***Chronicle of the Kings of Man and the Isles***, the island was divided into two halves following Godred's victory: the northern half was held from the king by the Manxmen, and the southern half was held by those islanders who supported Godred.

SLAVERY. Vikings in both eastern and western Europe, particularly **Ireland** and **Russia**, had a reputation for taking slaves during their raids, although little is known about how this trade functioned in detail. According to the ***Book of Settlements*** and other Icelandic sources, Irish and Scottish slaves were among the earliest colonists of Iceland and have left their traces in the place-names, personal names, and genetic inheritance of that island.

The Scandinavian evidence for the status of slaves or thralls (ON *þrællar*) is overwhelmingly medieval, based on the earliest preserved written **law-codes**. These law-codes suggest that, despite the Church's wish to improve conditions for slaves, the legal status of a slave was more or less identical to that of livestock and other property belonging to an individual. For example, the owner of a slave could buy, sell, and otherwise exchange him or her as they saw fit; owners were not liable before the law for hurting or killing a slave; and if the slave was harmed or killed by another person, that person paid compensation to the slave's owner, not to the slave's family as was normally the case. Some Christian influence is nevertheless evident; for example, Icelandic laws included an injunction on killing slaves during Lent.

The laws differ in their views on the marriage of slaves and the status of the children of slaves. Some Danish and Swedish provincial laws recognized slave marriages, and the Law of Uppland (eastern Sweden)

SNORRI STURLUSON (1179–1241) • 253

even contained provisions suggesting that any child of a Christian marriage was born free. However, it was more common for children to be given the status of his or her mother, and indeed most Scandinavian law-codes suggest that slavery was hereditary. The **Eddic** poem *Rígsþula* also supports the idea of slavery as being an inherited social position, as well as characterizing slaves as stupid and ugly and describing their daily activities as consisting of the heaviest and most unwelcome duties on a farm. Nevertheless, it was legally possible for slaves to be freed by their owners—and the Church appears to have encouraged manumission in the medieval period as an act of piety—or for slaves to buy their own freedom. Indeed, one Viking-Age runestone from Hørning in Denmark (DR 315) was raised by Toki the smith in memory of Thorgisl Gudmundsson, his former owner, who is said to have given him gold and freedom. Other Viking-Age evidence for the conditions of slaves is sparse and anecdotal: for example, the missionary **Ansgar** is said to have seen slaves chained together by the neck in **Hedeby** during the first half of the ninth century, and **Ibn Fadlan** describes the ritual sacrifice of a slave that took place in a Scandinavian **Rus** community in the early 10th century.

It appears that slavery had all but disappeared in Iceland and Norway by the end of the 12th century, but it persisted longer in Denmark and Sweden. Indeed, as late as 1335, the Skara Ordinance banned keeping Christians as slaves in southwestern Sweden. It appears that economic changes, which led to the development of a class of landless tenant farmers that was cheaper to employ than slaves, may account for the disappearance of slavery in Scandinavia.

SLEIPNIR. Odin's eight-legged horse, born to the god **Loki** after he was forced to take on the shape of a mare to distract the stallion Svaðilfari from completing building work on the walls of **Asgard**.

SLIESTHORP. *See* HEDEBY.

SNORRA EDDA. See PROSE EDDA; SNORRI STURLUSON.

SNORRI STURLUSON (1179–1241). Icelandic noble and historian, Snorri was born at Hvammr and was the son of Sturla Þórðarson (d. 1183) (Sturla features in the collection of sagas known as

Sturlunga Saga). Snorri was fostered by Jón Loptsson (d. 1197) of Oddi at the age of three and grew up there, in the educational and cultural center of **Iceland**. He married Herdís, the daughter of Bersi the Wealthy, at the age of 19, and when Bersi died in 1202, Snorri took over Bersi's estate at Borg. He also inherited the *goðorð* (*see* **goði**) of Mýrar from Bersi and subsequently acquired several more chieftaincies. In 1206, he moved to Reykholt, and left his wife Herdís. His nephew, also called Sturla Þórðarson, wrote in *Islendinga Saga* (one of the *Sturlunga* collection) that Snorri was promiscuous and had three children by other **women** as well as the two he had had with Herdís. However, Snorri remarried in 1224 and remained with his second wife, Hallveig Ormsdóttir ("the richest woman in Iceland" according to Sturla), until her death in 1241. As well as becoming the richest man in Iceland, Snorri acquired considerable secular power, serving as Law-Speaker at the **Althing** from 1215–1218 and again from 1222–1231 (or possibly even 1235).

In 1218, Snorri visited the court of the 14-year-old Norwegian king, Hákon Hákonarson (d. 1263), who ruled with his uncle, Earl Skúli Bárðarson. He was well received and when he returned to Iceland some two years later, he was given a **ship** and other splendid gifts by the **earl**, and became a royal retainer. He also promised to persuade the Icelanders to accept Norwegian rule. Snorri composed the final part of his ***Prose Edda***, known as ***Háttatal***, in honor of Hákon and Skúli. Snorri returned to Norway in 1237, following his expulsion from Reykholt by Sturla Sighvatsson, his nephew. However, Norway was in a state of political turmoil at this time, with Hákon and Skúli vying for the Norwegian throne. Snorri stayed with the earl and with the earl's son during his two-year stay in Norway and was apparently made an earl himself by Skúli. This earned Snorri Hákon's enmity, and the Norwegian king forbade Snorri to leave the country. However, Snorri ignored Hákon's command and returned to Iceland and his estate at Reykholt, as Sturla Sighvatsson had been killed in battle that summer. Civil war broke out in Norway at the same time and was only resolved in 1240 when Hákon won a victory over Skúli in the Battle of **Oslo**. Hákon then instructed the Icelander Gizurr Þorvaldsson, his newly appointed earl and Snorri's son-in-law, to ensure that the "traitor" Snorri returned to Norway or to kill him. Snorri was executed in the cellar of his home in Reykholt on 22 September 1241.

However, Snorri is most famous today for his writing, which preserves much of the history, **mythology**, and poetry of the North. His key works are a history of the kings of Norway called *Heimskringla*, his *Separate Saga of St. Olaf* (*see* **Sagas of St. Olaf**), and a handbook for skaldic poets, incorporating an account of pre-Christian Norse mythology, known as the *Prose Edda*. Some scholars believe that he may also have been the author of *Egil's Saga*, although this cannot be proved conclusively.

SPAIN (AND THE MEDITTERANEAN), VIKINGS IN. The first recorded **Viking** attack on Spain was in 844, when the Vikings based on the River Loire in **Frankia** sailed south and attacked the northwestern Spanish kingdom of Galicia. They then sailed farther south, sacking Lisbon in present-day Portugal, Seville in the Moorish kingdom of Andalusia, and Cadiz and Algeciras in present-day Morocco. These attacks and the Moorish response are recorded in a number of Spanish chronicles and Arabic sources. These also describe how these Vikings were pursued and resoundingly defeated by the emir of Cordoba, Abdurrhaman II (d. 852), who is credited with killing some five hundred of the **Majus** and capturing four of their **ships** in one of the subsequent battles on the River Guadalquivir. It was after this attack that the diplomat, **Al-Ghazal**, was supposedly sent by Abdurrhaman II to the court of the Majus king.

Thus discouraged, the Vikings did not return to Spain until 859 when another fleet, of 62 ships, sailed south from the Loire. Led by **Björn Ironside** and Hastein, this fleet spent some three years harrying in and around the Mediterranean, attacking the Spanish, Moroccan, and Italian coasts, with the ultimate target of looting Rome. However, having mistakenly plundered Luna in northern Italy rather than Rome, Björn and Hastein returned to Spain and suffered a notable defeat at the hands of the Moors in the Straits of Gibraltar off southern Spain. The Arabic ships were equipped with "Greek fire" or a form of napalm that could be catapulted on to the ships of their enemies. Only 20 Viking ships escaped from this confrontation, and they promptly returned to their base on the Loire. A further and final series of raids in northern Spain, including that on the shrine of St. James in Santiago de Compostela, were recorded in the late 960s. According to Spanish sources, the Vikings ruled Galicia for some three years, taking Christian **slaves** and killing the bishop of Santiago, Sisenand, who is said to have attacked the Vikings at Fornellos in March 970. However, they were finally defeated by the count of Galicia, Gonsalo Sancho, in 971. No further Viking raids are recorded in either Spanish or Arabic sources, although **Olaf Haraldsson** may have fought there in around 1014, and Snorri's *Heimskringla* relates that he was persuaded by a dream not to sail into the Straits of Gibraltar. *Knýtlinga Saga* also refers to a Danish **earl**, Ulf, who conquered Galicia in the 11th century.

SPILLINGS HOARD. The largest Viking-Age hoard currently known, discovered on the Baltic island of **Gotland** in the summer of 1999. The hoard contains 14,295 silver coins, 486 silver arm rings, and many other artifacts, totaling 85 kilograms. It is believed that the hoard was deposited around the year 870.

To date, some 1,400 of the coins have been examined. These include four Scandinavian coins, one from **Byzantium**, 23 from Persia (present-day Iran); the rest are Islamic coins. One of these Islamic coins (*c.* 830–840), from the kingdom of the Khazars in present-day southern **Russia**, bears an Arabic inscription "Moses is the messenger of God," which appears to be a Jewish variant of the Islamic credo "Mohammed is the messenger of God." Only four other coins are known to have this inscription, and it appears to confirm the belief that the Khazars converted to Judaism.

STAMFORD BRIDGE, BATTLE OF. Battle fought in East Yorkshire on 25 September 1066 between the invading Norwegian army of **Harald Hard-Ruler** and the English army under its king, Harold Godwinsson. Harald's army was supported by the forces of Tostig, the brother of the English king, and by **Earls** Paul and Erlend of **Orkney**. Stamford Bridge is situated on the River Derwent and lies just 12 kilometers east of **York**, where Harald's army had arrived some five days earlier after defeating the English at **Fulford Gate**. Harald's fleet of 300 ships was moored some 22 kilometers away from the battlefield at Riccall on the Ouse, while his army camped at Stamford Bridge apparently waiting for the hostages from York to be delivered to them. Harold Godwinsson's army marched from London, perhaps in as little as ten days, and took the Norwegians by surprise.

According to **Heimskringla**, in negotiations before the battle Harald Hard-Ruler demanded control of the north of England. Harold Godwinsson's famous reply was apparently "I will grant you seven feet of English ground, or as much more as you are taller than other men," i.e., the only English ground Harald would get would be that in which he was buried. The exact location of the battle is unknown, but an area of higher ground to the southeast of the present center of Stamford Bridge is known as Battle Flats. It is said that skeletons and **weapons** were found here in the 18th century, although none of these artifacts survive. According to a later Anglo-Norman tradition, inserted into the **Anglo-Saxon Chronicle**, the battle centered upon a wooden bridge over the Derwent that was held defiantly by one, huge **Viking berserker** until the very last. However, there is no genuine historical evidence for this detail. Harald was killed at Stamford Bridge by an arrow that pierced his throat, and the Norwegians suffered a massive defeat. According to the *Anglo-Saxon Chronicle*, just 24 ships were needed to carry the Norwegian survivors away from England. Stamford Bridge is sometimes described as the last major battle of the Viking Age in England. Certainly, coming as it did, just 19 days before the Battle of Hastings and the Norman Conquest of England, English political attention was forcibly shifted away from the North and southwards toward the European Continent.

STARAJA ("OLD") LADOGA (ON *Aldeigjuborg***).** Viking-Age trading center on the left bank of the River Volkhov, eight kilometers south of its confluence with Lake Ladoga in present-day **Russia**. This site was the main market and crafts center in northern Russia before being eclipsed by **Novgorod** and, later, **Kiev**. Staraja Ladoga was founded sometime in the mid-eighth century and seems to have been the initial focal point of the Scandinavian presence in European Russia, which ultimately led to the establishment of the state of the **Rus**. Excavations have revealed that the proto-town's population included Slavic, Scandinavian, Baltic, and Finnish elements, and the craft activities taking place on-site included the manufacture of goods made from glass, iron, bronze, bone, and amber. Trade with the East was also an important element of Ladoga's economy, and a hoard of Islamic dirhams from the 780s demonstrates that this trade was established during the early stages of the town's development. There is also evidence that repairs to **ships** and boats were made in Staraja Ladoga.

By the middle of the ninth century, a new trading center in northern Russia had been established farther up the River Volkhov at Novogorod. Part of the reason for this move may have been the vulnerability of Ladoga to Viking raids—excavations have revealed that a large part of the town was burned down in the 860s, although the precise cause of the fire is unknown. Nevertheless, Ladoga still retained some importance as the first port-of-call on the long route south from Scandinavia to the Black Sea and east to Baghdad in present-day Iraq. By the 10th century, Ladoga had been fortified and had its own royal palace. After the official conversion of Vladimir I (d. 1015) to **Christianity** in 988, eight churches and monasteries were built in and around Staraja Ladoga.

The most important evidence for a Scandinavian presence in Staraja Ladoga comes from one of its cemeteries, at Plakun on the right bank of the Volkhov, which contains what appear to be exclusively Scandinavian graves. Some 60 **burial** mounds can be found at Plakun, and seven or eight of these contained boat graves with cremations. A further mound, some distance from the main cemetery, contained a boat grave and an inhumation. It seems from this evidence that Scandinavian **women** as well as men were living in Staraja Ladoga. As well as finds from the cemeteries, Scandinavian artifacts have also been recovered from the trading center itself, including, for example, an eighth-century hoard of smith's tools, which also contained a bronze amulet that may represent the Norse god, **Odin**; a rune-inscribed (*see* **rune**) wooden stick from the ninth century; and Scandinavian-style combs and brooches from the 8th to the 10th century.

STIKLESTAD, BATTLE OF (ON *Stiklastaðir*). Stiklestad is approximately 80 kilometers northeast of present-day **Trondheim** in Norway. A battle was fought there by **Olaf Haraldsson** and some 3,000 supporters against an army of approximately 14,000 men, led by Norwegian chieftains and backed by **Cnut I the Great**, on 29 July 1030. Before the battle, Olaf had been in exile for two years, during which time Cnut was recognized as the country's king by all the most powerful chieftains. However, Cnut's nephew and governor, **Earl** Hákon, died in 1029, and Olaf decided to launch an attempt to win back the Norwegian throne with the help of the Swedish king, **Anund Jakob**. Olaf's half brother, **Harald Hard-Ruler**, fought alongside him in the battle. An account of the battle can be found in the 13th-century *Heimskringla*, which is in turn based upon **skaldic poetry** that is believed to have been composed shortly after the battle. Olaf died in the battle and is said to have been killed by wounds inflicted by Þórir hundr ("Hound") and Kálfr Árnason. *Heimskringla* describes how a wound that Þórir had received to his hand on the battlefield was then healed by Olaf's blood, and as a result Þórir was one of the first to spread the news of the dead Olaf's sanctity. Following Olaf's defeat and death, Cnut installed **Svein Cnutsson**, his own son by **Ælfgifu of Northampton**, as king of Norway. However, his rule was unpopular, and Kálfr Árnason was subsequently instrumental in the recalling of Olaf's son, **Magnus I the Good**, from his exile in Sweden.

STÖNG. Late Viking-Age farmstead in the Thjórsársalur valley, southern **Iceland**, which was buried in volcanic debris or tephra following the eruption of Mount Hekla. It was previously thought that the eruption of 1104 led to the abandonment of the farm, but it may be that occupation continued there some hundred years after this date, and the decisive eruption was therefore considerably later than 1104. The Stöng **house** was first excavated in 1939, and subsequent excavations revealed two further, earlier occupation levels below the Late Viking-Age remains. The tephra had helped preserve the turf roof and the long, low turf walls of the main house, which rested on a stone foundation. The turf provided good insulation, as did the extremely thick walls, and the use of turf also meant that the comparatively small supplies of wood available on Iceland could be conserved. There were wooden panels lining the inside of the hall to keep out the damp. There were no windows—the single external doorway and the smoke hole would provide the only source of light—which also minimized heat loss.

The house, just over 12 meters long, consisted of a main hall, with wide benches that could be used for sleeping, and a smaller living room. Two further small rooms were located on one side of the house, conventionally described as a dairy and lavatory but probably used for the processing of wool (urine was used to prepare the fleeces).

Three outbuildings, a cattle byre, what may have been a barn, and smithy, lay near to the farmhouse. Very few artifacts were found in the buildings, suggesting that its inhabitants had time to evacuate the farmstead before the eruption. A full-size reconstruction of the Stöng farmstead was built near the original buildings in 1974.

SUÐREYJAR ("Southern Islands"). Norse name for the **Hebrides**, which lie off the western coast of **Scotland**.

SVAÐILFARI. *See* ASGARD.

SVEALAND. East Swedish province and kingdom, centered on the modern counties of Uppland, Södermanland, and Västmanland (which surround the present-day capital, Stockholm). **Gamla Uppsala** was the **burial** place of the Svear kings and the site of a pagan ritual that may still have been performed as late as the second half of the 11th century. **Adam of Bremen** describes Svealand as being "rich in fruits and honey besides excelling all others in cattle raising [. . .] the whole region everywhere full of merchandise from foreign parts" in his *History of the Archbishops of Hamburg-Bremen*.

The Svear people gave their name to the country of Sweden (ON *Svea rike* or *Sverige* in modern Swedish), and traditionally the origins of a unified kingdom of Sweden were sought in Svealand. However, more recently, scholars have emphasized the importance of **Götaland** in the emergence of a united Sweden. Certainly, the Svear were converted to **Christianity** later than the Götar and resisted attempts at political unification by their kings.

SVEIN CNUTSSON (d. 1035). Son of **Cnut I the Great** and **Ælfgifu of Northampton**. King of Norway between 1030 and 1035, under Ælfgifu's wardship and, for that reason, also known as Svein Álfífuson. Svein and his mother were installed as Cnut's representatives in Norway following the Battle of **Stiklestad** and were driven out of Norway by the rebellion that followed the growth of the cult of **Olaf Haraldsson** of Norway. A **skaldic poem** by the poet Þórarinn loftunga ("Praise-Tongue"), called *Glælognskviða* ("Calm-Sea Lay"), advises Svein to support the worship of the dead king Olaf. Svein and Ælfgifu's short rule was harsh, with heavy taxation, and unpopular, and one of Svein's most prominent supporters, Kálfr Árnason, was instrumental in replacing him with Olaf's son, **Magnus I the Good**. According to *Heimskringla*, after being driven from Norway, Svein went to the court of his brother, **Harthacnut**, in Denmark, and they agreed to divide that kingdom between them. However, Svein is said to have died in Denmark shortly afterward, in the same winter that his father, Cnut, died.

SVEIN ESTRITHSSON (ON *Sveinn Estrîðsson*) **(d. 1074).** King of Denmark 1047–1074. Svein's claim to the Danish throne came from his mother, Estrith, who was the sister of **Cnut I the Great**, and hence he is normally known by his mother's name rather than his patronymic, Ulfsson. His father, Earl Ulf Þorgilsson (also Sprakalegsson), was made **earl** of Denmark by Cnut but was later killed by him at Roskilde. Svein was described in the *Roskilde Chronicle* (*c.* 1140) as Svein the Great, for his reorganization of the Danish church into eight regular bishoprics and for his work in bringing the kingdom of Denmark into the religious and political community of western Europe. Svein worked to strengthen links between the papacy and the Danish church, to reduce the influence of the German church in Denmark, and ultimately to establish an independent archbishopric in Denmark (this was finally achieved in 1104, with the elevation of **Lund**). Svein was one of the main informants used by **Adam of Bremen** for his *History of the Archbishops of Hamburg-Bremen*, and Adam praised the king for his learning, piety, and respect for Church law; a letter from Pope Gregory VII to Svein also mentions his superior "book-learning."

Politically, much of Svein's reign was spent in conflict with the kings of Norway. Since the death of **Harthacnut**, **Magnus I the Good** had been recognized as king of Denmark. The *Anglo-Saxon Chronicle* records that, in 1047, Svein asked for English help against Magnus, requesting some 50 **ships**. This was refused, and Svein was defeated in battle by Magnus shortly before the Norwegian king died. According to *Heimskringla*, Svein had allied himself with Magnus's uncle, **Harald Hard-Ruler**, but Harald was bought off by Magnus with the offer of half the kingdom of Norway. After Harald's accession to Magnus's kingdom in 1047, conflict continued with Norwegian attacks on Denmark in 1048, 1050, 1060 and a confrontation at

Nisås, off the Swedish coast, in 1062. In 1048, the *Anglo-Saxon Chronicle* records another appeal to Edward the Confessor (d. 1065) of England to send ships to support Svein; again this was refused. Svein was driven out of his kingdom at some point in this conflict, and according to Adam of Bremen spent twelve years in exile at the court of King **Anund Jakob** of Sweden. However, Svein and Harald came to terms in 1064, and Svein was finally recognized as king of Denmark. Secure in Denmark, Svein was keen to re-establish his uncle's North-Sea empire, and he planned an invasion of England in 1069. Although the people of **Northumbria** welcomed Svein and joined his army in a rebellion against William the Conqueror, the revolt was brutally crushed and Svein's ambitions came to nothing.

Svein married Gunnhild, the widow of Anund of Sweden, but according to Adam he agreed to the annulment of the marriage after Archbishop Adalbart of Hamburg-Bremen protested that they were too closely related. Svein, however, seems rather to have been forced into conformity by the intervention of the pope. Despite Adam's praise of the Danish king, he did also recognize Svein's weaknesses, described as gluttony and **women**. Indeed, Svein is known to have had at least 14 sons by a number of different mothers, and he was succeeded by five of these sons in turn: Harald Hén "Soft Whetstone" (d. 1080), St. **Knut II Sveinsson**, Olaf Hunger (d. 1095), Erik Ejegod "Ever-Good" (d. 1103), and Niels (d. 1134).

SVEIN FORKBEARD HARALDSSON (ON *Sveinn tvéskegg***) (d. 1014). King of Denmark** *c.* **987–1014.** Son of **Harald Blue-Tooth**, Svein deposed his father in what **Adam of Bremen** describes as a pagan backlash against Harald's rule. However, there is no other evidence that Svein was a pagan. He campaigned extensively in England during the late 10th and early 11th century, sometimes (in 991? and 994) in alliance with **Olaf Tryggvason** of Norway. According to Adam of Bremen, Svein was driven out of his kingdom by **Erik the Victorious** of Sweden and spent fourteen years in exile. While there is evidence of conflict, no other source refers to this long period of exile and it seems that Adam had misunderstood his informants.

Svein later challenged Olaf Tryggvason's rule of Norway, and formed an alliance with the Svear (*see* **Svealand**), marrying the widow of their king, Erik the Victorious. Together with his stepson,

Olof Skötkonung of Sweden, Svein defeated Olaf at the Battle of **Svöld** and restored Danish control of Norway.

There is, however, some confusion over Svein's marriages. In *Heimskringla*, Snorri writes that he was married twice. His first wife was called Gunnhild, who is described as the daughter of the Polish ruler, Boleslav, and the mother of Svein's sons, Harald and **Cnut I the Great**. She is said to have later died and Svein to have remarried. His second wife, **Sigrid the Proud**, is described as the mother of Olof Skötkonung by **Snorri Sturluson**. However, in Adam of Bremen, Gunnhild and Sigrid are amalgamated, and Svein is said to have only one (unnamed) wife, who was the mother of Olof, the sister of Boleslav, and the widow of Erik. **Thietmar of Merseburg** has the same information as Adam, but adds that Svein divorced his wife and sent her home to Poland (*Wendland*). This picture is further complicated by the fact that Svein also had a sister called Gunnhild and a sister called Thyre. Thyre is said to have been married to Boleslav of Poland, whom she left, and then subsequently to Olaf Tryggvason. Svein was therefore related by marriage to the Swedish, Norwegian, and Polish royal houses; his daughter, Gytha, was married to Erik, son of **Hákon Jarl** of **Lade**, and his other daughter, Estrith, to the Anglo-Saxon noble, Wulfsige (in Danish tradition, **Earl** Ulf).

Svein's sister, Gunnhild, and her husband, Pallig, were killed in the **St. Brice's Day massacre** of 1002, and it is possible that Svein's campaigns in **Wessex** and **East Anglia** in 1003–1004 were to avenge their deaths. The *Anglo-Saxon Chronicle* does not mention Svein's name in connection with the raids of 1006–1007 and 1009–1012, led by **Thorkell the Tall**, and it is not until August 1013 that he is said to have returned to England. After sailing up the **Humber** and down the River Trent to Gainsborough, Svein received the submission of **Northumbria**, Lindsey (north Lincolnshire), the **Five Boroughs**, and "all the raiding army to the north of **Watling Street**." Moving south, he received the submission of Oxford, Winchester, and the southwest, and finally **London**. At Christmas 1013, King **Æthelred II** left England to join his wife and children in exile in **Normandy**. However, Svein died in Gainsborough, Lincolnshire, on 3 February 1014. Svein was buried in England, but later his body was taken to the church he had built at Roskilde in Denmark and reburied. His son, **Cnut I the Great**, succeeded him, first as king of England and then as king of Denmark.

SVEN AGGESEN (b. *c.* 1140–1150). The author of *Brevis Historia Regum Dacie*, Sven Aggeson was a Danish nobleman, whose family included two archbishops of **Lund** and a bishop of Viborg. Sven appears to have studied in France and wrote at a time when Danish independence was threatened by German expansion. Sven was also a contemporary of the author of the most famous of Danish histories, **Saxo Grammaticus**.

SVÖLD, BATTLE OF (ON *Svölðr*). Sea battle fought at uncertain location by a Scandinavian coalition of **Svein Forkbeard**, **Olof Skötkonung**, and **Earl** Erik of **Lade** against **Olaf Tryggvason**. According to Snorri's *Heimskringla*, Olaf Tryggvason was tricked and ambushed by Sigvaldi Strút-Haraldsson, the leader of the **Jomsvikings**. Olaf Tryggvason was subsequently killed and defeated, and the victors are said in *Heimskringla* to have divided Norway between them. As a result of the battle, Norway was ruled by Svein Forkbeard and the Earls of Lade for 15 years, until the throne was claimed by **Olaf Haraldsson**.

– T –

TARA, BATTLE OF. Battle fought in Meath, to the northwest of **Dublin**, in 980. In this battle, the king of the southern Uí Néill, Máel Sechnaill II, defeated the **Vikings** of Dublin and the Isles (**Hebrides**) under their king, **Olaf Cúarán**. This "very great slaughter," which is recorded in the *Annals of Ulster*, was followed by Olaf's departure for the holy island of **Iona**, where he died as a monk in the following year. Máel Sechnaill was recognized as overlord of Dublin, ruling it through Olaf's son, *Glún Iairn* (Irish) or *Járnkné* (Norse) "Iron knee" (d. 989). After the defeat at Tara, the political independence of Dublin was never regained.

THANGBRAND (ON *Þangbrandr*). A Flemish or Saxon priest who, according to the *Book of the Icelanders*, was sent to **Iceland** by **Olaf Tryggvason** to teach the islanders **Christianity**. Despite converting a number of chieftains, including Hall Þorsteinsson of Sida and his household, Thangbrand apparently spent just a year or two in Iceland, before concluding that his efforts were in vain. The missionary priest is characterized as a militant preacher and is said to have killed two or three men for mocking him before leaving Iceland. Snorri's *Saga of King Olaf Tryggvason* in **Heimskringla** adds some more details, describing Thangbrand as a "passionate, ungovernable man, and a great man-slayer; but he was a good scholar, and a clever man." According to **Snorri Sturluson**, Thangbrand killed Thorvald Veile and Veterliði the Skald for composing a satire about him, as well as one other man, in his two-year stay.

Both Snorri and **Ari Thorgilsson** write that recent Icelandic converts, Gizurr the White and Hjalti Skeggjason, dissuaded the angry Olaf Tryggvason from killing all the Icelanders in Norway. They claimed that the Icelanders would convert to Christianity but, in Snorri's words, "Thangbrand proceeded [. . .] with violence and manslaughter and such conduct the people there would not submit to." Approximately one year after Thangbrand's return to Norway, the **Althing** accepted Christianity.

THEGN (ON Þegn). Term of rank, the meaning of which is much debated. The semantic range of the Old Norse word *þegn* has certainly been influenced by its use in Anglo-Saxon England, where thegns were royal servants in the 11th century. However, the evidence of **rune-stones** and **skaldic poetry** suggests that in Viking-Age Scandinavia, a thegn was simply a free man, a landholder, or a warrior. Although often linked with **drengs**, the runic evidence suggests that thegns were probably older as they tend to be commemorated by their children and wives rather than by their parents. There have been a number of attempts to portray the Scandinavian thegns (and drengs) as members of the royal retinue or administration, but although some thegns may have been in the service of kings, there is no Viking-Age evidence to support the idea that all thegns were royal servants.

THEODORICUS. *See HISTORIA DE ANTIQUITATE REGUM NORWAGENSIUM.*

THING (ON þing). Old Norse word for an open-air assembly or meeting where law and justice were discussed. Things were held at regular intervals and existed at local, regional, and national level. The thing about which the most is known is the Icelandic **Althing**, but regional assemblies are known from Norway and Denmark. Things were also established in Scandinavian colonies abroad, such as the **Isle of Man** (*see* **Tynwald**), and place-names, such as Dingwall (Sutherland, northeastern **Scotland**) and Thingwall (Cheshire, northwestern England), show that Scandinavian settlers had things in many parts of the British Isles.

THINGAMANNALIÐ (ON Þingamannalið**).** Also known as the *þingalið*. Medieval sources, such as **Sven Aggesen's** version of *Vederlov* (*see* **Hird**), uses this word for the bodyguard employed by **Cnut I the Great** in England. A **rune-stone** from Kålsta, Häggeby in Uppland (U 668), Sweden, commemorates a warrior called Gere, who is said to have served in the west in the *þingalið*, and there are a few references in **skaldic poetry** to *þingamaðr* (plural *þingamenn*), which is generally translated as "a man who served in the *þingalið*." The exact meaning of these compounds is unclear, although it has recently been suggested that they may derive from the verb *þinga* and mean "contracted" man or men. *See also* **LIÐ.**

THINGVELLIR (ON Þingvöllr **"assembly plain").** Location of the Icelandic **Althing**. Thingvellir lies in the valley of the River Öxára, some 50 kilometers east of Reykjavik.

THOR (ON Þórr**).** God of the **Æsir** family and said to be the brother of **Odin**. Thor lived in a hall called Bilskírnir in Þrúðheimr or Þrúðvangr and was said to ride across the sky in a chariot drawn by two male goats, Tanngrísnir and Tanngnóstr. He was married to Sif, whose hair was made of gold. In **mythological** literature, Thor appears as the defender of the gods' home, **Asgard**, and there are several tales that relate how he defeated the gods' enemies, the giants, with his mighty hammer, **Mjöllnir**. As well as this hammer, Thor also possessed a magic belt that doubled his strength and a pair of iron gloves. A well-known myth about Thor, preserved in both the *Prose Edda* and the **Eddic poem** *Hymiskviða*, relates to his fishing trip with the giant Hymir, during which Thor hooked the **Midgard serpent** using an ox head as bait. At **Ragnarök**, Thor is said to kill the Midgard serpent, but in doing so, is fatally poisoned by the serpent's venom.

Despite his strength, many of the myths about Thor depict the god in rather comical circumstances, such as the time he lost Mjöllnir to the giant Þrymr (*see Þrymskviða*). Indeed, while Odin appears to have been the god of the aristocracy, the common man worshiped Thor and the discovery of Thor's hammer amulets in Viking-Age graves testifies to his importance. He was the god of thunder and the weather and his association with the weather meant that he determined the fate of crops and sea voyages. In his account of the pagan ritual at **Gamla Uppsala**, **Adam of Bremen** describes Thor as the most important of the three gods (the other two are Odin and **Frey**). According to *Lokasenna*, Thor was the only god able to stop **Loki's** abuse of the Æsir. Thor gave his name to Thursday, and there are many Scandinavian personal and place-names containing the name Thor. *See also* HELGITHELEAN.

THORFINN KARLSEFNI (ON *Þorfinnr karlsefni*). A wealthy merchant from Reynisnes in northern **Iceland** who, according to the *Saga of the Greenlanders* and the *Saga of Erik the Red*, undertook an expedition to colonize **Vinland** in the early 11th century. Thorfinn decided to travel to Vinland after spending the winter at **Brattahlíð**, Erik the Red's farmstead in **Greenland**. According to the *Saga of Erik the Red*, he took with him three ships and some 160 people, including his new wife, Gudrid, who was the widow of Thorstein, one of Erik's sons. However, the *Saga of the Greenlanders* says that the expedition consisted of 60 men and five **women**. The two *Vinland sagas* also differ in their account of Thorfinn's expedition to the Vinland. While the *Saga of the Greenlanders* relates how Thorfinn simply settled at *Leifsbuðir* "Leif's houses," the *Saga of Erik the Red* describes a long exploratory voyage around the coast of **North America**, apparently going as far south as Hóp or "Tidal Pool," which has been identified with New York. However, both sagas agree that Thorfinn and Gudrid's son, Snorri, was born in Vinland (he is said in *Erik's Saga* to be three years old when they left, but in the *Saga of the Greenlanders*, the expedition lasted only two winters in its entirety); they also both describe (in rather different terms) how Thorfinn's attempt to colonize Vinland was ultimately abandoned because of hostile relations with the native **skrælings**. The *Saga of the Greenlanders* relates that Thorfinn, "a man of great distinction and nobility," Gudrid, and Snorri later settled in north Iceland, at Glumbæjarland. The very last paragraph of this saga describes the achievements of Thorfinn's descendants, concluding that he was "blest in his kin," and that he had given the best account of the Vinland voyages.

THORFINN THE MIGHTY SIGURDSSON (ON *Þorfinnr inn ríki Sigurðarsonr*) **(1014–c.1065).** Earl of **Orkney**, Thorfinn was the grandson of the Scottish king, Malcolm III Canmore, and grew up in his court. As the relatively detailed treatment of his rule in *Orkneyinga Saga* suggests, Thorfinn's rule was a significant period in the history of the earldom. As well as considerable territorial conquests in **Scotland** and the **Hebrides**, Thorfinn's rule marked a new stage in the relationship between Orkney and Norway. From the time of **Sigurd the Stout**, the **earls** had tended to look westward, marrying into western noble families and concentrating their energies on conquest in the west. However, Thorfinn married a Norwegian **woman** and maintained closer connections with the Norwegian court than previous earls of Orkney, visiting the king three times. Thorfinn's career also combined traditional **Viking** activities with the role of a Christian ruler: he raided in the British Isles; served in **Cnut I the Great's** þingamannalið; visited the Imperial court; made a pilgrimage to Rome; and is credited with establishing the first fixed bishop's see in Orkney *c.* 1050 at **Birsay**.

THORKELL THE TALL (ON *Þorkell inn hávi*) **(d. after 1023).** The son of Strút-Haraldr, **earl** of the Danish island of Sjælland. Before his arrival in England, Thorkell appears to have been one of the legendary **Jomsvikings**, fighting against the Norwegians at **Hjörungavágr** and possibly also at **Svöld**, as part of a Danish-Swedish alliance. However, Thorkell is best known as the leader of the "immense raiding army" that arrived at Sandwich in southeast England in August 1009. By 1011, the Scandinavian army had overrun **East Anglia**, Essex, Middlesex, Oxfordshire, Cambridgeshire, Hertfordshire, Buckinghamshire, Bedfordshire, half of Huntingdonshire and, to the south of the Thames, all Kent, Sussex, the district around Hastings, Surrey, Berkshire, Hampshire, and a great part of Wiltshire, according to the *Anglo-Saxon Chronicle*. This army was also responsible for the notorious occupation of Canterbury in September 1011, during which a number of prominent ecclesiasts were taken hostage. Most of these were ransomed for 48,000 pounds in tribute, paid in April 1012, but the archbishop, Ælfheah (St Alphege), refused and was martyred in the **Viking** camp at Greenwich on 19 April. According to Thietmar of Merseburg, Thorkell had tried to prevent the archbishop's death at the hand of drunken Vikings. Certainly following this episode, Thorkell's army dispersed, and 45 **ships** under Thorkell entered into the service of King **Æthelred II**, promising to defend England against the newly arrived army of **Svein Forkbeard**. These ships even carried Æthelred and his family into exile in 1013.

The tax that was levied in order to pay for the mercenaries, the *heregeld*, was imposed every year until 1051, and later became known as **Danegeld**. Interestingly, Thorkell's name appears on a Swedish **rune-stone**, raised in memory of Ulf of Borresta at Yttergärde in Uppland, Sweden. According to the inscription, Ulf received a share in the "geld" that Thorkell paid, presumably that of 1012, as well as shares in those gelds previously paid by Tosti (*see* **Sigrid the Proud**) and later paid by **Cnut I the Great**. This inscription therefore suggests that Swedes, as well as Danes, fought in Thorkell's army.

At some point, possibly following the death of Æthelred, Thorkell appears to have aligned himself with Svein's son, Cnut. Certainly he was subsequently rewarded with the newly created earldom of East Anglia in 1017, and he is placed first among the earls in witness lists to all the charters issued by Cnut in 1018 and 1019. However, just two years later, in November 1021, Cnut outlawed Thorkell for reasons unknown, and Thorkell seems to have returned to Denmark. Cnut was compelled to return to Denmark in 1022, probably to deal with trouble that Thorkell had initiated. A reconciliation between the two was effected in 1023, Cnut returning with Thorkell's son as hostage, while Thorkell was made regent of Denmark and in turn apparently entrusted with Cnut's son, **Harthacnut**. Nothing more is known about Thorkell after this date.

THORVI. *See* THYRE.

ÞRYMSKVIÐA ("The Lay of Þrymr"). One of the poems of the *Poetic Edda*, which describes how **Thor** lost and retrieved his hammer, **Mjöllnir**, from the giant Þrymr. The giant said that he would only return

Thor's hammer if the goddess **Freya** would become his wife. Freya refused, and so Thor disguised himself as Freya and traveled to Þrymr's hall, but he nearly gave himself away by eating and drinking vast quantities of food and drink (three casks of mead, one ox, eight salmon, and countless delicacies). As part of the wedding ceremony, the hammer was placed in the bride's lap and at this point Thor abandoned his disguise and attacked the giant.

THYRE. Danish queen in the first half of the ninth century, Thyre was married to **Gorm the Old** and was the mother of **Harald Blue-Tooth**. According to the *Saga of the Jomsvikings* (*see* **Jomsvikings**), she and Gorm also had another son, called Knut *Danaást* "Denmark's love," who died before his parents, although there is no contemporary evidence for this son. Thyre is commemorated by her husband and son in two runic inscriptions (DR 41 and 42) at the dynasty's seat in **Jelling**, and the **rune-stone** raised by her husband, Gorm, calls her "Denmark's adornment" (tanmarkaR : but :). Later Danish historians, such as **Saxo Grammaticus** and **Sven Aggesen**, as well as the Icelandic *Saga of the Jomsvikings* preserve similar epithets: *Danicae maiestatis caput* "the head of Danish sovereignty"; *Decus Datiæ* "Ornament of Denmark"; and *Danmarkarbót* "Denmark's adornment." They also recount a number of stories about Thyre to explain her nickname and her importance in Danish history: for Sven and Saxo, she earned her nickname by constructing the **Danevirke** and thus thwarting the ambitions of the German emperor, while the *Saga of the Jomsvikings* has her rescuing the Danes from a famine.

Saxo's account of Danish history states that Thyre outlived Gorm, a statement that would seem to be contradicted by the rune-stone Gorm raised at Jelling; Sven Aggesen's account does not make it clear who outlived whom. In recent years, it has been argued that Saxo's account might in fact preserve some truth, and that Gorm's monument to Thyre was actually raised by Harald Blue-Tooth. This argument has centered upon two further inscriptions from Læborg (DR 26) and Bække (DR 29) that were raised by Tue, Ravn's descendant, in memory of his queen, Thyre. It is argued that this was the same Thyre as appears on the Jelling stones, and that therefore she married Tue after Gorm had died. The Bække inscription adds that Tue made Thyre's [**burial**] mound and certainly there is no evidence that Thyre was buried at Jelling—the south "burial" mound there lacked any evidence of a grave. This interpretation sees Gorm and his son Harald Blue-Tooth as Tue's rivals for power in Jutland and Thyre as playing a key role in this political tug-of-war because of her family links to lands in Denmark (originally the name of the lands on the other side of the *Store Bælt*). Therefore, Harald was keen to stress his right to both his maternal and paternal inheritance, and the two rune-stones at Jelling were raised by him for this purpose; the south mound at Jelling may also have been constructed by him in order to mask the fact that Thyre was not buried with Gorm, who lay in the north mound.

TRELLEBORG FORTRESSES. The name given to four circular fortress constructed in Denmark *c*. 980, according to **dendrochronological** dates from the Trelleborg and Fyrkat fortresses. The name is taken from one of these fortresses, at Trelleborg on the island of Sjælland, which was the first to be found and excavated. Aggersborg, in northern Jutland, is the largest of the four; while the remains of the fortress at Nonnebakken on Fyn have been largely destroyed by a later monastery and suburban development. A reconstruction of one of the forts can be found at Fyrkat in northern Jutland. All four fortresses consisted of a circular turf rampart, topped with a timber palisade, and protected by an external ditch. The rampart had four gateways at the four points of the compass. The land inside the fortresses was divided into quarters (with four buildings in each quarter at Fyrkat and Trelleborg; and 12 buildings in each quarter at Aggersborg), and Aggersborg was then further subdivided into quarters again. The fort at Trelleborg also had a further 15 buildings constructed outside the rampart, following the lines of the rampart.

The purpose of these forts has been a matter of considerable speculation. The first suggestion was that they were camps for **Svein Forkbeard's** army, which invaded England at the end of the 10th century and the beginning of the 11th. However, several objections have been raised against this theory: firstly, the dendrochronological dates for the forts are too early for Svein's invasion, and it seems as though the forts were not occupied for more than 20 years. Secondly, the distribution of the forts is more closely linked to land routes and the Baltic than to the North Sea, with the exception of Aggersborg, which is located on Limfjörd. Finally, the finds from the forts themselves are not exclusively military in character: there is evidence that **women** and children lived there and that craft activities were taking place, although it should be pointed out that army camps often attracted followers of this nature. It has therefore been argued that these camps were rather associated with the reign of **Harald Blue-Tooth** and that they were centers of royal power, designed to secure his control of his newly won kingdom.

TRONDHEIM (ON *Niðaróss*). Coastal town in central Norway, located on the banks of the River Nid. According to *Heimskringla*, **Olaf Tryggvason** founded the town around 995, but recently scholars have begun to examine more critically archaeological evidence that suggests a trading settlement may have existed on the site from the early years of the 10th century. Excavations on the town's library site since 1973 have revealed details of this early settlement and the subsequent development of the town. Finds include *c.* 130 runic inscriptions (*see* **rune**) on small portable objects, particularly wooden sticks known as *rúnakefli*, dating to the very end of the Viking Age and the medieval period. Trondheim became the center of royal and ecclesiastical power in 11th-century Norway and is most famous for the shrine of St. **Olaf Haraldsson**, which became one of the most important pilgrim destinations in northern Europe after its establishment in 1075. The bishopric of Nidaros, founded 1029, was elevated to the status of an archbishopric in 1153, and work on the cathedral, Nidarosdomen, was begun shortly afterward. This was built on the site of **Olaf the Peaceful's** Christchurch, which in turn was built on the spot where Olaf Haraldsson was said to be buried after **Stiklestad**. Trondheim's position as Norway's "capital" was taken over by **Bergen** in the Middle Ages.

TURGEIS (ON Þ*orgils* or Þ*órgestr?*). Turgeis was a **Viking** leader, who is said in the *Annals of Ulster* to have established a base at Lough Ree on the River Shannon in western Ireland in 844. He was captured by the Irish high king, Máel Sechlainn, in the following year and was drowned in Lough Owel. Turgeis is particularly infamous in Irish history because the 12th-century *War of the Irish with* *the Foreigners* records dramatic details of his exploits in order to enhance the prestige of **Brian Boru**, a later descendant of Máel Sechlainn. In the more colorful accounts of Turgeis's life, he is said to have tried to convert the Irish to the worship of **Thor** and it is claimed that his wife performed witchcraft on the high altar of the church at Clocmacnoise.

TYNWALD. Tynwald was where the **Isle of Man's** Viking-Age assembly met. It is derived from ON *Þingvöllur* "assembly plain," and the name has a direct Icelandic parallel in **Thingvellir**, where the **Althing** met every summer. The present-day Manx parliament still meets at Tynwald every summer (5 July) to formally approve all the laws passed during the previous year.

TYR. God of the Æsir. Tyr was a god of war and battle whose importance appears to have been eclipsed by **Odin** by the Viking Age. Very little is known about Tyr, although **Snorri Sturluson** describes how he put his hand into the mouth of the wolf **Fenrir** while the gods chained it. This was as a guarantee to Fenrir that it would be released again; and when Fenrir realized that it had been tricked by the gods, the wolf bit off Tyr's arm. Tyr is also said to fight against another mythical wolf, Garm, at **Ragnarök** (while Odin battles with Fenrir). Tyr gave his name to Tuesday, the t-rune in the *fuþark* or runic alphabet (*see* **rune**), and his name is also found in some Scandinavian place-names.

– U –

UDAL, THE. Settlement site on the island of North Uist in the Outer **Hebrides**. Excavations at the Udal revealed a square fort and other **longhouses** immediately overlying and destroying an early Celtic township. The building of this fortification in the mid- or late ninth century was also accompanied by a complete shift in the material culture of the inhabitants, with characteristic Norse artifacts replacing those used previously. Interestingly, the first inhabitants used pottery, which although not found in Viking-Age Norway or the Northern Isles of **Orkney** and **Shetland** has parallels with that found on approximately 40 other sites in the Hebrides and is similar to the so-called Souterrain Ware of northeast **Ireland**. The inhabitants of the Udal practiced a mixed economy, centered on farming and fishing.

The fort seems to have been in use for only a short period, but the site continued in use, perhaps by the descendants of the first Viking settlers, until the end of the 12th century, when it appears that they were driven out by a Gaelic population. On the basis of this site, the excavator argued for a sudden and destructive Norse presence in the Hebrides, rather than the more extended period of contact and co-existence between Norse and native for which the excavators of sites such as **Buckquoy** and **Birsay** in Orkney have argued. The place-name is the English form of the Gaelic name *An t-Udal*, which is in turn the Gaelic form of a Norse name, probably *den Óðal*. Ironically, this name is derived from a word for inherited family land. An *óðal* man was a high-ranking freeholder, suggesting that the inhabitants of the Udal were fairly wealthy and important.

URNES. Scandinavian **art** style that takes its name from the 11th-century wooden portals that decorate the 12th-century stave church at Urnes, Sogn og Fjordane, western Norway. The main characteristics of this style are sleek greyhound-like beasts interlaced with tendrils and snakes. The art style dates from the very end of the Viking Age (*c.* 1050–1125), and it can be found on a number of Swedish **rune-stones** from the eastern province of Uppland. Some examples of the style are found outside Scandinavia, particularly in **Ireland**. The Cross of Cong, a processional metalwork cross that was commissioned by the King of Connacht around 1123, is one of the finest examples of the Urnes style.

– V –

VALHALLA. Mythological hall with 540 doors and a roof of shields, belonging to **Odin**. All heroes killed in battle were taken by **valkyries** to Valhalla, where they spent their days fighting and their nights feasting while they awaited **Ragnarök**. The heroes fed on the flesh of a mythical boar (*Sæhrimnir*) that constantly renewed itself, and the mead they drank flowed constantly from the udders of a mythical goat (*Heiðrun*).

VALKYRIE (ON *valkyrie*). Literally "chooser of the slain." **Mythological** female who chose which of the dead warriors on the battlefield were to go to **Valhalla**. The valkyries were closely associated with **Odin** and are sometimes called "Odin's maids." The **Eddic** poem, *Grímnismál*, lists the names of some 13 valkyries who are said to have served the warriors (known as the *einherjar* "those who fight alone") in Valhalla. Brynhild, one of **Sigurd the Dragon-Slayer's** lovers, is said to have been a valkyrie.

VÄLSGÄRDE. Site of a pagan cemetery on the west bank of the River Fyris in the central eastern Swedish province of Uppland. The cemetery seems to have been in use from *c*. 600 until the end of the Viking Age, and it includes a number of boat **burials** as well as often lavish grave goods accompanying the dead. A replica of one of the boats, a small five-oared rowing boat, has been reconstructed. The high-status nature of the site is particularly demonstrated by the armor found in some of the graves and the horses and hunting dogs that were buried with their owners in a number of cases.

VANAHEIM. *See* VANIR.

VANIR. The family of fertility gods, which included **Niord**, **Frey**, and **Freya**, who lived in Vanaheim. According to Snorri's ***Prose Edda*** and ***Ynglinga Saga***, the Vanir and the Æsir once engaged in a series of wars (the so-called Vanir wars). In the peace treaty that ended this conflict, hostages were swapped and Niord and Frey were exchanged for Hoenir.

VARANGIAN GUARD. Scandinavians who traveled to **Byzantium** to serve in the emperor's bodyguard were generally known as Varangians. Scandinavians had entered imperial service from as early as the mid-ninth century, under Michael III, but a separate unit was not established until 988, when Basil II recruited Scandinavian mercenaries from Vladimir I of **Kiev**. The Varangian Guard became an elite unit of Scandinavian mercenaries and was the highest paid among the imperial guard. The Norwegian, **Harald Hard-Ruler**, was perhaps the most famous member of this bodyguard. However, after 1066, when there was an influx of English exiles, the unit became less Scandinavian in character. The Varangian Guard survived until 1204, when Byzantium fell to the Fourth Crusade.

As well as referring to the imperial bodyguard, the *Russian Primary Chronicle* uses the word Varangian in a different and more general sense, describing how the Slavic people invited three Varangian princes to come and rule over them. Here it seems that Varangian simply meant Scandinavian, and there is therefore some confusion over the difference between Varangian and another word, **Rus**, which is also used to describe Scandinavians in **Russia** and the east. There is no evidence for the use of the word Varangian in Russia before the second half of the 10th century, and it has been argued that the Varangians were Scandinavians who came to Russia after the first influx of Swedes and the establishment of settlements around **Novgorod** and Kiev.

The etymology of the word Varangian (*varjagi* in Russian sources and *varangoi* in Byzantine sources) is unclear. The Old Norse word *várar* means pledge or oath, and the suffix -ing would give the meaning "men of the oath." Alternatively, the Russian word *varyag* means itinerant pedlar, trader (from *vara* "goods"), and the word Varangian may therefore have originally been associated with people who participated in trading enterprises.

VELLEKLA ("Shortage of gold"). Poem by the Icelandic skald, Einarr Helgason *skálaglamm* ("scale tinkle") in honor of the Norwegian ruler, **Hákon Jarl** of **Lade**. Einarr's nickname refers to the scales given to him by Hákon, which tinkled and foretold the future according to the *Saga of the Jomsvikings* (*see* **Jomsvikings**). Stanzas from the poem are quoted in *Heimskringla* and *Fagrskinna*, although the complete poem has not been preserved. *Vellekla* has been described as one of the most important **skaldic poems** of the 10th century and contains references to Hákon's battle for power with the sons of **Erik Blood-Ax**, his restoration of pagan cults in Norway, and Hákon's role in the battle **Harald Blue-Tooth** fought against Otto II of Germany. A number of stanzas describing the Battle of the Jomsvikings are often included in reconstructions of the poem, but their inclusion is debated.

VENDEL. Pagan cemetery on the east bank of the River Fyris in the central eastern Swedish province of Uppland. The cemetery seems to have been in use from *c.* 600 until the end of the Viking Age, and was apparently the resting place of a number of rulers of the Svear (*see* **Svealand**). The graves include lavishly decorated boat **burials**, accompanied by armor, glass, horse-fittings, hunting dogs, and even, in one case, a falcon. However, perhaps the most famous find from Vendel is an iron helmet found in a seventh-century boat burial—one of the very few extant examples of helmets known from the Scandinavian world.

The site has given its name to both a style of **art**, typified by the elaborate animal ornamentation found on many of the finds, and to a historic era: the Vendel period is the last phase of the Scandinavian Iron Age in Sweden, used to describe the centuries immediately before the Viking Age, running from *c.* 550–800.

VIKING (ON *víkingr*). The word *Viking* has come to be used in a general sense for people from the area covered by the modern Scandinavian countries of Sweden, Norway, and Denmark, in the period *c.* 800–*c.* 1100. However, it originally had a more specific meaning and was used in this narrower sense by the contemporaries of the Vikings.

The word *Viking* does not occur in Old Norse sources until the late 10th century, but this is not surprising as we have very few written sources for Scandinavia before that date. It is first found in an Old-English source dating to the eighth century, and it was used to describe Scandinavian people who were involved in raiding and trading in England at that time. The precise meaning and origin (etymology) of *Viking* is, however, uncertain. The two main interpretations are that it was either based on the Old Norse word for inlet, fjörd (*vík*), or that it comes from the Old English word *wic*, which means a camp or fort. The Vikings are said to have built temporary camps and fortifications during their campaigns in England. The suffix *ing* is generally accepted as meaning a person who belongs to a group. So, if the Old Norse etymology is correct, Viking would mean man or people from the fjörds, and if the Old English version is the correct one, then Viking would mean man or people from the camp. A further two possibilities are that Old Norse *vík* in this compound is derived from the name for the area around Oslofjörd in Norway—Viken; alternatively this first element might come from the OE word *wic*, which is often used in place-names with the sense of town or market, and that therefore the Vikings might have been distinguished by the fact that they frequented these trading places—for both raiding and trading.

Although the people who stayed at home in Scandinavia technically were not Vikings in the true sense of the word, it is often hard to distinguish the two groups of population clearly, as in the summer, people who had lived peacefully at home all winter may have turned to Viking activities.

The term *Viking* was in actual fact hardly used by the contemporaries of the Vikings. They used instead a wide range of other terms: in the Christian West they were often called "heathen," and in the Muslim regions, such as Spain, they were called ***majus***. Most common, however, were the geographical terms "Northmen" and "Danes" that were usually used irrespective of which part of Scandinavia from which they came.

VINLAND (ON *Vinland*). Region, also known as Vinland the Good, explored by Norse Greenlanders that is mentioned in a number of written sources, the most important of which are the Icelandic sagas, the ***Saga of the Greenlanders*** and the ***Saga of Erik the Red***. In these sagas, Vinland is described as having a plentiful supply of salmon; a mild climate so that livestock could graze all year round; days and nights of a more even length than in **Iceland** or **Greenland**; and a good supply of timber and wild grapes.

The geographical descriptions contained in these sagas make it clear that Vinland was located somewhere in **North America**, but there has been considerable scholarly debate about the exact location of the region. One of the earliest suggestions was made by C. C. Rafn in 1837, when he equated Vinland with Cape Cod, but New England, Nova Scotia, New Brunswick, and the St. Lawrence River valley have since also been put forward as possible locations for Vinland. However, following the archaeological discoveries at **L'Anse aux Meadows** in the 1960s, most scholars believed that Newfoundland was the Vinland of the sagas, although the absence of wild grapes in the region has caused a number of problems in identifying the excavated site with the descriptions of the sagas. More recent accounts have stressed the connection between L'Anse aux Meadows and the specific settlements or camps mentioned in the sagas, Leifsbuðir and

Straumfjörd, which were used as bases for exploration south. In this view, Vinland itself would be located to the south of Newfoundland, where grapes grew in the wild, perhaps in New Brunswick, the Bay of Fundy, or the St. Lawrence River valley.

VINLAND MAP. Yale University Press published *The Vinland Map and the Tartar Relation* by Raleigh A. Skelton, Thomas E. Marston, and George D. Painter on 11 October 1965 (the day before Columbus Day). It was found by an American bookseller, Lawrence Witten, of New Haven, and was purchased in 1957 by a man called Mellon. However, Witten had sworn not to reveal details of the map's previous ownership, so nothing else is known of its provenance. The map is a crude depiction of the world, drawn on antique vellum and dated by its authors to *c.* 1440 because of its discovery with an authentic and unrelated medieval text, the *Tartar Relation*. In the top left-hand corner of the map (in the northwest) was what appeared to be the first known depiction of **Vinland**, labeled *Winilanda* (or *Vinilanda*) *Insula*. A Latin inscription above this mentions *Byarnus* (**Bjarni Herjólfsson**) and *Leiphus* (**Leif Eriksson**) together explored *Winilanda*, and that *Henricus . . . epsicopus* (Bishop Eiríkr Gnúpsson?) went in search of Vinland in the early 12th century.

Norse voyages to Vinland are recorded in the Icelandic sagas, the **Saga of Erik the Red** and the **Saga of the Greenlanders**, and on the basis of the geographical descriptions in these sagas, Vinland had been identified as lying somewhere in **North America**. However, before the discovery of archaeological evidence for a Scandinavian presence in North America, many historians questioned the reliability of the sagas' evidence, as they were first and foremost literary rather than historical texts. The Vinland Map therefore seemed to substantiate saga evidence for pre-Columbian Europeans visiting the North American continent.

However, doubts concerning the authenticity of the map were raised from the time of its publication. Its view of the world was outside the mainstream of cartographic evolution, where the ocean is normally depicted as encircling the inhabited world on medieval maps, but this is not the case on the Vinland Map; unlike other medieval maps, the map is not oriented to the east; the depiction of **Greenland** was unparalleled in its accuracy before the 20th century;

and, of course, the map shows Greenland and part of North America, which otherwise do not appear on extant maps until the beginning of the 16th century, when they are depicted by Genovese cartographer, Nicolo Canerio (his map is dated to 1503–1505). Following scientific tests by Walter McCrone, the Vinland Map was dismissed as a forgery in 1974, as the ink with which it was drawn contained commercial titanium oxide, anatase, which was apparently unknown before 1917. However, later testing by Thomas A. Cahill, published in 1987, suggested that only trace elements of the chemical could be found, and that the map could therefore not be dismissed as a fake on the grounds of its ink. However, others contest this, and analysis of the specific ink used to draw the map is ongoing; it appears that it may be a common varnish-based printer's ink that needs to be heated to about 200 degrees Fahrenheit in order to remain stable on the page. The results of a fresh examination of the ink were published in 2002, and the scientists from University College London concluded that they were modern. However, the parchment on which the map is drawn is likely to be from the 15th century. Despite careful preservation, the ink pigment on the Vinland Map has been rapidly falling off since its discovery, so that no black lines can be seen today, just the stain of linseed that soaked into the vellum; such a rate of loss further suggests that the map is unlikely to have been medieval in date. Finally, the supposedly medieval date of the map partly rested on its discovery with the 15th-century *Tartar Relation*, but the binding with which the two were placed together is 18th-century in date.

Ironically, the map provides no real evidence to help scholars locate Vinland: it does not show **Markland** and **Helluland**, which the sagas say were visited by Scandinavians on their way south to Vinland, and scholars who argue for Hudson Bay, New England, or Newfoundland as the location of Vinland can all find some support in the map for their claims. Yet, at the time of the map's publication, clear archaeological evidence for Scandinavian settlement at **L'Anse aux Meadows** had just been discovered.

VINLAND SAGAS. Name given to the two *Icelandic sagas* that recount Norse voyages to **Vinland**. There are many similarities between the ***Saga of Erik the Red*** and the ***Saga of the Greenlanders*** but a number of differences too. The key difference between the two sagas is the role of **Leif the Lucky Eriksson**, son of **Erik the Red**. In the *Saga of Erik the Red*, Leif made the first accidental discovery of Vinland in 1000, whereas in the *Saga of the Greenlanders*, it was sighted by **Bjarni Herjólfsson** some 15 years earlier. The account in the *Saga of Erik the Red* also links Leif's discovery with the conversion of **Greenland** to **Christianity**, claiming that Leif was persuaded in Norway by **Olaf Tryggvason** to convert his countrymen. However, while sailing from Norway to Greenland, Leif was blown off course and thus discovered Vinland, before heading back to Greenland and then successfully converting the Norse colony to Christianity, and rescuing two shipwrecked sailors on the way.

Although the more polished *Saga of Erik the Red* was preferred by many 19th-century scholars, research published in the 1950s demonstrated that the story about Leif meeting Olaf Tryggvason and converting Greeland was the invention of an Icelandic monk, Gunnlaug Leifsson, in the late 12th century, when the traditional number of countries that Olaf is said to have converted, five (Norway, **Iceland**, **Orkney**, **Shetland**, and **Faroe Islands**), suddenly became six. Gunnlaug added Greenland to the list, and this new "tradition" was subsequently repeated in many 13th-century works. The *Saga of Erik the Red* was therefore seen as a deliberate revision of the older *Saga of the Greenlanders*, focusing on the role played by Erik's family. The writer of the *Saga of Erik the Red* had to try to reconcile all the evidence he had: on the one hand, the *Saga of the Greenlanders* recorded that Vinland was first accidentally sighted by Bjarni, but on the other, there was the later tradition that it was Leif who had discovered Vinland first. The result was that he discarded the Bjarni episode and was therefore also forced to discard the story about Leif's deliberate voyage to explore Vinland, which is given in the *Saga of the Greenlanders*. However, the details of this voyage were used but fitted into different places in the narrative in the *Saga of Erik the Red*. More recently, some scholars have argued against a written link between the two Vinland sagas, concluding instead that they both independently drew upon details of the Vinland voyages that were circulating in oral tradition.

VÖLSUNGA SAGA **("The Saga of the Volsungs")**. This saga is perhaps the most famous of the *Sagas of Ancient Times* and was the inspiration for German composer Richard Wagner's opera cycle *Ring des Nibelungen*. It was written in **Iceland** *c*. 1260–1270 and is preserved in just one vellum manuscript dating from *c*. 1400 but is believed to incorporate relics of a much older oral tradition. Indeed, some of the figures in the saga can be identified with known historical figures from the Migration Age (*c*. 400–550). For example, *Jörmunrekkr* in the saga appears to be the fourth-century king of the Goths, Ermanaric; and *Atli*, the fifth-century king of the Huns, Attila. However, the central figure in the saga is **Sigurd the Dragon-Slayer**, whose acquisition of a cursed treasure of gold leads to his death and a bitter and bloody series of feuds. Following Sigurd's own death, the cursed treasure passed into the possession of his brothers-in-law, Gunnar and Hogni. Their sister, Gudrun, remarried, taking Atli, brother of the **valkyrie** Brynhild, as her husband. Atli coveted the gold Gudrun's brothers owned and tricked and killed them both (Gunnar was put to death in a snake pit). Gudrun revenged the deaths of her brothers by tricking Atli into drinking the blood and eating the hearts of his sons, before killing him with the help of Hogni's son, Niflung. However, the curse of the gold followed Gudrun, whose daughter (by Sigurd), Svanhild, was trampled to death by horses at the instigation of her (Svanhild's) father-in-law.

VÖLUSPÁ ("The Prophecy of the Seeress"). The first and most famous of the **mythological** poems in the collection known as the *Elder* or *Poetic Edda*. The poem is preserved in two main manuscripts, the *Codex Regius* and *Hauksbók*, the texts and ordering of which are quite different; most modern editions follow the former, adding some four stanzas (34, 54, 65, and parts of 47 and 60) from *Hauksbók*, which gives the poem a total of 66 stanzas. Although the *Codex Regius* manuscript is dated to *c*. 1270, the poem itself is believed to be considerably older and may predate 1065, when the skald (*see* **skaldic poetry**) Arnórr Þórðarson jarlaskáld echoes stanza 57 of *Völuspá* in his *Þorfinnsdrápa*. A date as early as the beginning of the 10th century has been suggested, but it is also argued that the poem may reflect millennial anxieties surrounding the year 1000, when it was believed that the world would come to an end. *Völuspá* is presented as a series of visions recounted by a seeress or sybil to **Odin** and it provides an account of the beginning and end of the Norse mythological world. **Snorri Sturluson** used this poem for his own account of Norse mythology and cosmology in the ***Prose Edda***. The extent to which the poem reflects Christian influence has been much debated, with particular attention paid to the poem's account of the end of the world, the reference to the coming of "The Mighty One," and the idea of punishment or reward after death.

– W –

WALES, VIKINGS IN (ON *Bretland*). It appears that Wales escaped serious **Viking** raiding until the mid-ninth century. Its coastline, with treacherous currents and difficult approaches, certainly made it difficult for hostile forces to attack. However, following the establishment of permanent Viking settlements in **Ireland** and the **Hebrides**, Scandinavian raiders made some attempt to gain a foothold in Wales. Particularly attractive was the island of Anglesey off the northwestern coast of Wales. However, Rhodri Mawr, prince of the northern Welsh kingdom of Gwynedd, (844–878) managed to resist Scandinavian attempts to establish settlements on Anglesey and killed the Viking leader, Gorm, in an important campaign in 855. Excavations at Llanbedrgoch on Anglesey since the 1990s have revealed a huge defended enclosure that may have been constructed during Rhodri's reign or that of his son's in response to Viking pressure. However, the artifacts found at Llanbedrgoch also suggest that there was trading contact with Scandinavians active in the Irish Sea region, and it may even be possible that the settlement was taken over by Vikings at some point. During the last years of Rhodri's reign, he was forced into exile in Ireland following a series of Danish victories; and in 878, the Vikings first overwintered in Wales, in the southwestern district of Pembrokeshire.

The expulsion of the **Dublin** Norse in 902 renewed Scandinavian interest in Wales and, in particular, Anglesey. However, Ingimundr's army was driven from the island and was eventually given land around Chester by Æthelflæd, Lady of the Mercians. The restoration of Scandinavian power in Ireland in 914 was followed by a further attack on Anglesey, which was repelled by Hywel Dda (*c*. 915–950), grandson of Rhodri Mawr. South Wales suffered rather more during this period. Pembrokeshire offered a relatively easy line of entry into the country through Milford Haven; there were sporadic raids and there may have been some limited settlement along the Haven. In 914, two Viking **earls** from **Brittany**, Ohter and Hroald, ravaged the Welsh coast and moved inland along the Wye Valley as far as Archenfield. Here they captured the bishop of Llandaff, Bishop Cyfeiliog, who was ransomed for £40 by Edward the Elder of England.

There was a lull in Scandinavian activity in Wales during the second quarter of the 10th century during Hywel's reign, and by 942, Hywel was ruler of virtually the whole country. However, this interlude was followed by a dramatic new development in Welsh relations with the Vikings. Until this time, Wales was the only kingdom in the British Isles that had been able to avoid intense raiding and conceding tracts of land to the Scandinavians. But Hywel Dda's death in 950 ignited a disastrous period of internal conflict in Wales, and this was taken advantage of by the Vikings. Some Welsh princes used Scandinavian mercenaries in their own campaigns for political dominance within Wales. For example, Maredudd ap Owain (986–999), ruler of the south Welsh kingdom of Dyfed, used Viking mercenaries but was later forced by them to pay a penny a head for Welsh prisoners that they had taken. Some 14 or 15 raids are recorded in the 50 years that followed the death of Hywel Dda: on Dyfed, Anglesey, and the Lleyn Peninsula, and in the Bristol Channel area. Monasteries were obvious and vulnerable targets, for example, St. David's was attacked in 982, 988, and 999; and the kingdom of Gwynedd suffered from its proximity to Viking bases in Ireland and the **Isle of Man**, with attacks recorded on Holyhead (961) and Towyn (963). However, again, Anglesey appears to have suffered most. In 971, Magnus Haraldsson, leader of the Manx Vikings, attacked Penmon, and further attacks by Magnus's brother, Godfrey, are recorded in 972, 980, and 987. In 972, Godfrey was apparently the temporary lord of Anglesey. The ferocious attack in 987 was recorded in Irish and Welsh annals, where some thousand Welshmen are said to have been killed and a further two thousand taken captive.

By around the year 1000, Viking activity across the border from England increased with intensified campaigning there. Pressure from the east became the dominant issue in Welsh politics, a trend that was intensified after the Norman Conquest of England in 1066. However, Gruffydd ap Llewelyn (1039–1063) largely resisted these incursions successfully, until defeated by Harald Godwinsson in 1063. Gruffydd was actually assisted by a Norwegian fleet, under **Magnus Haraldsson**, son of **Harald Hard-Ruler** in 1058. By this time, distinctions between Celt and Norseman were becoming blurred, and it is possible to talk of an Irish-Sea political circle. For example, Gruffydd ap Cynan, ruler of Gwynedd from 1075, was said to have been born in exile in Ireland in 1054 or 1055 and to have been brought up in the Scandinavian settlement there.

After 1066, the new Norman earls of Hereford, Chester, and Shrewsbury supported Norman expansion into the west. Hugh Lupus of Chester, with Hugh Montgomery of Shrewsbury, made a decisive attempt to win control of north Wales in 1098. The native Welsh princes were forced to withdraw to Anglesey and employed Hiberno-Norse mercenaries to help control the seas. The mercenaries betrayed their Welsh lords, and Gruffydd ap Cynan was forced to flee to Ireland. It was at this point that the last real Viking intervention in Welsh affairs came, with the appearance of King **Magnus Bare-Foot** and a Norwegian fleet off the island of Priestholm. After a confrontation in the Menai Straits and a Norwegian victory, both the Norwegians and the Normans withdrew from Wales.

The impact of the Vikings on Wales was relatively slight when compared to other parts of the British Isles. There was virtually no Scandinavian influence on the Welsh language: *iarll* "earl" and *gardd* "enclosure" may be examples of Scandinavian loanwords, but it is also possible that they were loaned via English. There is no explicit mention of Scandinavian settlement in Wales in any sources, apart from the very problematic 12th-century legendary *Saga of the Jomsvikings* (*see* **Jomsvikings**), which mentions a Danish colony that was established in *Bretland* before *c.* 930 and which existed throughout the 10th century. There are several examples of Scandinavian place-names, but these are generally navigation points and the names of small islands around the Welsh coast, such as Bardsey, Holyhead, the Skerries, Priestholm and Orme's Head in the north, and Ramsey, Grassholm, and Skokholm in the south. Anglesey itself, which is consistently called *Mon* in Welsh, seems to be a Scandinavian name meaning "Ongull's island," although no Viking leader called Ongull can be identified in any of the written sources. Names inland around Milford (itself derived from ON *-fjörðr*) do, however, hint at some kind of Scandinavian settlement in the interior of Wales. Swansea is undoubtedly Scandinavian "Svein's island," but there are also many names, such as Womanby Street in Cardiff (from Hundmanby), that may reflect later Anglo-Scandinavian influence rather than Scandinavian influence.

WANTAGE CODE. *See* DANELAW, WAPENTAKE.

WAPENTAKE (ON *vápnatak* OE *wæpentac* "weapon-taking"). A local administrative and legal division found in parts of **Danelaw**, which largely corresponds with the English hundred (a hundred notionally consisted of 100 hides, a hide being the amount of land needed to support one family and the basic unit of taxation in England). In 1086, Domesday Book records wapentakes in the territory of the **Five Boroughs**, parts of Northamptonshire, and in the West and North Ridings of Yorkshire (East Yorkshire, however, is divided into hundreds). The word is first found in English sources in 962, in the laws of King Edgar (959–975), concerning the buying and selling of goods "in a borough or a wapentake." Wapentake assemblies were held regularly, usually in the open air, and they appear to have been the most important legal and judicial unit in the administration of the Five Boroughs in Æthelred II's Wantage Code. In **Iceland**, the *vápnatak* was a ceremony performed at the end of the **Althing**, in which **weapons** were beaten to confirm the decisions of the assembly. Weapons were outlawed at the Althing in 1154, but it seems that this law was largely ignored. There is no Scandinavian evidence for the use of the term "wapentake" to describe an administrative district.

WAR OF THE IRISH WITH THE FOREIGNERS (Irish *Cogadh Gaedhel re Gallaibh*). Twelfth-century Irish rhetorical account of Norse-Irish relations, written as a piece of propaganda for the Uí Briain dynasty descended from **Brian Boru**. Divided into two sections, the work begins with a colorful description of **Viking** raids and plundering that afflicted **Ireland** during the eighth and ninth centuries, and then goes on to describe in heroic terms the defeat of the Vikings at the hands of the Uí Briain kings of Dál Cais, paying particular attention to Brian and his brother, Mathgamain. The *War of the Irish with the Foreigners* culminates with a vivid description of the Battle of **Clontarf**, in which the "foreigners" are depicted as, among a long series of pejorative adjectives, "cunning, warlike, poisonous, murderous, hostile," while the Irish under Brian are "bright, fresh, never-weary, valiant, victorious heroes." Despite the clearly propagandist nature of the work, it has had considerable influence on perceptions of the importance of the Battle of Clontarf.

WATLING STREET. Name of the Roman road that ran from **London** in the southeast to Chester in northwest England. During the Viking period, Watling Street appears to have functioned as a boundary between the area of Scandinavian settlement and the area that remained under English control. Watling Street was mentioned in **Alfred the Great** and **Guthrum's** treaty at **Wedmore**, although the treaty itself does not actually specify that the boundary ran along the whole length of Watling Street to Chester. Instead, it merely states that the dividing line between Alfred's and Guthrum's territories should first follow the River Thames, then the River Lea to its source, then run in a direct line to Bedford, and then up the River Ouse to Watling Street. It is not until later on, in the ***Anglo-Saxon Chronicle*** for 1013, that we have some contemporary evidence that Watling Street had come to be generally recognized as the dividing line between Anglo-Scandinavian and English England. The distribution of Scandinavian place-names also largely follows this dividing line.

WEAPONS AND ARMOR. **Viking** warriors were generally armed with a shield, spear, a sword or an ax, and a short knife attached to their belts. The warrior shown on the **Middleton cross** is equipped with all of these weapons and is also wearing a helmet. Very few helmets have survived from the Viking Age, although depictions of warriors in Viking **art** suggest that conical helmets were common. The horned and winged helmets associated with the Vikings in popular mythology were the invention of 19th-century Romanticism. It has been suggested that Viking helmets may have been made from leather, as well as from iron. The best-preserved Viking helmet is that from Gjermundbu in Norway, which is more elaborate than the simple conical design, with protection around the eyes and for the nose.

A further rare find from Gjermundbu is one of the most complete chain-mail shirts yet found, and although there are indications that mail was worn by kings and the wealthiest warriors, leather jerkins were probably worn as protection by most Viking warriors.

Shields were circular, up to a meter in diameter, wooden, often edged with iron or leather, and had a raised iron boss in their center, behind which was the hand-grip. Literature, some archaeological finds (normally only the shield boss survives due to problems with the preservation of wood), and stone sculpture suggest that shields were painted and decorated. For example, the shields found in the **Gokstad ship burial** were painted in alternating yellow and black segments; and there is a subgenre of **skaldic poetry**, known as "shield poems," that describes scenes painted on shields (*see* **Bragi**).

Spears could be thrown or thrust at an enemy and had wooden (ash) shafts, measuring 2–3 meters in length, that were tipped with iron blades. These iron spearheads are generally all that survive in pagan Scandinavian burials, as the wood has normally perished. In Norse **mythology**, **Odin's** weapon was the spear, and throwing a spear over enemy warriors was said to dedicate them to Odin or, in other words, bring about their death in battle.

The ax might be a simple hand ax, which could be used as a tool in woodworking, or a more elaborate broadax, with a crescent-shaped blade, like those said to have been used in the Battle of Hastings (1066) by Harold Godwinsson's **housecarls**. According to **Snorri Sturluson's** *Prose Edda*, axes were often named after she-trolls. Axes are found more often than any other weapon in Norwegian Viking-Age graves.

Swords were also given names, although these were generally rather poetic and encapsulated the qualities of a good sword, such as **Magnus Bare-Foot's** sword Legbiter. Most Viking swords had double-edged blades and, during the early Viking Age, were pattern-welded; later swords were more commonly inlaid with symbols or letters. Some Viking swords had elaborate hilts, which might be decorated in gold, silver, copper, or niello (Legbiter's hilt is said to have been of ivory), but most had simple hilts, with unadorned blades measuring 70–80 centimeters in length and 5–6 centimeters in width. A sword was nevertheless an expensive weapon to produce, and a good sword was apparently prized by successive generations of warriors. Swords are certainly found less frequently in male graves than other weapons. Viking-Age swords are more commonly found in Norway and Denmark than they are in Sweden, where spears appear to have been more popular than in western Scandinavia. There is some evidence from Viking burials for the deliberate and possibly ritual "killing" of swords, which involved the blade being bent so that it was unusable. This may have served a practical function in deterring any grave robbers from disturbing the burial in order to get one of these costly weapons.

WEDMORE, TREATY OF. Name given to the treaty that **Alfred the Great** and **Guthrum**, leader of the Danes, are believed to have signed in 878 following Alfred's victory at **Edington**. Wedmore lies in the modern English county of Wiltshire, southwest England. The treaty outlined the border between Alfred's and Guthrum's respective spheres of influence: along the Rivers Thames, Lea, and Ouse until reaching the old Roman road, **Watling Street**. Although many scholars regard this treaty as dividing England into two halves, Danish and English England, and formally establishing the area that was later known as **Danelaw**, the treaty does not specify that the boundary continued along Watling Street through the East Midlands to the Irish Sea. The treaty was renewed in 886, following Guthrum's breaking of the terms; it is the text of this later treaty that has survived.

WENDS. Collective name for the West Slavic people living on the coast of the south Baltic, in the area between the River Oder in the east and the River Elbe in the west. The **Abodrites** are among the Wendish people with whom Scandinavians had contact. A Wendish town, *Reric* (*see* **Hedeby**), was destroyed by **Godfred** of Denmark at the beginning of the ninth century, and later Scandinavian kings (**Harald Blue-Tooth**, **Erik the Victorious**, **Svein Forkbeard**, and **Olaf Tryggvason**) are known to have both fought against and allied themselves with rulers of the Wends, such as Boleslav of Poland. **Wolin**, identified with the **Jomsviking** stronghold of *Jómsborg*, lay in Wendland, and the settlement at **Fribrødre River** has been interpreted as a Wendish colony under Scandinavian control. During the 12th century, Danish kings launched a series of crusades against the pagan Wends.

WESSEX. Anglo-Saxon kingdom that by the Viking Age consisted of most of England south of the River Thames and the southwestern peninsula. At the beginning of the Viking Age, following the Battle of Ellandun in 825, Wessex surpassed the neighboring kingdom of **Mercia** and emerged as the dominant kingdom within England. It was the only kingdom to survive intact the **Viking** settlements of the ninth century, and indeed it increased both its territory and authority under **Alfred I the Great** and his successors. Before the emergence of **London** as the capital city of England in the 11th century, Winchester in the heart of West-Saxon territory appears to have been the most important town in the kingdom.

The first recorded Viking attack on southern England (at Portland in Dorset) is described by the *Anglo-Saxon Chronicle* in the entry for 789; although confusingly it is stated there that the raid took place in the reign of Beorhtric of Wessex, a period between 786–802. However, an attack on Sheppey by "the heathen" in 835 signaled the real beginning of the Viking Age in southern England. The *Chronicle* subsequently records a series of raids on southern England, variously attributed to Danes (*Deniscan*), "the heathen" (*hæþene men*), and "the army" (*se here*) (in 836, 838, 840, 841, 842, 843?, 845?, 851). The Danish army first wintered in England in 851 on the Isle of Thanet. More attacks on southern England followed in 853, 860, and 865, before the armies temporarily transferred their activities to **East Anglia**, Nottingham, and **York**. However, in 871 the Danish army returned to Wessex and fought with the English at Englefield, Reading, Ashdown, Basing, *Meretun*, and Wilton, before the West Saxons made peace with them. The same year saw Alfred the Great take over the West Saxon leadership, inaugurating a period of effective resistance to Viking attacks.

Following the Viking defeat at Edington in 878 and the subsequent settlement between Alfred and **Guthrum** at **Wedmore**, there was a lull in hostilities. A short-lived series of raids in the 890s were effectively repelled following the introduction of a number of defensive measures by Alfred. Unlike the rest of England, therefore, southern England was not subject to large-scale Scandinavian settlement in the Viking Age. While there is consequently little place-name evidence to testify to the presence of Scandinavians in this part of the country, written evidence about the Viking period is comparatively plentiful.

To judge from the *Anglo-Saxon Chronicle*, southern England appears to have enjoyed a comparatively peaceful 10th century, until the resumption of Viking attacks in 980 during the reign of **Æthelred II**. Indeed, Alfred's son, Edward the Elder, was strong enough to embark upon the reconquest of the Danelaw, a process that was largely complete by the 920s. The death of Edward the Elder's sister, Æthelflæd in 918, saw the absorption of English Mercia into Wessex, and certainly, by the time Alfred's grandson, **Athelstan**, was king, the king of Wessex was king of England.

WESTERN SETTLEMENT. *See* GREENLAND.

WESTNESS. Westness is on the southwest coast of the **Orkney** island of Rousay. Archaeological excavation of the site began in 1968, following the discovery of a richly furnished female **burial** on Moa Ness. This grave is dated to the ninth century and contained the skeleton of a young **woman** and a newborn child, accompanied by a range of household and personal items and three brooches. Four seasons of excavation have revealed a Viking farm, with a boathouse and a graveyard nearby. The farm, consisting of a large dwelling **house** and two byres, is a substantial one and the cemetery, with its 30 or more graves, has yielded two boat burials, a huge boat-shaped stone-setting, and a number of richly-furnished pagan graves. The cemetery was in use from the seventh to the ninth century and the pagan Norse burials are preceded by unaccompanied cist burials, believed to be those of the pre-existing native population. Unfortunately the excavations have not yet been published in detail, and it is not yet certain whether the farm, cemetery, and boathouse are contemporary. Nor is it clear whether the excavations revealed the full extent of the site: there may be more graves farther up the slopes of Moa Ness, and other farms may also have existed in the area.

WIDUKIND. Widukind was the author of *Rerum Gestarum Saxonicarum* "History of the Saxons," the first version of which was completed around 968. According to Widukind, the Danes had been Christian for some time before the reign of **Harald Blue-Tooth**, although they still worshipped pagan idols. He claims that Henry I the Fowler (919–936) of Germany had defeated the Danes in 934, and forced their king, Chnuba, to convert to **Christianity** (*see* **Olaf Dynasty**). However, the *Annals of Corvey*, upon which Widukind's account is based, do not refer to Chnuba's baptism and so the truth of this episode is doubtful. Widukind's famous account of Harald Blue-Tooth's conversion attributes the king's change of religion to the Saxon priest, Poppo, who is said to have convinced the Danish leader through ordeal, by carrying a piece of red-hot iron.

WILLIAM OF JUMIÈGES. Norman monk and author of a Latin history of the dukes of **Normandy**, the *Gesta Normannorum ducum* ("Deeds of the Dukes of Normandy"), written between the late 1050s and *c*. 1070. The first four books of William's history revised and updated the earlier history of the dukes by **Dudo of St-Quentin**, which covered **Rollo**, **William I Longsword**, and Richard I the Fearless (d. 996). To these, William added three further books covering the reigns of Richard II the Good (d. 1026), Robert the Magnificent (d. 1035), and William the Conqueror (d. 1087). He is the first authority to mention the figure *Lothbroc*, who may be the legendary **Ragnar Loðbrók**, and his history contains a unique reference to **Björn Ironside**. William's history shows several indications that he used (Anglo-)Scandinavian sources, including the **skaldic** verses composed by **Sighvatr Þórðarson** in honor of **Olaf Haraldsson**.

WILLIAM I LONGSWORD (d. 943). William was the son of **Rollo** and the second ruler of **Normandy**. He succeeded his father *c*. 925, when Rollo is said to have abdicated. According to **Dudo of St-Quentin**, William was the son of Rollo by his wife, Popa of Bayeux, but the *Plaintsong* composed after William's death suggests that his mother was a Christian from overseas. In Norse tradition too, Rollo is said to have had a child, called Kathleen, while he was in **Scotland**; as this name suggests a Christian Celtic mother, it is possible that William too may have been the child of Rollo and an unknown Celtic **woman**. The *Plaintsong* also records that William was a Christian, and that Rollo "stuck to the pagan error."

William expanded yet further the territory of the Normans and, according to contemporary annalist, Flodoard of Reims (893–894–*c*. 966), was granted "the territory of the Bretons at the edge of the sea" by the Franks in 933. This area probably included the Cotentin

Peninsula and Avranchin, although the extent of the 933 grant has been much debated. Dudo of St-Quentin even suggests that William put down a revolt in **Brittany** in 931, a claim that was probably designed to retrospectively make good Norman claims to Brittany at the time Dudo was writing. The grant of Cotentin and Avranchin made "Normandy" approximately three times the size of the original grant made to Rollo and about the same size of the duchy at the time of William the Conqueror's conquest of England in 1066.

William was murdered by Count Arnulf I of Flanders (918–965). His sister, Gerloc (also known as Adela) appears to have commissioned the *Plaintsong*, mourning the death of William (described as count of Rouen). Flodoard records that Louis IV (d. 954) of France granted "the land of the Normans" to Richard ("the Fearless"), William's 10-year old son by Sprota, his Breton concubine. Nevertheless, William's death unleashed civil war in Normandy. Louis IV, Richard, and a Danish exile called Aigrold, who William had allowed to settle the Cotentin shortly before his death, together confronted the French duke, Hugh the Great (d. 956). Hugh's campaign was backed by Scandinavian pagans, Sigtrygg and Tormod, who were, however, killed at Rouen by Louis in 943. By 947, Richard, son of William Longsword, was undisputed ruler of Normandy, and he married Emma, daughter of Hugh the Great, in 960.

WILLIBRORD, ST. (658–739). Northumbrian missionary, brought up in the monastery of Ripon, who was known as "the Apostle of the Frisians" after his missionary work there in 690. Willibrord was made archbishop of Utrecht in 695, and, in 698, he founded a monastery at Echternach, in present-day Luxembourg, where he was later buried.

Willibrord led the earliest recorded mission to Scandinavia, visiting Denmark in the early eighth century. This is briefly described in Willibrord's *Life* (*Vita Willibrordi*), written by another Northumbrian, **Alcuin**, who described the Danes as a "very savage people." Willibrord attempted to convert Denmark's king, **Angantyr**, but failed. He did, however, bring back from Denmark 30 boys, probably in order to bring them up as Christian missionaries, although they may simply have been captives he found and ransomed in Denmark.

WOLIN. Located on an island between the estuaries of the Rivers Oder and Dziwna in present-day Poland, Wolin was called *Jumne* in the histories of **Adam of Bremen** and **Saxo Grammaticus**. In Norse tradition, it is identified with *Jómsborg*, the headquarters of the semi-legendary **Jomsvikings** during the 10th century. *Jumne* is said to have been ceded by the Jomsvikings to the Slavic **Wends** in the 980s, and Adam of Bremen describes it as a Slavic town, with a population of merchants from as far away as Greece.

Although a fishing settlement from the seventh century has been identified at Wolin, the town grew in importance during the second half of the 9th and the 10th centuries. A long wooden waterfront was built *c.* 860, a regular grid of **house** plots laid out, and the town was surrounded with a semicircular defensive rampart. Artifacts recovered from Wolin are similar to those from **Hedeby** and **Birka**, with evidence of, for example, bone- and antler working, smithing, shipbuilding, and amber working taking place. The pottery is, however, almost exclusively Slavonic in character, and a Slavic temple, dated to 966, has also been excavated on the site. At its peak, Wolin was one of the largest settlements on the Baltic coast, covering an area of about 20 hectares, and it may have had as many as 10,000 inhabitants. Extensive cemeteries lie to the north and south of the town, and the northern one contains approximately 2,000 cremation and inhumation graves dating from the 10th to the 12th centuries.

WOMEN. Primary evidence for the status of women in Viking-Age Scandinavia can be found in runic inscriptions (*see* **rune**) and archaeological evidence. The former suggests that women were able to inherit wealth, to commission costly stone monuments, and that they were also commemorated by runic memorials. Some runic memorials contain further snippets of anecdotal information about the lives of Viking-Age women. For example, one rune-stone (U 605 from Uppland in Sweden) suggests that some women at least could contemplate traveling to Jerusalem on a pilgrimage; and others record that skill with handicrafts (N 68 from Dynna in Norway) and good house management (Vs 24 from Västmanland in Sweden) were qualities for which women were praised. However, the vast majority of runic inscriptions were raised by men in memory of men, a fact that probably reflects the superior social and economic status of men, perhaps particularly in connection with rights of inheritance to land and property.

Evidence from graves also suggests that Viking-Age women could enjoy very high status. The **Oseberg** ship **burial** contains the bodies of two women, placed inside a burial chamber on the **ship** and surrounded with a wealth of grave goods. These reflect both the status of the women being buried (although one of the bodies is traditionally interpreted as that of a **slave**) and the wealth of her family, who could afford to dispose of these possessions. The grave goods found in the Oseberg ship, like other less splendid burials, also provide some indication of social expectations about what women would do in the afterlife. In clear contrast to male graves—which traditionally contain **weapons**, implements associated with farming or trading, and gaming sets—women's graves usually contain objects associated with the home, such as keys, and with domestic activities, such as weaving, cooking, sewing.

The depiction of women in later written sources, particularly *Sagas of the Icelanders*, has been very influential in forming modern views of women in the Viking Age. However, the strong female characters found in these sagas, who are shown inciting their men to take revenge and perpetuate bloody feuds, primarily appear to fulfill a literary function and are often rather stock characters. Moreover, the world of these sagas is primarily male—there are far fewer female than male characters, there is no saga with a woman as the main character, and the viewpoint of the saga writer is male and medieval. However, *Laxdœla Saga* is perhaps an exception to this general rule, containing so many female characters of different types and centering on the unfulfilled love of the beautiful and intelligent Gudrun, that it has been suggested that it may either have been written by a woman or for a female audience. The more historical *Kings' Sagas* mention the names of wives and daughters of the main characters but little more on the whole. Some notable exceptions are **Gunnhild**, the wife of **Erik Blood-Ax**, **Sigrid the Proud**, and **Ingibjorg**, the daughter of **Olaf Haraldsson** and the wife of **Jaroslav the Wise**. Although there are many female characters in his *History of the Danes*, Saxo **Grammaticus** shows strong disapproval for women who act outside the bounds of what medieval churchmen thought as appropriate behavior and social roles (those of wife, mother, and daughter): the free and proud women warriors he describes in his account of pre-Christian Denmark are heathen pirates who are ultimately defeated. Moreover, active and independent women are almost totally absent from his account of Denmark after its conversion to **Christianity**.

Gudrun, the heroine of *Laxdœla Saga*, dies a nun, a social role that first became possible for women in the late Viking Age. Indeed, the evidence of rune-stones from eastern Sweden suggests that women were enthusiastic supporters of the new religion. For example, women were responsible for a large proportion of the so-called bridge rune-stones, connected with the building of "bridges" or roads, an activity that was encouraged by the missionary church in order to improve internal communications. It has been argued that one of the main reasons for women's support of early Christianity was the opportunities that the new religion gave them, particularly the option of avoiding marriage if they wished, a decision that would give them the protection of the Church if opposed by their families.

WULFSTAN. Wulfstan is known from his account of Scandinavian geography that was incorporated into the Old English translation of Paulus Orosius's *Seven Books of History against the Pagans*. This revised translation of Orosius was commissioned by **Alfred the Great** at the end of the ninth century, who also supplemented it with a geography of northern Europe, derived from, among others, **Ohthere** and Wulfstan. Wulfstan describes his journey from **Hedeby** to Truso, a port in the Vistula Delta that can probably be identified with Elblag in present-day Poland. A cemetery on the outskirts of Elblag provides evidence of a permanent Scandinavian presence in the settlement. Wulfstan's account includes a list of islands and regions in the Baltic and he also provides important evidence on which countries claimed these lands. For example, he writes that the island of **Bornholm** (part of present-day Denmark) had its own kings.

– Y –

YAROSLAV. *See* JAROSLAV THE WISE.

YGGDRASIL (ON *Yggdrasill*). Also known as the world tree or the world ash, Yggdrasil was the giant evergreen ash tree that held the various worlds of Nordic **mythology** together by its roots. The name *Yggdrasil* literally means "Ygg's horse" and Ygg is one of the many other names by which **Odin** is known. This may be a possible reference to the occasion when Odin hung on a tree as a sacrifice for gaining wisdom and the knowledge of **runes**: the "horse" of the hanged was the gallows.

The tree is said to support a selection of mythical creatures: an eagle sits in its branches; a dragon (**Nidhogg**) and numerous snakes gnaw at its roots; a squirrel (**Ratatosk**) runs up and down the trunk of the tree acting as a messenger between the eagle and the dragon; and four deer graze in the branches of the tree. At the foot of Yggdrasil there are three springs: Urd's well, Mimir's well, and **Hvergelmir**. In Snorri's *Gylfaginning*, Hvergelmir is said to be under the root of the tree that reaches down to **Niflheim**; Mimir's well is under the root that leads to the land of the frost giants; and Urd's well is found underneath the third root of the tree, which extends upwards to the sky. A similar description is found in the **Eddic** poem, *Grímnismál*, where the three roots of the tree are said to reach into the worlds of men, giants, and **Hel**; but *Völuspá* only refers to one spring underneath the tree, Urd's well.

YNGLINGA SAGA **("The Saga of the Ynglingar").** The first saga in Snorri's *Heimskringla*, which gives an account of the Swedish Yngling dynasty from its mythical beginnings to the mid-ninth century. Snorri traces the descent of the dynasty from the pagan gods or Æsir, who are said to have moved to Scandinavia from Asia. According to this saga, the name of the dynasty was derived from the god **Frey**, who was also known as Yngvi-Frey.

Although the dynasty is particularly associated with the Svear (*see* **Svealand**) cultic and **burial** place at **Gamla Uppsala**, King **Harald Fine-Hair** of Norway also claimed descent from the Ynglingar (hence the inclusion of *Ynglinga Saga* in a history of the kings of Norway). Indeed, one of Snorri's key sources for this saga was *Ynglingatal*, composed by a Norwegian poet to glorify the kings of Vestfold in southeastern Norway. *Historia Norwegiae* and the *Book of the Icelanders* also contain lists of the Ynglingar kings, but the precise relationship between *Ynglingatal*, *Historia Norwegiae*, the *Book of the Icelanders*, and *Ynglinga Saga* is unclear.

YNGLINGATAL. Ninth-century poem composed by the Norwegian Thjodolf (*Þjóðólfr*) of Hvin for King Rögnvald the Highly-Honored (*heiðumhæri*) of Vestfold in southeastern Norway. This poem was the main source for **Snorri Sturluson**'s *Ynglinga Saga*, in which it is preserved. Some 27 ancestors of Rögnvald are listed in the poem, with descriptions of their deaths and **burial** places, linking the king with the legendary Yngling dynasty of **Gamla Uppsala** in Sweden.

YNGVARR INN VÍÐFÖRLA. *See* INGVAR THE FAR-TRAVELED.

YORK (ON *Jórvík*). The Old Norse name for this town appears to be a corruption of Anglo-Saxon *Eoforwic*, itself in turn a corruption of Latin *Eboracum*. Located on the River Ouse, York was the principal town of northern England and administrative capital of the kingdom of **Northumbria** in the Viking Age. The Romans had established a fort in York around 71 AD and by 314 the town was a bishop's see. However, little is known about York in the post-Roman/early Anglian period from written sources, apart from its location within the kingdom of Deira, stretching from the **Humber** to the River Tees. During the seventh and eighth centuries, a little more is known thanks to the *Anglo-Saxon Chronicle* and Bede's *Ecclesiastical History*, although these details are principally the names of kings and bishops. In 735, York was raised to the status of an archiepiscopal see. There is little archaeological evidence for settlement within the town walls during the early Anglo-Saxon period.

The **Great Army** captured York in 866–867. Following this, the town was under Danish control but nothing is known about this rule until the **Viking** leader, **Halfdan**, apparently assumed direct control in 875, when his army settled in Northumbria, "plowing and providing for themselves" according to the *Anglo-Saxon Chronicle*. The first definite Scandinavian king of York was Guthfrith, whose death on 24 August 895 was recorded by *The Chronicle of Æthelweard*, and who appears to have become king at some point between 880 and 885. Guthfrith was converted to **Christianity** *c*. 883. Coins from York provide the names of two kings who appear to have ruled York shortly after Guthfrith: Cnut and Siefrid; and the *Anglo-Saxon Chronicle* records that Æthelwold, the nephew of King **Alfred the Great**, revolted against his cousin, Edward the Elder, after Alfred's death and was accepted as king of Northumbria by the Danish army in 899. He was later also acknowledged as leader by the Vikings in Essex before being killed by Edward the Elder's army.

In the first half of the 10th century, there was a three-way struggle for control of the town between the English, the Dublin Norse, and the Anglo-Scandinavian population of Northumbria. In 909, Edward the Elder of England campaigned throughout Northumbria, and the town submitted to his sister, Æthelflæd, Lady of the Mercians, in 918. However, coins from York suggest that a Hiberno-Norse leader, **Ragnald**, may have ruled the town for a period around the year 914 or earlier. Shortly afterward York became the joint capital of a Norse kingdom centered on **Dublin** and York, following the recapture of the town by Ragnald in 919 (923 according to the *Anglo-Saxon Chronicle*). However, King **Athelstan** of England then captured York from the Norse in 927, driving out its king, Guthfrith, and it took Olaf Guthfrithsson of Dublin some 11 years to reassert Norse control over the town. Olaf seems to have enjoyed the support of Wulfstan (d. 955), the Archbishop of York, who accompanied him on his campaigns in the **Five Boroughs** in 940. However, just five years later, in 944, the English had recaptured the town once again, and two Scandinavian kings of York, **Olaf Cúarán** and Ragnald Guthfrithsson, were expelled on this occasion. The most famous Scandinavian king of York was **Erik Blood-Ax**, who defeated Irish and English rivals for the town in 948, once more with the support of Archbishop Wulfstan. Erik was deserted by the Northumbrians shortly afterward, and paid compensation to the English king, Eadred, for their disloyalty. However, Olaf Cúarán returned to York in 949 and ruled there until 952, when Erik Blood-Ax regained the town. He struggled to control York for a further two years, before being driven out of the town by the Northumbrians in 954. *Egil's Saga* contains a description of a meeting between Erik and his archenemy, Egill Skallagrimsson, in the town.

The town's fortunes appear to have been revived following the Scandinavian settlement of Northumbria. This Anglo-Scandinavian settlement was concentrated in the area to the south of the Roman fort, and, by around 1000, the town probably had a population of around 10,000–15,000. Excavations at York Minster between 1967–1973 have revealed that the Viking-Age cathedral church was not located directly underneath the present Minster, but that it must have been nearby as a 10th- to 11th-century graveyard was found, along with decorated gravestones marking the **burials**. No remains of the hall of the Viking-Age kings of York have been found, but it is believed to have been located at King's Square—a name first recorded in the 13th century as *Kuningesgard* (from ON *Konungsgarðr*)—by one of the main gateways into the Roman fortress. This site was not used by the later **earls** of Northumbria or the Norman rulers of York, and, according to the *Anglo-Saxon Chronicle*, Earl Siward (d. 1055) was buried in the church of St. Olaf (dedicated to the Scandinavian saint, **Olaf Haraldsson**) at *Galmanho* or *Earlsburgh* "the earls' residence." Coinage issued by the Viking-Age kings of York provides the names of some kings not found in other documentary records, particularly in the shadowy 9th and early 10th centuries. It also reveals that around the year 1000, about 75 percent of the moneyers names were of Scandinavian origin, and by 1066, this figure had reached 100 percent.

Archaeological excavations have revealed that the trading contacts of Viking York extended from **Ireland** to the Middle East, and that it was an important center of production. Many of the street names of York are derived from the various trading and craft activities that took place. Evidence of glassmaking, textile manufacture, metalwork, amber and jet working, as well as wood-, bone-, leather-, and antler working have been found in the extensive excavations undertaken in the town since 1972. These were concentrated in the Coppergate area of York and are presented in the famous Jorvik Museum. The excellent preservation conditions at 16–22 Coppergate allowed the recovery of wood, textiles, and other organic matter, and excavations revealed traces of 10th-century buildings built on regular plots that are largely the same as present-day property boundaries in the area.

After Erik Blood-Ax's departure and subsequent murder on Stainmore, York was ruled in principle by Eadred, the king of England, and his successors. However, the earls of Northumbria in reality often exercised considerable independence. York did not fall to another Viking army until 1066, when **Harald Hard-Ruler** of Norway launched his invasion of England and defeated York's forces in the Battle of **Fulford** in September 1066. His subsequent defeat and death in the Battle of **Stamford Bridge**, however, put an end to Scandinavian control of the town. After the Norman Conquest, there were further Scandinavian attempts to win the English throne, and York was targeted in the northern uprising of 1069 after the invasion of **Svein Estrithsson** of Denmark. However, despite further Danish expeditions in 1070 and 1075, York remained in the hands of the kings of England.

YOUNGER EDDA.** See **PROSE EDDA.

Bibliography

CONTENTS

INTRODUCTION

There are a huge number of books and articles about the Vikings and this selection is but a small drop in the ocean. The interdisciplinary nature of the subject also means that scholarship on the Viking Age is very wide-ranging, encompassing among other things historical, archaeological, literary, textual, religious, and linguistic studies. This bibliography focuses almost exclusively on English-language publications as it is primarily designed for those who cannot read the Scandinavian or other languages. This, however, does unfortunately mean that the sections on Scandinavia and the European continent are rather underrepresented when compared to the British Isles and the North Atlantic, although some attempt to counter this has been made in section XVIII, which contains a selection of important works in the Scandinavian languages. The bibliographies listed under I. Reference Works will fill in some of the inevitable gaps, and by consulting the bibliographies of the articles and books that are included, students and researchers will also be able to find further references to particular topics. Please note that works by Icelandic scholars are listed under their surnames rather than their forenames.

Although its focus is primarily on the period after the end of the Viking Age, the multiauthored *Medieval Scandinavia: An Encyclopedia* is an invaluable source of reference for those seeking detailed information about Scandinavia and its North Atlantic colonies and contains bibliographies for each entry. It is particularly useful for finding out more about individual literary and historical works produced in the Scandinavian world in the medieval period that, for reasons of space, it has not always been possible to include in this dictionary. Readers of the Scandinavian languages are also directed to the 22-volume *Kulturhistorisk leksikon for nordisk middelalder* (section XVII), which, although now somewhat dated, provides extremely useful summaries of scholarship on various aspects of medieval Scandinavia. Similarly, the *Dictionary of Northern Mythology* by Rudolf Simek provides a fairly substantial account of the individual deities, mythological works, and religious practices of pagan Scandinavia, with select references for each entry. Those looking for additional works on the Viking period in general are strongly recommended to consult Martin Syrett's annotated bibliography, *Scandinavian History in the Viking Age*. This was produced for students in the Department of Anglo-Saxon, Norse, and Celtic at the University of Cambridge, and focuses on modern English-language scholarship, although not exclusively. It is divided into five main sections: textbooks, reference works, and written sources; political and social history; the Viking expansion; religion; and archaeology. Simon Keynes's bibliography of *Anglo-Saxon England* also contains particularly useful sections on Scandinavian sources relating to England, the Danelaw, and the Danish kings of England.

Section II, Primary Sources, contains only English translations, or editions with translations, of the most important sources for Viking-Age Scandinavia. Francis Tschan's translation of Adam of Bremen's *History of the Archbishops of Hamburg-Bremen* is perhaps one of the most useful of these primary sources, containing as it does much information on Scandinavian geography, society, religious practices, and rulers that is not found elsewhere. There are separate sections on religion and mythology (XII), literature (XIII), and runes (XVI) that contain secondary works and scholarship relating to many of these primary sources. In addition to this, the final section in this bibliography, Scandinavian-language sources, contains some of the most important editions of primary source material that is not available in English, including, for example, the corpus of runic inscriptions from Denmark, Norway, and Sweden.

Peter Sawyer's *Age of the Vikings* remains a seminal and essential work some 30 years after the second edition was published. It marked the birth of modern Viking studies through its questioning of many long-held assumptions about the period, such as the size of the Viking armies, the reliability of primary source material, and the reasons underlying the Viking expansion. Although not all scholars agree with all of Sawyer's conclusions, much of what he wrote in *Age of the Vikings* and its sequel, *Kings and Vikings*, forms the basis of modern debate on the period. It is especially good for its critical discussion of key written sources and for using often-neglected numismatic evidence. Else Roesdahl's *The Vikings* gives a more up-to-date and less controversial overview and pays more attention to the nature of Scandinavian society and to the archaeological evidence for the Vikings at home and abroad. *The Viking World*, edited by James Graham-Campbell, also provides a good starting point for students, with lots of high-quality illustrations that bring the period to life. It is divided into short thematic rather than chronological sections and gives clear and basic introductions to subjects such as Viking ships, Viking art, and trade and towns.

There are very few English-language monographs on Scandinavian history during the Viking Age, as opposed to Viking activity in the period, and much of the material in Section IV is therefore in the form of specialized articles. An exception is Birgit and Peter Sawyer's *Medieval Scandinavia*, although as the longer time span of this volume (800–1500) suggests, there is also a good deal of material that relates to the period after the end of the Viking Age. A good political survey of the Viking period by Niels Lund is available in volume 2 of *The New Cambridge Medieval History* and there is a separate short bibliography on Scandinavia at the back of the volume, pp. 913–14, which includes many Scandinavian-language sources. Although not available at the time of writing, Cambridge University Press also has a multiauthored *Cambridge History of Scandinavia*, by Knut Helle *et al.*, scheduled for publication in August 2003. Scandinavian-language surveys of the individual countries can be found in section XVII, and readers are particularly referred to Peter Sawyer's *Da Danmark blev Danmark* and *När Sverige blev Sverige* (updated Swedish version of *The Making of Sweden*) and to Per Sveaas Andersen's *Samlingen av Norge og kristningen av landet 800–1130*.

In recent years, there has been a good deal of new archaeological work on the North Atlantic colonies established by the Vikings in the British Isles, the Faroe Isles, Iceland, and Greenland, as well as renewed interest in the Viking discovery of North America *c.* AD 1000 that accompanied the celebrations of the new millennium in 2000. The collection of articles in *Vikings: The North Atlantic Saga*, edited by William Fitzhugh and Elisabeth Ward, accompanied by a large bibliography, is particularly good for its account of new archaeological work in North America, Greenland, Iceland, and the Faroe Isles. However, it also contains useful survey articles on Scandinavia, Finland, Frankia, and Britain and Ireland.

Section VI, The British Isles, is the largest single section of the bibliography, reflecting both the diversity of the Viking experience in different parts of Britain and Ireland and the huge scholarly output in this area. Recent works to single out are the collections of papers found in *Vikings and the Danelaw*, *Cultures in Contact: Scandinavian Settlement in England in the Ninth and Tenth Centuries*, *The Vikings in Ireland*, and *Ireland*

and Scandinavia in the Early Viking Age, which contain introductory surveys alongside more detailed and discursive articles on individual aspects of the Viking experience in these regions. No survey of the British Isles has been published since Henry Loyn's *The Vikings in Britain*, so for more up-to-date accounts incorporating recent archaeological evidence in particular, readers are instead referred to surveys of the individual countries: James Graham-Campbell and Colleen Batey's *Vikings in Scotland: An Archaeological Survey*, Mark Redknap's *Vikings in Wales: An Archaeological Quest*, and Julian Richards's *Viking Age England*. Barbara Crawford's *Scandinavian Scotland* is a key work for students of the Vikings in Scotland and is particularly useful because it deals with written and place-name evidence, as well as archaeological material. Gillian Fellows-Jensen's work on the place-names of the British Isles is an essential starting point for anyone interested in onomastics and in the density of Scandinavian settlement in the British Isles, although it should be noted that her views have developed and changed over the period since she began publishing.

In addition to the items listed in section VII, readers of French are also directed to Lucien Musset's *Les Invasions: Le second assaut contre l'Europe chrétienne (VIIe–XIe siècles)*. Published in 1971 (Paris: Presses universitaires de France), this remains a classic work on the European experience during the Viking Age. The recently-published collection of papers, *L'héritage maritime des Vikings en Europe de l'Ouest* (Caen: Presses universitaires de Caen, 2002), edited by Elisabeth Ridel contains several articles on the Vikings in Normandy, including work on ships and the maritime vocabulary of the region. Most articles also have short English summaries for those who do not read French.

Recent years have seen fresh archaeological work on Scandinavian activity in Eastern Europe, which has led to a reassessment of the nature and role of the Rus in the mixed society of European Russia. Simon Franklin and Jonathan Shephard's *The Emergence of the Rus* is a recent and authoritative account of the Scandinavian contribution.

Those seeking a general introduction to the range of Viking ships and navigation techniques are directed to the articles by Jan Bill and Arne Emil Christensen in section IX. Olaf Olsen and Ole Crumlin-Pedersen's *Five Viking Ships from Roskilde Fjord* provides a good introduction to these important finds. Judith Jesch's book is a critical account of the vocabulary used in skaldic poetry and runic inscriptions to describe Viking ships and their crews. Seán McGrail's *Ancient Boats* is a technical and comparative account of the ships of northwest Europe and is recommended for those who require a more in-depth and contextual view of Viking ships and ship-building. Ian Heath and Angus McBride's *The Vikings* is part of a popular series on the "history, organization, appearance, and equipment of famous fighting men of the past and present" and contains color illustrations of how Viking warriors and weapons may have looked, as well as plates showing some of the more famous archaeological finds of weapons and armor. There is a small bibliography at the end of this book, but this is very general and somewhat outdated; those seeking more detail and more references are advised to consult the entries "Weapons" and "Warfare" in *Medieval Scandinavia: An Encyclopedia* (see section I).

Much of the evidence for Scandinavian society postdates the Viking Age and comes from Iceland, rather than Denmark, Norway, or Sweden. *Saga and Society*, the English translation of Preben Meulengracht Sørensen's 1977 Danish classic *Saga og Samfund*, provides an excellent introduction into the literary evidence for Icelandic society in the medieval period. However, runic inscriptions and skaldic poetry provide some information about conditions in Scandinavia before *c*. AD 1100. Judith Jesch's books on Viking women and men deal with both types of this evidence, as well as other kinds. However, while *Women in the Viking Age* is written as an introduction that can be read by both the beginner and the more experienced researcher, *Ships and Men in the Late Viking Age* is more detailed and more technical in its discussion and focuses on the precise meaning of social ranks that are referred to in inscriptions and poetry. Ruth Mazo Karras's book on slavery remains the classic work on this subject.

Helen Clarke and Björn Ambrosiani's *Towns in the Viking Age* contains accounts of individual towns across northern Europe, as well as more general information about the development of urban communities in this period, and remains the best starting point for layman and scholar alike. *Viking-Age Coinage in Northern Lands* includes an introductory article by A. E. Lieber on "International trade and coinage in the northern lands during the early Middle Ages" (pp. 1–34). Readers of the Scandinavian languages are also encouraged to consult the entries "Coins and mints" and "Hoards" in *Medieval Scandinavia: An Encyclopedia* (see section I), which includes a comprehensive bibliography of works, many of which are written in Danish, Norwegian, or Swedish.

Those seeking a good introduction to Norse mythology could start with R. I. Page's *Norse Myths*, a slim volume that nevertheless manages to survey all the major sources, tales, and provides a useful annotated select bibliography. More detail about scholarship on the subject can be found in John Lindow's "Mythology and mythography." Anthony Faulkes's translation of Snorri Sturluson's *Prose Edda* (see section II) is essential for those who wish to consult one of the two major primary sources for this mythology. Translations of the *Poetic Edda* are more difficult to recommend; Carolyne Larrington's (see section II) is the most recently-published, but see the review in *Saga-Book* 25, 1998, pp. 92–95. *The Christianisation of Scandinavia* by Birgit Sawyer, Peter Sawyer, and Ian Wood provides a vey useful introduction to the sources and debates surrounding the conversion of the Vikings. In both Sweden and Norway, research projects on the conversion process have produced a number of important works in the Scandinavian languages that are included in section XVII. In particular, readers are directed to *Kristnandet i Sverige*, edited by Bertil Nilsson, which includes English summaries of most articles, and to *Fra hedendom til kristendom: Perspektiver på religionsskiftet i Norge*, edited by Magnus Rindal.

The number of books and articles on Old Norse prose and poetry is huge, and the list included in section XIII is extremely selective. Perhaps the single best survey is Carol Clover and John Lindow's *Old-Norse Literature: A Critical Guide*, which contains substantial articles by experts in the fields on most of the major saga genres and on skaldic and Eddic poetry. Jónas Kristjansson's *Eddas and Sagas* is a much shorter, illustrated introduction to the subject, for those who require a more basic survey of the major sources.

Ole Klindt-Jensen and David Wilson's *Viking Art*, although published many years ago, remains the classic work of reference on the subject, although it is not particularly lavishly illustrated. The chapter on Viking art in *The Viking World*, edited by James Graham-Campbell (see Section III), has short accounts of each major art style and includes color illustrations. Much of the published work on sculpture deals with England, where stone monuments were produced in large numbers following the Scandinavian settlements. The series, *Corpus of Anglo-Saxon Stone Sculpture*, is a major source of reference, providing as it does a detailed catalog of all the stone sculpture from the areas settled by Vikings, accompanied by illustrations. A less detailed but nevertheless invaluable survey, which dis-

cusses the significance of the material as a whole, can be found in Richard
Bailey's *Viking Age Sculpture in Northern England.*

The section on language and place-names is dominated by work on
the British Isles, where the continued debate on the scale of Scandinavian settlement has made this material particularly important. As mentioned above, Gillian Fellows-Jensen's work is a necessary starting
point for anyone interested in this subject. R. I. Page's and David Parsons's articles on "How long did the Scandinavian language survive in
England" are key works on this difficult question. More recently and
in more detail, Matthew Townend has discussed the question of linguistic contact in England and includes a full account of the sources for
this topic in his *Language and History in Viking Age England.* Much of
the work on language and place-names in Scandinavia is published
in the Scandinavian languages, and readers are advised to consult
Gillian Fellows-Jensen's article with bibliography "Place-name research in Scandinavia 1960–1982," and *Medieval Scandinavia: An Encyclopedia* (see section I), under personal names and language for
further details. In addition to this, the classic works on place-names in
Denmark, Norway, and Sweden have been included in section XVII.

Those readers seeking a general introduction to the evidence of runic inscriptions should consult Ray Page's *Runes,* which includes material from
Viking-Age Scandinavia alongside that from Anglo-Saxon England and
Dark-Age Europe. More detailed surveys of the runes of Denmark
and Sweden can be found in Erik Moltke and Sven B. F. Jansson respectively, both of which remain classic works. Unfortunately, there is no similar English-language counterpart for the Viking-Age inscriptions from
Norway, although admittedly there are far fewer runic inscriptions
from this part of Scandinavia. Michael Barnes's and Ray Page's work on
the runic inscriptions of the British Isles is authoritative and scholarly, although both are primarily concerned with establishing the corpus and correct readings of texts. Katherine Holman's book is, as the title suggests, a
consideration of the historical significance of these inscriptions, but does
also contain a list of all the known Scandinavian runic inscriptions in
Britain. Birgit Sawyer has recently published *The Viking-Age Rune-Stones,*
which brings together a number of Sawyer's theories about the historical
significance of 2,307 Viking-Age rune-stones from Scandinavia and centers around her main argument that the entire corpus can be viewed as the
result of concern for inheritance and property. The published editions of

Scandinavian runic inscriptions are listed in section XVIII for those who read the Scandinavian languages.

I. REFERENCE WORKS

A. Dictionaries and Encyclopedias

Cleasby, Richard, and Gudbrand Vigfusson. *An Icelandic-English Dictionary*. 2nd ed. Supplement by William A. Craigie. Oxford: Clarendon Press, 1957.

Ekwall, Eilert. *The Concise Oxford Dictionary of English Place-Names*. 4th ed. Oxford: Clarendon Press, 1960.

Haywood, John. *Encyclopedia of the Viking Age*. London: Thames & Hudson, 2000.

Lapidge, Michael, with John Blair, Simon Keynes, and Donald Scragg, eds. *The Blackwell Encyclopaedia of Anglo-Saxon England*. Oxford: Blackwell, 1999.

Pulsiano, Philip, ed. *Medieval Scandinavia: An Encyclopedia*. New York: Garland, 1993.

Simek, Rudolf, ed. *Dictionary of Northern Mythology*. Translated by Angela Hall. Cambridge: D. S. Brewer, 1993.

Williams, Ann, Alfred P. Smyth, and D. P. Kirby. *A Biographical Dictionary of Dark Age Britain: England, Scotland and Wales, c. 500–c. 1050*. London: Seaby, 1991.

B. Bibliographies

Bekker-Nielsen, Hans. *Old Norse-Icelandic Studies: A Select Bibliography*. Toronto: University of Toronto Press, 1967.

Fry, Donald K. *Norse Sagas Translated into English: A Bibliography*. New York: AMS, 1980.

Keynes, Simon. *Anglo-Saxon England: A Bibliographical Handbook for Students of Anglo-Saxon History*. 2nd ed. Cambridge: Department of Anglo-Saxon, Norse, and Celtic, University of Cambridge, 2001.

Syrett, Martin. *Scandinavian History in the Viking Age: A Select Bibliography*. Cambridge: Department of Anglo-Saxon, Norse, and Celtic, University of Cambridge, 2001.

II. PRIMARY SOURCES

A. General

Allen, W. E. D. "The poet and the spae-wife: An attempt to reconstruct Al-Ghazal's embassy to the Vikings." *Saga-Book* 15:3 (1960): 1–102.

Page, R. I. *Chronicles of the Vikings: Records, Memorials and Myths*. London: British Museum, 1995.

B. Scandinavia

Adam of Bremen. *History of the Archbishops of Hamburg-Bremen*. Translated with introduction and notes by Francis J. Tschan; with new introduction and selected bibliography by Timothy Reuter. New York: Columbia University Press, 2002.

Ágrip af Nóregskonungasögum. Edited and translated by M. J. Driscoll. London: Viking Society for Northern Research, 1995.

The Book of Settlements. Translated by Herman Pálsson and Paul Edwards. University of Manitoba Icelandic Studies, 1. Winnipeg: University of Manitoba, 1972.

Dennis, Andrew, et al., trans. *Laws of Early Iceland: Grágás*. Winnipeg: University of Manitoba Press, 1980.

Egil's Saga. Translated by Herman Pálsson and Paul Edwards. Harmondsworth: Penguin, 1976.

Eyrbyggja Saga. Translated by Herman Pálsson and Paul Edwards. Harmondsworth: Penguin, 1989.

Færeyinga Saga, or the Tale of Thrond of Gate. Translated by F. York Powell. London: David Nutt, 1896. Facsimile reprint by Felinfach: Llanerch, 1995.

Göngu-Hrolf's Saga. Translated by Hermann Pálsson and Paul Edwards. Edinburgh: Canongate, 1980.

Grettir's Saga. Translated by Denton Fox and Hermann Pálsson. Toronto: University of Toronto Press, 1974.

Knýtlinga Saga: The History of the Kings of Denmark. Translated by Hermann Pálsson and Paul Edwards. Odense: Odense University Press, 1986.

Laxdæla Saga. Translated by Magnus Magnusson and Hermann Pálsson. Harmondsworth: Penguin, 1969.

Morkinskinna. Edited by Theodore M. Andersson and Kari Ellen Gade. Ithaca, NY: Cornell University Press, 2000.

Njal's Saga. Translated by Magnus Magnusson and Hermann Pálsson. Harmondsworth: Penguin, 1960.

The Norse Atlantic Saga [includes the *Book of the Icelanders*]. Translated by Gwyn Jones. 2nd ed. Oxford: Oxford University Press, 1986.

The Poetic Edda. Translated by Carolyne Larrington. Oxford: Oxford University Press, 1996.

Runes. *See* SECTION XVI.

The Saga of the Jómsvikings. Translated by Lee M. Hollander. Austin: University of Texas Press, 1955.

The Saga of the Volsungs: The Norse Epic of Sigurd the Dragon Slayer. Translated by Jesse L. Byock. Berkeley, CA: University of California Press, 1990.

Saxo Grammaticus. *The History of the Danes: Books I–IX.* Translated by Peter Fisher, edited and commentary by Hilda Ellis Davidson. Cambridge: D. S. Brewer, 1979–80.

Skaldic Poetry. *See* SECTION XIII.

Snorri Sturluson. *Prose Edda.* Translated by Anthony Faulkes. London: J. M. Dent, 1987.

——. *Heimskringla: Sagas of the Norse Kings.* 3 vols. Translated by Samuel Laing. London: Dent, 1961–64.

Theodericus Monachus: Historia de antiquitate regum Norwagensium. An Account of the Ancient History of the Norwegian Kings. Translated by David and Ian McDougall, and introduction by Peter Foote. London: Viking Society for Northern Research, 1998.

Two Voyagers at the Court of King Alfred: Ohthere and Wulfstan. Edited by Niels Lund, translated by Christine E. Fell, with essays by Ole Crumlin-Pedersen, P. H. Sawyer, and Christine E. Fell. York: William Sessions, 1984.

The Vinland Sagas: The Norse Discovery of America. Grænlendinga saga and Eirik's saga. Translated by Magnus Magnusson and Hermann Pálsson. Harmondsworth: Penguin, 1965.

The Works of Sven Aggesen, Twelfth-Century Danish Historian. Translated by Eric Christiansen. London: Viking Society for Northern Research, 1992.

C. British Isles

Alfred the Great: Asser's Life of King Alfred *and Other Contemporary Sources.* Translated by Simon Keynes and Michael Lapidge. London: Penguin, 1983.

The Anglo-Saxon Chronicle. Translated and edited by Michael J. Swanton. London: J. M. Dent, 1996.

The Annals of Ulster (to AD 1131). Translated and edited by Seán Mac Airt and Gearóid Mac Niocaill. Dublin: Dublin Institute of Advanced Studies, 1983.

Ashdown, Margaret. *English and Norse Documents Relating to the Reign of Ethelred the Unready.* Cambridge: Cambridge University Press, 1930.

Early Sources of Scottish History A.D. 500–1286. 2 vols. Collected and translated by Alan Orr Anderson. Edinburgh: Oliver & Boyd, 1922.

Encomium Emmae Reginae. Edited and translated by Alistair Campbell, with new introduction by Simon Keynes. Camden Classic Reprints, 4. Cambridge: Cambridge University Press, 1998.

Orkneyinga Saga. Translated by Hermann Pálsson and Paul Edwards. London: Penguin, 1981.

Rollason, David, with Derek Gore, and Gillian Fellows-Jensen. *Sources for York History to AD 1100*. The Archaeology of York, 1. York: York Archaeological Trust, 1998.

"Translatio Sancti Ælfegi Cantuariensis archiespiscopi et martyris: Osbern's account of the translation of St. Ælfheah's relics from London to Canterbury, 8–11 June 1023." An annotated edition by Alexander R. Rumble with a translation of the text of Rosemary Morris and Alexander R. Rumble in *The Reign of Cnut: King of England, Denmark and Norway*, edited by Alexander R. Rumble, 283–315. London: Leicester University Press, 1994.

War of the Gaedhil with the Gaill, or The Invasion of Ireland by the Danes and other Norsemen. Translated and introduced by J. H. Todd. Rerum Britannicarum medii ævi scriptores, 48. London: Rolls Series, 1867.

Whitelock, Dorothy, ed. *English Historical Documents c. 500–1042*. 2nd ed. London: Eyre & Spottiswoode, 1979.

D. Continental Western Europe

The Annals of Fulda. Translated and annotated by Timothy Reuter. Ninth-Century Histories, 2. Manchester: Manchester University Press, 1992.

The Annals of St-Bertin. Translated and annotated by Janet L. Nelson. Ninth-Century Histories, 1. Manchester: Manchester University Press, 1991.

Dudo of St-Quentin. *History of the Normans*. Translated by Eric Christiansen. Woodbridge: Boydell, 1998.

The Gesta Normannorum Ducum of William of Jumièges, Orderic Vitalis, and Robert of Torigni. Edited and translated by Elisabeth M. C. van Houts. Oxford: Clarendon Press, 1992–95.

van Houts, Elisabeth, trans. and ed. *The Normans in Europe*. Manchester: Manchester University Press, 2000.

Scholz, Walter Bernard, with Barbara Rogers, trans. *Carolingian Chronicles: Royal Frankish Annals and Nithard's Histories*. Ann Arbor: University of Michigan Press, 1970.

Stefansson, Jón, trans. "The Vikings in Spain from Arabic (Moorish) and Spanish sources." *Saga-Book* 6 (1909): 31–46.

E. Eastern Europe

Constantine Porphyrogenitos. *De Administrando Imperio*. Edited by G. Moravcsik, translated by R. J. H. Jenkins. Washington DC: Dumbarton Oaks Center for Byzantine Studies, 1967.

Russian Primary Chronicle: Laurentian Text. Edited and translated by Samuel H. Cross and Olgerd P. Sherbowitz-Wetzor. Cambridge, MA: Medieval Academy of America, 1953.

Smyser, H. M. "Ibn Fadlan's account of the Rus with some commentary and some allusions to Beowulf." In *Medieval and Linguistic Studies in Honor of Francis Peabody Magoun, Jr.*, edited by Jess B. Bessinger Jr. and Robert P. Creed, 92–119. London: Allen & Unwin, 1965.

Vikings in Russia: Yngvar's Saga *and* Eymund's Saga. Translated by Hermann Pálsson and Paul Edwards. Edinburgh: Polygon, 1989.

Zenkovsky, Serge A., trans. and ed. *Medieval Russia's Epics, Chronicles, and Tales.* Rev. ed. New York: Penguin, 1974. [includes *Russian Primary Chronicle*].

III. GENERAL SURVEYS OF THE THE VIKING AGE

A. Monographs

Foote, Peter G., and David M. Wilson. *The Viking Achievement.* 2nd ed. London: Sidgewick & Jackson, 1980.

Graham-Campbell, James, ed. *Cultural Atlas of the Viking World.* Oxford: Andromeda, 1994.

———. *The Viking World.* 2nd ed. London: Windward and Frances Lincoln, 1989.

Haywood, John. *The Penguin Historical Atlas of the Vikings.* London: Penguin, 1995.

Jones, Gwyn. *A History of the Vikings.* 2nd ed. Oxford: Oxford University Press, 1984.

Logan, F. Donald. *The Vikings in History.* 2nd ed. London: Routledge, 1991.

Roesdahl, Else. *The Vikings.* Rev. ed. London: Penguin, 1998.

Sawyer, P. H. *Kings and Vikings.* London: Methuen, 1982.

———. *The Age of the Vikings.* 2nd ed. London: Edward Arnold, 1971.

Turville-Petre, G. *The Heroic Age of Scandinavia.* London: Hutchison, 1951.

Wilson, David M. *The Vikings and Their Origins.* London: Thames & Hudson, 1970.

B. Collections of Articles

Almqvist, Bo, and David Greene, eds. *Proceedings of the Seventh Viking Congress, Dublin, 15–21 August 1973.* Dublin: Royal Irish Academy, 1976.

Ambrosiani, Björn, and Helen Clarke, eds. *The Twelfth Viking Congress: Developments Around the Baltic and the North Sea in the Viking Age*. Birka Studies, 3. Stockholm: Riksantikvarieämbetet and Statens Historiska Museer, 1994.

Andersson, Thorsten, and Karl Inge Sandred, eds. *The Vikings: Proceedings of the Symposium of the Faculty of Arts of Uppsala University, June 6–9, 1977*. Stockholm: Almqvist & Wiksell, 1978.

Bekker-Nielsen, Hans, Peter Foote, and Olaf Olsen, eds. *Proceedings of the Eighth Viking Congress, Århus, 24–31 August 1977*. Odense: Odense University Press, 1981.

Eldjárn, Kristján, ed. *Þriðji Vikingafundur: Third Viking Congress, Reykjavík 1956*. Árbók hins íslenzka fornleifafélags fylgirit 1958. Reykjavik: Ísafoldarprentsmiðja, 1958.

Falck, Kjell, ed. *Annen Viking Kongress Bergen 1953*. Universitet i Bergen årbok 1955, Historisk-antikvarisk Rekke 1. Bergen: Universitet i Bergen, 1955.

Farrell, R. T., ed. *The Vikings*. London: Phillimore, 1982.

Faulkes, Anthony, and Richard Perkins, eds. *Viking Revaluations*. London: Viking Society for Northern Research, 1993.

Fitzhugh, William W., and Elisabeth I. Ward, eds. *Vikings: The North Atlantic Saga*. Washington DC: Smithsonian Institution, 2000.

Foote, Peter, and Dag Strömbäck, eds. *Proceedings of the Sixth Viking Congress, Uppsala 3–10 August 1969, Bonäs, Dalarna 10–12 August 1969*. Stockholm: Almqvist & Wiksell, 1971.

Knirk, James E., ed. *Proceedings of the Tenth Viking Congress, Larkollen, Norway, 1985*. Universitets Oldsaksamlings Skrifter, new series, 9. Oslo: Universitets Oldsaksamling, 1987.

Larsen, Anne-Christine, ed. *The Vikings in Ireland*. Roskilde: The Viking Ship Museum, 2001.

Niclasen, Bjarni, ed. *The Fifth Viking Congress, Tórshavn, July 1965*. Tórshavn: Føroya Landsstýri, Tórshavnar Býráð, Føroya Fróðskaparfelag, and Føroya Fornminnissavn, 1968.

Roesdahl, Else, and David M. Wilson, eds. *From Viking to Crusader: Scandinavia and Europe 800–1200*. The 22nd Council of Europe Exhibition. Copenhagen: Nordic Council of Ministers and The Council of Europe, 1992.

Sawyer, Peter, ed. *The Oxford Illustrated History of the Vikings*. Oxford: Oxford University Press, 1997.

Simpson, W. Douglas, ed. *The Viking Congress, Lerwick, July 1950*. Aberdeen University Studies, 132. Edinburgh: Oliver & Boyd, 1954.

Small, Alan, ed. *The Fourth Viking Congress, York, August 1961*. Aberdeen University Studies, 149. Edinburgh: Oliver & Boyd, 1965.

C. Articles

Eldjárn, Kristján. "The Vikings: Some introductory remarks." In *The Vikings: Proceedings of the Symposium of the Faculty of Arts of Uppsala University, June 6–9, 1977*, edited by Thorsten Andersson and Karl Inge Sandred, 11–20. Stockholm: Almqvist & Wiksell, 1978.

Fell, Christine E. "Old English *wicing*: A question of semantics." *Proceedings of the British Academy* 72 (1986): 295–316.

———. "Modern English *Viking*." *Leeds Studies in English* 18 (1987): 111–23.

Hødnebø, Finn. "Who were the first Vikings?" In *Proceedings of the Tenth Viking Congress, Larkollen, Norway, 1985*, edited by James E. Knirk, 43–54. Universitets Oldsaksamlings Skrifter, new series, 9. Oslo: Universitets Oldsaksamling, 1987.

Lund, Niels. "Allies of God or man? The Viking expansion in a European perspective." *Viator* 20 (1989): 45–59.

———. "Peace and non-peace in the Viking Age: Ottar in Biarmaland, the Rus in Byzantium, and Danes and Norwegians in England." In *Proceedings of the Tenth Viking Congress, Larkollen, Norway, 1985*, edited by James E. Knirk, 255–69. Universitets Oldsaksamlings Skrifter, new series, 9. Oslo: Universitets Oldsaksamling, 1987.

Sawyer, Peter H. "Causes of the Viking Age." In *The Vikings*, edited by R. T. Farrell, 1–7. London: Phillimore, 1992.

Thorson, P. "A new interpretation of 'viking'." In *Proceedings of the Sixth Viking Congress*, edited by Peter Foote and Dag Strömbäck, 101–4. Uppsala: Almqvist & Wiksell, 1969.

Wormald, C. P. "Viking studies: Whence and whither?" In *The Vikings*, edited by R. T. Farrell, 128–53. London: Phillimore, 1982.

IV. SCANDINAVIA

A. General

Lund, Niels. "Scandinavia, c. 700–1066." In *The New Cambridge Medieval History*, vol. 2, c. 700–c. 900, edited by Rosamond McKitterick, 202–27. Cambridge: Cambridge University Press, 1995.

Page, R. I. "Scandinavian society, 800–1100: The contribution of runic studies." In *Viking Revaluations*, edited by Anthony Faulkes and Richard Perkins, 145–59. London: Viking Society for Northern Research, 1993.

Price, Neil S. "The Scandinavian landscape: People and environment." In *Vikings: The North Atlantic Saga*, edited by William W. Fitzhugh and Elisabeth I. Ward, 31–41. Washington DC: Smithsonian Institution, 2000.

Roesdahl, Else. "The Scandinavian kingdoms." In *From Viking to Crusader: Scandinavia and Europe 800–1200*, edited by Else Roesdahl and David M. Wilson, 32–41. The 22nd Council of Europe Exhibition. Copenhagen: Nordic Council of Ministers and The Council of Europe, 1992.

Sawyer, Birgit and Peter. *Medieval Scandinavia: From Conversion to Reformation, circa 800–1500*. Minneapolis: University of Minnesota Press, 1993.

Sawyer, Peter. "Scandinavia in the Viking Age." In *Vikings: The North Atlantic Saga*, edited by William W. Fitzhugh and Elisabeth I. Ward, 27–30. Washington DC: Smithsonian Institution, 2000.

———. "Cnut's Scandinavian empire." In *The Reign of Cnut: King of England, Denmark and Norway*, edited by Alexander R. Rumble, 10–26 [including an appendix on "The evidence of Scandinavian runic inscriptions" by Birgit Sawyer]. London: Leicester University Press, 1994.

Zachrisson, Inger. "Saamis and Scandinavians: Examples of interaction." In *The Twelfth Viking Congress: Developments Around the Baltic and the North Sea in the Viking Age*, edited by Björn Ambrosiani and Helen Clarke, 173–79. Birka Studies, 3. Stockholm: Riksantikvarieämbetet and Statens Historiska Museer, 1994.

B. Denmark

Becker, C. J. "Viking Age villages and 'manors' in Denmark: Recent discoveries." In *Proceedings of the Eighth Viking Congress, Århus, 24–31 August 1977*, edited by Hans Bekker-Nielsen, Peter Foote, and Olaf Olsen, 25–36. Odense: Odense University Press, 1981.

Feveile, Claus. "The latest news from Viking Age Ribe: Archaeological excavations 1993." In *The Twelfth Viking Congress: Developments Around the Baltic and the North Sea in the Viking Age*, edited by Björn Ambrosiani and Helen Clarke, 91–99. Birka Studies, 3. Stockholm: Riksantikvarieämbetet and Statens Historiska Museer, 1994.

Jensen, Jørgen Steen. "Do the coin finds of recent years change our ideas about the character of monetary circulation in Denmark in the Viking Age?" In *The Twelfth Viking Congress: Developments Around the Baltic and the North Sea in the Viking Age*, edited by Björn Ambrosiani and Helen Clarke, 237–41. Birka Studies, 3. Stockholm: Riksantikvarieämbetet and Statens Historiska Museer, 1994.

Jensen, Stig. *The Vikings of Ribe*. Ribe: Den antikvariske Samling, 1991.

Lund, Niels. "Cnut's Danish kingdom." In *The Reign of Cnut: King of England, Denmark and Norway*, edited by Alexander R. Rumble, 27–42. London: Leicester University Press, 1994.

——. "Danish military organization." In *The Battle of Maldon: Fiction and Fact*, edited by Janet Cooper, 109–26. London: Hambledon, 1993.

Madsen, H. J. "Introduction to Viking Århus." In *Proceedings of the Eighth Viking Congress, Århus, 24–31 August 1977*, edited by Hans Bekker-Nielsen, Peter Foote, and Olaf Olsen, 69–72. Odense: Odense University Press, 1981.

Randsborg, Klavs. *The Viking Age in Denmark: The Formation of a State*. London: Duckworth, 1980.

Roesdahl, Else. "Dendrochronology and Viking studies in Denmark, with a note on the beginning of the Viking Age." In *The Twelfth Viking Congress: Developments Around the Baltic and the North Sea in the Viking Age*, edited by Björn Ambrosiani and Helen Clarke, 106–16. Birka Studies, 3. Stockholm: Riksantikvarieämbetet and Statens Historiska Museer, 1994.

——. "Pagan beliefs, Christian impact and archaeology: A Danish view." In *Viking Revaluations*, edited by Anthony Faulkes and Richard Perkins, 128–36. London: Viking Society for Northern Research, 1993.

——. "Aggersborg in the Viking Age." In *Proceedings of the Eighth Viking Congress, Århus, 24–31 August 1977*, edited by Hans Bekker-Nielsen, Peter Foote, and Olaf Olsen, 107–22. Odense: Odense University Press, 1981.

Sørensen, John Kousgård. "Toponymic evidence for administrative divisions in Denmark in the Viking Age." In *The Vikings: Proceedings of the Symposium of the Faculty of Arts of Uppsala University, June 6–9, 1977*, edited by Thorsten Andersson and Karl Inge Sandred, 133–41. Stockholm: Almqvist & Wiksell, 1978.

C. Norway

Andersen, Per Sveaas. *Vikings of the West: The Expansion of Norway in the Early Middle Ages*. 2nd ed. Sandnes: Aase Grafiske, 1985.

Blindheim, Charlotte. "Introduction [to Viking-Age Viken, in southeast Norway]." In *Proceedings of the Tenth Viking Congress, Larkollen, Norway, 1985*, edited by James E. Knirk, 27–42. Universitets Oldsaksamlings Skrifter, new series, 9. Oslo: Universitets Oldsaksamling, 1987.

Bonde, Niels, and Arne Emil Christensen. "Dendrochronological dating of the Viking Age ship burials at Oseberg, Gokstad and Tune, Norway." *Antiquity* 67 (1993): 575–83.

Halvorsen, Eyvind Fjeld. "East Norway in the sagas." In *Proceedings of the Tenth Viking Congress, Larkollen, Norway, 1985*, edited by James E. Knirk, 55–67. Universitets Oldsaksamlings Skrifter, new series, 9. Oslo: Universitets Oldsaksamling, 1987.

Helle, Knut. "A history of the early Viking Age in Norway." In *Ireland and Scandinavia in the Early Viking Age*, edited by Howard B. Clarke et al., 239–58. Dublin: Four Courts, 1998.

———. "Norway, 800–1200." In *Viking Revaluations*, edited by Anthony Faulkes and Richard Perkins, 1–14. London: Viking Society for Northern Research, 1993.

Kaland, Sigrid H. H. "Viking/medieval settlement in the heathland area of Nordhordland." In *Proceedings of the Tenth Viking Congress, Larkollen, Norway, 1985*, edited by James E. Knirk, 171–90. Universitets Oldsaksamlings Skrifter, new series, 9. Oslo: Universitets Oldsaksamling, 1987.

Martens, Irmelin. "Norwegian Viking Age weapons: Some questions concerning their production and distribution." In *The Twelfth Viking Congress: Developments Around the Baltic and the North Sea in the Viking Age*, edited by Björn Ambrosiani and Helen Clarke, 180–82. Birka Studies, 3. Stockholm: Riksantikvarieämbetet and Statens Historiska Museer, 1994.

———. "Iron extraction, settlement and trade in the Viking and early Middle Ages in south Norway." In *Proceedings of the Tenth Viking Congress, Larkollen, Norway, 1985*, edited by James E. Knirk, 69–80. Universitets Oldsaksamlings Skrifter, new series, 9. Oslo: Universitets Oldsaksamling, 1987.

Munch, Gerd Stamsø, Olav Sverre Johansen, and Ingegerd Larsen. "Borg in Lofoten: A chieftain's farm in Arctic Norway." In *Proceedings of the Tenth Viking Congress, Larkollen, Norway, 1985*, edited by James E. Knirk, 149–70. Universitets Oldsaksamlings Skrifter, new series, 9. Oslo: Universitets Oldsaksamling, 1987.

Myhre, Bjørn. "The archaeology of the early Viking Age in Norway." In *Ireland and Scandinavia in the Early Viking Age*, edited by Howard B. Clarke et al., 3–36. Dublin: Four Courts, 1998.

Resi, Heid Gjøstein. "Reflections on Viking Age local trade in stone products." In *Proceedings of the Tenth Viking Congress, Larkollen, Norway, 1985*, edited by James E. Knirk, 95–102. Universitets Oldsaksamlings Skrifter, new series, 9. Oslo: Universitets Oldsaksamling, 1987.

Stalsberg, Anne. "The Russian-Norwegian sword project." In *The Twelfth Viking Congress: Developments Around the Baltic and the North Sea in the Viking Age*, edited by Björn Ambrosiani and Helen Clarke, 183–89. Birka Studies, 3. Stockholm: Riksantikvarieämbetet and Statens Historiska Museer, 1994.

Wamers, Egon. "Insular finds in Viking Age Scandinavia and the state formation of Norway." In *Ireland and Scandinavia in the Early Viking Age*, edited by Howard B. Clarke et al., 37–72. Dublin: Four Courts, 1998.

Weber, Birthe. "Vesle Hjerkinn—A Viking Age mountain lodge?: A preliminary report." In *Proceedings of the Tenth Viking Congress, Larkollen, Norway,*

1985, edited by James E. Knirk, 103–11. Universitets Oldsaksamlings Skrifter, new series, 9. Oslo: Universitets Oldsaksamling, 1987.

D. Sweden

Ambrosiani, Björn. "Royal manors and towns in central Sweden." In *Proceedings of the Tenth Viking Congress, Larkollen, Norway, 1985*, edited by James E. Knirk, 247–53. Universitets Oldsaksamlings Skrifter, new series, 9. Oslo: Universitets Oldsaksamling, 1987.

———. "Birka: A planted town serving an increasing agricultural population." In *Proceedings of the Eighth Viking Congress, Århus, 24–31 August 1977*, edited by Hans Bekker-Nielsen, Peter Foote, and Olaf Olsen, 19–24. Odense: Odense University Press, 1981.

Ambrosiani, Björn, and Helen Clarke, eds. *Early Investigations and Future Plans*. Birka Studies, 1. Stockholm: Riksantikvarieämbetet och Statens Historiska Museer, 1992.

———. *Investigations in the Black Earth 1990*. Birka Studies, 2. Stockholm: Riksantikvarieämbetet och Statens Historiska Museer, 1995.

Arwidsson, Greta. "Viking society in central Sweden: Traditions, organization and economy." In *The Vikings: Proceedings of the Symposium of the Faculty of Arts of Uppsala University, June 6–9, 1977*, edited by Thorsten Andersson and Karl Inge Sandred, 154–60. Stockholm: Almqvist & Wiksell, 1978.

Göransson, Sölve. "Viking Age traces in Swedish systems for territorial organization and land division." In *The Vikings: Proceedings of the Symposium of the Faculty of Arts of Uppsala University, June 6–9, 1977*, edited by Thorsten Andersson and Karl Inge Sandred, 142–53. Stockholm: Almqvist & Wiksell, 1978.

Lindkvist, Thomas. "Social and political power in Sweden 1000–1300: Predatory incursions, royal taxation, and the formation of a feudal state." In *Social Approaches to Viking Studies*, edited by Ross Samson, 137–46. Glasgow: Cruithne, 1991.

Löfving, Carl. "Who ruled the region east of the Skagerrak in the eleventh century?" In *Social Approaches to Viking Studies*, edited by Ross Samson, 147–56. Glasgow: Cruithne, 1991.

Sawyer, P. H. *The Making of Sweden*. Alingsås: Viktoria, 1988.

V. NORTH ATLANTIC COLONIES (EXCLUDING THE BRITISH ISLES)

A. General

Batey, Collen E., Judith Jesch, and Christopher D. Morris, eds. *The Viking Age in Caithness, Orkney and the North Atlantic: Select Papers from the Pro-*

ceedings of the Eleventh Viking Congress, Thurso and Kirkwall, 22 August–1 September 1989. Edinburgh: Edinburgh University Press, 1993.

Bertlesen, Reidar, and Raymond G. Lamb. "Settlement mounds in the North Atlantic." In *The Viking Age in Caithness, Orkney and the North Atlantic*, edited by Colleen Batey et al., 544–54. Edinburgh: Edinburgh University Press, 1993.

Buckland, Paul C. "The North Atlantic environment." In *Vikings: The North Atlantic Saga*, edited by William W. Fitzhugh and Elisabeth I. Ward, 146–53. Washington DC: Smithsonian Institution, 2000.

Buckland, Paul C., Jon P. Sadler, and David N. Smith. "An insect's eye-view of the Norse farm." In *The Viking Age in Caithness, Orkney and the North Atlantic*, edited by Colleen Batey et al., 506–27. Edinburgh: Edinburgh University Press, 1993.

Fitzhugh, William W., and Elisabeth I. Ward, eds. *Vikings: The North Atlantic Saga*. Washington DC: Smithsonian Institution, 2000.

Magnússon, Thór, Símun V. Arge, and Jette Arneborg. "New lands in the North Atlantic." In *From Viking to Crusader: Scandinavia and Europe 800–1200*, edited by Else Roesdahl and David M. Wilson, 52–61. The 22nd Council of Europe Exhibition. Copenhagen: Nordic Council of Ministers and The Council of Europe, 1992.

Morris, Christopher D., and D. James Rackham, eds. *Norse and Later Settlement and Subsistence in the North Atlantic*. Glasgow: Department of Archaeology, University of Glasgow, 1992.

Rafnsson, Sveinbjörn. "The Atlantic islands." In *The Oxford Illustrated History of the Vikings*, edited by Peter Sawyer, 110–33. Oxford: Oxford University Press, 1997.

B. Faroe Islands

Arge, Símun V. "Vikings in the Faeroe Islands." In *Vikings: The North Atlantic Saga*, edited by William W. Fitzhugh and Elisabeth I. Ward, 154–63. Washington DC: Smithsonian Institution, 2000.

———. "On the landnam of the Faroe Islands." In *The Viking Age in Caithness, Orkney and the North Atlantic*, edited by Colleen Batey et al., 465–72. Edinburgh: Edinburgh University Press, 1993.

Dahl, Sverri. "The Norse settlement of the Faroe Islands." *Medieval Archaeology* 14 (1970): 60–73.

Debes, Hans Jacob. "Problems concerning the earliest settlement in the Faroe Islands." In *The Viking Age in Caithness, Orkney and the North Atlantic*, edited by Colleen Batey et al., 454–64. Edinburgh: Edinburgh University Press, 1993.

Hansen, Steffen Stummann. "Viking-Age Faroe Islands and their southern links in the light of recent finds at Toftanes, Leirvik." In *The Viking Age in Caithness,*

Orkney and the North Atlantic, edited by Colleen Batey et al., 473–86. Edinburgh: Edinburgh University Press, 1993.

Mahler, Ditlev L. D. "Shielings and their role in the the Viking-Age economy: New evidence from the Faroe Islands." In *The Viking Age in Caithness, Orkney and the North Atlantic*, edited by Colleen Batey et al., 487–505. Edinburgh: Edinburgh University Press, 1993.

Thorsteinsson, Arne. "On the development of Faroese settlements." In *Proceedings of the Eighth Viking Congress, Århus, 24–31 August 1977*, edited by Hans Bekker-Nielsen, Peter Foote, and Olaf Olsen, 189–202. Odense: Odense University Press, 1981.

C. Iceland

Aðalsteinsson, Jón Hnefill. *Under the Cloak: The Acceptance of Christianity in Iceland with Particular Reference to the Attitudes Prevailing at the Time*. Uppsala: Etnologiska institutionen, Uppsala universitet, 1978.

Benediktsson, Jakob. "Some problems in the history of the settlement of Iceland." In *The Vikings: Proceedings of the Symposium of the Faculty of Arts of Uppsala University, June 6–9, 1977*, edited by Thorsten Andersson and Karl Inge Sandred, 161–65. Stockholm: Almqvist & Wiksell, 1978.

Byock, Jesse L. *Viking Age Iceland*. London: Penguin, 2001.

———. *Medieval Iceland: Society, Sagas, and Power*. Enfield: Hisarlik, 1993.

Foote, P. G. "On the conversion of the Icelanders." In *Aurvandilstá*, edited by Michael P. Barnes et al., 56–64. Odense: Odense University Press, 1984.

Jóhannesson, Jón. *Íslendinga Saga: The History of the Old Icelandic Commonwealth*. Winnipeg: University of Manitoba Press, 1974.

Kristjánsson, Jónas. *Eddas and Sagas: Iceland's Medieval Literature*. Reykjavik: Hið íslenska bókmenntafélag, 1997.

Ólafsson, Guðmundur. "Þingnes by Elliðavatn: The first local assembly in Iceland?" In *Proceedings of the Tenth Viking Congress, Larkollen, Norway, 1985*, edited by James E. Knirk, 343–49. Universitets Oldsaksamlings Skrifter, new series, 9. Oslo: Universitets Oldsaksamling, 1987.

Sigurðsson, Gísli. *Gaelic Influence in Iceland: Historical and Literary Contacts*. 2nd ed. Reykjavik: University of Iceland Press, 2000.

Thorláksson, Helgi. "The Icelandic Commonwealth period: Building a new society." In *Vikings: The North Atlantic Saga*, edited by William W. Fitzhugh and Elisabeth I. Ward, 175–85. Washington DC: Smithsonian Institution, 2000.

Turville-Petre, E. O. Gabriel. *Origins of Icelandic Literature*. Oxford: Clarendon Press, 1953.

Vésteinsson, Orri. "The archaeology of *landnám*: Early settlement in Iceland." In *Vikings: The North Atlantic Saga*, edited by William W. Fitzhugh and Elisabeth I. Ward, 164–74. Washington DC: Smithsonian Institution, 2000.

D. Greenland

Arneborg, Jette. "Greenland and Europe." In *Vikings: The North Atlantic Saga*, edited by William W. Fitzhugh and Elisabeth I. Ward, 304–17. Washington DC: Smithsonian Institution, 2000.

Arneborg, Jette, and Kirsten A. Seaver. "Norse Greenland: From Vikings to Norsemen." In *Vikings: The North Atlantic Saga*, edited by William W. Fitzhugh and Elisabeth I. Ward, 281–84. Washington DC: Smithsonian Institution, 2000.

Berglund, Joel. "The Farm Beneath the Sand." In *Vikings: The North Atlantic Saga*, edited by William W. Fitzhugh and Elisabeth I. Ward, 295–303. Washington DC: Smithsonian Institution, 2000.

Buckland, P. C., T. H. McGovern, J. P. Sadler, and P. Skidmore. "Twig layers, floors and middens: Recent palaeoecological research in the Western Settlement, Greenland." In *The Twelfth Viking Congress: Developments Around the Baltic and the North Sea in the Viking Age*, edited by Björn Ambrosiani and Helen Clarke, 132–43. Birka Studies, 3. Stockholm: Riksantikvarieämbetet and Statens Historiska Museer, 1994.

Gulløv, Hans Christian. "Natives and Norse in Greenland." In *Vikings: The North Atlantic Saga*, edited by William W. Fitzhugh and Elisabeth I. Ward, 318–26. Washington DC: Smithsonian Institution, 2000.

Halldórsson, Ólafur. "The conversion of Greenland in written sources." In *Proceedings of the Eighth Viking Congress, Århus, 24–31 August 1977*, edited by Hans Bekker-Nielsen, Peter Foote, and Olaf Olsen, 203–16. Odense: Odense University Press, 1981.

Lynnerup, Niels. "Life and death in Norse Greenland." In *Vikings: The North Atlantic Saga*, edited by William W. Fitzhugh and Elisabeth I. Ward, 285–94. Washington DC: Smithsonian Institution, 2000.

McGovern, Thomas H. "The demise of Norse Greenland." In *Vikings: The North Atlantic Saga*, edited by William W. Fitzhugh and Elisabeth I. Ward, 327–39. Washington DC: Smithsonian Institution, 2000.

Stoklund, Marie. "Greenland runes: Isolation or cultural contact?" In *The Viking Age in Caithness, Orkney and the North Atlantic*, edited by Colleen Batey et al., 528–43. Edinburgh: Edinburgh University Press, 1993.

E. North America

Cox, Steven L. "A Norse penny from Maine." In *Vikings: The North Atlantic Saga*, edited by William W. Fitzhugh and Elisabeth I. Ward, 206–7. Washington DC: Smithsonian Institution, 2000.

Foote, P. G. "On the Vínland legends on *The Vinland Map*." *Saga-Book* 17:1 (1966): 73–89.

Haugen, Einar. "Was Vinland in Newfoundland?" In *Proceedings of the Eighth Viking Congress, Århus, 24–31 August* 1977, edited by Hans Bekker-Nielsen, Peter Foote, and Olaf Olsen, 3–8. Odense: Odense University Press, 1981.

Ingstad, Anne Stine. *The Discovery of a Norse Settlement in America: Excavations at L'Anse aux Meadows, Newfoundland 1961–1968*. Oslo: Norwegian University Press, 1977.

Ingstad, Helge. *Westward to Vinland: The Discovery of Pre-Columbian Norse House-Sites in North America*. London: BCA, 1969.

Perkins, R. M. "Norse implications." In H. Wallis et al. "The Strange Case of the Vinland Map." *The Geographical Journal* 140 (1974): 199–205.

Schledermann, Peter. "Ellesmere: Vikings in the Far North." In *Vikings: The North Atlantic Saga*, edited by William W. Fitzhugh and Elisabeth I. Ward, 248–56. Washington DC: Smithsonian Institution, 2000.

Sigurðsson, Gísli. "A introduction to the *Vinland Sagas: Greenlanders' Saga* and *Erik the Red's Saga*." In *Vikings: The North Atlantic Saga*, edited by William W. Fitzhugh and Elisabeth I. Ward, 219–24. Washington DC: Smithsonian Institution, 2000.

——. "The quest for Vinland in saga scholarship." In *Vikings: The North Atlantic Saga*, edited by William W. Fitzhugh and Elisabeth I. Ward, 232–37. Washington DC: Smithsonian Institution, 2000.

Sutherland, Patricia D. "The Norse and Native North Americans." In *Vikings: The North Atlantic Saga*, edited by William W. Fitzhugh and Elisabeth I. Ward, 238–47. Washington DC: Smithsonian Institution, 2000.

Wahlgren, Erik. *The Vikings and America*. London: Thames & Hudson, 1986.

Wallace, Birgitta Linderoth. "The Viking settlement at L'Anse aux Meadows." In *Vikings: The North Atlantic Saga*, edited by William W. Fitzhugh and Elisabeth I. Ward, 208–16. Washington DC: Smithsonian Institution, 2000.

——. "An archaeologist's interpretation of the *Vinland Sagas*." In *Vikings: The North Atlantic Saga*, edited by William W. Fitzhugh and Elisabeth I. Ward, 225–31. Washington DC: Smithsonian Institution, 2000.

——. "The Vikings in North America: Myth and reality." In *Social Approaches to Viking Studies*, edited by Ross Samson, 206–20. Glasgow: Cruithne, 1991.

Washburn, W., ed. *Proceedings of the Vinland Map Conference*. Chicago: University of Chicago Press, 1971.

VI. THE BRITISH ISLES

A. General

Barnes, Michael P. "Aspects of the Scandinavian runes of the British Isles." In *Roman, Runes and Ogham*, edited by John Higgitt et al., 103–11. Donington: Shaun Tyas, 2001.

———. "Norse in the British Isles." In *Viking Revaluations*, edited by Anthony Faulkes and Richard Perkins, 65–85. London: Viking Society for Northern Research, 1993.

Batey, Colleen, and John Sheehan. "Viking expansion and cultural blending in Britain and Ireland." In *Vikings: The North Atlantic Saga*, edited by William W. Fitzhugh and Elisabeth I. Ward, 127–41. Washington DC: Smithsonian Institution, 2000.

Crawford, Barbara E., ed. *Conversion and Christianity in the North Sea World*. St. John's House Publications, 8. St. Andrews: Committee for Dark Ages Studies, University of St. Andrews, 1998.

———. *Scandinavian Settlement in Northern Britain*. London: Leicester University Press, 1995.

Fellows-Jensen, Gillian. "The Vikings' relationship with Christianity in the British Isles: The evidence of place-names containing the element *kirkja*." In *Proceedings of the Tenth Viking Congress, Larkollen, Norway, 1985*, edited by James E. Knirk, 295–307. Universitets Oldsaksamlings Skrifter, new series, 9. Oslo: Universitets Oldsaksamling, 1987.

Hall, Richard A. *Viking Age Archaeology in Britain and Ireland*. Princes Risborough: Shire, 1990.

Holman, Katherine. "Scandinavian runic inscriptions as a source for the history of the British Isles: The St. Paul's rune-stone." In *Runeninschriften als Quellen interdisziplinärer Forschung*, edited by Klaus Düwel, 629–38. Berlin: Walter de Gruyter, 1998.

———. *Scandinavian Runic Inscriptions in the British Isles: Their Historical Context*. Senter for middelalder studier, 4. Trondheim: Tapir, 1996.

Loyn, H. R. *The Vikings in Britain*. London: BCA, 1977.

Smyth, Alfred P. *Scandinavian Kings in the British Isles, 850–880*. Oxford: Oxford University Press, 1977.

Wilson, David M., with Richard Hall. "The Scandinavians in Britain and Ireland." In *From Viking to Crusader: Scandinavia and Europe 800–1200*, edited by Else Roesdahl and David M. Wilson, 96–105. The 22nd Council of Europe Exhibition. Copenhagen: Nordic Council of Ministers and The Council of Europe, 1992.

B. England

Abrams, Lesley. "Edward the Elder's Danelaw." In *Edward the Elder 899–924*, edited by N. J. Higham and D. H. Hill, 128–43. London: Routledge, 2001.

———. "The conversion of the Danelaw." In *Vikings and the Danelaw: Select Papers from the Proceedings of the Thirteenth Viking Congress*, edited by James Graham-Campbell et al., 31–44. Oxford: Oxbow, 2001.

———. "Conversion and assimilation." In *Cultures in Contact: Scandinavian Settlement in England in the Ninth and Tenth Centuries*, edited by Dawn M. Hadley and Julian D. Richards, 135–53. Turnhout: Brepols, 2000.

Ashdown, Margaret. *English and Norse Documents Relating to the Reign of Ethelred the Unready*. Cambridge: Cambridge University Press, 1930.

Baldwin, John R., and Ian D. Whyte, eds. *The Scandinavians in Cumbria*. Edinburgh: Scottish Society for Northern Studies, 1985.

Barrow, Julia. "Survival and mutation: Ecclesiastical institutions in the Danelaw in the ninth and tenth centuries." In *Cultures in Contact: Scandinavian Settlement in England in the Ninth and Tenth Centuries*, edited by Dawn M. Hadley and Julian D. Richards, 155–76. Turnhout: Brepols, 2000.

Biddle, Martin, and Birthe Kjølbye-Biddle. "Repton and the 'great heathen army', 873–4." In *Vikings and the Danelaw: Select Papers from the Proceedings of the Thirteenth Viking Congress*, edited by James Graham-Campbell et al., 45–96. Oxford: Oxbow, 2001.

Binns, A. L. *The Viking Century in East Yorkshire*. East Yorkshire Local History Society, no. 15. York: East Yorkshire Local History Society, 1963.

Blackburn, Mark. "Expansion and control: Aspects of Anglo-Scandinavian minting south of the Humber." In *Vikings and the Danelaw: Select Papers from the Proceedings of the Thirteenth Viking Congress*, edited by James Graham-Campbell et al., 125–42. Oxford: Oxbow, 2001.

Cameron, Kenneth. "The minor names and field-names of the Holland division of Lincolnshire." In *The Vikings: Proceedings of the Symposium of the Faculty of Arts of Uppsala University, June 6–9, 1977*, edited by Thorsten Andersson and Karl Inge Sandred, 81–88. Stockholm: Almqvist & Wiksell, 1978.

———, ed. *Place-name Evidence for the Anglo-Saxon Invasion and Scandinavian Settlements*. Nottingham: English Place-Name Society, 1977.

———. *English Place-Names*. Rev. ed. London: Batsford, 1977.

Campbell, James, ed. *The Anglo-Saxons*. London: Penguin, 1991.

Cavill, Paul, Stephen E. Harding, and Judith Jesch. *Wirral and Its Viking Heritage*. Nottingham: English Place-Name Society, 2000.

Coupland, Simon. "The Vikings in Francia and Anglo-Saxon England to 911." In *The New Cambridge Medieval History*, vol. 2, *c. 700–c. 900*, edited by Rosamond McKitterick, 190–201. Cambridge: Cambridge University Press, 1995.

Crook, John. "'A worthy antiquity': The movement of King Cnut's bones in Winchester Cathedral." In *The Reign of Cnut: King of England, Denmark and Norway*, edited by Alexander R. Rumble, 165–92. London: Leicester University Press, 1994.

Davidson, Michael R. "The (non)submission of the northern kings in 920." In *Edward the Elder 899–924*, edited by N. J. Higham and D. H. Hill, 200–11. London: Routledge, 2001.

DeVries, Kelly. *The Norwegian Invasion of England in 1066*. Woodbridge: Boydell, 1999.

Dolley, Michael. *Viking Coins of the Danelaw and of Dublin*. London: British Museum, 1965.

Edwards, B. J. N. *Vikings in North West England: The Artifacts*. Lancaster: Centre for North-West Regional Studies, University of Lancaster, 1998.

Evison, Martin Paul. "All in the genes? Evaluating the biological evidence of contact and migration." In *Cultures in Contact: Scandinavian Settlement in England in the Ninth and Tenth Centuries*, edited by Dawn M. Hadley and Julian D. Richards, 277–94. Turnhout: Brepols, 2000.

Fell, Christine E. "Anglo-Saxon saints in Old Norse sources and vice versa." In *Proceedings of the Eighth Viking Congress, Århus, 24–31 August* 1977, edited by Hans Bekker-Nielsen, Peter Foote, and Olaf Olsen, 95–106. Odense: Odense University Press, 1981.

Fellows-Jensen, Gillian. "In the steps of the Vikings." In *Vikings and the Danelaw: Select Papers from the Proceedings of the Thirteenth Viking Congress*, edited by James Graham-Campbell et al., 279–88. Oxford: Oxbow, 2001.

——. "Scandinavian settlement in Yorkshire: Through the rear-view mirror." In *Scandinavian Settlement in Northern Britain*, edited by Barbara E. Crawford, 170–86. London: Leicester University Press, 1995.

——. "Danish place-names and personal names in England: The influence of Cnut?" In *The Reign of Cnut: King of England, Denmark and Norway*, edited by Alexander R. Rumble, 125–40. London: Leicester University Press, 1994.

——. *Scandinavian Settlement Names in the North-West*. Copenhagen: C. A. Reitzel, 1985.

——. "Scandinavian settlement in Cumbria and Dumfriesshire: The place-name evidence." In *The Scandinavians in Cumbria*, edited by John R. Baldwin and Ian D. Whyte, 65–82. Edinburgh: Scottish Society for Northern Studies, 1985.

Fellows-Jensen, Gillian. "Scandinavian settlement in the Isle of Man and northwest England: The place-name evidence." In *The Viking Age in the Isle of Man*, edited by Christine E. Fell et al., 37–52. London: Viking Society for Northern Research, 1983.

——. "Scandinavian settlement in the Danelaw in the light of the place-names of Denmark." In *Proceedings of the Eighth Viking Congress, Århus, 24–31 August* 1977, edited by Hans Bekker-Nielsen, Peter Foote, and Olaf Olsen, 133–45. Odense: Odense University Press, 1981.

——. "Place-name evidence for Scandinavian settlement in the Danelaw: A re-assessment." In *The Vikings: Proceedings of the Symposium of the Faculty of Arts of Uppsala University, June 6–9, 1977*, edited by Thorsten Andersson and Karl Inge Sandred, 89–98. Stockholm: Almqvist & Wiksell, 1978.

———. *Scandinavian Settlement Names in the East Midlands*. Navnestudier udgivet af Institut for Navneforskning, 16. Copenhagen: Akademisk Forlag, 1978.

———. "The Vikings in England: A review." *Anglo-Saxon England* 4 (1975): 181–206.

———. *Scandinavian Settlement Names in Yorkshire*. Navnestudier udgivet af Institut for Navneforskning, 11. Copenhagen: Akademisk Forlag, 1972.

———. *Scandinavian Personal Names in Lincolnshire and Yorkshire*. Navnestudier udgivet af Institut for Navneforskning, 7. Copenhagen: Akademisk Forlag, 1968.

Frank, Roberta. "King Cnut in the verse of his skalds." In *The Reign of Cnut: King of England, Denmark and Norway*, edited by Alexander R. Rumble, 106–24. London: Leicester University Press, 1994.

Garmonsway, G. N. *Canute and His Empire*. Dorothea Coke Memorial Lecture in Northern Studies. London: Viking Society for Northern Research, 1964.

Gelling, Margaret. "Scandinavian settlement in Cheshire: The evidence of place-names." In *Scandinavian Settlement in Northern Britain*, edited by Barbara E. Crawford, 187–94. London: Leicester University Press, 1995.

Gore, Derek. *The Vikings and Devon*. Exeter: Mint, 2001.

Graham-Campbell, James. "The northern hoards: From Cuerdale to Bossall/Flaxton." In *Edward the Elder 899–924*, edited by N. J. Higham and D. H. Hill, 212–29. London and New York: Routledge, 2001.

———. "Pagan Scandinavian burial in the central and southern Danelaw." In *Vikings and the Danelaw: Select Papers from the Proceedings of the Thirteenth Viking Congress*, edited by James Graham-Campbell et al., 105–23. Oxford: Oxbow, 2001.

———, ed. *Viking Treasure from the North West: The Cuerdale Hoard in Its Context*. National Museums and Galleries on Merseyside, Occasional Papers, Liverpool Museum, 5. Liverpool: Liverpool Museum, 1992.

Graham-Campbell, James, et al., eds. *Vikings and the Danelaw: Select Papers from the Proceedings of the Thirteenth Viking Congress*. Oxford: Oxbow, 2001.

Griffiths, David. "The north-west frontier." In *Edward the Elder 899–924*, edited by N. J. Higham and D. H. Hill, 167–87. London: Routledge, 2001.

Hadley, Dawn M. "In search of the Vikings: The problems and possibilities of interdisciplinary approaches." In *Vikings and the Danelaw: Select Papers from the Proceedings of the Thirteenth Viking Congress*, edited by James Graham-Campbell et al., 13–30. Oxford: Oxbow, 2001.

———. *The Northern Danelaw: Its Social Structure, c. 800–1100*. London: Leicester University Press, 2000.

———. "'Hamlet and the Princes of Denmark': Lordship in the Danelaw, *c*. 860–954." In *Cultures in Contact: Scandinavian Settlement in England in the Ninth and Tenth Centuries*, edited by Dawn M. Hadley and Julian D. Richards, 107–32. Turnhout: Brepols, 2000.

Hadley, Dawn M., and Julian D. Richards. "Introduction: Interdisciplinary approaches to the Scandinavian settlement." In *Cultures in Contact: Scandinavian Settlement in England in the Ninth and Tenth Centuries*, edited by Dawn M. Hadley and Julian D. Richards, 3–15. Turnhout: Brepols, 2000.

———, eds. *Cultures in Contact: Scandinavian Settlement in England in the Ninth and Tenth Centuries*. Turnhout: Brepols, 2000.

Hald, Kristian. "*A*-mutation in Scandinavian words in England." In *The Vikings: Proceedings of the Symposium of the Faculty of Arts of Uppsala University, June 6–9, 1977*, edited by Thorsten Andersson and Karl Inge Sandred, 99–106. Stockholm: Almqvist & Wiksell, 1978.

Hall, Richard A. "A kingdom too far: York in the early tenth century." In *Edward the Elder 899–924*, edited by N. J. Higham and D. H. Hill, 188–99. London: Routledge, 2001.

———. "Anglo-Scandinavian urban development in the East Midlands." In *Vikings and the Danelaw: Select Papers from the Proceedings of the Thirteenth Viking Congress*, edited by James Graham-Campbell et al., 143–55. Oxford: Oxbow, 2001.

———. "Anglo-Scandinavian attitudes: Archaeological ambiguities in late ninth- to mid-eleventh-century York." In *Cultures in Contact: Scandinavian Settlement in England in the Ninth and Tenth Centuries*, edited by Dawn M. Hadley and Julian D. Richards, 311–24. Turnhout: Brepols, 2000.

———. *Viking York*. London: B. T. Batsford, 1994.

———. "Vikings gone west? A summary review." In *The Twelfth Viking Congress: Developments Around the Baltic and the North Sea in the Viking Age*, edited by Björn Ambrosiani and Helen Clarke, 32–49. Birka Studies, 3. Stockholm: Riksantikvarieämbetet and Statens Historiska Museer, 1994.

Halsall, Guy. "The Viking presence in England? The burial evidence reconsidered." In *Cultures in Contact: Scandinavian Settlement in England in the Ninth and Tenth Centuries*, edited by Dawn M. Hadley and Julian D. Richards, 259–76. Turnhout: Brepols, 2000.

Hart, Cyril. *The Danelaw*. London: Hambledon, 1992.

Higham, Mary C. "Scandinavian settlement names in north-west England, with a special study of *Ireby* names." In *Scandinavian Settlement in Northern Britain*, edited by Barbara E. Crawford, 195–205. London: Leicester University Press, 1995.

Higham, N. J., and D. H. Hill, eds. *Edward the Elder 899–924*. London: Routledge, 2001.

Hill, David. "An urban policy for Cnut?" In *The Reign of Cnut: King of England, Denmark and Norway*, edited by Alexander R. Rumble, 101–05. London: Leicester University Press, 1994.

———. *An Atlas of Anglo-Saxon England*. Oxford: Blackwell, 1981.

Holman, Katherine. "Defining the Danelaw." In *Vikings and the Danelaw: Select Papers from the Proceedings of the Thirteenth Viking Congress*, edited by James Graham-Campbell et al., 1–11. Oxford: Oxbow, 2001.

Hooper, Nicholas. "Military developments in the reign of Cnut." In *The Reign of Cnut: King of England, Denmark and Norway*, edited by Alexander R. Rumble, 89–100. London: Leicester University Press, 1994.

Innes, Matthew. "Danelaw identities: Ethnicity, regionalism, and political allegiance." In *Cultures in Contact: Scandinavian Settlement in England in the Ninth and Tenth Centuries*, edited by Dawn M. Hadley and Julian D. Richards, 65–88. Turnhout: Brepols, 2000.

Jesch, Judith. "England and *Orkneyinga saga*." In *The Viking Age in Caithness, Orkney and the North Atlantic*, edited by Colleen Batey et al., 222–39. Edinburgh: Edinburgh University Press, 1993.

———. "Skaldic verse in Scandinavian England." In *Vikings and the Danelaw: Select Papers from the Proceedings of the Thirteenth Viking Congress*, edited by James Graham-Campbell et al., 313–25. Oxford: Oxbow, 2001.

Jonsson, Kenneth. "The coinage of Cnut." In *The Reign of Cnut: King of England, Denmark and Norway*, edited by Alexander R. Rumble, 193–230. London: Leicester University Press, 1994.

Kershaw, Paul. "The Alfred-Guthrum treaty: Scripting accommodation and interaction in Viking Age England." In *Cultures in Contact: Scandinavian Settlement in England in the Ninth and Tenth Centuries*, edited by Dawn M. Hadley and Julian D. Richards, 43–64. Turnhout: Brepols, 2000.

Keynes, Simon. "The Vikings in England." In *The Oxford Illustrated History of the Vikings*, edited by Peter Sawyer, 48–82. Oxford: Oxford University Press, 1997.

———. "Cnut's earls." In *The Reign of Cnut: King of England, Denmark and Norway*, edited by Alexander R. Rumble, 43–88. London: Leicester University Press, 1994.

Lawson, M. K. "Archbishop Wulfstan and the homiletic element in the laws of Æthelred II and Cnut." In *The Reign of Cnut: King of England, Denmark and Norway*, edited by Alexander R. Rumble, 141–64. London: Leicester University Press, 1994.

———. *Cnut: The Danes in England in the Early Eleventh Century*. London: Longman, 1993.

Leahy, Kevin, and Caroline Paterson. "New light on the Viking presence in Lincolnshire: The artefactual evidence." In *Vikings and the Danelaw: Select*

Papers from the Proceedings of the Thirteenth Viking Congress, edited by James Graham-Campbell et al., 181–202. Oxford: Oxbow, 2001.

Lund, Niels. "The armies of Swein Forkbeard and Cnut: 'leding' or 'lið'?" *Anglo-Saxon England* 15 (1986): 105–18.

———. "The settlers: Where do we get them from—and do we need them?" In *Proceedings of the Eighth Viking Congress, Århus, 24–31 August* 1977, edited by Hans Bekker-Nielsen, Peter Foote, and Olaf Olsen, 147–71. Odense: Odense University Press, 1981.

———. "King Edgar and the Danelaw." *Mediaeval Scandinavia* 9 (1976): 181–95.

McIntosh, Angus. "Middle English word geography: Its potential role in the study of the long-term impact of the Scandinavians settlements upon English." In *The Vikings: Proceedings of the Symposium of the Faculty of Arts of Uppsala University, June 6–9, 1977*, edited by Thorsten Andersson and Karl Inge Sandred, 124–30. Stockholm: Almqvist & Wiksell, 1978.

McKinnell, John. "Eddic poetry in Anglo-Scandinavian northern England." In *Vikings and the Danelaw: Select Papers from the Proceedings of the Thirteenth Viking Congress*, edited by James Graham-Campbell et al., 327–44. Oxford: Oxbow, 2001.

Morris, Christopher D. "Viking and native in northern England: A case study." In *Proceedings of the Eighth Viking Congress, Århus, 24–31 August* 1977, edited by Hans Bekker-Nielsen, Peter Foote, and Olaf Olsen, 223–44. Odense: Odense University Press, 1981.

Page, R. I. "A most vile people": *Early English Historians on the Vikings*. The Dorothea Coke Memorial Lecture in Northern Studies, University College London, 19 March 1986. London: Viking Society for Northern Research, 1987.

———. "How long did the Scandinavian language survive in England? The epigraphical evidence." In *England before the Conquest: Studies in Primary Sources Presented to Dorothy Whitelock*, edited by Peter Clemoes and Kathleen Hughes, 165–81. Cambridge: Cambridge University Press, 1971.

Parsons, David N. "How long did the Scandinavian language survive in England? Again." In *Vikings and the Danelaw: Select Papers from the Proceedings of the Thirteenth Viking Congress*, edited by James Graham-Campbell et al., 299–312. Oxford: Oxbow, 2001.

Richards, Julian D. "Boundaries and cult centres: Viking burial in Derbyshire." In *Vikings and the Danelaw: Select Papers from the Proceedings of the Thirteenth Viking Congress*, edited by James Graham-Campbell et al., 97–104. Oxford: Oxbow, 2001.

———. "Finding the Vikings: The search for Anglo-Scandinavian rural settlement in the northern Danelaw." In *Vikings and the Danelaw: Select Papers from the Proceedings of the Thirteenth Viking Congress*, edited by James Graham-Campbell et al., 269–77. Oxford: Oxbow, 2001.

———. "Identifying Anglo-Scandinavian settlements." In *Cultures in Contact: Scandinavian Settlement in England in the Ninth and Tenth Centuries*, edited by Dawn M. Hadley and Julian D. Richards, 295–309. Turnhout: Brepols, 2000.

———. *Viking Age England*. London: BCA, 1991.

Roesdahl, Else, et al., eds. *The Vikings in England and in their Danish Homeland*. London: The Anglo-Danish Viking Project, 1981.

Rumble, Alexander R. "Introduction: Cnut in context." In *The Reign of Cnut: King of England, Denmark and Norway*, edited by Alexander R. Rumble, 1–9. London: Leicester University Press, 1994.

———, ed. *The Reign of Cnut: King of England, Denmark and Norway*. London: Leicester University Press, 1994.

Sandred, Karl Inge. "Viking administration in the Danelaw: A look at Scandinavian and English place names in Norfolk." In *The Twelfth Viking Congress: Developments Around the Baltic and the North Sea in the Viking Age*, edited by Björn Ambrosiani and Helen Clarke, 269–76. Birka Studies, 3. Stockholm: Riksantikvarieämbetet and Statens Historiska Museer, 1994.

———. "The Vikings in Norfolk: Some observations on the place-names in-*by*." In *Proceedings of the Tenth Viking Congress, Larkollen, Norway, 1985*, edited by James E. Knirk, 309–24. Universitets Oldsaksamlings Skrifter, new series, 9. Oslo: Universitets Oldsaksamling, 1987.

Sawyer, Peter H. *From Roman Britain to Norman England*. 2nd ed. London: Routledge, 1998.

———. *Anglo-Saxon Lincolnshire*. Lincoln: History of Lincolnshire Committee, 1998.

———. "Conquest and colonisation: Scandinavians in the Danelaw and in Normandy." In *Proceedings of the Eighth Viking Congress, Århus, 24–31 August 1977*, edited by Hans Bekker-Nielsen, Peter Foote, and Olaf Olsen, 123–31. Odense: Odense University Press, 1981.

Sidebottom, Phil. "Viking Age stone monuments and social identity in Derbyshire." In *Cultures in Contact: Scandinavian Settlement in England in the Ninth and Tenth Centuries*, edited by Dawn M. Hadley and Julian D. Richards, 213–35. Turnhout: Brepols, 2000.

Smyth, Alfred P. *Scandinavian York and Dublin: The History and Archaeology of Two Related Viking Kingdoms*. Dublin: Irish Academic Press, 1987.

Stafford, Pauline. *Queen Emma and Queen Edith: Queenship and Women's Power in Eleventh-Century England*. Oxford: Blackwell, 1997.

———. *Unification and Conquest: A Political and Social History of England in the Tenth and Eleventh Centuries*. London: Edward Arnold, 1989.

———. *The East Midlands in the Early Middle Ages*. Leicester: Leicester University Press, 1985.

Stenton, F. M. *Anglo-Saxon England*. 3rd ed. Oxford: Clarendon Press, 1971.

Stocker, David. "Monuments and merchants: Irregularities in the distribution of stone sculpture in Lincolnshire and Yorkshire in the tenth century." In *Cultures in Contact: Scandinavian Settlement in England in the Ninth and Tenth Centuries*, edited by Dawn M. Hadley and Julian D. Richards, 179–212. Turnhout: Brepols, 2000.

Stocker, David, and Paul Everson. "Five towns funerals: Decoding diversity in Danelaw stone sculpture." In *Vikings and the Danelaw: Select Papers from the Proceedings of the Thirteenth Viking Congress*, edited by James Graham-Campbell et al., 223–43. Oxford: Oxbow, 2001.

Styles, Tania. "Scandinavian elements in English place-names: Some semantic problems." In *Vikings and the Danelaw: Select Papers from the Proceedings of the Thirteenth Viking Congress*, edited by James Graham-Campbell et al., 289–98. Oxford: Oxbow, 2001.

Syrett, Martin. *The Vikings in England: The Evidence of Runic Inscriptions*. Cambridge: Department of Anglo-Saxon, Norse, and Celtic, University of Cambridge, 2002.

Thomas, Gabor. "Anglo-Scandinavian metalwork from the Danelaw: Exploring social and cultural interaction." In *Cultures in Contact: Scandinavian Settlement in England in the Ninth and Tenth Centuries*, edited by Dawn M. Hadley and Julian D. Richards, 237–55. Turnhout: Brepols, 2000.

Townend, Matthew. "Viking Age England as a bilingual society." In *Cultures in Contact: Scandinavian Settlement in England in the Ninth and Tenth Centuries*, edited by Dawn M. Hadley and Julian D. Richards, 89–105. Turnhout: Brepols, 2000.

Trafford, Simon. "Ethnicity, migration theory, and the historiography of the Scandinavian settlement of England." In *Cultures in Contact: Scandinavian Settlement in England in the Ninth and Tenth Centuries*, edited by Dawn M. Hadley and Julian D. Richards, 17–39. Turnhout: Brepols, 2000.

Turville-Petre, Thorlac. "Representations of the Danelaw in Middle English literature." In *Vikings and the Danelaw: Select Papers from the Proceedings of the Thirteenth Viking Congress*, edited by James Graham-Campbell et al., 345–55. Oxford: Oxbow, 2001.

Vince, Alan. "Lincoln in the Viking Age." In *Vikings and the Danelaw: Select Papers from the Proceedings of the Thirteenth Viking Congress*, edited by James Graham-Campbell et al., 157–79. Oxford: Oxbow, 2001.

Wainwright, F. T. "The Scandinavians in Lancashire." *Transactions of the Lancashire and Cheshire Antiquarian Society* 58 (1945–46): 71–116.

Watts, Victor. "Northumberland and Durham: The place-name evidence." In *Scandinavian Settlement in Northern Britain*, edited by Barbara E. Crawford, 206–13. London: Leicester University Press, 1995.

Wawn, Andrew. "Hereward, the Danelaw and the Victorians." In *Vikings and the Danelaw: Select Papers from the Proceedings of the Thirteenth Viking Congress*, edited by James Graham-Campbell et al., 357–68. Oxford: Oxbow, 2001.

Whitelock, Dorothy, ed. *English Historical Documents c. 500–1042*. 2nd ed. London: Eyre & Spottiswoode, 1979.

C. Scotland (including the Northern and Western Isles and the Isle of Man)

Andersen, Per Sveas. "Norse settlement in the Hebrides: What happened to the natives and what happened to the Norse immigrants?" In *People and Places in Northern Europe 500–1600: Essays in Honour of Peter Hayes Sawyer*, edited by Ian Wood and Niels Lund, 131–47. Woodbridge: Boydell, 1991.

Bangor-Jones, Malcolm. "Norse settlement in south-east Sutherland." In *Scandinavian Settlement in Northern Britain*, edited by Barbara E. Crawford, 80–91. London: Leicester University Press, 1995.

Barnes, Michael P. *The Norn Language of Orkney and Shetland*. Lerwick: Shetland Times, 1998.

———. "Norse in the British Isles." In *Viking Revaluations*, edited by Anthony Faulkes and Richard Perkins, 65–85. London: Viking Society for Northern Research, 1993.

———. *The Runic Inscriptions of Maeshowe, Orkney*. Runrön, 8. Uppsala: Institutionen för nordiska språk, Uppsala universitet, 1994.

———. "Orkney and Shetland Norn." In *Language in the British Isles*, edited by Peter Trudgill, 352–66. Cambridge: Cambridge University Press, 1984.

Batey, Colleen E. "Viking and Late Norse Caithness: The archaeological evidence." In *Proceedings of the Tenth Viking Congress, Larkollen, Norway, 1985*, edited by James E. Knirk, 131–48. Universitets Oldsaksamlings Skrifter, new series, 9. Oslo: Universitets Oldsaksamling, 1987.

Batey, Colleen E., Judith Jesch, and Christopher D. Morris, eds. *The Viking Age in Caithness, Orkney and the North Atlantic*. Edinburgh: Edinburgh University Press, 1993.

Bertlesen, Reidar, and Raymond G. Lamb. "Settlement mounds in the North Atlantic." In *The Viking Age in Caithness, Orkney and the North Atlantic*, edited by Colleen Batey et al., 544–54. Edinburgh: Edinburgh University Press, 1993.

Bigelow, Gerald F. "Archaeological and ethnohistoric evidence of a Norse island food custom." In *The Viking Age in Caithness, Orkney and the North At-*

lantic, edited by Colleen Batey et al., 441–53. Edinburgh: Edinburgh University Press, 1993.

Christensen, Arne Emil. "Boats and boat-building in western Norway and the Islands." In *The Northern and Western Isles in the Viking World: Survival, Continuity and Change*, edited by Alexander Fenton and Hermann Pálsson, 85–95. Edinburgh: John Donald, 1984.

Crawford, Barbara E., ed. *Conversion and Christianity in the North Sea World*. St John's House Publications, 8. St Andrews: Committee for Dark Ages Studies, University of St Andrews, 1998.

———, ed. *Scandinavian Settlement in Northern Britain*. London: Leicester University Press, 1995.

———. "Norse earls and Scottish bishops in Caithness: A clash of cultures." In *The Viking Age in Caithness, Orkney and the North Atlantic*, edited by Colleen Batey et al., 129–47. Edinburgh: Edinburgh University Press, 1993.

———. *Scandinavian Scotland*. Leicester: Leicester University Press, 1987.

———, ed. *Essays in Shetland History: Heiðursrit to T. M. Y. Manson*. Lerwick: Shetland Times, 1984.

Crawford, Iain A. "War or peace: Viking colonisation in the Northern and Western Isles of Scotland reviewed." In *Proceedings of the Eighth Viking Congress, Århus, 24–31 August* 1977, edited by Hans Bekker-Nielsen, Peter Foote, and Olaf Olsen, 259–69. Odense: Odense University Press, 1981.

Dolley, Michael. "The palimpsest of Viking settlement on Man." In *Proceedings of the Eighth Viking Congress, Århus, 24–31 August* 1977, edited by Hans Bekker-Nielsen, Peter Foote, and Olaf Olsen, 173–81. Odense: Odense University Press, 1981.

Fell, Christine E., et al., eds. *The Viking Age in the Isle of Man*. London: Viking Society for Northern Research, 1983.

Fellows-Jensen, Gillian. "Some Orkney personal names." In *The Viking Age in Caithness, Orkney and the North Atlantic*, edited by Colleen Batey et al., 397–407. Edinburgh: Edinburgh University Press, 1993.

———. "Scandinavian settlement in Cumbria and Dumfriesshire: The place-name evidence." In *The Scandinavians in Cumbria*, edited by John R. Baldwin and Ian D. Whyte, 65–82. Edinburgh: Scottish Society for Northern Studies, 1985.

———. "Viking settlement in the Northern and Western Isles: The place-name evidence as seen from Denmark and the Danelaw." In *The Northern and Western Isles in the Viking World: Survival, Continuity and Change*, edited by Alexander Fenton and Hermann Pálsson, 148–68. Edinburgh: John Donald, 1984.

———. "Scandinavian settlement in the Isle of Man and north-west England: The place-name evidence." In *The Viking Age in the Isle of Man*, edited by

Christine E. Fell, et al., 37–52. London: Viking Society for Northern Research, 1983.

Fenton, Alexander. "Orkney Norn: A survey of 'taboo' terms." In *The Viking Age in Caithness, Orkney and the North Atlantic*, edited by Colleen Batey et al., 381–87. Edinburgh: Edinburgh University Press, 1993.

Fenton, Alexander, and Hermann Pálsson, eds. *The Northern and Western Isles in the Viking World*. Edinburgh: John Donald, 1984.

Fraser, Ian. "Norse settlement on the north-west seaboard." In *Scandinavian Settlement in Northern Britain*, edited by Barbara E. Crawford, 92–107. London: Leicester University Press, 1995.

Gelling, Margaret. "Norse and Gaelic in medieval Man: The place-name evidence." In *The Vikings: Proceedings of the Symposium of the Faculty of Arts of Uppsala University, June 6–9, 1977*, edited by Thorsten Andersson and Karl Inge Sandred, 107–118. Stockholm: Almqvist & Wiksell, 1978.

Gelling, Peter S. "The Norse buildings at Skaill, Deerness, Orkney, and their immediate predecessor." In *The Northern and Western Isles in the Viking World: Survival, Continuity and Change*, edited by Alexander Fenton and Hermann Pálsson, 12–39. Edinburgh: John Donald, 1984.

Graham-Campbell, James. "The early Viking Age in the Irish Sea area." In *Ireland and Scandinavia in the Early Viking Age*, edited by Howard B. Clarke et al., 104–30. Dublin: Four Courts, 1998.

Graham-Campbell, James, and Colleen E. Batey. *Vikings in Scotland: An Archaeological Survey*. Edinburgh: Edinburgh University Press, 1998.

Guðmundsson, Finnbogi. "On the writing of *Orkneyinga saga*." In *The Viking Age in Caithness, Orkney and the North Atlantic*, edited by Colleen Batey et al., 204–11. Edinburgh: Edinburgh University Press, 1993.

Holman, Katherine. "Reading the runes: Epigraphy and history in the Northern Isles." In *Roman, Runes and Ogham*, edited by John Higgitt et al., 112–20. Donington: Shaun Tyas, 2001.

———. "The dating of Scandinavian runic inscriptions from the Isle of Man." In *Innskrifter og datering*, edited by Audun Dybdahl and Jan Ragnar Hagland, 43–54. Senter for middelalderstudier, Skrifter, 8. Tapir: Trondheim 1998.

Hunter, John R., Julie M. Bond, and Andrea M. Smith. "Some aspects of early Viking settlement in Orkney." In *The Viking Age in Caithness, Orkney and the North Atlantic*, edited by Colleen Batey et al., 272–84. Edinburgh: Edinburgh University Press, 1993.

Hunter, John, and Christopher D. Morris. "Recent excavations at the Brough of Birsay, Orkney." In *Proceedings of the Eighth Viking Congress, Århus, 24–31 August 1977*, edited by Hans Bekker-Nielsen, Peter Foote, and Olaf Olsen, 245–58. Odense: Odense University Press, 1981.

Jesch, Judith. "England and *Orkneyinga saga*." In *The Viking Age in Caithness, Orkney and the North Atlantic*, edited by Colleen Batey et al., 222–39. Edinburgh: Edinburgh University Press, 1993.

Johnston, Anne. "Norse settlement patterns in Coll and Tiree." In *Scandinavian Settlement in Northern Britain*, edited by Barbara E. Crawford, 108–26. London: Leicester University Press, 1995.

Kaland, Sigrid H. H. "The settlement of Westness, Rousay." In *The Viking Age in Caithness, Orkney and the North Atlantic*, edited by Colleen Batey et al., 308–17. Edinburgh: Edinburgh University Press, 1993.

Lamb, Raymond G. "Carolingian Orkney and its transformation." In *The Viking Age in Caithness, Orkney and the North Atlantic*, edited by Colleen Batey et al., 260–71. Edinburgh: Edinburgh University Press, 1993.

Liestøl, Aslak. "Runes." In *The Northern and Western Isles in the Viking World: Survival, Continuity and Change*, edited by Alexander Fenton and Hermann Pálsson, 224–38. Edinburgh: John Donald, 1984.

———. "An Iona rune stone and the world of Man and the Isles." In *The Viking Age in the Isle of Man*, edited by Christine E. Fell et al., 85–93. London: Viking Society for Northern Research, 1983.

Morris, Christopher D. "Raiders, traders and settlers: The early Viking Age in Scotland." In *Ireland and Scandinavia in the Early Viking Age*, edited by Howard B. Clarke et al., 73–103. Dublin: Four Courts, 1998.

———. "The Brough of Deerness, Orkney—Excavations 1975–7: A summary report." In *Proceedings of the Tenth Viking Congress, Larkollen, Norway, 1985*, edited by James E. Knirk, 113–29. Universitets Oldsaksamlings Skrifter, new series, 9. Oslo: Universitets Oldsaksamling, 1987.

Morris, Christopher D., James H. Barrett, and Colleen E. Batey. "The Viking and Early Settlement Archaeological Research Project: Past, present and future." In *The Twelfth Viking Congress: Developments Around the Baltic and the North Sea in the Viking Age*, edited by Björn Ambrosiani and Helen Clarke, 144–58. Birka Studies, 3. Stockholm: Riksantikvarieämbetet and Statens Historiska Museer, 1994.

Mundal, Else. "The Orkney earl and scald Torf-Einarr and his poetry." In *The Viking Age in Caithness, Orkney and the North Atlantic*, edited by Colleen Batey et al., 248–59. Edinburgh: Edinburgh University Press, 1993.

Ó Corráin, Donnchadh, "Ireland, Wales, Man, and the Hebrides." In *The Oxford Illustrated History of the Vikings*, edited by Peter Sawyer, 83–109. Oxford: Oxford University Press, 1997.

Oftedal, Magne. "Names of lakes on the Isle of Lewis in the Outer Hebrides." In *Proceedings of the Eighth Viking Congress, Århus, 24–31 August 1977*, edited by Hans Bekker-Nielsen, Peter Foote, and Olaf Olsen, 183–87. Odense: Odense University Press, 1981.

O'Meadhra, Uaininn. "Viking-Age sketches and motif-pieces from the northern earldoms." In *The Viking Age in Caithness, Orkney and the North Atlantic*, edited by Colleen Batey et al., 423–40. Edinburgh: Edinburgh University Press, 1993.

Oram, Richard D. "Scandinavian settlement in south-west Scotland with a special study of Bysbie." In *Scandinavian Settlement in Northern Britain*, edited by Barbara E. Crawford, 127–40. London: Leicester University Press, 1995.

Owen, Olwyn A., and Magnar Dalland. *Scar: A Viking Boat Burial on Sanday, Orkney*. East Linton: Tuckwell, 1999.

Owen, Olwyn A. "Tuquoy, Westray, Orkney: A challenge for the future?" In *The Viking Age in Caithness, Orkney and the North Atlantic*, edited by Colleen Batey et al., 318–39. Edinburgh: Edinburgh University Press, 1993.

Page, R. I. "Some thoughts on Manx runes." *Saga-Book* 20 (1980): 179–99.

———. "The Manx rune-stones." In *The Viking Age in the Isle of Man*. Edited by Christine E. Fell et al., 133–46. London: Viking Society for Northern Research, 1983.

Rendboe, Laurits. "The Lord's Prayer in Orkney and Shetland Norn." In *The Viking Age in Caithness, Orkney and the North Atlantic*, edited by Colleen Batey et al., 388–96. Edinburgh: Edinburgh University Press, 1993.

Ritchie, Anna. *Viking Scotland*. London: B. T. Batsford and Historic Scotland, 1993.

Smith, Brian. "Scandinavian place-names in Shetland with a study of the district of Whiteness." In *Scandinavian Settlement in Northern Britain*, edited by Barbara E. Crawford, 26–41. London: Leicester University Press, 1995.

Smyth, Alfred P. *Warlords and Holy Men: Scotland AD 80–1000*. Edinburgh: Edinburgh University Press, 1984.

Taylor, Simon. "The Scandinavians in Fife and Kinross: The onomastic evidence." In *Scandinavian Settlement in Northern Britain*, edited by Barbara E. Crawford, 141–68. London: Leicester University Press, 1995.

Thomson, William P. L. "Orkney farm-names: A re-assessment of their chronology." In *Scandinavian Settlement in Northern Britain*, edited by Barbara E. Crawford, 42–63. London: Leicester University Press, 1995.

Waugh, Doreen. "Settlement names in Caithness with particular reference to Reay parish." In *Scandinavian Settlement in Northern Britain*, edited by Barbara E. Crawford, 64–79. London: Leicester University Press, 1995.

———. "Caithness: An onomastic frontier zone." In *The Viking Age in Caithness, Orkney and the North Atlantic*, edited by Colleen Batey et al., 120–28. Edinburgh: Edinburgh University Press, 1993.

Weber, Birthe. "Iron Age combs: Analyses of raw material." In *The Twelfth Viking Congress: Developments Around the Baltic and the North Sea in the Viking Age*, edited by Björn Ambrosiani and Helen Clarke, 190–93. Birka Studies, 3. Stockholm: Riksantikvarieämbetet and Statens Historiska Museer, 1994.

D. Wales

Charles, B. G. *Old Norse Relations with Wales*. Cardiff: University of Wales Press, 1934.

Davies, Wendy. *Wales in the Early Middle Ages*. Leicester: Leicester University Press, 1982.

Graham-Campbell, James. "The early Viking Age in the Irish Sea area." In *Ireland and Scandinavia in the Early Viking Age*, edited by Howard B. Clarke et al., 104–30. Dublin: Four Courts, 1998.

Loyn, Henry. *The Vikings in Wales*. The Dorothea Coke Memorial Lecture in Northern Studies, University College London, 1976. London: University College London, 1977.

Ó Corráin, Donnchadh, "Ireland, Wales, Man, and the Hebrides." In *The Oxford Illustrated History of the Vikings*, edited by Peter Sawyer, 83–109. Oxford: Oxford University Press, 1997.

Redknap, Mark. *Vikings in Wales: An Archaeological Quest*. Cardiff: National Museums and Galleries of Wales, 2000.

E. Ireland

Abrams, Lesley. "The conversion of the Scandinavians of Dublin." *Anglo-Norman Studies* 20 (1998): 1–29.

Almqvist, Bo, and D. Greene, eds. *Proceedings of the Seventh Viking Congress Dublin, 15–21 August 1973*. Dublin: Royal Irish Academy, 1976.

Ambrosiani, Björn. "Ireland and Scandinavia in the early Viking Age: An archaeological response." In *Ireland and Scandinavia in the Early Viking Age*, edited by Howard B. Clarke et al., 405–20. Dublin: Four Courts, 1998.

Barnes, Michael P., Jan Ragnar Hagland, and R. I. Page. *The Runic Inscriptions of Viking Age Dublin*. National Museum of Ireland, Medieval Dublin Excavations 1962–81, series B, 5. Dublin: Royal Irish Academy, 1997.

Bourke, Cormac. "A view of the early Irish Church." In *The Vikings in Ireland*, edited by Anne-Christine Larsen, 77–86. Roskilde: The Viking Ship Museum, 2001.

Clarke, Howard B. "Proto-towns and towns in Ireland and Britain in the ninth and tenth centuries." In *Ireland and Scandinavia in the Early Viking*

Age, edited by Howard B. Clarke et al., 331–80. Dublin: Four Courts, 1998.

Clarke, Howard B., Máire Ní Mhaonaigh, and Raghnall Ó Floinn, eds. *Ireland and Scandinavia in the Early Viking Age*. Dublin: Four Courts, 1998.

de Paor, Liam. "The Viking towns of Ireland." In *Proceedings of the Seventh Viking Congress, Dublin, 15–21 August 1973*, edited by Bo Almqvist and David Greene, 29–37. Dublin: Royal Irish Academy, 1976.

Doherty, Charles. "The Viking impact upon Ireland." In *The Vikings in Ireland*, edited by Anne-Christine Larsen, 29–35. Roskilde: The Viking Ship Museum, 2001.

———. "The Vikings in Ireland: A review." In *Ireland and Scandinavia in the Early Viking Age*, edited by Howard B. Clarke et al., 288–330. Dublin: Four Courts, 1998.

Dolley, Michael. *Viking Coins of the Danelaw and of Dublin*. London: British Museum, 1965.

Etchingham, Colmán. *Viking Raids on Irish Church Settlements in the Ninth Century*. Maynooth Monographs, Series Minor, 1. Maynooth: The Department of Old and Middle Irish, St. Patrick's College, 1996.

Fellows-Jensen, Gillian. "Nordic names and loanwords in Ireland." In *The Vikings in Ireland*, edited by Anne-Christine Larsen, 107–13. Roskilde: The Viking Ship Museum, 2001.

———. "Scandinavian place-names of the Irish Sea province." In *Viking Treasure from the North West: The Cuerdale Hoard in its Context*, edited by James Graham-Campbell, 31–42. Liverpool: Liverpool Museum, 1992.

Graham-Campbell, James. "The early Viking Age in the Irish Sea area." In *Ireland and Scandinavia in the Early Viking Age*, edited by Howard B. Clarke et al., 104–30. Dublin: Four Courts, 1998.

———. "The Viking-Age silver hoards of Ireland." In *Proceedings of the Seventh Viking Congress, Dublin, 15–21 August 1973*, edited by Bo Almqvist and David Greene, 39–74. Dublin: Royal Irish Academy, 1976.

Greene, David. "The evidence of language and place-names in Ireland." In *The Vikings: Proceedings of the Symposium of the Faculty of Arts of Uppsala University, June 6–9, 1977*, edited by Thorsten Andersson and Karl Inge Sandred, 119–23. Stockholm: Almqvist & Wiksell, 1978.

———. "The influence of Scandinavian on Irish." In *Proceedings of the Seventh Viking Congress, Dublin, 15–21 August 1973*, edited by Bo Almqvist and David Greene, 75–82. Dublin: Royal Irish Academy, 1976.

Hagland, Jan Ragnar. "The Dublin runes." In *The Twelfth Viking Congress: Developments Around the Baltic and the North Sea in the Viking Age*, edited by Björn Ambrosiani and Helen Clarke, 302–4. Birka Studies, 3. Stockholm: Riksantikvarieämbetet and Statens Historiska Museer, 1994.

Harrison, Stephen H. "Viking graves and grave-goods in Ireland." In *The Vikings in Ireland*, edited by Anne-Christine Larsen, 61–75. Roskilde: The Viking Ship Museum, 2001.

Hughes, Kathleen. *Early Christian Ireland: Introduction to the Sources*. London: Sources of History and Hodder & Stoughton, 1972.

Kristjánsson, Jónas. "Ireland and the Irish in Icelandic tradition." In *Ireland and Scandinavia in the Early Viking Age*, edited by Howard B. Clarke et al., 259–76. Dublin: Four Courts, 1998.

Larsen, Anne-Christine. "The exhibition: The Vikings in Ireland." In *The Vikings in Ireland*, edited by Anne-Christine Larsen, 127–48. Roskilde: The Viking Ship Museum, 2001.

———, ed. *The Vikings in Ireland*. Roskilde: The Viking Ship Museum, 2001.

Larsen, Anne-Christine, and Steffen Stummann Hansen. "Viking Ireland and the Scandinavian communities in the North Atlantic." In *The Vikings in Ireland*, edited by Anne-Christine Larsen, 115–26. Roskilde: The Viking Ship Museum, 2001.

McTurk, R. W. "Ragnarr Loðbrók in the Irish annals?" In *Proceedings of the Seventh Viking Congress, Dublin, 15–21 August 1973*, edited by Bo Almqvist and David Greene, 93–123. Dublin: Royal Irish Academy, 1976.

Ní Mhaonaigh, Máire. "The Vikings in medieval Irish literature." In *The Vikings in Ireland*, edited by Anne-Christine Larsen, 99–105. Roskilde: The Viking Ship Museum, 2001.

———. "Friend and foe: Vikings in ninth- and tenth-century Irish literature." In *Ireland and Scandinavia in the Early Viking Age*, edited by Howard B. Clarke et al., 381–402. Dublin: Four Courts, 1998.

O'Brien, Elizabeth. "The location and context of Viking burials at Kilmainham and Islandbridge, Dublin." In *Ireland and Scandinavia in the Early Viking Age*, edited by Howard B. Clarke et al., 203–21. Dublin: Four Courts, 1998.

Ó Corráin, Donnchadh. "The Vikings in Ireland." In *The Vikings in Ireland*, edited by Anne-Christine Larsen, 17–27. Roskilde: The Viking Ship Museum, 2001.

———. "Viking Ireland: Afterthoughts." In *Ireland and Scandinavia in the Early Viking Age*, edited by Howard B. Clarke et al., 421–52. Dublin: Four Courts, 1998.

———. "Ireland, Wales, Man, and the Hebrides." In *The Oxford Illustrated History of the Vikings*, edited by Peter Sawyer, 83–109. Oxford: Oxford University Press, 1997.

———. "The semantic development of Old Norse *jarl* in Old and Middle Irish." In *Proceedings of the Tenth Viking Congress, Larkollen, Norway, 1985*, edited by James E. Knirk, 287–93. Universitets Oldsaksamlings Skrifter, new series, 9. Oslo: Universitets Oldsaksamling, 1987.

——— . *Ireland before the Normans*. Dublin: Gill & Macmillan, 1972.

Ó Cróinín, Dáibhí. *Early Medieval Ireland 400–1200*. London: Longman, 1995.

Ó Floinn, Raghnall. "Irish and Scandinavian art in the early medievial period." In *The Vikings in Ireland*, edited by Anne-Christine Larsen, 87–97. Roskilde: The Viking Ship Museum, 2001.

——— . "The archaeology of the early Viking Age in Ireland." In *Ireland and Scandinavia in the Early Viking Age*, edited by Howard B. Clarke et al., 131–65. Dublin: Four Courts, 1998.

Oftedal, Magne. "Scandinavian place-names in Ireland." In *Proceedings of the Seventh Viking Congress, Dublin, 15–21 August 1973*, edited by Bo Almqvist and David Greene, 125–33. Dublin: Royal Irish Academy, 1976.

Ó Riordáin, Breandán. "The High Street excavations." In *Proceedings of the Seventh Viking Congress, Dublin, 15–21 August 1973*, edited by Bo Almqvist and David Greene, 135–41. Dublin: Royal Irish Academy, 1976.

Ó Riordáin, Breandán, Elisabeth Okasha, G. R. Coope, and Hilary Murray. "Aspects of Viking Dublin." In *Proceedings of the Eighth Viking Congress, Århus, 24–31 August 1977*, edited by Hans Bekker-Nielsen, Peter Foote, and Olaf Olsen, 43–68. Odense: Odense University Press, 1981.

Rekdal, Jan Erik. "Parallels between the Norwegian legend of St. Sunniva and Irish voyage tales." In *Ireland and Scandinavia in the Early Viking Age*, edited by Howard B. Clarke et al., 277–87. Dublin: Four Courts, 1998.

Sawyer, Peter. "The Vikings and Ireland." In *Ireland in Early Medieval Europe*, edited by Dorothy Whitelock, R. McKitterick, and David N. Dumville, 345–61. Cambridge: Cambridge University Press, 1982.

Sheehan, John. "Ireland's Viking Age hoards: Sources and contacts." In *The Vikings in Ireland*, edited by Anne-Christine Larsen, 51–59. Roskilde: The Viking Ship Museum, 2001.

——— . "Early Viking Age silver hoards from Ireland and their Scandinavian elements." In *Ireland and Scandinavia in the Early Viking Age*, edited by Howard B. Clarke et al., 166–202. Dublin: Four Courts, 1998.

Smyth, Alfred P. *Scandinavian York and Dublin: The History and Archaeology of Two Related Viking Kingdoms*. Dublin: Irish Academic Press, 1987.

Wallace, Patrick. "Ireland's Viking towns." In *The Vikings in Ireland*, edited by Anne-Christine Larsen, 37–50. Roskilde: The Viking Ship Museum, 2001.

——— . "The layout of later Viking Age Dublin: Indications of its regulation and problems of continuity." In *Proceedings of the Tenth Viking Congress, Larkollen, Norway, 1985*, edited by James E. Knirk, 271–85. Universitets Oldsaksamlings Skrifter, new series, 9. Oslo: Universitets Oldsaksamling, 1987.

Walsh, Aidan. "A summary classification of Viking Age swords in Ireland." In *Ireland and Scandinavia in the Early Viking Age*, edited by Howard B. Clarke et al., 222–35. Dublin: Four Courts, 1998.

VII. CONTINENTAL WESTERN EUROPE

A. General

Morris, Christopher D. "The Viking Age in Europe." In *Vikings: The North Atlantic Saga*, edited by William W. Fitzhugh and Elisabeth I. Ward, 99–102. Washington DC: Smithsonian Institution, 2000.

Musset, Lucien. "The Scandinavians and the Western European continent." In *From Viking to Crusader: Scandinavia and Europe 800–1200*, edited by Else Roesdahl and David M. Wilson, 88–95. The 22nd Council of Europe Exhibition. Copenhagen: Nordic Council of Ministers and The Council of Europe, 1992.

B. Frankia, Normandy, and Brittany

Bates, David. *Normandy before 1066*. London: Longman, 1982.

Breese, Lauren Wood. "The persistence of Scandinavian connections in Normandy in the tenth and early eleventh centuries." *Viator* 8 (1977): 47–61.

Coupland, Simon. "The Vikings in Francia and Anglo-Saxon England to 911." In *The New Cambridge Medieval History*, vol. 2, *c*. 700–*c*. 900, edited by Rosamond McKitterick, 190–201. Cambridge: Cambridge University Press, 1995.

Douglas, D. C. "Rollo of Normandy." *English Historical Review* 57 (1942): 417–36.

———. "The rise of Normandy." *Proceedings of the British Academy* 33 (1947): 101–30.

Fellows-Jensen, Gillian. "Scandinavian place-names and Viking settlement in Normandy." *Namn och bygd* 76 (1988): 113–37.

The Gesta Normannorum Ducum of William of Jumièges, Orderic Vitalis, and Robert of Torigni. Edited and translated by Elisabeth M. C. van Houts. Oxford: Clarendon Press, 1992–95.

Gibson, Margaret T., and Janet Nelson, eds. *Charles the Bald: Court and Kingdom*. 2nd rev. ed. Aldershot: Variorum, 1990.

van Houts, Elisabeth, trans. and ed. *The Normans in Europe*. Manchester: Manchester University Press, 2000.

McKitterick, Rosamond. *The Frankish Kingdoms under the Carolingians 751–987*. London: Longman, 1983.

Nelson, Janet L. "The Frankish empire." In *The Oxford Illustrated History of the Vikings*, edited by Peter Sawyer, 19–47. Oxford: Oxford University Press, 1997.

———. *Charles the Bald*. London: Longman, 1992.

Price, Neil S. "'Laid waste, plundered, and burned': Vikings in Frankia." In *Vikings: The North Atlantic Saga*, edited by William W. Fitzhugh and Elisabeth I. Ward, 116–26. Washington DC: Smithsonian Institution, 2000.

———. "The Vikings in Brittany." *Saga-Book* 22 (1989): 321–440.

Searle, Eleanor. "Fact and pattern in heroic history: Dudo of St. Quentin." *Viator* 15 (1984): 119–37.

———. *Predatory Kinship and the Creation of Norman Power, 840–1066*. Berkeley: University of California Press, 1988.

Wallace-Hadrill, J. M. *The Vikings in Francia*. The Stenton Lecture, 1974. Reading: Department of History, University of Reading, 1975.

C. Spain and the Meditteranean

Stefansson, Jón, trans. "The Vikings in Spain from Arabic (Moorish) and Spanish sources." *Saga-Book* 6 (1909): 31–46.

VIII. EASTERN EUROPE

A. General

Jansson, Ingmar, with Evgenij N. Nosov. "The way to the East." In *From Viking to Crusader: Scandinavia and Europe 800–1200*, edited by Else Roesdahl and David M. Wilson, 74–83. The 22nd Council of Europe Exhibition. Copenhagen: Nordic Council of Ministers and The Council of Europe, 1992.

Melnikova, Elena A. "Runic inscriptions as a source for the relation of northern and eastern Europe in the Middle Ages." In *Runeninschriften als Quellen interdisziplinärer Forschung*, edited by Klaus Düwel, 647–59. Berlin: Walter de Gruyter, 1998.

———. *The Eastern World of the Vikings: Eight Essays about Scandinavia and Eastern Europe in the Early Middle Ages*. Gothenburg Old Norse Studies, 1. Gothenburg: Litteraturvetenskapliga institutionen, Gothenburg University, 1996.

Noonan, Thomas S. "The Vikings in the East: Coins and commerce." In *The Twelfth Viking Congress: Developments Around the Baltic and the North Sea in the Viking Age*, edited by Björn Ambrosiani and Helen Clarke, 215–36. Birka Studies, 3. Stockholm: Riksantikvarieämbetet and Statens Historiska Museer, 1994.

B. Russia

Avdusin, D. "Smolensk and the Varangians according to the archaeological data." *Norwegian Archaeological Review* 2 (1969): 52–62.

Brisbane, Mark A., ed. *The Archaeology of Novgorod, Russia: Recent Results from the Town and Its Hinterland*. Lincoln: Society for Medieval Archaeology, 1992.

Callmer, Johan. "The archaeology of Kiev to the end of the earliest urban phase." *Harvard Ukrainian Studies* 11 (1987): 323–53.

Constantine Porphyrogenitos. *De Administrando Imperio*. Edited by G. Moravcsik, translated by R. J. H. Jenkins. Washington DC: Dumbarton Oaks Center for Byzantine Studies, 1967.

Cross, Samuel H. "Yaroslav the Wise in Norse tradition." *Speculum* 4 (1929): 177–97.

Dolukhanov, Pavel Markovich. *The Early Slavs: Eastern Europe from the Initial Settlement to the Kievan Rus*. London: Longman, 1996.

Franklin, Simon, and Jonathan Shepard. *The Emergence of Rus, 750–1200*. London: Longman, 1996.

Jansson, Ingmar, with Evgenij N. Nosov. "The way to the East." In *From Viking to Crusader: Scandinavia and Europe 800–1200*, edited by Else Roesdahl and David M. Wilson, 74–83. The 22nd Council of Europe Exhibition. Copenhagen: Nordic Council of Ministers and The Council of Europe, 1992.

Klejn, L. S. "Soviet archaeology and the role of the Vikings in the early history of the Slavs." *Norwegian Archaeological Review* 6 (1973): 1–4.

Lebedev, G. S., and V. A. Nazarenko. "The connections between Russians and Scandinavians in the 9th–11th centuries." *Norwegian Archaeological Review* 6 (1973): 5–9.

Lichacev, D. S. "The legend of the calling-in of the Varangians, and political purposes in Russian chronicle-writing from the second half of the eleventh to the the beginning of the thirteenth century." In *Varangian Problems*, edited by K. R. Schmidt, 170–85. Scando-Slavica Supplementum, 1. Copenhagen: Munskgaard, 1970.

Medieval Russia's Epics, Chronicles, and Tales. Rev. ed. Translated and edited by Serge A. Zenkovsky. New York: Penguin, 1974.

Melnikova, Elena. "New finds of Scandinavian runic inscriptions from the USSR." In *Runor och Runinskrifter*, 163–73. Stockholm: Almqvist & Wiksell, 1987.

Noonan, Thomas S. "Scandinavians in European Russia." In *The Oxford Illustrated History of the Vikings*, edited by Peter Sawyer, 134–55. Oxford: Oxford University Press, 1997.

———. "The Vikings in the East: Coins and commerce." In *The Twelfth Viking Congress: Developments Around the Baltic and the North Sea in the Viking Age*, edited by Björn Ambrosiani and Helen Clarke, 215–36. Birka Studies, 3. Stockholm: Riksantikvarieämbetet and Statens Historiska Museer, 1994.

———. "The Vikings and Russia: Some new directions and approaches to an old problem." In *Social Approaches to Viking Studies*, edited by Ross Samson, 201–06. Glasgow: Cruithne, 1991.

———. "Kievan Rus." In *Dictionary of the Middle Ages*, edited by Joseph R. Strayer, vol. 7, 244–52. New York: Scribner, 1982–89.

Pritzak, O. *The Origin of Rus I: Old Scandinavian Sources Other than the Sagas*. Cambridge, MA: Harvard Ukrainian Research Institute, 1981.

Russian Primary Chronicle: Laurentian Text. Edited and translated by Samuel H. Cross and Olgerd P. Sherbowitz-Wetzor. Cambridge, MA: Medieval Academy of America, 1953.

Schmidt, K. R. "The Varangian problem: A brief history of the controversy." In *Varangian Problems*, edited by K. R. Schmidt, 7–20. Scando-Slavica Supplementum, 1. Copenhagen: Munskgaard, 1970.

———, ed. *Varangian Problems: Report on the First International Symposium on the Theme 'The Eastern Connections of the Nordic Peoples in the Viking Period and Early Middle Ages'*. Scando-Slavica Supplementum, 1. Copenhagen: Munskgaard, 1970.

Shepard, Jonathan. "The Rhos guests of Louis the Pious: Whence and wherefore?" *Early Medieval Europe* 4 (1995): 41–60.

———. "Yngvarr's expedition to the east and a Russian inscribed stone cross." *Saga-Book* 21 (1984–85): 222–92.

Smyser, H. M. "Ibn Fadlan's account of the Rus with some commentary and some allusions to Beowulf." In *Medieval and Linguistic Studies in Honor of Francis Peabody Magoun, Jr.*, edited by Jess B. Bessinger Jr. and Robert P. Creed, 92–119. London: Allen & Unwin, 1965.

Stalsberg, Anne. "The Scandinavian Viking Age finds in Rus: Overview and analysis." *Bericht der Römisch-Germanischen Kommission* 69 (1988): 448–71.

Vasiliev, Alexander A. *The Russian Attack on Constantinople in 860*. Cambridge, MA: Medieval Academy of America, 1946.

Vikings in Russia: Yngvar's Saga *and* Eymund's Saga. Translated by Hermann Pálsson and Paul Edwards. Edinburgh: Polygon, 1989.

C. Byzantium

Blöndal, Sigfús, and Benedikt S. Benedikz. *The Varangians of Byzantium*. Cambridge: Cambridge University Press, 1978.

Ellis Davidson, H. R. *The Viking Road to Byzantium*. London: Allen & Unwin, 1976.

Schmidt, K. R., ed. *Varangian Problems: Report on the First International Symposium on the Theme 'The Eastern Connections of the Nordic Peoples in the Viking Period and Early Middle Ages'*. Scando-Slavica Supplementum, 1. Copenhagen: Munskgaard, 1970.

Vasiliev, Alexander A. *The Russian Attack on Constantinople in 860*. Cambridge, MA: Medieval Academy of America, 1946.

IX. SHIPS AND WARFARE

A. Ships

Bill, Jan. "Ships and seamanship." In *The Oxford Illustrated History of the Vikings*, edited by Peter Sawyer, 182–201. Oxford: Oxford University Press, 1997.

Binns, Alan L. *Viking Voyagers: Then and Now*. London: Heinemann, 1980.

———. "The ships of the vikings, were they 'Viking ships'?" In *Proceedings of the Eighth Viking Congress, Århus, 24–31 August 1977*, edited by Hans Bekker-Nielsen, Peter Foote, and Olaf Olsen, 287–94. Odense: Odense University Press, 1981.

Bonde, Niels, and Arne Emil Christensen. "Dendrochronological dating of the Viking Age ship burials at Oseberg, Gokstad and Tune, Norway." *Antiquity* 67 (1993): 575–83.

Brøgger, A. W., and Haakon Shetelig. *The Viking Ships: Their Ancestry and Evolution*. Oslo: Dreyer, 1951.

Christensen, Arne Emil. "Ships and navigation." In *Vikings: The North Atlantic Saga*, edited by William W. Fitzhugh and Elisabeth I. Ward, 86–97. Washington DC: Smithsonian Institution, 2000.

———. "Boats and boat-building in western Norway and the Islands." In *The Northern and Western Isles in the Viking World: Survival, Continuity and Change*, edited by Alexander Fenton and Hermann Pálsson, 85–95. Edinburgh: John Donald, 1984.

———. "Viking Age ships and shipbuilding." *Norwegian Archaeological Review* 15 (1982): 19–28.

Crumlin-Pedersen, Ole. "Ship types and sizes AD 800–1400." In *Aspects of Maritime Scandinavia AD 200–1200*, edited by Ole Crumlin-Pedersen, 69–82. Roskilde: Roskilde Ship Museum, 1991.

———, ed. *Aspects of Maritime Scandinavia AD 200–1200*. Roskilde: Roskilde Ship Museum, 1991.

———. "Viking shipbuilding and seamanship." In *Proceedings of the Eighth Viking Congress, Århus, 24–31 August 1977*, edited by Hans Bekker-Nielsen,

Peter Foote, and Olaf Olsen, 271–86. Odense: Odense University Press, 1981.

——. "The ships of the Vikings." In *The Vikings: Proceedings of the Symposium of the Faculty of Arts of Uppsala University, June 6–9, 1977*, edited by Thorsten Andersson and Karl Inge Sandred, 32–41. Stockholm: Almqvist & Wiksell, 1978.

Crumlin-Pedersen, Ole, Mogens Schou Jørgensen, and Torsten Edgren. "Ships and travel." In *From Viking to Crusader: Scandinavia and Europe 800–1200*, edited by Else Roesdahl and David M. Wilson, 42–51. The 22nd Council of Europe Exhibition. Copenhagen: Nordic Council of Ministers and The Council of Europe, 1992.

Hallberg, Peter. "The ship: Reality and image in Old Norse poetry." In *The Vikings: Proceedings of the Symposium of the Faculty of Arts of Uppsala University, June 6–9, 1977*, edited by Thorsten Andersson and Karl Inge Sandred, 42–56. Stockholm: Almqvist & Wiksell, 1978.

Jesch, Judith. *Ships and Men in the Late Viking Age*. Woodbridge: Boydell & Brewer, 2001.

McGrail, Seán. *Ancient Boats in North-West Europe: The Archaeology of Water Transport to AD 1500*. London: Longman, 1987.

Olsen, Olaf, and Ole Crumlin-Pedersen. *Five Viking Ships from Roskilde Fjord*. Copenhagen: National Museum, 1978.

B. Armor, Weapons, and Battles

DeVries, Kelly. *The Norwegian Invasion of England in 1066*. Woodbridge: Boydell, 1999.

Griffith, Paddy. *The Viking Art of War*. London: Greenhill, 1995.

Heath, Ian, and Angus McBride. *The Vikings*. Elite Series, 3. London: Osprey, 1985.

Lehtosalo-Hilander, Pirkko-Liisa. "Weapons and their use." In *From Viking to Crusader: Scandinavia and Europe 800–1200*, edited by Else Roesdahl and David M. Wilson, 194–95. The 22nd Council of Europe Exhibition. Copenhagen: Nordic Council of Ministers and The Council of Europe, 1992.

Martens, Irmelin. "Norwegian Viking Age weapons: Some questions concerning their production and distribution." In *The Twelfth Viking Congress: Developments Around the Baltic and the North Sea in the Viking Age*, edited by Björn Ambrosiani and Helen Clarke, 180–82. Birka Studies, 3. Stockholm: Riksantikvarieämbetet and Statens Historiska Museer, 1994.

Stalsberg, Anne. "The Russian-Norwegian sword project." In *The Twelfth Viking Congress: Developments Around the Baltic and the North Sea in the Viking Age*, edited by Björn Ambrosiani and Helen Clarke, 183–89. Birka

Studies, 3. Stockholm: Riksantikvarieämbetet and Statens Historiska Museer, 1994.

Walsh, Aidan. "A summary classification of Viking Age swords in Ireland." In *Ireland and Scandinavia in the Early Viking Age*, edited by Howard B. Clarke et al., 222–35. Dublin: Four Courts, 1998.

C. Military Organization

Hooper, Nicholas. "Military developments in the reign of Cnut." In *The Reign of Cnut: King of England, Denmark and Norway*, edited by Alexander R. Rumble, 89–100. London: Leicester University Press, 1994.

Jørgensen, Anne Nørgård, and Birthe L. Clausen. *Military Aspects of Scandinavian Society in a European Perspective, AD 1–1300*. Studies in Archaeology and History, 2. Copenhagen: National Museum, 1997.

Lund, Niels. "If the Vikings knew a *leding*, what was it like?" In *The Twelfth Viking Congress: Developments Around the Baltic and the North Sea in the Viking Age*, edited by Björn Ambrosiani and Helen Clarke, 100–05. Birka Studies, 3. Stockholm: Riksantikvarieämbetet and Statens Historiska Museer, 1994.

———. "Danish military organization." In *The Battle of Maldon: Fiction and Fact*, edited by Janet Cooper, 109–26. London: Hambledon, 1993.

———. "The armies of Swein Forkbeard and Cnut: 'leding' or 'lið'?" *Anglo-Saxon England* 15 (1986): 105–18.

X. SOCIETY

Arwidsson, Greta. "Viking society in central Sweden: Traditions, organization and economy." In *The Vikings: Proceedings of the Symposium of the Faculty of Arts of Uppsala University, June 6–9, 1977*, edited by Thorsten Andersson and Karl Inge Sandred, 154–60. Stockholm: Almqvist & Wiksell, 1978.

Brink, Stefan. "Social order in the early Scandinavian landscape." In *Settlement and Landscape: Proceedings of a Conference in Århus, Denmark, May 4–7 1998*, edited by Charlotte Fabech and Jytte Ringtved, 423–39. Højbjerg: Jutland Archaeological Society, 1999.

Byock, Jesse L. *Medieval Iceland: Society, Sagas, and Power*. Enfield: Hisarlik, 1993.

Christophersen, Axel. "Drengs, thegns, landmen and kings." *Meddelanden från Lunds Universitets Historiska Museum* 4 (1982): 115–34.

Dommasnes, Liv Helga. "Women, kinship, and the basis of power in the Norwegian Viking Age." In *Social Approaches to Viking Studies*, edited by Ross Samson, 65–73. Glasgow: Cruithne, 1991.

Einarsson, B. "On the status of free men in society and sagas." *Mediaeval Scandinavia* 7 (1974): 45–55.

Fenger, Ole. "Scandinavian society." In *From Viking to Crusader: Scandinavia and Europe 800–1200*, edited by Else Roesdahl and David M. Wilson, 120–25. The 22nd Council of Europe Exhibition. Copenhagen: Nordic Council of Ministers and The Council of Europe, 1992.

Jesch, Judith. *Ships and Men in the Late Viking Age*. Woodbridge: Boydell & Brewer, 2001.

——. "Women and ships in the Viking world." *Northern Studies* 36 (2001): 1–20.

——. *Women in the Viking Age*. Woodbridge: Boydell & Brewer, 1991.

——. "Skaldic verse and Viking semantics." In *Viking Revaluations*, edited by Anthony Faulkes and Richard Perkins, 160–71. London: Viking Society for Northern Research, 1993.

——. "Runic inscriptions and social history: Some problems of method." In *Proceedings of the Third International Symposium on Runes and Runic Inscriptions, Grindaheim, Norway, 8–12 August 1990*, edited by James E. Knirk, 149–62. Runrön, 9. Uppsala: Institutionen för nordiska språk, Uppsala universitet, 1994.

Jochens, Jenny. *Women in Old Norse Society*. Ithaca, NY: Cornell University Press, 1995.

Jørgensen, Lars. "Political organization and social life." In *Vikings: The North Atlantic Saga*, edited by William W. Fitzhugh and Elisabeth I. Ward, 72–85. Washington DC: Smithsonian Institution, 2000.

Karlsson, Gunnar. "A century of research on early Icelandic society." In *Viking Revaluations*, edited by Anthony Faulkes and Richard Perkins, 15–25. London: Viking Society for Northern Research, 1993.

Karras, Ruth Mazo. *Slavery and Society in Medieval Scandinavia*. New Haven, CT: Yale University Press, 1988.

——. "Concubinage and slavery in the Viking Age." *Scandinavian Studies* 62 (1990): 141–62.

Kristensen, Anne K. G. "Danelaw institutions and Danish society in the Viking Age: *Sochemanni, liberi homines*, and *Königsfreie*." *Mediaeval Scandinavia* 8 (1975): 27–85.

Page, R. I. "Scandinavian society 800–1100: The contribution of runic studies." In *Viking Revaluations*, edited by Anthony Faulkes and Richard Perkins, 145–59. London: Viking Society for Northern Research, 1993.

Samson, Ross, ed. *Social Approaches to Viking Studies*. Glasgow: Cruithne, 1991.

Sawyer, Birgit. *The Viking-Age Rune-Stones: Custom and Commemoration in Early Medieval Scandinavia*. Oxford: Oxford University Press, 2000.

———. "Viking Age rune-stones as a source for legal history." In *Runeninschriften als Quellen interdisziplinärer Forschung*, edited by Klaus Düwel, 766–77. Berlin: Walter de Gruyter, 1998.

———. "Women as bridge-builders: The role of women in Viking-Age Scandinavia." In *People and Places in Northern Europe 500–1600: Essays in Honour of Peter Hayes Sawyer*, edited by Ian Wood and Niels Lund, 211–24. Woodbridge: Boydell, 1991.

———. *Property and Inheritance in Viking Scandinavia: The Runic Evidence*. Alingsås: Viktoria, 1988.

Skyum-Nielsen, Niels. "Nordic slavery in an international setting." *Mediaeval Scandinavia* 11 (1978–79): 126–48.

Sørensen, Preben Meulengracht. "Social institutions and belief systems of medieval Iceland (*c*. 870–1400) and their relations to literary production." In *Old Icelandic Literature and Society*, edited by Margaret Clunies Ross, 8–29. Cambridge: Cambridge University Press, 2000.

———. *Saga and Society: An Introduction to Old Norse Literature*. Odense: Odense University Press, 1993.

Stalsberg, Anne. "Women as actors in North European Viking Age trade." In *Social Approaches to Viking Studies*, edited by Ross Samson, 75–83. Glasgow: Cruithne, 1991.

Strid, Jan Paul. "Runic Swedish drengs and thegns." In *Runor och runinskrifter. Föredrag vid Rikantikvarieämbetets och Vitterhetsakademiens symposium 8–11 september 1985*, 301–16. Stockholm: Almqvist & Wiksell, 1987.

Syrett, Martin. "Drengs and thegns again." *Saga-Book* 25:3 (2000): 243–71.

Vestergaard, Torben A. "Marriage exchange and social structure in Old Norse mythology." In *Social Approaches to Viking Studies*, edited by Ross Samson, 21–34. Glasgow: Cruithne, 1991.

———. "The system of kinship in early Norwegian law." *Mediaeval Scandinavia* 12 (1988): 160–93.

XI. ECONOMY

A. General

Kaland, Sigrid H. H., and Irmelin Martens. "Farming and daily life." In *Vikings: The North Atlantic Saga*, edited by William W. Fitzhugh and Elisabeth I. Ward, 42–54. Washington DC: Smithsonian Institution, 2000.

Morris, Christopher D. "The Vikings in the British Isles: Some aspects of their settlement and economy." In *The Vikings*, edited by R. T. Farrell, 70–94. London: Phillimore, 1982.

Sawyer, Peter. "Resources and settlements." In *From Viking to Crusader: Scandinavia and Europe 800–1200*, edited by Else Roesdahl and David M. Wilson, 126–35. The 22nd Council of Europe Exhibition. Copenhagen: Nordic Council of Ministers and The Council of Europe, 1992.

B. Towns, Trade, and Crafts

Ambrosiani, Björn. "Royal manors and towns in central Sweden." In *Proceedings of the Tenth Viking Congress, Larkollen, Norway, 1985*, edited by James E. Knirk, 247–53. Universitets Oldsaksamlings Skrifter, new series, 9. Oslo: Universitets Oldsaksamling, 1987.

———. "Birka: A planted town serving an increasing agricultural population." In *Proceedings of the Eighth Viking Congress, Århus, 24–31 August 1977*, edited by Hans Bekker-Nielsen, Peter Foote, and Olaf Olsen, 19–24. Odense: Odense University Press, 1981.

Ambrosiani, Björn, and Helen Clarke, eds. *Early Investigations and Future Plans*. Birka Studies, 1. Stockholm: Riksantikvarieämbetet och Statens Historiska Museer, 1992.

———. *Investigations in the Black Earth 1990*. Birka Studies, 2. Stockholm: Riksantikvarieämbetet och Statens Historiska Museer, 1995.

Arwidsson, Greta. "Viking society in central Sweden: Traditions, organization and economy." In *The Vikings: Proceedings of the Symposium of the Faculty of Arts of Uppsala University, June 6–9, 1977*, edited by Thorsten Andersson and Karl Inge Sandred, 154–60. Stockholm: Almqvist & Wiksell, 1978.

Avdusin, D. "Smolensk and the Varangians according to the archaeological data." *Norwegian Archaeological Review* 2 (1969): 52–62.

Blindheim, Charlotte. "The emergence of urban communities in Viking Age Scandinavia." In *The Vikings*, edited by R. T. Farrell, 42–69. London: Phillimore, 1982.

———. "Trade problems in the Viking Age: Some reflections on insular metalwork found in Norwegian graves of the Viking Age." In *The Vikings: Proceedings of the Symposium of the Faculty of Arts of Uppsala University, June 6–9, 1977*, edited by Thorsten Andersson and Karl Inge Sandred, 166–76. Stockholm: Almqvist & Wiksell, 1978.

Brisbane, Mark A., ed. *The Archaeology of Novgorod, Russia: Recent Results from the Town and its Hinterland*. Lincoln: Society for Medieval Archaeology, 1992.

Callmer, Johan. "Urbanization in Scandinavia and the Baltic region *c*. AD 700–1100: Trading places, centres and early urban sites." In *The Twelfth*

Viking Congress: Developments Around the Baltic and the North Sea in the Viking Age, edited by Björn Ambrosiani and Helen Clarke, 50–90. Birka Studies, 3. Stockholm: Riksantikvarieämbetet and Statens Historiska Museer, 1994.

———. "The archaeology of Kiev to the end of the earliest urban phase." *Harvard Ukrainian Studies* 11 (1987): 323–53.

Clarke, Helen, and Björn Ambrosiani. *Towns in the Viking Age*. Rev. ed. London: Leicester University Press, 1995.

Clarke, Howard B. "Proto-towns and towns in Ireland and Britain in the ninth and tenth centuries." In *Ireland and Scandinavia in the Early Viking Age*, edited by Howard B. Clarke et al., 331–80. Dublin: Four Courts, 1998.

Feveile, Claus. "The latest news from Viking Age Ribe: Archaeological excavations 1993." In *The Twelfth Viking Congress: Developments Around the Baltic and the North Sea in the Viking Age*, edited by Björn Ambrosiani and Helen Clarke, 91–99. Birka Studies, 3. Stockholm: Riksantikvarieämbetet and Statens Historiska Museer, 1994.

Helle, Knut. "Descriptions of Nordic towns and town-like settlements in early literature." In *The Twelfth Viking Congress: Developments Around the Baltic and the North Sea in the Viking Age*, edited by Björn Ambrosiani and Helen Clarke, 20–31. Birka Studies, 3. Stockholm: Riksantikvarieämbetet and Statens Historiska Museer, 1994.

Jensen, Stig. *The Vikings of Ribe*. Ribe: Den antikvariske Samling, 1991.

Martens, Irmelin. "Iron extraction, settlement and trade in the Viking and early Middle Ages in south Norway." In *Proceedings of the Tenth Viking Congress, Larkollen, Norway, 1985*, edited by James E. Knirk, 69–80. Universitets Oldsaksamlings Skrifter, new series, 9. Oslo: Universitets Oldsaksamling, 1987.

Noonan, Thomas S. "The Vikings in the East: Coins and commerce." In *The Twelfth Viking Congress: Developments Around the Baltic and the North Sea in the Viking Age*, edited by Björn Ambrosiani and Helen Clarke, 215–36. Birka Studies, 3. Stockholm: Riksantikvarieämbetet and Statens Historiska Museer, 1994.

Ó Riordáin, Breandán. "The High Street excavations." In *Proceedings of the Seventh Viking Congress, Dublin, 15–21 August 1973*, edited by Bo Almqvist and David Greene, 135–41. Dublin: Royal Irish Academy, 1976.

Ó Riordáin, Breandán, Elisabeth Okasha, G. R. Coope, and Hilary Murray. "Aspects of Viking Dublin." In *Proceedings of the Eighth Viking Congress, Århus, 24–31 August 1977*, edited by Hans Bekker-Nielsen, Peter Foote, and Olaf Olsen, 43–68. Odense: Odense University Press, 1981.

de Paor, Liam. "The Viking towns of Ireland." In *Proceedings of the Seventh Viking Congress, Dublin, 15–21 August 1973*, edited by Bo Almqvist and David Greene, 29–37. Dublin: Royal Irish Academy, 1976.

Resi, Heid Gjøstein. "Reflections on Viking Age local trade in stone products." In *Proceedings of the Tenth Viking Congress, Larkollen, Norway, 1985*, edited by James E. Knirk, 95–102. Universitets Oldsaksamlings Skrifter, new series, 9. Oslo: Universitets Oldsaksamling, 1987.

Sawyer, P. H. "Wics, kings and Vikings." In *The Vikings: Proceedings of the Symposium of the Faculty of Arts of Uppsala University, June 6–9, 1977*, edited by Thorsten Andersson and Karl Inge Sandred, 23–31. Stockholm: Almqvist & Wiksell, 1978.

Skovgaard-Petersen, Inge. "The historical context of the first towns in northern and eastern Europe." In *Proceedings of the Eighth Viking Congress, Århus, 24–31 August* 1977, edited by Hans Bekker-Nielsen, Peter Foote, and Olaf Olsen, 9–18. Odense: Odense University Press, 1981.

Stalsberg, Anne. "Women as actors in North European Viking Age trade." In *Social Approaches to Viking Studies*, edited by Ross Samson, 75–83. Glasgow: Cruithne, 1991.

Wallace, Patrick. "Ireland's Viking towns." In *The Vikings in Ireland*, edited by Anne-Christine Larsen, 37–50. Roskilde: The Viking Ship Museum, 2001.

———. "The layout of later Viking Age Dublin: Indications of its regulation and problems of continuity." In *Proceedings of the Tenth Viking Congress, Larkollen, Norway, 1985*, edited by James E. Knirk, 271–85. Universitets Oldsaksamlings Skrifter, new series, 9. Oslo: Universitets Oldsaksamling, 1987.

C. Coins, Hoards, Jewelry, and Treasure

Blackburn, Mark. "Expansion and control: Aspects of Anglo-Scandinavian minting south of the Humber." In *Vikings and the Danelaw: Select Papers from the Proceedings of the Thirteenth Viking Congress*, edited by James Graham-Campbell et al., 125–42. Oxford: Oxbow, 2001.

Blackburn, Mark, and D. M. Metcalf. *Viking-Age Coinage in Northern Lands*. BAR International Series, 122. Oxford: B.A.R., 1981.

Blindheim, Charlotte. "Trade problems in the Viking Age: Some reflections on insular metalwork found in Norwegian graves of the Viking Age." In *The Vikings: Proceedings of the Symposium of the Faculty of Arts of Uppsala University, June 6–9, 1977*, edited by Thorsten Andersson and Karl Inge Sandred, 166–76. Stockholm: Almqvist & Wiksell, 1978.

Blindheim, Martin. "The Ranuaik reliquary in Copenhagen: A short study." In *Proceedings of the Tenth Viking Congress, Larkollen, Norway, 1985*, edited by James E. Knirk, 203–18. Universitets Oldsaksamlings Skrifter, new series, 9. Oslo: Universitets Oldsaksamling, 1987.

Dolley, Michael. *Viking Coins of the Danelaw and of Dublin*. London: British Museum, 1965.

Gaimster, Märit. "Money and media in Viking Age Scandinavia." In *Social Approaches to Viking Studies*, edited by Ross Samson, 113–22. Glasgow: Cruithne, 1991.

Graham-Campbell, James. "Western pennanular brooches and their Viking Age copies in Norway: A new classification." In *Proceedings of the Tenth Viking Congress, Larkollen, Norway, 1985*, edited by James E. Knirk, 231–46. Universitets Oldsaksamlings Skrifter, new series, 9. Oslo: Universitets Oldsaksamling, 1987.

———. "Viking silver hoards: An introduction." In *The Vikings*, edited by R. T. Farrell, 32–41. London: Phillimore, 1982.

———. "The Viking-Age silver hoards of Ireland." In *Proceedings of the Seventh Viking Congress, Dublin, 15–21 August 1973*, edited by Bo Almqvist and David Greene, 39–74. Dublin: Royal Irish Academy, 1976.

Jensen, Jørgen Steen. "Do the coin finds of recent years change our ideas about the character of monetary circulation in Denmark in the Viking Age?" In *The Twelfth Viking Congress: Developments Around the Baltic and the North Sea in the Viking Age*, edited by Björn Ambrosiani and Helen Clarke, 237–41. Birka Studies, 3. Stockholm: Riksantikvarieämbetet and Statens Historiska Museer, 1994.

Lagerqvist, Lars O. "Scandinavian coins." In *From Viking to Crusader: Scandinavia and Europe 800–1200*, edited by Else Roesdahl and David M. Wilson, 220–21. The 22nd Council of Europe Exhibition. Copenhagen: Nordic Council of Ministers and The Council of Europe, 1992.

Malmer, Brita. *King Canute's Coinage in the Northern Countries*. Dorothea Coke Memorial Lecture. London: Viking Society for Northern Research, 1974.

Metcalf, D. M. "The beginnings of coinage in the North Sea coastlands: A Pirenne-like hypothesis." In *The Twelfth Viking Congress: Developments Around the Baltic and the North Sea in the Viking Age*, edited by Björn Ambrosiani and Helen Clarke, 196–214. Birka Studies, 3. Stockholm: Riksantikvarieämbetet and Statens Historiska Museer, 1994.

Noonan, Thomas S. "The Vikings in the East: Coins and commerce." In *The Twelfth Viking Congress: Developments Around the Baltic and the North Sea in the Viking Age*, edited by Björn Ambrosiani and Helen Clarke, 215–36. Birka Studies, 3. Stockholm: Riksantikvarieämbetet and Statens Historiska Museer, 1994.

O'Hara, Michael Dennis (with a contribution by Elizabeth Pirie and the collaboration of Peter Thornton-Pett). "An iron reverse die of the reign of Cnut." In *The Reign of Cnut: King of England, Denmark and Norway*, edited by Alexander R. Rumble, 231–82. London: Leicester University Press, 1994.

Sheehan, John. "Ireland's Viking Age hoards: Sources and contacts." In *The Vikings in Ireland*, edited by Anne-Christine Larsen, 51–59. Roskilde: The Viking Ship Museum, 2001.

———. "Early Viking Age silver hoards from Ireland and their Scandinavian elements." In *Ireland and Scandinavia in the Early Viking Age*, edited by Howard B. Clarke et al., 166–202. Dublin: Four Courts, 1998.

Skaare, Kolbjørn. *Coins and Coinage in Viking-Age Norway*. Oslo: Universitetsforlaget, 1976.

———. "Mints in Viking-Age Scandinavia." In *Proceedings of the Eighth Viking Congress, Århus, 24–31 August* 1977, edited by Hans Bekker-Nielsen, Peter Foote, and Olaf Olsen, 37–42. Odense: Odense University Press, 1981.

Thomas, Gabor. "Anglo-Scandinavian metalwork from the Danelaw: Exploring social and cultural interaction." In *Cultures in Contact: Scandinavian Settlement in England in the Ninth and Tenth Centuries*, edited by Dawn M. Hadley and Julian D. Richards, 237–55. Turnhout: Brepols, 2000.

XII. RELIGION AND MYTHOLOGY

Abrams, Lesley. "The conversion of the Danelaw." In *Vikings and the Danelaw: Select Papers from the Proceedings of the Thirteenth Viking Congress*, edited by James Graham-Campbell et al., 31–44. Oxford: Oxbow, 2001.

———. "Conversion and assimilation." In *Cultures in Contact: Scandinavian Settlement in England in the Ninth and Tenth Centuries*, edited by Dawn M. Hadley and Julian D. Richards, 135–53. Turnhout: Brepols, 2000.

———. "The conversion of the Scandinavians of Dublin." *Anglo-Norman Studies* 20 (1998): 1–29.

Aðalsteinsson, Jón Hnefill. *Under the Cloak: The Acceptance of Christianity in Iceland with Particular Reference to the Attitudes Prevailing at the Time*. Uppsala: Etnologiska institutionen, Uppsala universitet, 1978.

Clunies Ross, Margaret. "The conservation and reinterpretation of myth in medieval Icelandic writings." In *Old Icelandic Literature and Society*, edited by Margaret Clunies Ross, 116–39. Cambridge: Cambridge University Press, 2000.

———. "Pseudo-procreation myths in Old Norse: An anthropological approach." In *Social Approaches to Viking Studies*, edited by Ross Samson, 35–44. Glasgow: Cruithne, 1991.

Crawford, Barbara E., ed. *Conversion and Christianity in the North Sea World*. St. John's House Publications, 8. St. Andrews: Committee for Dark Ages Studies, University of St. Andrews, 1998.

Dronke, Ursula. "[Pagan beliefs and Christian impact:] The contribution of Eddic studies." In *Viking Revaluations*, edited by Anthony Faulkes and

Richard Perkins, 121–27. London: Viking Society for Northern Research, 1993.

Edwards, Diana. "Christian and pagan references in eleventh-century Norse poetry: The case of Arnórr jarlaskáld." *Saga-Book* 21:1–2 (1982–83): 34–53.

Ellis Davidson, H. R. *Gods and Myths of Northern Europe*. Harmondsworth: Penguin, 1964.

Fell, Christine E. "Anglo-Saxon saints in Old Norse sources and vice versa." In *Proceedings of the Eighth Viking Congress, Århus, 24–31 August 1977*, edited by Hans Bekker-Nielsen, Peter Foote, and Olaf Olsen, 95–106. Odense: Odense University Press, 1981.

Fidjestøl, Bjarne. "[Pagan beliefs and Christian impact:] The contribution of scaldic studies." In *Viking Revaluations*, edited by Anthony Faulkes and Richard Perkins, 100–20. London: Viking Society for Northern Research, 1993.

Foote, Peter G. "Historical studies: Conversion moment and conversion period." In *Viking Revaluations*, edited by Anthony Faulkes and Richard Perkins, 137–44. London: Viking Society for Northern Research, 1993.

——. "On the conversion of the Icelanders." In *Aurvandilstá*, edited by Michael P. Barnes et al., 56–64. Odense: Odense University Press, 1984.

Gräslund, Anne-Sofie. "Religion, art, and runes." In *Vikings: The North Atlantic Saga*, edited by William W. Fitzhugh and Elisabeth I. Ward, 55–69. Washington DC: Smithsonian Institution, 2000.

——. "Thor's hammers, pendant crosses and other amulets." In *From Viking to Crusader: Scandinavia and Europe 800–1200*, edited by Else Roesdahl and David M. Wilson, 190–91. The 22nd Council of Europe Exhibition. Copenhagen: Nordic Council of Ministers and The Council of Europe, 1992.

——. "Some aspects of Christianisation in central Sweden." In *Social Approaches to Viking Studies*, edited by Ross Samson, 45–52. Glasgow: Cruithne, 1991.

——. "Pagan and Christian in the age of conversion." In *Proceedings of the Tenth Viking Congress, Larkollen, Norway, 1985*, edited by James E. Knirk, 81–94. Universitets Oldsaksamlings Skrifter, new series, 9. Oslo: Universitets Oldsaksamling, 1987.

Gräslund, Anne-Sofie, and Michael Müller-Wille. "Burial customs in Scandinavia during the Viking Age." In *From Viking to Crusader: Scandinavia and Europe 800–1200*, edited by Else Roesdahl and David M. Wilson, 186–87. The 22nd Council of Europe Exhibition. Copenhagen: Nordic Council of Ministers and The Council of Europe, 1992.

Halldórsson, Ólafur. "The conversion of Greenland in written sources." In *Proceedings of the Eighth Viking Congress, Århus, 24–31 August 1977*, edited by Hans Bekker-Nielsen, Peter Foote, and Olaf Olsen, 203–16. Odense: Odense University Press, 1981.

Hultgård, Anders. "Ragnarok and Valhalla: Eschatological beliefs among the Scandinavians of the Viking period." In *The Twelfth Viking Congress: Developments Around the Baltic and the North Sea in the Viking Age*, edited by Björn Ambrosiani and Helen Clarke, 288–93. Birka Studies, 3. Stockholm: Riksantikvarieämbetet and Statens Historiska Museer, 1994.

Lindow, John. "Mythology and mythography." In *Old Norse-Literature: A Critical Guide*, edited by Carol J. Clover and John Lindow, 21–67. Islandica, 45. Ithaca, NY: Cornell University Press, 1985.

Olsen, Olaf. "Christianity and churches." In *From Viking to Crusader: Scandinavia and Europe 800–1200*, edited by Else Roesdahl and David M. Wilson, 152–61. The 22nd Council of Europe Exhibition. Copenhagen: Nordic Council of Ministers and The Council of Europe, 1992.

Roesdahl, Else. "Pagan beliefs, Christian impact and archaeology: A Danish view." In *Viking Revaluations*, edited by Anthony Faulkes and Richard Perkins, 128–36. London: Viking Society for Northern Research, 1993.

Sawyer, Birgit, Peter Sawyer, and Ian Wood, eds. *The Christianization of Scandinavia*. Alingsås: Viktoria, 1987.

Steinsland, Gro. "Scandinavian paganism." In *From Viking to Crusader: Scandinavia and Europe 800–1200*, edited by Else Roesdahl and David M. Wilson, 144–51. The 22nd Council of Europe Exhibition. Copenhagen: Nordic Council of Ministers and The Council of Europe, 1992.

Strömback, Dag. *The Conversion of Iceland: A Survey*. London: Viking Society for Northern Research, 1974.

Sørensen, Preben Meulengracht. "Religions old and new." In *The Oxford Illustrated History of the Vikings*, edited by Peter Sawyer, 202–24. Oxford: Oxford University Press, 1997.

Tegnér, Göran. "Christian graves and funerary monuments." In *From Viking to Crusader: Scandinavia and Europe 800–1200*, edited by Else Roesdahl and David M. Wilson, 188–89. The 22nd Council of Europe Exhibition. Copenhagen: Nordic Council of Ministers and The Council of Europe, 1992.

Turville-Petre, E. O. G. *Myth and Religion of the North*. London: Weidenfeld & Nicolson, 1964.

XIII. LITERATURE

A. Prose

1. General

Byock, Jesse L. *Feud in the Icelandic Saga*. Berkeley: University of California Press, 1982.

Clover, Carol J. *The Medieval Saga*. Ithaca, NY: Cornell University Press, 1982.

Clover, Carol J., and John Lindow. *Old Norse-Literature: A Critical Guide*. Islandica, 45. Ithaca, NY: Cornell University Press, 1985.

Clunies Ross, Margaret, ed. *Old Icelandic Literature and Society*. Cambridge: Cambridge University Press, 2000.

Kristjánsson, Jónas. *Eddas and Sagas: Iceland's Medieval Literature*. Reykjavik: Hið íslenska bókmenntafélag, 1997.

———. "Preface: Vikings and sagas." In *From Viking to Crusader: Scandinavia and Europe 800–1200*, edited by Else Roesdahl and David M. Wilson, 18–23. The 22nd Council of Europe Exhibition. Copenhagen: Nordic Council of Ministers and The Council of Europe, 1992.

The Norse Atlantic Saga [includes the *Book of the Icelanders*]. Translated by Gwyn Jones. 2nd ed. Oxford: Oxford University Press, 1986.

Ólafsson, Haraldur. "Sagas of western expansion." In *Vikings: The North Atlantic Saga*, edited by William W. Fitzhugh and Elisabeth I. Ward, 142–45. Washington DC: Smithsonian Institution, 2000.

Pálsson, Gísli, ed. *From Sagas to Society: Comparative Approaches to Early Iceland*. Enfield Lock: Hisarlik, 1992.

Sørensen, Preben Meulengracht. "Social institutions and belief systems of medieval Iceland (*c*. 870–1400) and their relations to literary production." In *Old Icelandic Literature and Society*, edited by Margaret Clunies Ross, 8–29. Cambridge: Cambridge University Press, 2000.

———. "Historical reality and literary form." In *Viking Revaluations*, edited by Anthony Faulkes and Richard Perkins, 172–81. London: Viking Society for Northern Research, 1993.

———. *Saga and Society: An Introduction to Old Norse Literature*. Odense: Odense University Press, 1993.

———. "Some methodological considerations in connection with the study of sagas." In *From Sagas to Society: Comparative Approaches to Early Iceland*, edited by Gísli Pálsson, 27–42. Enfield Lock: Hisarlik, 1992.

The Vinland Sagas: The Norse Discovery of America. Grænlendinga saga and Eirik's saga. Translated by Magnus Magnusson and Hermann Pálsson. Harmondsworth: Penguin, 1965.

2. Kings' Sagas

Andersson, Theodore. "Norse Kings' Sagas." In *Dictionary of the Middle Ages*, edited by Joseph R. Strayer, vol. 9, 175–78. New York: Scribner, 1982–89.

———. "Kings' Sagas." In *Old Norse-Literature: A Critical Guide*, edited by Carol J. Clover and John Lindow, 197–238. Islandica, 45. Ithaca, NY: Cornell University Press, 1985.

Bagge, Sverre. "From sagas to society: The case of *Heimskringla*." In *From Sagas to Society: Comparative Approaches to Early Iceland*, edited by Gísli Pálsson, 61–75. Enfield Lock: Hisarlik, 1992.

———. *Society and Politics in Snorri Sturluson's* Heimskringla. Berkeley: University of California Press, 1991.

Guðmundsson, Finnbogi. "On the writing of *Orkneyinga saga*." In *The Viking Age in Caithness, Orkney and the North Atlantic*, edited by Colleen Batey et al., 204–11. Edinburgh: Edinburgh University Press, 1993.

Knýtlinga Saga: The History of the Kings of Denmark. Translated by Hermann Pálsson and Paul Edwards. Odense: Odense University Press, 1986.

Morkinskinna. Edited by Theodore M. Andersson and Kari Ellen Gade. Ithaca, NY: Cornell University Press, 2000.

Orkneyinga Saga. Translated by Hermann Pálsson and Paul Edwards. London: Penguin, 1981.

Snorri Sturluson. *Heimskringla: Sagas of the Norse Kings*. 3 vols. Translated by Samuel Laing. London: Dent, 1961–64.

Whaley, Diana. "A useful past: Historical writing in medieval Iceland." In *Old Icelandic Literature and Society*, edited by Margaret Clunies Ross, 161–202. Cambridge: Cambridge University Press, 2000.

———. "The Kings' Sagas." In *Viking Revaluations*, edited by Anthony Faulkes and Richard Perkins, 43–64. London: Viking Society for Northern Research, 1993.

———. *Heimskringla: An Introduction*. London: Viking Society for Northern Research, 1991.

———. "The miracles of S. Olaf in Snorri Sturluson's *Heimskringla*." In *Proceedings of the Tenth Viking Congress, Larkollen, Norway, 1985*, edited by James E. Knirk, 325–42. Universitets Oldsaksamlings Skrifter, new series, 9. Oslo: Universitets Oldsaksamling, 1987.

3. Family Sagas or Sagas of Icelanders

Clover, Carol J. "Icelandic family sagas." In *Old Norse-Literature: A Critical Guide*, edited by Carol J. Clover and John Lindow, 239–315. Islandica, 45. Ithaca, NY: Cornell University Press, 1985.

Egil's Saga. Translated by Herman Pálsson and Paul Edwards. Harmondsworth: Penguin, 1976.

Einarsson, Bjarni. "The last hour of Hallfreðr vandræðaskáld as described in *Hallfreðarsaga*." In *Proceedings of the Eighth Viking Congress, Århus, 24–31 August 1977*, edited by Hans Bekker-Nielsen, Peter Foote, and Olaf Olsen, 217–21. Odense: Odense University Press, 1981.

Eyrbyggja Saga. Translated by Herman Pálsson and Paul Edwards. Harmondsworth: Penguin, 1989.

Færeyinga Saga, or the Tale of Thrond of Gate. Translated by F. York Powell. London: David Nutt, 1896. Facsimile reprint by Felinfach: Llanerch, 1995.

Glauser, Jürg. "Sagas of Icelanders (*Íslendinga sögur*) and *þættir* as the literary representation of new social space." In *Old Icelandic Literature and Society*, edited by Margaret Clunies Ross, 203–20. Cambridge: Cambridge University Press, 2000.

Laxdæla Saga. Translated by Magnus Magnusson and Hermann Pálsson. Harmondsworth: Penguin, 1969.

Njal's Saga. Translated by Magnus Magnusson and Hermann Pálsson. Harmondsworth: Penguin, 1960.

Ólason, Vésteinn. "The Sagas of Icelanders." In *Viking Revaluations*, edited by Anthony Faulkes and Richard Perkins, 26–42. London: Viking Society for Northern Research, 1993.

4. Sagas of Ancient Times

Göngu-Hrolf's Saga. Translated by Hermann Pálsson and Paul Edwards. Edinburgh: Canongate, 1980.

Grettir's Saga. Translated by Denton Fox and Hermann Pálsson. Toronto: University of Toronto Press, 1974.

Hallberg, Peter. "Some aspects of the Fornaldarsögur as a corpus." *Arkiv för nordisk filologi* 97 (1982): 1–35.

Pálsson, Hermann. "*Förnaldarsögur.*" In *Dictionary of the Middle Ages*, edited by Joseph R. Strayer, vol. 5, 137–43. New York: Scribner, 1982–89.

Pálsson, Hermann, and Paul Edwards. *Legendary Fiction in Medieval Iceland.* Studia Islandica, 30. Reykjavik: Heimspekideild Háskóla Íslands, Menningarsjóður, 1971.

The Saga of the Jómsvikings. Translated by Lee M. Hollander. Austin: University of Texas Press, 1955.

The Saga of the Volsungs: The Norse Epic of Sigurd the Dragon Slayer. Translated by Jesse L. Byock. Berkeley: University of California Press, 1990.

B. Poetry

1. Skaldic

Campbell, Alistair. *Skaldic Verse and Anglo-Saxon History.* Dorothea Coke Memorial Lecture in Northern Studies, 1970. London: University College London, 1971.

Edwards, Diana. "Christian and pagan references in eleventh-century Norse poetry: The case of Arnórr jarlaskáld." *Saga-Book* 21:1–2 (1982–83): 34–53.
Einarsson, Bjarni. "The blood-eagle once more: *Blóðörn*—An observation on
the ornithological aspect." *Saga-Book* 22:3 (1990): 80–81.
———. "The last hour of Hallfreðr vandræðaskáld as described in *Hall-
freðarsaga*." In *Proceedings of the Eighth Viking Congress, Århus, 24–31
August 1977*, edited by Hans Bekker-Nielsen, Peter Foote, and Olaf Olsen,
217–21. Odense: Odense University Press, 1981.
Fell, Christine E. "Víkingavísur." In *Speculum Norroenum*, edited by Ursula
Dronke et al., 106–22. Odense: Odense University Press, 1981.
Fidjestøl, Bjarne. "[Pagan beliefs and Christian impact:] The contribution of
skaldic studies." In *Viking Revaluations*, edited by Anthony Faulkes and
Richard Perkins, 100–20. London: Viking Society for Northern Research,
1993.
Foote, P. G. "Wrecks and rhymes." In *Aurvandilstá*, edited by Michael P.
Barnes et al., 222–35. Odense: Odense University Press, 1984.
Frank, Roberta. "King Cnut in the verse of his skalds." In *The Reign of Cnut:
King of England, Denmark and Norway*, edited by Alexander R. Rumble,
106–24. London: Leicester University Press, 1994.
———. "The blood-eagle once more: Ornithology and the interpretation of
skaldic verse." *Saga-Book* 23:2 (1990): 81–83.
———. "Did Anglo-Saxon audiences have a skaldic tooth?" *Scandinavian Stud-
ies* 59 (1987): 338–55.
———. "Skaldic poetry." In *Old Norse-Literature: A Critical Guide*, edited by
Carol J. Clover and John Lindow, 157–196. Islandica, 45. Ithaca, NY: Cor-
nell University Press, 1985.
———. "Viking atrocity and skaldic verse: The rite of the blood-eagle." *English
Historical Review* 99 (1984): 332–43.
———, ed. and trans. *Old Norse Court Poetry: The Dróttkvætt Stanza*. Is-
landica, 42. Ithaca, NY: Cornell University Press, 1978.
Gade, Kari Ellen. "Poetry and its changing importance in medieval Icelandic
culture." In *Old Icelandic Literature and Society*, edited by Margaret Clunies
Ross, 61–95. Cambridge: Cambridge University Press, 2000.
Hallberg, Peter. "The ship: Reality and image in Old Norse poetry." In *The
Vikings: Proceedings of the Symposium of the Faculty of Arts of Uppsala
University, June 6–9, 1977*, edited by Thorsten Andersson and Karl Inge
Sandred, 42–56. Stockholm: Almqvist & Wiksell, 1978.
Hollander, Lee M., trans. *The Skalds: A Selection of Their Poems*. 2nd ed. Ann
Arbor: University of Michigan Press, 1968.
Jesch, Judith. *Ships and Men in the Late Viking Age*. Woodbridge: Boydell &
Brewer, 2001.

———. "Skaldic verse in Scandinavian England." In *Vikings and the Danelaw: Select Papers from the Proceedings of the Thirteenth Viking Congress*, edited by James Graham-Campbell et al., 313–25. Oxford: Oxbow, 2001.

———. "Skaldic studies." *Collegium Medievale* 11 (1998): 105–17.

———. "Skaldic and runic vocabulary and the Viking Age: A research project." In *The Twelfth Viking Congress: Developments Around the Baltic and the North Sea in the Viking Age*, edited by Björn Ambrosiani and Helen Clarke, 294–301. Birka Studies, 3. Stockholm: Riksantikvarieämbetet and Statens Historiska Museer, 1994.

———. "Skaldic verse and Viking semantics." In *Viking Revaluations*, edited by Anthony Faulkes and Richard Perkins, 160–71. London: Viking Society for Northern Research, 1993.

Kristjánsson, Jónas. "Scaldic poetry." In *From Viking to Crusader: Scandinavia and Europe 800–1200*, edited by Else Roesdahl and David M. Wilson, 172–75. The 22nd Council of Europe Exhibition. Copenhagen: Nordic Council of Ministers and The Council of Europe, 1992.

Mundal, Else. "The Orkney earl and scald Torf-Einarr and his poetry." In *The Viking Age in Caithness, Orkney and the North Atlantic*, edited by Colleen Batey et al., 248–59. Edinburgh: Edinburgh University Press, 1993.

Poole, Russell. *Viking Poems on War and Peace: A Study in Skaldic Narrative*. Toronto: University of Toronto Press, 1991.

———. "Skaldic verse and Anglo-Saxon history. Some aspects of the period 1009–1016." *Speculum* 62 (1987): 265–98.

Turville-Petre, E. O. Gabriel. *Scaldic Poetry*. Oxford: Clarendon Press, 1976.

Whitelock, Dorothy, ed. *English Historical Documents c. 500–1042*. 2nd ed. London: Eyre & Spottiswoode, 1979 [pp. 324–41 contain English translations of a number of poems that refer to events in England].

2. Eddic

Dronke, Ursula. "[Pagan beliefs and Christian impact:] The contribution of Eddic studies." In *Viking Revaluations*, edited by Anthony Faulkes and Richard Perkins, 121–27. London: Viking Society for Northern Research, 1993.

Glendinning, Robert J., and Haraldur Bessason, eds. *Edda: A Collection of Essays*. University of Manitoba Studies, 4. Winnipeg: University of Manitoba Press, 1983.

Harris, Joseph. "Eddic poetry." In *Old Norse-Literature: A Critical Guide*, edited by Carol J. Clover and John Lindow, 68–156. Islandica, 45. Ithaca, NY: Cornell University Press, 1985.

Kellogg, Robert. "Literacy and orality in the Poetic Edda." In *Vox intexta: Orality and Textuality in the Middle Ages*, edited by A. N. Doane and

Carol Braun Pasternack, 89–101. Madison: University of Wisconsin Press, 1991.

Kristjánsson, Jónas. *Eddas and Sagas: Iceland's Medieval Literature*. Reykjavik: Hið íslenska bókmenntafélag, 1997.

McKinnell, John. "Eddic poetry in Anglo-Scandinavian northern England." In *Vikings and the Danelaw: Select Papers from the Proceedings of the Thirteenth Viking Congress*, edited by James Graham-Campbell et al., 327–44. Oxford: Oxbow, 2001.

The Poetic Edda. Translated by Carolyne Larrington. Oxford: Oxford University Press, 1996.

XIV. ART AND SCULPTURE

Bailey, Richard N. *Viking Age Sculpture in Northern England*. London: Collins, 1980.

———. "Aspects of Viking-Age sculpture in Cumbria." In *The Scandinavians in Cumbria*, edited by John R. Baldwin and Ian D. Whyte, 53–63. Edinburgh: Scottish Society for Northern Studies, 1985.

Bailey, Richard N., and Rosemary J. Cramp. *Corpus of Anglo-Saxon Stone Sculpture II: Cumberland, Westmorland and Lancashire North-of-the-Sands*. Oxford: Oxford University Press, 1988.

Collingwood, William G. *Northumbrian Crosses of the Pre-Norman Age*. London: Faber & Gwyer, 1927.

Cramp, Rosemary J. *Grammar of Anglo-Saxon Ornament: A General Introduction to the Corpus of Anglo-Saxon Stone Sculpture*. Oxford: Oxford University Press, 1984.

———. *Corpus of Anglo-Saxon Stone Sculpture I: County Durham and Northumberland*. Oxford: Oxford University Press, 1984.

———. "The Viking image." In *The Vikings*, edited by R. T. Farrell, 8–19. London: Phillimore, 1982.

Everson, Paul, and David Stocker. *Corpus of Anglo-Saxon Stone Sculpture V: Lincolnshire*. Oxford: Oxford University Press, 1999.

Fuglesang, Signe Horn. "Swedish runestones of the eleventh century: Ornament and dating." In *Runeninschriften als Quellen interdisziplinärer Forschung*, edited by Klaus Düwel, 197–218. Berlin: Walter de Gruyter, 1998.

———. "Art." In *From Viking to Crusader: Scandinavia and Europe 800–1200*, edited by Else Roesdahl and David M. Wilson, 176–84. The 22nd Council of Europe Exhibition. Copenhagen: Nordic Council of Ministers and The Council of Europe, 1992.

———. "'The personal touch': On the identification of workshops." In *Proceedings of the Tenth Viking Congress, Larkollen, Norway, 1985*, edited by James E. Knirk, 219–30. Universitets Oldsaksamlings Skrifter, new series, 9. Oslo: Universitets Oldsaksamling, 1987.

———. "Crucifixion iconography in Viking Scandinavia." In *Proceedings of the Eighth Viking Congress, Århus, 24–31 August 1977*, edited by Hans Bekker-Nielsen, Peter Foote, and Olaf Olsen, 73–94. Odense: Odense University Press, 1981.

———. *Some Aspects of the Ringerike Style: A Phase of 11th Century Scandinavian Art*. Medieval Scandinavia, Supplements 1. Odense: Odense University Press, 1980.

Graham-Campbell, James. "Viking art." In *The Viking World*, edited by James Graham-Campbell, 130–53. 2nd ed. London: Frances Lincoln, 1989.

Gräslund, Anne-Sofie. "Religion, art, and runes." In *Vikings: The North Atlantic Saga*, edited by William W. Fitzhugh and Elisabeth I. Ward, 55–69. Washington DC: Smithsonian Institution, 2000.

———. "Rune stones: On ornamentation and chronology." In *The Twelfth Viking Congress: Developments Around the Baltic and the North Sea in the Viking Age*, edited by Björn Ambrosiani and Helen Clarke, 117–31. Birka Studies, 3. Stockholm: Riksantikvarieämbetet and Statens Historiska Museer, 1994.

Klindt-Jensen, Ole and Wilson, David M. *Viking Art*. London: Allen & Unwin, 1966.

Lang, James T. "The hogback: A Viking colonial monument." *Anglo-Saxon Studies in Archaeology and History* 3 (1984): 86–176.

———. *Anglo-Saxon Sculpture*. Princes Risborough: Shire, 1988.

———. *Corpus of Anglo-Saxon Stone Sculpture III: York and Eastern Yorkshire*. Oxford: Oxford University Press, 1991.

Ó Floinn, Raghnall. "Irish and Scandinavian art in the early medieval period." In *The Vikings in Ireland*, edited by Anne-Christine Larsen, 87–97. Roskilde: The Viking Ship Museum, 2001.

O'Meadhra, Uaininn. "Viking-Age sketches and motif-pieces from the northern earldoms." In *The Viking Age in Caithness, Orkney and the North Atlantic*, edited by Colleen Batey et al., 423–40. Edinburgh: Edinburgh University Press, 1993.

Owen, Olwyn. "The strange beast that is the English Urnes style." In *Vikings and the Danelaw: Select Papers from the Proceedings of the Thirteenth Viking Congress*, edited by James Graham-Campbell et al., 203–222. Oxford: Oxbow, 2001.

Sidebottom, Phil. "Viking Age stone monuments and social identity in Derbyshire." In *Cultures in Contact: Scandinavian Settlement in England in the*

Ninth and Tenth Centuries, edited by Dawn M. Hadley and Julian D. Richards, 213–35. Turnhout: Brepols, 2000.

Stocker, David. "Monuments and merchants: Irregularities in the distribution of stone sculpture in Lincolnshire and Yorkshire in the tenth century." In *Cultures in Contact: Scandinavian Settlement in England in the Ninth and Tenth Centuries*, edited by Dawn M. Hadley and Julian D. Richards, 179–212. Turnhout: Brepols, 2000.

Stocker, David, and Paul Everson. "Five towns funerals: Decoding diversity in Danelaw stone sculpture." In *Vikings and the Danelaw: Select Papers from the Proceedings of the Thirteenth Viking Congress*, edited by James Graham-Campbell et al., 223–43. Oxford: Oxbow, 2001.

XV. LANGUAGE AND PLACE-NAMES

A. General

Elmevik, Lennart. "[The Nordic languages as borrowers and lenders in the Viking Age and early Middle Ages:] Introduction." In *The Twelfth Viking Congress: Developments Around the Baltic and the North Sea in the Viking Age*, edited by Björn Ambrosiani and Helen Clarke, 244–46. Birka Studies, 3. Stockholm: Riksantikvarieämbetet and Statens Historiska Museer, 1994.

Fellows-Jensen, Gillian. "From Scandinavia to the British Isles and back again: Linguistic give-and-take in the Viking period." In *The Twelfth Viking Congress: Developments Around the Baltic and the North Sea in the Viking Age*, edited by Björn Ambrosiani and Helen Clarke, 253–68. Birka Studies, 3. Stockholm: Riksantikvarieämbetet and Statens Historiska Museer, 1994.

Sellevold, Berit Jansen, and Jan Ragnar Hagland. "People and language." In *From Viking to Crusader: Scandinavia and Europe 800–1200*, edited by Else Roesdahl and David M. Wilson, 116–19. The 22nd Council of Europe Exhibition. Copenhagen: Nordic Council of Ministers and The Council of Europe, 1992.

B. Scandinavia

Brink, Stefan. "The place-names of Markim-Orkesta." In *The Twelfth Viking Congress: Developments Around the Baltic and the North Sea in the Viking Age*, edited by Björn Ambrosiani and Helen Clarke, 277–79. Birka Studies, 3. Stockholm: Riksantikvarieämbetet and Statens Historiska Museer, 1994.

Fellows-Jensen, Gillian. "Place-name research in Scandinavia 1960–1982, with a select bibliography." *Names* 32 (1964): 267–324.

Holmberg, Bente. "Recent research into sacral names." In *The Twelfth Viking Congress: Developments Around the Baltic and the North Sea in the Viking Age*, edited by Björn Ambrosiani and Helen Clarke, 280–87. Birka Studies, 3. Stockholm: Riksantikvarieämbetet and Statens Historiska Museer, 1994.

Sørensen, John Kousgård. "Toponymic evidence for administrative divisions in Denmark in the Viking Age." In *The Vikings: Proceedings of the Symposium of the Faculty of Arts of Uppsala University, June 6–9, 1977*, edited by Thorsten Andersson and Karl Inge Sandred, 133–41. Stockholm: Almqvist & Wiksell, 1978.

C. British Isles

Barnes, Michael P. *The Norn Language of Orkney and Shetland*. Lerwick: Shetland Times, 1998.

———. "Norse in the British Isles." In *Viking Revaluations*, edited by Anthony Faulkes and Richard Perkins, 65–85. London: Viking Society for Northern Research, 1993.

———. "Orkney and Shetland Norn." In *Language in the British Isles*, edited by Peter Trudgill, 352–66. Cambridge: Cambridge University Press, 1984.

Baugh, Albert C., and Thomas Cable. *A History of the English Language*. 4th ed. Englewood Cliffs, NJ: Prentice-Hall, 1993.

Björkman, Erik. *Scandinavian Loan-Words in Middle English*. Studien zur englischen Philologie 7. Halle: Max Niemeyer, 1900.

Cameron, Kenneth. *English Place-Names*. Rev. ed. London: Batsford, 1977.

Cameron, Kenneth. "The minor names and field-names of the Holland division of Lincolnshire." In *The Vikings: Proceedings of the Symposium of the Faculty of Arts of Uppsala University, June 6–9, 1977*, edited by Thorsten Andersson and Karl Inge Sandred, 81–88. Stockholm: Almqvist & Wiksell, 1978.

———, ed. *Place-name Evidence for the Anglo-Saxon Invasion and Scandinavian Settlements*. Nottingham: English Place-Name Society, 1977.

von Feilitzen, Olof. *The Pre-Conquest Personal Names of Domesday Book*. Uppsala: Almqvist & Wiksell, 1937.

Fellows-Jensen, Gillian. "In the steps of the Vikings." In *Vikings and the Danelaw: Select Papers from the Proceedings of the Thirteenth Viking Congress*, edited by James Graham-Campbell et al., 279–88. Oxford: Oxbow, 2001.

———. "Nordic names and loanwords in Ireland." In *The Vikings in Ireland*, edited by Anne-Christine Larsen, 107–13. Roskilde: The Viking Ship Museum, 2001.

———. "Scandinavian settlement in Yorkshire: Through the rear-view mirror." In *Scandinavian Settlement in Northern Britain*, edited by Barbara E. Crawford, 170–86. London: Leicester University Press, 1995.

——. "Danish place-names and personal names in England: The influence of Cnut?" In *The Reign of Cnut: King of England, Denmark and Norway*, edited by Alexander R. Rumble, 125–40. London: Leicester University Press, 1994.

——. "Some Orkney personal names." In *The Viking Age in Caithness, Orkney and the North Atlantic*, edited by Colleen Batey et al., 397–407. Edinburgh: Edinburgh University Press, 1993.

——. "Scandinavian place-names of the Irish Sea province." In *Viking Treasure from the North West: The Cuerdale Hoard in its Context*, edited by James Graham-Campbell, 31–42. Liverpool: Liverpool Museum, 1992.

——. "Scandinavian place-names and Viking settlement in Normandy." *Namn och bygd* 76 (1988): 113–37.

——. *Scandinavian Settlement Names in the North-West*. Copenhagen: C. A. Reitzel, 1985.

——. "Scandinavian settlement in Cumbria and Dumfriesshire: The place-name evidence." In *The Scandinavians in Cumbria*, edited by John R. Baldwin and Ian D. Whyte, 65–82. Edinburgh: Scottish Society for Northern Studies, 1985.

——. "Viking settlement in the Northern and Western Isles: The place-name evidence as seen from Denmark and the Danelaw." In *The Northern and Western Isles in the Viking World: Survival, Continuity and Change*, edited by Alexander Fenton and Hermann Pálsson, 148–68. Edinburgh: John Donald, 1984.

——. "Scandinavian settlement in the Isle of Man and north-west England: The place-name evidence." In *The Viking Age in the Isle of Man*, edited by Christine E. Fell et al., 37–52. London: Viking Society for Northern Research, 1983.

——. "Scandinavian settlement in the Danelaw in the light of the place-names of Denmark." In *Proceedings of the Eighth Viking Congress, Århus, 24–31 August 1977*, edited by Hans Bekker-Nielsen, Peter Foote, and Olaf Olsen, 133–45. Odense: Odense University Press, 1981.

——. "Place-name evidence for Scandinavian settlement in the Danelaw: A re-assessment." In *The Vikings: Proceedings of the Symposium of the Faculty of Arts of Uppsala University, June 6–9, 1977*, edited by Thorsten Andersson and Karl Inge Sandred, 89–98. Stockholm: Almqvist & Wiksell, 1978.

——. *Scandinavian Settlement Names in the East Midlands*. Navnestudier udgivet af Institut for Navneforskning 16. Copenhagen: Akademisk Forlag, 1978.

——. "The Vikings in England: A review." *Anglo-Saxon England* 4 (1975): 181–206.

——. *Scandinavian Settlement Names in Yorkshire*. Navnestudier udgivet af Institut for Navneforskning 11. Copenhagen: Akademisk Forlag, 1972.

———. *Scandinavian Personal Names in Lincolnshire and Yorkshire*. Navnes-tudier udgivet af Institut for Navneforskning 7. Copenhagen: Akademisk Forlag, 1968.

Fenton, Alexander. "Orkney Norn: A survey of 'taboo' terms." In *The Viking Age in Caithness, Orkney and the North Atlantic*, edited by Colleen Batey et al., 381–87. Edinburgh: Edinburgh University Press, 1993.

Geipel, John. *The Viking Legacy: The Scandinavian Influence on the English and Gaelic Languages*. Newton Abbot: David & Charles, 1971.

Gelling, Margaret. "Scandinavian settlement in Cheshire: The evidence of place-names." In *Scandinavian Settlement in Northern Britain*, edited by Barbara E. Crawford, 187–94. London: Leicester University Press, 1995.

———. *Signposts to the Past*. 2nd ed. Chichester: Phillimore, 1988.

———. "Norse and Gaelic in medieval Man: The place-name evidence." In *The Vikings: Proceedings of the Symposium of the Faculty of Arts of Uppsala University, June 6–9, 1977*, edited by Thorsten Andersson and Karl Inge San-dred, 107–118. Stockholm: Almqvist & Wiksell, 1978.

Greene, David. "The evidence of language and place-names in Ireland." In *The Vikings: Proceedings of the Symposium of the Faculty of Arts of Uppsala University, June 6–9, 1977*, edited by Thorsten Andersson and Karl Inge San-dred, 119–23. Stockholm: Almqvist & Wiksell, 1978.

———. "The influence of Scandinavian on Irish." In *Proceedings of the Seventh Viking Congress, Dublin, 15–21 August 1973*, edited by Bo Almqvist and David Greene, 75–82. Dublin: Royal Irish Academy, 1976.

Hald, Kristian. "*A*-mutation in Scandinavian words in England." In *The Vikings: Proceedings of the Symposium of the Faculty of Arts of Uppsala University, June 6–9, 1977*, edited by Thorsten Andersson and Karl Inge San-dred, 99–106. Stockholm: Almqvist & Wiksell, 1978.

McIntosh, Angus. "Middle English word geography: Its potential role in the study of the long-term impact of the Scandinavians settlements upon Eng-lish." In *The Vikings: Proceedings of the Symposium of the Faculty of Arts of Uppsala University, June 6–9, 1977*, edited by Thorsten Andersson and Karl Inge Sandred, 124–30. Stockholm: Almqvist & Wiksell, 1978.

Ó Corráin, Donnchadh. "The semantic development of Old Norse *jarl* in Old and Middle Irish." In *Proceedings of the Tenth Viking Congress, Larkollen, Norway, 1985*, edited by James E. Knirk, 287–93. Universitets Oldsaksamlings Skrifter, new series, 9. Oslo: Universitets Oldsaksamling, 1987.

Oftedal, Magne. "Names of lakes on the Isle of Lewis in the Outer Hebrides." In *Proceedings of the Eighth Viking Congress, Århus, 24–31 August 1977*, edited by Hans Bekker-Nielsen, Peter Foote, and Olaf Olsen, 183–87. Odense: Odense University Press, 1981.

——. "Scandinavian place-names in Ireland." In *Proceedings of the Seventh Viking Congress, Dublin, 15–21 August 1973*, edited by Bo Almqvist and David Greene, 125–33. Dublin: Royal Irish Academy, 1976.

Page, R. I. "How long did the Scandinavian language survive in England? The epigraphical evidence." In *England before the Conquest: Studies in Primary Sources Presented to Dorothy Whitelock*, edited by Peter Clemoes and Kathleen Hughes, 165–81. Cambridge: Cambridge University Press, 1971.

Parsons, David N. "How long did the Scandinavian language survive in England? Again." In *Vikings and the Danelaw: Select Papers from the Proceedings of the Thirteenth Viking Congress*, edited by James Graham-Campbell et al., 299–312. Oxford: Oxbow, 2001.

Rendboe, Laurits. "The Lord's Prayer in Orkney and Shetland Norn." In *The Viking Age in Caithness, Orkney and the North Atlantic*, edited by Colleen Batey et al., 388–96. Edinburgh: Edinburgh University Press, 1993.

Sandred, Karl Inge. "Viking administration in the Danelaw: A look at Scandinavian and English hundred-names in Norfolk." In *The Twelfth Viking Congress: Developments Around the Baltic and the North Sea in the Viking Age*, edited by Björn Ambrosiani and Helen Clarke, 269–76. Birka Studies, 3. Stockholm: Riksantikvarieämbetet and Statens Historiska Museer, 1994.

——. "The Vikings in Norfolk: Some observations on the place-names in *-by*." In *Proceedings of the Tenth Viking Congress, Larkollen, Norway, 1985*, edited by James E. Knirk, 309–24. Universitets Oldsaksamlings Skrifter, new series, 9. Oslo: Universitets Oldsaksamling, 1987.

Smith, Brian. "Scandinavian place-names in Shetland with a study of the district of Whiteness." In *Scandinavian Settlement in Northern Britain*, edited by Barbara E. Crawford, 26–41. London: Leicester University Press, 1995.

Styles, Tania. "Scandinavian elements in English place-names: Some semantic problems." In *Vikings and the Danelaw: Select Papers from the Proceedings of the Thirteenth Viking Congress*, edited by James Graham-Campbell et al., 289–98. Oxford: Oxbow, 2001.

Taylor, Simon. "The Scandinavians in Fife and Kinross: The onomastic evidence." In *Scandinavian Settlement in Northern Britain*, edited by Barbara E. Crawford, 141–68. London: Leicester University Press, 1995.

Thomson, William P. L. "Orkney farm-names: A re-assessment of their chronology." In *Scandinavian Settlement in Northern Britain*, edited by Barbara E. Crawford, 42–63. London: Leicester University Press, 1995.

Townend, Matthew. *Language and History in Viking Age England: Linguistic Relations between Speakers of Old Norse and Old English*. Turnhout: Brepols, 2002.

——. "Viking Age England as a bilingual society." In *Cultures in Contact: Scandinavian Settlement in England in the Ninth and Tenth Centuries*, edited by Dawn M. Hadley and Julian D. Richards, 89–105. Turnhout: Brepols, 2000.

Waugh, Doreen. "Settlement names in Caithness with particular reference to Reay parish." In *Scandinavian Settlement in Northern Britain*, edited by Barbara E. Crawford, 64–79. London: Leicester University Press, 1995.

——. "Caithness: An onomastic frontier zone." In *The Viking Age in Caithness, Orkney and the North Atlantic*, edited by Colleen Batey et al., 120–28. Edinburgh: Edinburgh University Press, 1993.

XVI. RUNES AND RUNIC INSCRIPTIONS

A. General

Barnes, Michael P. "On types of argumentation in runic studies." In *Proceedings of the Third International Symposium on Runes and Runic Inscriptions, Grindaheim, Norway, 8–12 August 1990*, edited by James E. Knirk, 11–29. Runrön, 9. Uppsala: Institutionen för nordiska språk, Uppsala universitet, 1994.

Elliot, Ralph W. V. *Runes: An Introduction*. 2nd ed. Manchester: Manchester University Press, 1989.

Gräslund, Anne-Sofie. "Religion, art, and runes." In *Vikings: The North Atlantic Saga*, edited by William W. Fitzhugh and Elisabeth I. Ward, 55–69. Washington DC: Smithsonian Institution, 2000.

Haugen, Einar. "The dotted runes: From parsimony to plenitude." In *Proceedings of the Seventh Viking Congress, Dublin, 15–21 August 1973*, edited by Bo Almqvist and David Greene, 83–92. Dublin: Royal Irish Academy, 1976.

Jesch, Judith. "Runic inscriptions and social history: Some problems of method." In *Proceedings of the Third International Symposium on Runes and Runic Inscriptions, Grindaheim, Norway, 8–12 August 1990*, edited by James E. Knirk, 149–62. Runrön, 9. Uppsala: Institutionen för nordiska språk, Uppsala universitet, 1994.

——. "Skaldic and runic vocabulary and the Viking Age: A research project." In *The Twelfth Viking Congress: Developments Around the Baltic and the North Sea in the Viking Age*, edited by Björn Ambrosiani and Helen Clarke, 294–301. Birka Studies, 3. Stockholm: Riksantikvarieämbetet and Statens Historiska Museer, 1994.

Liestol, Aslak. "The Viking runes: The transition from the older to the younger *futhark*." *Saga-Book* 20 (1981): 247–66.

Moltke, Erik. *Runes and their Origins: Denmark and Elsewhere*. Copenhagen: National Museum, 1985.

Page, R. I. *Runes and Runic Inscriptions: Collected Essays on Anglo-Saxon and Viking Runes*. Edited by David N. Parsons. Woodbridge: Boydell, 1995.

——. "Runes and rune-stones." In *From Viking to Crusader: Scandinavia and Europe 800–1200*, edited by Else Roesdahl and David M. Wilson, 162–65.

The 22nd Council of Europe Exhibition. Copenhagen: Nordic Council of Ministers and The Council of Europe, 1992.

——. *Runes*. London: British Museum, 1987.

Runor och runinskrifter. Föredrag vid Rikantikvarieämbetets och Vitterhet-sakademiens symposium 8–11 september 1985. Stockholm: Almqvist & Wiksell, 1987.

Söderberg, Barbro. "Cultural progression: Latin and runic writing." In *The Twelfth Viking Congress: Developments Around the Baltic and the North Sea in the Viking Age*, edited by Björn Ambrosiani and Helen Clarke, 247–52. Birka Studies, 3. Stockholm: Riksantikvarieämbetet and Statens Historiska Museer, 1994.

B. Scandinavia

Gräslund, Anne-Sofie. "Rune stones: On ornamentation and chronology." In *The Twelfth Viking Congress: Developments Around the Baltic and the North Sea in the Viking Age*, edited by Björn Ambrosiani and Helen Clarke, 117–31. Birka Studies, 3. Stockholm: Riksantikvarieämbetet and Statens Historiska Museer, 1994.

Jansson, Sven B. F. *The Runes of Sweden*. Rev. ed. Stockholm: Gidlunds, 1987.

Jesch, Judith. "Still standing in Ågersta: Textuality and literacy in late Viking-Age rune stone inscriptions." In *Runeninschriften als Quellen interdisziplinärer Forschung*, edited by Klaus Düwel, 462–75. Berlin: Walter de Gruyter, 1998.

Knirk, James E. "Recently found runestones from Toten and Ringerike." In *Proceedings of the Tenth Viking Congress, Larkollen, Norway, 1985*, edited by James E. Knirk, 191–202. Universitets Oldsaksamlings Skrifter, new series, 9. Oslo: Universitets Oldsaksamling, 1987.

Larsson, Mats G. "Runic inscriptions as a source for the history of settlement." In *Runeninschriften als Quellen interdisziplinärer Forschung*, edited by Klaus Düwel, 639–46. Berlin: Walter de Gruyter, 1998.

Peterson, Lena. "Scandinavian runic-text data base: A presentation." In *The Twelfth Viking Congress: Developments Around the Baltic and the North Sea in the Viking Age*, edited by Björn Ambrosiani and Helen Clarke, 305–09. Birka Studies, 3. Stockholm: Riksantikvarieämbetet and Statens Historiska Museer, 1994.

Sawyer, Birgit. *The Viking-Age Rune-Stones: Custom and Commemoration in Early Medieval Scandinavia*. Oxford: Oxford University Press, 2000.

——. "Viking Age rune-stones as a source for legal history." In *Runenin-schriften als Quellen interdisziplinärer Forschung*, edited by Klaus Düwel, 766–77. Berlin: Walter de Gruyter, 1998.

———. *Property and Inheritance in Viking Scandinavia: The Runic Evidence.* Alingsås: Viktoria, 1988.

Williams, Henrik. "Runic inscriptions as sources of personal names." In *Runeninschriften als Quellen interdisziplinärer Forschung*, edited by Klaus Düwel, 601–10. Berlin: Walter de Gruyter, 1998.

C. Iceland, Greenland, and North America

Hall, Robert A. *The Kensington Rune-Stone is Genuine.* Columbia: Hornbeam, 1981.

Landsverk, O. G. *The Kensington Runestone.* Glendale: Church Press, 1961.

Stoklund, Marie. "Greenland runes: Isolation or cultural contact?" In *The Viking Age in Caithness, Orkney and the North Atlantic*, eds. Colleen Batey et al., 528–43. Edinburgh: Edinburgh University Press, 1993.

Wahlgren, Erik. "American runes: From Kensington to Spirit Pond." *Journal of English and Germanic Philology* 81 (1982): 157–85.

D. British Isles

Barnes, Michael P. "Aspects of the Scandinavian runes of the British Isles." In *Roman, Runes and Ogham*, edited by John Higgitt et al., 103–11. Donington: Shaun Tyas, 2001.

———. *The Runic Inscriptions of Maeshowe, Orkney.* Runrön, 8. Uppsala: Institutionen för nordiska språk, Uppsala universitet, 1994.

Barnes, Michael P., Jan Ragnar Hagland, and R. I. Page. *The Runic Inscriptions of Viking Age Dublin.* National Museum of Ireland, Medieval Dublin Excavations 1962–81, series B, 5. Dublin: Royal Irish Academy, 1997.

Elliot, Ralph W. V. *Runes: An Introduction.* 2nd ed. Manchester: Manchester University Press, 1989.

Hagland, Jan Ragnar. "The Dublin runes." In *The Twelfth Viking Congress: Developments Around the Baltic and the North Sea in the Viking Age*, edited by Björn Ambrosiani and Helen Clarke, 302–04. Birka Studies, 3. Stockholm: Riksantikvarieämbetet and Statens Historiska Museer, 1994.

Holman, Katherine. "Reading the runes: Epigraphy and history in the Northern Isles." In *Roman, Runes and Ogham*, edited by John Higgitt et al., 112–20. Donington: Shaun Tyas, 2001.

———. "The dating of Scandinavian runic inscriptions from the Isle of Man." In *Innskrifter og datering*, edited by Audun Dybdahl and Jan Ragnar Hagland, 43–54. Senter for middelalderstudier, Skrifter, 8. Tapir: Trondheim 1998.

———. "Scandinavian runic inscriptions as a source for the history of the British Isles: The St. Paul's rune-stone." In *Runeninschriften als Quellen interdisziplinärer Forschung*, edited by Klaus Düwel, 629–38. Berlin: Walter de Gruyter, 1998.

———. *Scandinavian Runic Inscriptions in the British Isles: Their Historical Context.* Senter for middelalder studier, 4. Trondheim: Tapir, 1996.

Jansson, Sven B. F. *Swedish Vikings in England: The Evidence of the Rune Stones.* The Dorothea Coke Memorial Lecture in Northern Studies, 1965. London: H. K. Lewis, 1965.

Liestøl, Aslak. "Runes." In *The Northern and Western Isles in the Viking World: Survival, Continuity and Change*, edited by Alexander Fenton and Hermann Pálsson, 224–38. Edinburgh: John Donald, 1984.

———. "An Iona rune stone and the world of Man and the Isles." In *The Viking Age in the Isle of Man*, edited by Christine E. Fell et al., 85–93. London: Viking Society for Northern Research, 1983.

Page, R. I. *An Introduction to English Runes.* 2nd ed. Woodbridge: Boydell, 1999.

———. "The Manx rune-stones." In *The Viking Age in the Isle of Man.* Edited by Christine E. Fell et al., 133–46. London: Viking Society for Northern Research, 1983.

———. "Some thoughts on Manx runes." *Saga-Book* 20 (1980): 179–99.

———. "How long did the Scandinavian language survive in England? The epigraphical evidence." In *England before the Conquest: Studies in Primary Sources Presented to Dorothy Whitelock*, edited by Peter Clemoes and Kathleen Hughes, 165–81. Cambridge: Cambridge University Press, 1971.

Parsons, David. "Sandwich: The oldest Scandinavian rune-stone in England?" In *The Twelfth Viking Congress: Developments Around the Baltic and the North Sea in the Viking Age*, edited by Björn Ambrosiani and Helen Clarke, 310–20. Birka Studies, 3. Stockholm: Riksantikvarieämbetet and Statens Historiska Museer, 1994.

Syrett, Martin. *The Vikings in England: The Evidence of Runic Inscriptions.* Cambridge: Department of Anglo-Saxon, Norse, and Celtic, University of Cambridge, 2002.

E. Other

Melnikova, Elena A. "Runic inscriptions as a source for the relation of northern and eastern Europe in the Middle Ages." In *Runeninschriften als Quellen interdisziplinärer Forschung*, edited by Klaus Düwel, 647–59. Berlin: Walter de Gruyter, 1998.

———. "New finds of Scandinavian runic inscriptions from the USSR." In *Runor och Runinskrifter*, 163–73. Stockholm: Almqvist & Wiksell, 1987.

XVII. SELECT SCANDINAVIAN-LANGUAGE SOURCES

Ælnoths Krønike. Translated by Erling Albrectsen. Odense: Odense Universitetsforlag, 1984.

Andersen, Per Sveaas. *Samlingen av Norge og kristningen av landet 800–1130*. Oslo: Universitetsforlaget, 1977.

Danmarks gamle personnavne. Edited by Gunnar Knudsen, Marius Kristensen, and Rikard Hornby. 2 vols. Copenhagen: G. E. C. Gads, 1936–64.

Danmarks runeindskrifter. 3 vols. Edited by Lis Jacobsen and Erik Moltke. Copenhagen: Ejnar Munksgaard, 1941–42.

Gräslund, Anne-Sofie. "'Gud hjälpe nu väl hennes själ': Om runstenskvinnorna, deras roll vid kristnandet och deras plats i familj och samhälle." *Tor* 22 (1988–89): 223–44.

Jónsson, Finnur, ed. *Den norsk-islandske skjaldedigtning*. 4 vols. Copenhagen: Gyldendal, 1912–15.

Jørgensen, Bent. *Dansk Stednavneleksikon*. 3 vols. Copenhagen: Gyldendal, 1981–83.

Kulturhistorisk leksikon for nordisk middelalder. 22 vols. Copenhagen: Rosenkilde & Bagger, 1956–78.

Lidén, Hans-Emil, ed. *Møtet mellom hedendom og kristendom i Norge*. Oslo: Universitetsforlaget, 1995.

Mortensen, Peder, and Birgit M. Rasmussen, eds. *Fra stamme til stat i Danmark*. 2 vols. Århus: Aarhus Universitetsforlag, 1988–91.

Nilsson, Bertil, ed. *Kristnandet i Sverige: Gamla källor och nya perspektiv*. Projektet Sveriges Kristnande, Publikationer, 5. Uppsala: Lunne Böcker, 1996.

Norges innskrifter med de yngre runer. 6 vols. Edited by Magnus Olsen, Aslak Liestøl, and James Knirk. Oslo: Norsk Historisk Kjeldeskrift-Institutt, 1941–in progress.

Palm, Rune. *Runor och regionalitet: Studier av variation i de nordiska minnesinskrifterna*. Runrön, 7. Uppsala: Institutionen för nordiska språk, Uppsala universitet, 1992.

Palme, S. U. *Kristendoms genombrott i Sverige*. Stockholm: Bonniers, 1959.

Pamp, Bengt. *Ortnamnen i Sverige*. 5th ed. Lundastudier i nordisk språkvetenskap, B2. Lund: Studentlitteratur, 1988.

Peterson, Lena. *Svenskt Runordsregister*. 2nd ed. Runrön, 2. Uppsala: Institutionen för nordiska språk, Uppsala unversitet, 1994.

Rindal, Magnus, ed. *Fra hedendom til kristendom: Perspektiver på religionsskiftet i Norge*. Oslo: Ad notam Gyldendal, 1996.

Rumar, Lars, ed. *Helgonet i Nidaros: Olavskult och kristnande i Norden*. Skrifter utgivna av Riksarkivet, 3. Stockholm: Riksarkivet, 1997.

Sandnes, Jorn, and Ola Stemshaug, eds. *Norsk Stadnamnleksikon*. 2nd ed. Oslo: Det Norske Samlaget, 1980.

Sawyer, Peter. *När Sverige blev Sverige*. Alingsås: Viktoria, 1991.

——. *Da Danmark blev Danmark*. Danmarkshistorie, 3. Copenhagen: Gyldendal & Politiken, 1988.

Seip, Didrik Arup. *Norsk språkhistorie til omkring 1370*. 2nd ed. Oslo: Aschehoug, 1955.

Skautrup, Peter. *Det danske sprogs historie*. 5 vols. Copenhagen: Gyldendal, 1944–70.

Steinsland, Gro, *et al.*, eds. Nordisk *hedendom: Et symposium*. Odense: Odense universitetsforlag, 1991.

Stemshaug, Ola. *Namn i Noreg: Ei innføring i norsk stadnamngransking*. 2nd ed. Oslo: Det Norske Samlaget, 1976.

Sveriges Runinskrifter (1900–in progress). Kungl. Vitterhets Historie och Antikvitets Akademien, Stockholm:

   I: *Ölands Runinskrifter* (1900–6). Edited by Sven Söderberg and Erik Brate.

   II: *Östergötlands Runinskrifter* (1911–18). Edited by Erik Brate.

   III: *Södermanlands Runinskrifter* (1924–36). Edited by Erik Brate and Elias Wessén.

   IV: *Smålands Runinskrifter* (1935–61). Edited by Ragnar Kinander.

   V: *Västergötlands Runinskrifter* (1940–71). Edited by Hugo Jugner and Elisabeth Svärdström.

   VI–IX: *Upplands Runinskrifter* (1940–58). Edited by Elias Wessén and Sven B. F. Jansson.

   X–XII: *Gotlands Runinskrifter* (1962–78). Edited by Sven B. F. Jansson, Elias Wessén and Elisabeth Svärdström.

   XIII: *Västmanlands Runinskrifter* (1964). Edited by Sven B. F. Jansson.

   XIV: *Närkes Runinskrifter. Värmlands Runinskrifter* (1975–78). Edited by Sven B. F. Jansson.

   XV: *Gästriklands Runinskrifter* (1981). Edited by Sven B. F. Jansson.

Wessén, Elias. *Svensk språkhistoria*. 3 vols. Stockholm: Almqvist & Wiksell, 1965.

Appendix: Museums with Viking Collections

An asterisk indicates large or important collections.

CANADA

L'Anse Aux Meadows, Newfoundland
L'Anse Aux Meadows Museum
Parks Canada
Canadian Heritage
PO Box 70
St Lunaire-Griquet, Newfoundland
A0K 2XO

DENMARK

Århus
Moesgård Museum*
Moesgård Allé 20
DK-8270 Højbjerg

Copenhagen
National Museum of Denmark (Danmarks Nationalmuseum)*
Fredriksholm Kanal 12
DK-1220 Copenhagen K

Fyrkat
Vikingcenter Fyrkat-Hobro
Fyrkatvej 37b
DK-9500 Hobro

Ladby
Kerteminde Museum
Strandgade 7
DK-5300 Kerteminde

Lindholm Høje
Lindholm Høje Museum
Vendilavej 11
DK-9400 Nørresundby

Roskilde
Viking Ship Museum (Vikingeskibshallen)*
Vindeboder 12
DK-4000 Roskilde

GERMANY

Schleswig (Hedeby)
Wikinger Museum Haithabu
Schloss Gottorf
D-24837 Schleswig

ICELAND

Reykjavik
National Museum of Iceland*
Suðurgata 41
IS-101 Reykjavik

Árni Magnússon Institute (Stofnun Árna Magnússonar)*
Árnagarður, V/Suðurgata
IS-101 Reykjavik

NORWAY

Bergen
Historisk Museum
Universitetet i Bergen

Haakon Sheteligs plass 3
N-5007 Bergen

Oslo
Universitetets Oldsaksamling*
Fredriks gate 2
N-0130 Oslo

Viking Ship Museum, Bygdøy*
Huk Aveny 35
N-0287 Oslo

Stiklestad
Stiklestad National Culture House
N-7650 Verdal

Trondheim
Museum of Natural History and Archaeology (Vitenskapsmuseet)
NTNU
Erling Skakkes gate 47
N-7491 Trondheim

POLAND

Wolin
Muzeum Regionalne im.
Kaube ul. Zamkowa 24
PL-72500 Wolin

Muzeum Narodowe
Ul. Staromlynska 27
PL-70561 Szczecin

SWEDEN

Stockholm
National Museum of Antiquities (Statens Historiska Museum)*
Narvavägen 13-17
SE-114 84 Stockholm

Uppsala (Gamla)
Gamla Uppsala Historiskt Centrum
Disavägen
SE-754 40 Uppsala

Visby, Gotland
Historical Museum of Gotland (Gotlands Fornsal)*
Strandgatan 12
SE-621 56 Visby

UNITED KINGDOM

Douglas, Isle of Man
Manx Museum and Manx National Heritage
Douglas IM1 3LY

Dublin, Ireland
National Museum of Ireland*
Kildare Street
Dublin 2

Edinburgh, Scotland
Museum of Scotland*
Chambers Street
Edinburgh EH1 1JF

London, England
British Museum*
Great Russell Street
London WC1B 3DG

York, England
Jorvik Viking Centre
Coppergate
York YO1 1NT

Yorkshire Museum
Museum Gardens
York YO1 2DR

About the Author

Katherine Holman (B.A., Hull University; Ph.D., Nottingham University) was formerly lecturer in Scandinavian studies and assistant director of European Studies at the University of Hull. Her research interests are in the Viking-Age and early medieval history of Britain and Scandinavia, particularly the nature and extent of the Scandinavian settlement in the various regions of the British Isles and how deeply it affected these regions. She also has a special interest in the Viking-Age and medieval inscriptions of Scandinavia and the historical, social, and cultural information they can provide about places and people that are not found in other written documents. She is a council member of the Viking Society for Northern Research, a consultant to *Viking Heritage* magazine, and she has contributed to a number of journals, including the *International Medieval Bibliography*, *Saga-Book*, and *Scandinavica*. Her other publications include *Scandinavian Runic Inscriptions in the British Isles: Their Historical Context* (1996), and with Jon Adams, she has recently edited a collection of conference papers on the theme *Scandinavia and Europe: Contact, Conflict, and Co-Existence 800–1350*.